New England Frontier

Puritans and Indians

1620-1675

D1430608

New England Frontier

Puritans and Indians

1620–1675

Third Edition

ALDEN T. VAUGHAN

ILLUSTRATED

UNIVERSITY OF OKLAHOMA PRESS
Norman

By Alden T. Vaughan

New England Frontier (Boston, 1965)
Chronicles of the American Revolution (New York, 1965)
America before the Revolution, 1725–1775 (Englewood Cliffs, N.J., 1967)
The American Colonies in the Seventeenth Century (New York, 1971)
The Puritan Tradition in America, 1620–1730 (New York, 1972)
American Genesis: Captain John Smith and the Founding of Virginia (Boston, 1975)
(with Edward W. Clark) *Puritans among the Indians* (Cambridge, Mass., 1981)
Narratives of North American Indian Captivity: A Selective Bibliography (New York, 1983)
(with Virginia Mason Vaughan) *Shakespeare's Caliban* (New York, 1991)
Roots of American Racism (New York, 1995)

Library of Congress Cataloging-in-Publication Data

Vaughan, Alden T., 1929–
  New England frontier : Puritans and Indians, 1620–1675 / Alden T.
Vaughan. — 3rd ed.
    p. cm.
  Includes bibliographical references (p.   ) and index.
  ISBN: 978-0-80612-718-7
    1. New England—History—Colonial period, 1600–1775. 2. In-
dians of North America—New England—Government relations—To
1789. 3. Indians of North America—New England—History.
4. Indians, Treatment of—New England. I. Title.
F7.V3 1994
974/.02—dc20   94-35277
                                                                   CIP

The paper in this book meets the guidelines for permanence and dura-
bility of the Committee on Production Guidelines for Book Longevity of
the Council on Library Resources, Inc. ∞

Contents

Illustrations

Statue of Massasoit (d. 1662). Twentieth century bronze by Cyrus Dallin. Courtesy the Dicksons, Plymouth, Massachusetts.

Indians making snowshoes. Detail from model of Algonquian village. Courtesy Robert S. Peabody Foundation for Archaeology, Phillips Academy, Andover, Massachusetts.

Indians making canoe. Detail from model of Algonquian village. Courtesy Robert S. Peabody Foundation for Archaeology, Phillips Academy, Andover, Massachusetts.

Indians making pottery. Detail from model of Algonquian village. Courtesy Robert S. Peabody Foundation for Archaeology, Phillips Academy, Andover, Massachusetts.

Algonquian wigwams. Detail from model of Algonquian village. Courtesy Peabody Museum of Archaeology and Ethnology, Harvard University, Cambridge, Massachusetts.

The Indian College, Harvard, about 1677. Detail from model in the Widener Library. Courtesy Harvard College Library.

Fort Saybrook, 1636. From an engraving, after a drawing, origin not known. Courtesy Emmett Collection, New York Public Library.

Reconstruction of the Pilgrims' Fort and Meetinghouse. Courtesy Plimouth Plantation, Plymouth, Massachusetts.

William Pynchon (1590-1662). From an oil portrait, artist unknown. Courtesy Essex Institute, Salem, Massachusetts.

Edward Winslow (1595-1655). From an oil portrait attributed to Robert Walker. Courtesy Pilgrim Society, Plymouth, Massachuetts.

John Endicott (1589-1665). From an oil portrait attributed to John Smibert. Courtesy Essex Institute, Salem, Massachusetts.

John Underhill (c. 1597-1672). From an oil portrait, artist unknown. Courtesy Society for the Preservation of Long Island Antiquities, Setauket, Long Island.

Introduction to the Second Edition

A PERSISTENT AMERICAN tragedy has been the inability of European colonists and their descendants to live equitably with the aboriginal population. Several recent events have emphasized this problem's agelessness—the "second battle" of Wounded Knee, disruptions at the Bureau of Indian Affairs, protests against the use of Indian logotypes by colleges and professional athletic teams, and litigation to reclaim tribal territories—while disproportionate poverty and high mortality continue to afflict Native Americans. Our ancestors failed to solve the infinite problems of racial adjustment; perhaps modern America is not doing much better.

New England Frontier, first published in 1965, explored the roots of Indian-European contact in one section of British America. The book's purpose was neither to defend nor to rationalize early English colonization, but rather to explain how the Puritan settlers of New England from 1620 to 1675 viewed the Indians and how their perceptions shaped their conduct toward the natives. My assessment of early Puritan attitudes and actions was on the whole favorable, arguing that until 1675 the New Englanders generally respected the Indians (though not Indian culture) and tried sincerely to win them to English ways and beliefs. The Puritans' ultimate goal was assimilation of the natives into Anglo-American society. Accordingly, the colonists—especially those with political or ecclesiastical authority—sought peaceful and equitable methods of acquiring land and furs, administering justice, and recruiting converts. The Puritans' effort was not flawless, and their goal was fundamentally presumptuous, but in the context of the seventeenth century, I contended, the Puritan record deserved a more affirmative judgment than it had usually received.

The initial reaction to *New England Frontier* was generally favorable. Some reviewers challenged specific points and a few took umbrage at the basic thesis; however, the overall response was gratifying. But times have changed and with them historians' perceptions. *New England Frontier* has increasingly been chided for sins of commission and omission, primarily for giving the Puritans more credit than they deserve, and I too have long harbored dissatisfaction with certain aspects of the book.[1] This new edition affords me an opportunity to restate my interpretation of the Puritans' Indian policy in the half century before King Philip's War, to answer some of the criticisms leveled

---

[1] For examples of favorable reviews see Edmund S. Morgan in the *New York Herald Tribune Book Week* (September 19, 1965); Malcolm Freiberg in the *Boston Sunday Globe* (October 18, 1965); Marion L. Starkey in the *New York Times Book Review* (November 7, 1965); and William C. Keissel in *American Historical Review*, LXXXI (1966). Also, *New England Frontier* was the selection of the History Book Club for September 1965, and was chosen as one of the best history paperbacks of 1967 by the *New York Times*. Major criticism emerged, perhaps predictably, in the late 1960s and early 1970s, and took two overlapping but distinct forms: (1) essentially objective and temperate reassessments of my interpretation, based on somewhat different assumptions and occasionally on a different reading of the evidence—for example, in the works of Wilcomb E. Washburn and James Axtell; and (2) heavily polemical attacks on the book and on the Puritan record, based on anti-Puritan bias and what seems to me a frequent misreading of the evidence—for example, in the writings of Francis Jennings and the earlier works of Neal E. Salisbury. See subsequent notes for citations.

against the original edition, and to rewrite a few passages of the book to reflect more accurately my current views.

*   *   *

Like most New England children, I early learned that the Pilgrims and their successors "fell first on their knees and then on the aborigines."[2] That quip said succinctly what many writers expounded at length: that despite whatever admirable qualities the early New Englanders may have possessed, they made short work of the natives—mostly by the sword, sometimes by slavery, and frequently by demon rum. The Puritans were said to have appropriated the natives' land, bargained unscrupulously for their furs, and abused individual Indians with impunity. A few authors admitted that Plymouth Colony had enjoyed amicable relations with Massasoit and Squanto, but most of the books I read in school and in subsequent years condemned unreservedly the Indian policies of Massachusetts and Connecticut. According to the prevailing version, Puritans believed that Indians consorted with the devil and therefore deserved whatever maltreatment they received from the godly. Puritan policy was, by popular and scholarly accord, indefensible.[3]

Many years later I began to write the story of Anglo-Indian relations in early New England. The impetus came

[2] Slightly varying versions of this shibboleth have been attributed to William Maxwell Evarts, Oliver Wendell Holmes, James Russell Lowell, George Frisbie Hoar, and Bill Nye.

[3] This version could be found, for example, in George E. Ellis, "The Indians of Eastern Massachusetts," in Justin Winsor, ed., *The Memorial History of Boston*, I (Boston, 1880); Clark Wissler, *The Indians of the United States* (Garden City, N. Y., 1940; reissued 1956), 63–66; and Jennings C. Wise, *The Red Man in the New World* (New York, 1931; rev. ed. 1971), 75–83. Recent works that offer a similar interpretation

not from doubt about the accuracy of the generalizations I had learned, but from curiosity about the details of a relatively neglected aspect of American Puritanism.[4] No single book told the whole story. The events of Puritan-Indian contact in New England appeared as side issues in histories of the entire sweep of Indian-European relations (for example, in William C. MacLeod's *American Indian Frontier*) or as almost parenthetical episodes in histories of New England (for instance, James Truslow Adams's *Founding of New England*). Some major works on New England—most notably Perry Miller's magisterial study of the New England mind—ignored the Indian altogether. Much detailed information could be found in John Gorham Palfrey's multivolume *History of New England*, but his filiopietistic view of the Puritans raised doubts about his objectivity.[5] There was need, I concluded, for a modern narrative and analysis of the Puritans' Indian policy.

My first step was to examine Pilgrim-Indian relations during the early years of Plymouth Colony. To my sur-

---

include Richard Slotkin, *Regeneration through Violence: The Mythology of the American Frontier, 1600–1860* (Middletown, Conn., 1973), chs. 2–6; and Francis Jennings, *The Invasion of America: Indians, Colonialism, and the Cant of Conquest* (Chapel Hill, N. C., 1975), part II.

[4] Influenced by the writings of Samuel Eliot Morison, Perry Miller, Edmund S. Morgan, and others, my principal interest in early New England lay in the Puritan experiment: its origins, character, and eventual demise. I therefore stated in my preface, clearly enough I thought, that *New England Frontier* was primarily a chapter in Puritan history, not in ethnohistory or Indian history, though of course it partook somewhat of both. Some critics have deplored or misrepresented my explicit intentions while at the same time presenting essentially European-focused accounts themselves. See, for example, Jennings, *Invasion of America*, especially 14 and 59.

[5] William C. MacLeod, *The American Indian Frontier* (New York, 1928) and James Truslow Adams, *The Founding of New England* (Boston, 1921) were both highly critical of the Puritans' Indian policy. The

prise, the evidence suggested a more humane and equitable treatment of the natives—at least in diplomatic negotiations, land acquisition, and the administration of justice—than I had expected.[6] I closed my draft of a chapter on Plymouth's first decade with an expression of regret that the subsequent settlers of New England had not followed the Pilgrims' commendable example. Then I delved into the materials on New England from 1630 to 1675, attempting to read every significant reference to Puritan-Indian relations in the surviving records. I encountered, as I had expected, much that reflected discredit on the early settlers: their arrogant assumption of religious and cultural superiority, their avarice for land and profitable trade, their brutality in war. But these were vices they shared with virtually all seventeenth-century Englishmen, probably with all seventeenth-century Europeans, perhaps with most seventeenth-century humans. What increasingly impressed me as different about the Puritans was their attempt, marked by failure in the long run but partly successful in the early years, to deal justly and peacefully with their Indian neighbors. For example, in 1638 Plymouth Colony hanged three Englishmen for murdering an Indian. That same year, Connec-

---

indexes to Perry Miller's *The New England Mind: The Seventeenth Century* (Cambridge, Mass., 1939) and *The New England Mind: From Colony to Province* (Cambridge, Mass., 1953) have no entries for "Indians." Similarly, Edmund S. Morgan's excellent *Puritan Dilemma: The Story of John Winthrop* (Boston, 1958) overlooks Winthrop's substantial involvement in Indian affairs. Palfrey's defense of Puritan policy appears in his *History of New England* (5 vols., Boston, 1865–1890).

[6] Until recently the Pilgrims have generally received more favorable assessment of their Indian policies than have their neighbors in Massachusetts and Connecticut. The best modern history of Plymouth, which gives considerable attention to Indian affairs, is George D. Langdon, Jr., *Pilgrim Colony: A History of New Plymouth, 1620–1691* (New Haven, 1966).

ticut's General Court rejected the protest of Wethersfield inhabitants who demanded revenge on a local chief for conspiracy in the killing of several English settlers; the colonial magistrates decided that an earlier though lesser violation of Indian rights by the settlers themselves justified the lethal retaliation. And even in 1675, when wartime passions generated virulent animosities, Massachusetts executed two colonists for murdering Indian non-combatants.

In their educational and judicial systems and in their missionary efforts, the Puritans revealed a paternalistic but genuine concern for the Indians—rather than hostility or indifference. By mid-century, Harvard College welcomed Indian students, as the colony's common and grammar schools had for many years. The college's purpose, according to its charter of 1650, was "the education of the English and Indian Youth of this Country"; before 1675 several Indians attended Harvard, though far fewer than the Puritans had hoped. The Puritans made somewhat comparable efforts, also futile in the long run, to involve Indians in their judicial system in cases involving Indian litigants. In the "praying towns" set up for voluntary converts to Christianity, all but the gravest crimes were adjudicated by Indian magistrates, and several Indians served on colonial juries in the 1670s. The praying towns were also the centers of the Puritan missionary effort: by 1675 fourteen villages had been formed, with more than one thousand inhabitants. Meanwhile, John Eliot, the most prominent missionary in seventeenth-century British America, had mastered the Massachusetts Algonquian language, created an alphabetical version of it, translated the Bible, and helped to print it on the Cambridge Press. He also published more than a score of religious and educational tracts for distribution to the natives. Seventeenth-century New England records revealed numerous other attempts to assimilate rather than expel or maltreat the Indians. Their cumulative evidence seemed to belie the stereotype I had long accepted.

The book that emerged from my research exhibited the pendulum effect. In attempting to straighten the record, I magnified—unintentionally but persistently—the Puritans' benign aims and mitigated their less admirable accomplishments. Many readers considered my version a necessary antidote to earlier accounts. But a colleague suggested that I was presenting a lawyer's brief, and a reviewer objected that my book "doth protest too much." I agree. Were I to rewrite *New England Frontier* in its entirety, I would give more attention to the Puritans' failures, less to their fleeting virtues, and would temper its exculpatory tone. I would also further emphasize the incompatibility of the Puritans' cultural imperialism with the survival, for any appreciable time, of tribal societies.[7]

*   *   *

Although my current interpretation of Puritan-Indian relations between 1620 and 1675 differs considerably in

---

[7] A year and a half after the publication of *New England Frontier* I addressed a meeting of the Colonial Society of Massachusetts on reactions to the book. In preparation for that talk I read the book for the first time without interruptions to revise or to check sources. That reading convinced me that I had overargued my case, and I so stated to my audience. I also rejected the contention of some listeners that overstatement was desirable, even necessary, to counteract earlier interpretations. I wrote the first draft of this introduction in 1970, when it became evident that the economic realities of the publishing industry precluded a complete resetting of *New England Frontier*. This edition retains the original text except for the correction of some typographical errors, the modification of several phrases, and the recasting of a few paragraphs, notably in the final chapter.

emphasis, only a few substantive particulars have changed. I offer here a brief summary of Puritan attitudes and policies as I now see them, and a discussion of several of the major themes and episodes that have spurred scholarly debate during the past fifteen years.

Seventeenth-century Puritans, more than other European settlers, sought to create in America a model society. Their New Jerusalem was based on the assumption that God had prescribed one faith, one fundamental form of government, and one basic style of life, which the Puritans believed they alone practiced. Leaders of the New England Zion welcomed new recruits but demanded adherence to its precepts by everyone—European or native—within their jurisdiction. Indians, especially, were desirable additions to the Puritan experiment, because their conversion would signal the approaching millennium and demonstrate God's approval of the Puritan exodus. However, the Indians must become complete Puritans, not autonomous neighbors or even partial carriers of aboriginal culture. They must forsake their theology, their language, their political and economic structures, their habitations and clothing, their social mores, their customs of work and play. The Puritans brooked no compromise. In anthropological terms, the Indian was expected not merely to acculturate by blending his traditional ways with those of the new society, but to transculturate: to repudiate totally his Indianness and become in every way an American Puritan.[8] Some natives—perhaps a few thousand—made substantial efforts to meet the Puritans' stern demands. Most refused, choosing to re-

---

[8]I here use "transculturation" somewhat differently than does A. Irving Hallowell in "American Indians, White and Black: The Phenomenon of Transculturalization," *Current Anthropology,* IV (1963), 519–531. He em-

main as they were except for several borrowings from European technology and a few from European customs.

Especially vulnerable to the Puritans' assault on Indian culture were the natives who chose to associate closely, either as individuals or as tribes, with the New England colonists. Yet it is clear from the frustratingly sparse evidence that no matter how thoroughly an Indian tried to effect transculturation, he seldom if ever gained full acceptance into Puritan society. Too many vestiges of his original affiliation clung to the convert. Perhaps if the bitterness caused by the holocaust of the 1670s had not destroyed the experiment in ethnic amalgamation, a greater proportion of the Indians would have been substantially integrated into colonial society. But in the period under consideration here, 1620–1675, Puritan policy kept the Indians, even the "praying Indians," at arm's length. The result was predictable. Both Puritans and Indians sensed the implicit inequality, and the Indians inevitably resented their subservient status.

At the same time, stringent laws forbade English settlers to join Indian society. Frequent warnings against tainting themselves with Indian habits, even hair styles, reminded the colonists that God wanted Englishmen to "civilize" the Indians, never the reverse. To admit that the Indians, without Christianity and without English customs, had a viable culture would have undermined the centrality of those influences; the Puritans could not approve Indian ways without repudiating their own. Thus the gap between "savagery" and "civilization" grew still wider in the Puritan

---

ploys the term to mean any degree of individual acculturation; I intend it to mean virtually complete acculturation.

mind as it evolved from an ethnocentric perception into a legal and psychological imperative.[9]

To encourage Indians in the transition to English society, John Eliot's praying towns removed potential converts from the "evil" influences of the native village, especially its chiefs and powwows, and isolated them from corrupting members of the English community. The praying Indians eventually produced their own preachers, teachers, magistrates, and minor officials, although Eliot and his associates hovered nearby, imposing a gentle but real curb on Indian autonomy. Eliot's sincerity can scarcely be questioned; his paternalism is nonetheless unmistakable.[10] Moreover, despite Eliot's partial success in gaining converts and changing their customs, most of his compatriots increasingly

---

[9] For a modern analysis of Europeans who "went Indian," see James Axtell, "The White Indians of Colonial America," *William and Mary Quarterly*, 3 ser. XXXII (1975), 55–88. There have been several recent attempts to probe the psychological component of Puritan perceptions and actions. All are built on shreds of evidence, but some are at least provocative. See, for example, Roy Harvey Pearce, *Savagism and Civilization: A Study of the Indian and the American Mind* (Baltimore, 1953 [entitled *Savages of America*]: rev. ed., 1965), 19–35; Neal E. Salisbury, "Conquest of the 'Savage': Puritans, Puritan Missionaries, and Indians, 1620–1680" (Ph.D. dissertation, University of California, Los Angeles, 1972); and Slotkin, *Regeneration through Violence*, chs. 2–6. Underlying these interpretations is the dubious premise that the Puritans were especially fearful and contemptuous of the Indians and bent on their physical destruction.

[10] Francis Jennings has questioned Eliot's sincerity, but his evidence is at best circumstantial, and his blatant animus toward the English in general and the Puritans in particular contributes to the abrasive tone of his analysis. See especially his "Goals and Functions of Puritan Missions to the Indians," *Ethnohistory*, XVIII (1971), 197–212, and *Invasion of America*, ch. 14. For other critical interpretations of Eliot see Neal E. Salisbury, "Red Puritans: The 'Praying Indians' of Massachusetts Bay and John Eliot," *William and Mary Quarterly*, 3 ser. XXXI (1974), 27–54; and same author, "Prospero in New England: The Puritan Missionary as Colonist," in William Cowan, ed., *Papers of the Sixth Algonquian Conference, 1974* (Ottawa, 1975), 253–273.

doubted the Indians' ability to complete the required religious and social transformation. The problem was not color prejudice: not until the eighteenth century did Puritan spokesmen seriously question the Indians' descent from the ten lost tribes of Israel or some other Old World stock, nor did they doubt the testimony of Eliot, Roger Williams, and others that' Indians were born white. Their tawny skin came from stains and the sun, not from heredity.[11] Rather, the "Indian problem" in early New England was firmly lodged in the colonists' cultural absolutism.

Ethnocentricity was not, of course, a Puritan monopoly. It was common to all colonizing nations, and probably, though to a lesser degree, to all Indian tribes. European captives were hastily transmuted—symbolically and often behaviorally—into neo-Indians. Under the pressure of war-

---

[11] Most scholars, even some of the new anti-Puritans, recognize the absence of color categories, with their implications of inherent racial bias, in seventeenth-century New England's Anglo-Indian contact. (The Puritans were not unique in this matter; most European commentators throughout the sixteenth and seventeenth centuries described the Indians as innately white.) One exception is G. E. Thomas, "Puritans, Indians, and the Concept of Race," *New England Quarterly*, XLVIII (1975), 3–27, which concludes that "racial characteristics turned out to be the one insurmountable barrier. No matter how hard the Puritan tried to transform the Indian or how completely the Indian conformed, the cause was ultimately hopeless because the Indian could never become white." The argument is anachronistic, and the article is also marred by serious misquotations, inaccurate citations, and inept research. Its publication is puzzling and unfortunate. Also unfortunate, because it subtly encourages such an interpretation, is the almost universal use by modern scholars (including me, I regret, in this book and elsewhere) of "reds" and "red men" for seventeenth-century Indians and "whites" for the English. The cost of removing such terms from this edition was prohibitive. Puritan perceptions of Africans, by contrast, were essentially racial from the outset. See Winthrop D. Jordan, *White over Black: American Attitudes toward the Negro, 1550–1812* (Chapel Hill, N. C., 1968); and Alden T. Vaughan, "Blacks in Virginia: A Note on the First Decade," *William and Mary Quarterly*, 3 ser. XXIX (1972), 469–478.

time captivity, many Puritan children and a few adults forsook their religion, customs, language, and clothing for those of their captors. All recorded instances of English conversion occurred after 1675, but earlier some colonists voluntarily forsook Puritan society to live among the Indians.[12] Such renegades discovered what many of their compatriots must have dimly perceived—that Indian society had virtues of its own and that Puritan antipathy to it reflected self-doubt as well as cultural myopia.

Throughout the colonial period the pressure for civil and religious conversion was usually in the other direction, as the Puritans strove to make all Indians into neo-Englishmen. For the Indians, the choices were few and disheartening. They could comply with this demand and lose their political and cultural identity; they could attempt to adopt a portion of English culture without destroying the integrity of their own (an unacceptable solution, in the long run, to Puritan authorities); they could push westward in search of vacant land and hope that other Indians and other Europeans would not resist them; or they could defy English encroachment on their culture and territory, by force of arms if necessary. In 1675 several tribes took the last

---

12 Little is known about the fate of most captives, despite the impressive efforts of Emma Lewis Coleman to follow the careers of those who were taken to Canada. See her *New England Captives Carried to Canada*, (2 vols., Portland, Maine, 1925). James Axtell, "The Scholastic Philosophy of the Wilderness," *William and Mary Quarterly*, 3 ser. XXIX (1972), 361, estimates that between 1689 and 1713, approximately fifteen per cent of the English captives "chose" to become "full-fledged Indians." Preliminary findings from an analysis that Daniel K. Richter and I are making of Coleman's evidence suggest a much lower figure. The overwhelming majority of those who succumbed to transculturation were children; that a few adults rejected their original culture, however, must have deeply upset Puritan society. See also Slotkin, *Regeneration through Violence*, chs. 4 and 5.

course, with tragic results for them and, indirectly, for all of New England's Indians. But some form of resistance or exodus was probably inevitable, for by the 1660s—certainly by 1676—the more perceptive Indians and the more candid Puritans must have realized that despite the good intentions of most missionaries and civil authorities, Puritanism was a culturally closed system. The Indian would never truly become a part of it so long as he remained in any sense an Indian. The Puritans' expectations, although understandably dictated by their own world view, were implausible and insensitive.

My discussions of several other facets of the Puritans' Indian policy call for some restatement. The account of New England's judicial system, for example, stressed its impartiality and the use of Indian jurors. Both points need to be more rigorously qualified, for although the courts may have adjudicated specific cases without discernible ethnic prejudice, Puritan justice was inherently biased against Indians. Its concepts of right and wrong were the Puritans', never the Indians'; its laws were recorded and administered in English, never Algonquian; its procedures and sentences reflected the Englishman's customs, never the native's. Indians who had voluntarily submitted to colonial authority may have accepted such drawbacks, but the many Indians brought into colonial courts who were members of independent tribes or of tribes that had come unwillingly under Puritan jurisdiction must have resented judgment by an alien system. And the instances of Indian jurors were few in number and highly circumscribed in character. Only Indians acceptable to the English served; they never comprised the majority of a jury; and they sat only on cases in which both litigants were Indians. Whatever the Puritans' intentions, their administration of justice helped to make the Indians a separate and almost voiceless minority and to undermine Indian cultural integrity.[13]

Underlying Puritan legal policy was the assumption, shared by all colonizing groups, that a royal charter conferred jurisdiction over everyone within its stipulated boundaries. For pragmatic reasons, Puritan authorities often left powerful tribes alone, but in principle, colonial laws applied to the entire population, Indian as well as English. Only one prominent Puritan challenged the orthodox view. In 1648 William Pynchon, of Springfield, Massachusetts, denied that Bay Colony magistrates could rightfully apprehend and pass judgment on several Indians in western Massachusetts who had allegedly murdered other Indians. "I grant they are all within the line of the patent," he wrote to Deputy-Governor Thomas Dudley, "but yet you cannot say, that therefore they are within your jurisdiction, until they have fully subjected themselves to your government (which I know they have not) and until you have bought their land; until this be done, they must be esteemed as an independent free people. . . ."[14] Pynchon's reasoning, so ripe with possibilities for more peaceful and equitable Anglo-Indian relations, fell on deaf ears.

---

[13] Recent assessments of Puritan jurisprudence include James P. Ronda, "Red and White at the Bench: Indians and the Law in Plymouth Colony, 1620–1691," *Essex Institute Historical Collections*, CX (1974), 200–215; and Yasuhide Kawashima, "Forced Conformity: Puritan Criminal Justice and Indians," *Kansas Law Review*, XXV (1977), 361–373. Lyle Koehler, in a paper delivered to the American Society for Ethnohistory (Chicago, 1976), argues that Indians were assigned harsher punishments than colonists for similar crimes, especially after 1660. If true, the erosion of Puritan justice in the sixties and seventies helps to explain King Philip's War. See below, pp. xxv–xxix.

[14] Pynchon to Dudley (5 July 1648), in Henry Morris, *Early History of Springfield, 1636–1675* (Springfield, Mass., 1876), 68–71.

Military conflict is another aspect of Puritan-Indian relations that engenders vociferous debate. Some historians have charged the Puritans with waging an especially brutal brand of warfare, even with committing genocide, and with forcing the Indians into conflicts that would satisfy the settlers' lust for more land and fewer Indian inhabitants.[15]

---

[15] Aspects of Anglo-Indian warfare in New England have recently been discussed from widely different approaches by Slotkin, *Regeneration through Violence*, especially ch. 3; Jennings, *Invasion of America*, especially chs. 9, 13, and 17; Douglas Edward Leach, *The Northern Colonial Frontier, 1607–1763* (New York, 1966), especially 36f., 53–61; same author, *Arms for Empire: A Military History of the British Colonies in North America, 1607–1763* (New York, 1973), especially 44–47, 59–67; Anne Kusener Nelson, "King Philip's War and the Hubbard-Mather Rivalry," *William and Mary Quarterly*, 3 ser. XXVII (1976), 615–629; Patrick M. Malone, "Changing Military Technology among the Indians of Southern New England, 1660–1677," *American Quarterly*, XXV (1973), 48–63; and Karen Ordahl Kupperman, "English Perceptions of Treachery, 1538–1640: The Case of the American 'Savages'," *The Historical Journal*, XX (1977), 263–287. A controversial episode is judiciously treated in John A. Sainsbury, "Miantonomo's Death and New England Politics, 1630–1645," *Rhode Island History*, XXX (1971), 111–123. On the hoary historical problem of which race first practiced scalping, see two persuasive articles: James Axtell, "Who Invented Scalping?" *American Heritage*, XXVIII, no. 3 (April 1977), 96–99; and Axtell and William C. Sturtevant, "The Unkindest Cut of All; or, Who Invented Scalping?" *William and Mary Quarterly* (forthcoming). The latter essay is a more extensive and documented version of the former. The Puritans are accused of genocide explicitly in Anna R. Monguia, "The Pequot War Reexamined," *American Indian Culture and Research Journal*, I, no. 3 (1975), 20, a brief article that badly misuses historical evidence, and implicitly in Lazar Ziff, *Puritanism in America: New Culture in a New World* (New York, 1973), which erroneously states that "The Puritan colonists . . . wanted the very lives of the entire tribe . . . [and they] achieved this extermination. . . . An entire tribe was obliterated" (p. 91). Ziff was apparently deceived by Puritan wartime hyperbole. Hundreds of Pequots survived to be distributed in 1638 among the Mohegans, the Narragansetts, and the English. The tribe was later reconstituted, and it aided the colonists in King Philip's War. In 1674 Daniel Gookin estimated the number of Pequot men as about 300, which suggests (in light of the very heavy mor-

Puritan warfare was certainly brutal: the military technology of the Europeans in New England, as elsewhere, vastly increased the human cost of war, and Puritans in New England and Old pursued their enemies with self-righteous vigor. The Indians, of course, had fought among themselves before Europeans arrived in America and continued to afterward. But Indian wars had seldom incurred heavy mortality; most tribes were too small to bear high losses without jeopardizing their survival, and the relative abundance of land and shortage of material goods virtually eliminated wars of conquest. Accordingly, Indian warfare, compared with European, required less destruction and more symbolic satisfactions—such as the torture of some captives, the assimilation of the rest, and occasional ritualistic cannibalism. By contrast, Europeans had become relatively inured to heavy casualties by centuries of incredible carnage. Thus they thought the Indians too lackadaisical in battle; as one Puritan soldier contemptuously observed, "They might fight seven years and not kill seven men."[16] In 1637 New England's armies gave their Pequot opponents a painful lesson in European military practices. The

tality of adult males in 1637) a total population of perhaps 1500–2000. —*Historical Collections of the Indians in New England* (Boston, 1792; repr. New York, 1972), 7. For a sound assessment of Puritan attitudes after 1675, see Peter N. Carroll, *Puritanism and the Wilderness: The Intellectual Significance of the New England Frontier* (New York, 1969), especially 214f.

The most authoritative estimate of Indian casualties is Sherburne F. Cook, "Interracial Warfare and Population Decline among the New England Indians," *Ethnohistory*, XX (1973), 1–24, which attributes eleven per cent of the Indian population decline between 1620 and 1676 to military action. Cook includes the Dutch war of 1643–1644.

[16] John Underhill, "News from America," *Mass. Hist. Soc. Coll.*, 3 ser. VI (1837), 26.

resulting carnage does not, however, justify charges by some historians—both amateur and professional—that in putting a palisaded village to the torch the Puritans intended genocide. Rather, the resort to such a drastic tactic reveals the Puritans' determination to crush the enemy by any means at hand, because the war's outcome was still very much in doubt and they were confident that in fighting the Lord's battle any means was legitimate. Fire was already a universal weapon. Europeans had used it against one another for centuries; Indians had occasionally used it against opposing tribes, perhaps for centuries, and they would frequently employ it against European strongholds.[17] It still, alas, plays a major role in armed conflicts.

The Puritans, from their perspective, deplored what they considered the Indians' unparalleled cruelty in raids on undefended settlements, torture ceremonies, and cannibalism. The reasons for differences in English and Indian approaches to war, and the double standard implicit in English perceptions of Indian cruelty, are important topics for further study. But what we already know about war and torture in seventeenth-century Europe and America suggests that cruelty was rather evenly distributed among peoples and nations. Its forms varied, but its presence appears to have been distressingly universal: whichever side had the upper hand exhibited little charity or compassion. Both

---

[17] For an early (1530s) account of North American Indian use of fire as a weapon, see John Florio, trans., *A Shorte and Briefe Narration of the Two Navigations and Discoveries to the Northwest Partes Called Newe Fraunce* (London, 1580), 57; also in Henry S. Burrage, ed., *Early English and French Voyages* . . . (New York, 1906), 66. There is no conclusive evidence, however, that New England Indians used fire before 1675.

sides often slew indiscriminately, both at times tortured captives, and both displayed parts of the victims as trophies of victory. The propensity for cruelty probably depended more on circumstances and individual psyches than on national or racial norms.[18]

Equally controversial are the causes of hostilities, especially New England's conflicts of 1623, 1637, and 1675–1676. The first episode, Miles Standish's massacre of several Massachusetts Indians at Wessagusett, should perhaps be labeled a raid rather than a war, although it indirectly led to substantial casualties among other Indians and cost several English lives as well. Who was to blame for this clash between Plymouth Colony and the Massachusetts tribe? William Bradford claimed to have intelligence from Massasoit, bolstered by reports from the small English settlement at Wessagusett, that some of the Massachusetts Indians were conspiring to annihilate the scattered English plantations. Standish therefore slew the presumed conspirators before they could launch a coordinated attack. Depending on the validity of the suspicion, that was either cold-blooded murder or a callous, though perhaps necessary, preventive assault. The evidence, of course, is all from the English side. Some historians refuse to accept it; instead they interpret the records as a fumbling attempt by the Pilgrims to

---

[18] Many of the narratives of men and women captured by Indians testify to the wide variety of treatment, ranging from kindness to cruelty, within a single tribe. See for example Mary White Rowlandson, *The Soveraignty and Goodness of God . . . Being a Narrative of the Captivity and Restoration of Mrs. Mary Rowlandson* (Boston, 1682); and John Gyles, *Memoirs of Odd Adventures, Strange Deliverances, etc. . . .* (Boston, 1736). Both are reprinted in Alden T. Vaughan and Edward W. Clark, eds., *Puritans among the Indians: Accounts of Captivity and Redemption, 1676–1724* (Cambridge, Mass., 1981).

justify their own pointless aggression.[19] After rereading the surviving evidence, I remain convinced that Plymouth was in real jeopardy. The Pilgrims would have gained nothing by inventing such a plot except further enmity, nor could they have predicted that posterity would castigate them for what they did. Nonetheless, I am also convinced that Plymouth's strategy was unconscionably hasty and brutal. A better option would have been to enlist Massasoit's aid in a united front against the belligerent tribes. The combination of Massasoit's numbers and Plymouth's firearms almost certainly could have thwarted the attempts to destroy Wessagusett, Plymouth, and other outposts. The English colony, I suspect, chose its course of action on a different principle: a recent devastating Indian attack on the Virginia settlements suggested that the best defense was a bold offense.[20]

The Pequot War was more complex. I have recounted the causal events twice—first in a journal article, then in this book. As some critics have noticed, my versions do not completely coincide. While both assign the bulk of the blame to the Pequots, the article stresses the complicity of

---

[19] See George F. Willison, *Saints and Strangers: Being the Lives of the Pilgrim Fathers* . . . (New York, 1945), ch. 15; and Jennings, *Invasion of America*, 186–187. Jennings accepts Willison's undocumented charge that Edward Winslow falsified the record of the Pilgrims' role in the incident and chides me for not accepting it too. Willison's and Jennings's interpretations rest on what seems to me an implausible reading of the evidence.

[20] For decades after the Virginia massacre of 1622, New England attempted to draw lessons from it. So did English writers such as Philip Vincent, who in 1638 applauded the New Englanders for insuring peace "by killing the barbarians, better than our English Virginians were by being killed by them."—"A True Relation of the Late Battel Fought in New England, between the English and the Pequet Salvages," *Mass. Hist. Soc. Coll.*, 3 ser. VI (1837), 42.

the Massachusetts government, accusing it of gross over-retaliation for the murder of John Oldham and of an unwarranted extension of its jurisdiction over the southern Connecticut Valley. That conduct does not totally exonerate the Pequots, however. Their frequent clashes with both Europeans and Indians helped to create the circumstances to which Massachusetts, already brittle from internal contention, overreacted. The article concludes with the judgment that "the blame lies somewhat more heavily upon the Pequots than the Puritans." The book is less explicit in assigning responsibility but implicitly attributes most of it to the Pequots.

I am less sure than I was fifteen years ago that the Pequots deserve the burden of blame. (The alterations made in this edition of the book partly correct the balance.) Certainly, Massachusetts initiated hostilities through John Endicott's excessive use of force on Block Island and in Pequot territory. On the other hand, I find somewhat fanciful a recent interpretation that lays all the blame on the "Puritan oligarchy" and accuses John Winthrop and the other Bay Colony leaders of destroying the evidence of their own guilt.[21] That interpretation overlooks more plausible explanations. For example, the contention that the Puritans abrogated the 1635 treaty with the Pequots, and then made sure no copy of it survived to reveal their duplicity, ignores a less dramatic and less conspiratorial explanation: each

---

[21] My earlier versions appeared in "Pequots and Puritans: The Causes of the War of 1637," *William and Mary Quarterly*, 3 ser. XXI (1964), 256–269; and in chs. 4 and 5 of the original edition of this book. Jennings, *Invasion of America*, chs. 11–12, begins a discussion of the Pequot War (pp. 180ff.) with a distorted account of "traditional assumptions," including mine, and offers a rather conspiratorial interpretation of the causes.

side understood the terms somewhat differently, which is hardly surprising—then or now—in negotiations between drastically different cultures and in the absence of skilled interpreters. Nor is the disappearance of the treaty remarkable. The survival rate of colonial sources is poor, for obvious reasons.

The question remains, however, of why Massachusetts and Connecticut assaulted the Pequots. The answer, I think, lies primarily in the Puritans' determination to curb any tribe that threatened the colony's stability or jurisdiction. In 1636 Massachusetts authorities were reeling from the Roger Williams and Anne Hutchinson controversies; concurrently they dreaded the growing movement in London to annul their charter. Convinced that the Pequot tribe was in some measure responsible for the murders of Captain Stone, his crew, and John Oldham, and that it had violated an earlier treaty, Massachusetts tried to frighten the Pequots into submission. The results were not what the Puritans expected, but their total victory in the ensuing war encouraged a more imperious treatment of other tribes. Cotton Mather later explained the outcome with typically Puritan rhetoric: "The marvellous Providence of God immediately extinguished that *War*, by prospering the *New-English* Arms, unto the utter subduing of the Quarrelsome Nation, and affrighting of all the other Natives."[22]

The causes of King Philip's War, which ravaged New

---

[22] For recent analyses of the Pequot-Mohegan tribe and of the Pequot War of 1637 see, in addition to the works cited in note 21, William Burton and Richard Lowenthal, "The First of the Mohegans," *American Ethnologist*, I (1974), 589–599; Richard P. Metcalf, "Who Should Rule at Home? Native American Politics and Indian-White Relations," *Journal of American History*, LXI (1974–1975), 651–655; Slotkin, *Regeneration through Violence, passim;* Monguia, "Pequot War Re-

England in 1675–1676 and drastically altered the pattern of Puritan-Indian relations, are even more complex than the events of the 1620s. No explanation seems wholly convincing, but I am more impressed than before by Rhode Island Deputy-Governor John Easton's "Relacion of the Indyan Warre," which sympathetically reported the Indians' viewpoint.[23] Once again the blame may not be entirely on one side; it is likely—though far from certain—that the Christian Indian John Sassamon was murdered by his Indian enemies for reporting a Wampanoag conspiracy against Plymouth.[24] But the colonists, not Philip, drew first blood. Moreover, they had almost insured hostilities by demanding the Wampanoags' guns, appropriating their lands (in pay-

---

examined"; Charles M. Segal and David C. Stineback, *Puritans, Indians and Manifest Destiny* (New York, 1977), ch. 3; Wilcomb E. Washburn, *The Indian in America* (New York, 1975), 129f.; and *Handbook of North American Indians*, XV: *Northeast*, edited by Bruce G. Trigger (Washington, 1978), esp. 89f., 172f. Alvin M. Josephy is currently reassessing the causes of the Pequot War from an economic standpoint (forthcoming). The Cotton Mather quote is from his *Magnalia Christi Americana* (London, 1702; repr. New York, 1972), 24 (1st pagination).

[23] Easton's "Relacion" is in Charles H. Lincoln, ed., *Narratives of the Indian Wars, 1675–1699* (New York, 1913). Although Easton's account has an impressive ring of truth, as a Quaker and a Rhode Islander he had abundant reasons to be unsympathetic to Plymouth and Massachusetts, and he therefore must be read with some caution. The most extensive recent interpretation of the causes of the war is Jennings, *Invasion of America*, ch. 17, which labels it "The Second Puritan Conquest." For Puritan reactions to the war see Richard Slotkin and James K. Folsom, eds., *So Dreadful a Judgment: Puritan Responses to King Philip's War, 1676–1677* (Middletown, Conn., 1979). Slotkin and Folsom's introduction distorts in several particulars my own interpretation.

[24] For a thorough examination of the evidence in this case see James P. and Jeanne Ronda, "The Death of John Sassamon: An Exploration in Writing New England Indian History," *American Indian Quarterly*, I (1974), 91–102.

ment of fines), and ignoring the Indians' accumulated grievances. The Wampanoag Indians complained, according to Easton, "that thay had a great fear to have ani of ther indians . . . be Caled or forsed to be Christian indians." They also protested that "if 20 of there [h]onest indians testefied that a Englishman had dun them rong, it was as nothing, and if but one of ther worst indians testefied against ani indian or ther king when it plesed the English that was sufitiant." The Wampanoags protested too against damage by English horses, against land swindles, and against their exclusion from participation in all but a very few trials of accused Indians. Easton urged impartial arbitration of the Indians' grievances by an Indian chief and Governor Edmund Andros of New York; Philip agreed, but Massachusetts and Plymouth did not seriously consider a solution in which the godly community would be judged by an Anglican and a heathen.[25] The immediate cause of the war is perhaps of little consequence. The essential ingredients of mortal conflagration—deeply felt Indian grievances and intransigent colonial officials—needed only a spark to ignite them.

If Easton's assessment is correct, the earlier Puritan policy had eroded badly by 1675. For several interlocking reasons, the majority of the settlers had lost their former determination—however imperfect—to treat the Indians fairly. The relative equity of the first decades, I believe, had stemmed principally from optimistic expectations of the Indians' religious and social conversion. Perhaps, too, the early settlers were more cautious about neighbors whose power they had

---

[25] Easton in Lincoln, *Narratives of the Indian Wars*, 1of.

not tested. And undoubtedly, the first wave of immigrants accepted to a greater degree than their successors the dictates of civil and ecclesiastical leaders. By 1675 much had changed. The Indians had proved largely impervious to Puritan anglicizing; thus they could no longer serve as living evidence of the Lord's favors to New England. In fact, their demise would reveal His intention to spread the godly over heathen lands, as He had earlier made room for them by the plagues of 1616–1617 and 1633–1634. And the settlers, now considerably more numerous than their potential foes, and beguiled by their overwhelming victory in 1637, no longer feared Indian power. (They would soon learn the folly of that judgment.) The later leaders of the New England colonies were, moreover, less flexible and more militaristic than Bradford and Winthrop, who like most of the other early Puritan statesmen had been clerical in outlook if not in occupation. Some of the early leaders—Winthrop, for example—had almost entered the ministry, and several gave lay sermons or wrote quasi-religious tracts. Winthrop's "Model of Christian Charity" exemplifies the former, Bradford's *History of Plymouth Plantation* the latter. And unlike so many of their contemporaries, few of the early New England magistrates had military experience. The one notable exception was John Endicott, whose destructive campaign against Block Island and Pequot Harbor triggered the war of 1637. Significantly, in 1675 the governors of both Massachusetts and Plymouth were veterans of the English civil wars, and both quickly resorted to armed force when trouble arose with the Indians. Equally important, the fading power of the clergy over an increasingly secular and heterodox population meant a lessening of benign control over Indian policy. In short, Puritan attitudes toward the Indians shifted significantly during the half century before King Philip's War.[26] That change needs to be documented and clarified, for only then does New England's war against the Wampanoags and their allies become understandable. Puritan attitudes and policies were never as static as *New England Frontier* implied. They deteriorated gradually, if unevenly, toward massive conflict.

One presumably altruistic aspect of Puritan policy that gained momentum in the decades before 1675 may have contributed to the eventual hostilities: the social and religious proselytizing of John Eliot, Thomas Mayhew, and the other missionaries. It has recently become fashionable to charge New England's missionaries with nefarious intentions. One historian concludes that Eliot was "an apostle who was not of peace," that he was essentially an agent of Puritan expansion who deliberately undermined Indian political and social cohesion in the interest of territorial aggradizement and political imperialism. Eliot is even accused of arming his converts and sending them on offensive campaigns against the Iroquois.[27] Thus the one New England colonist who used to draw praise from even the most anti-Puritan writers has become a prime target for modern critics.

Eliot and the other missionaries were unquestionably de-

---

[26] The existence of anti-Indian sentiment appeared, for example, in the aftermath of the Pequot War when Plymouth executed Arthur Peach and his cohorts for murdering an Indian. According to William Bradford (*History of Plymouth Plantation*, edited by Worthington C. Ford [2 vols., Boston, 1912], II, 267–268) "some of the rude and ignorant sorte murmured that any English should be put to death for the Indeans." Bradford's comment suggests that such a view was confined to a few and that they were among the least influential members of the colony.

[27] Jennings, "Goals and Functions of Puritan Missions," 197–212.

structive of Indian culture—as all proselyting clergy attack
other peoples' central beliefs. And the Puritans' insistence
on total religious and civil conversion was certainly a major
threat to tribal customs and cohesion. But the evidence of
forced conversion, of military aggression, and of hypocritical motives is circumstantial at best. Rather, the missionaries posed a more subtle and less militant peril: they undermined tribal leadership, reduced tribal strength, and cut ties
of kinship. In that sense, the missionaries were clearly detri-
mental rather than ameliorative to Indian-European relations. Many individual Indians saw the matter differently.
To the several hundred who accepted, for whatever reasons, the missionaries' message, the Puritans offered a viable
alternative life style and belief system.[28] Perhaps the increasing division of the Indian population into Christian
Indians and those who rejected or ignored anglicization
added to the likelihood of war between the latter and the
English colonies. That was not the missionaries' intention,
but Philip's comments (as reported by Easton) suggest that
the missionaries' eager search for converts may have indi-

---

[28] Explanations of Puritanism's appeal to some of the Indians are
offered in the two articles by Salisbury cited in note 10, and in William
S. Simmons, "Conversion from Indian to Puritan" (forthcoming). Ken-
neth M. Morrison, " 'That Art of Coyning Christians': John Eliot and the
Praying Indians of Massachusetts," in *Ethnohistory*, XXI (1974), 77–92,
is a flawed attempt to explain both Eliot's appeal and his failure; far
more persuasive and wide-ranging are James Axtell, "The European
Failure to Convert the Indians: An Autopsy," in Cowan, *Papers of the
Sixth Algonquian Conference*, 274–290; and James P. Ronda, " 'We are
Well As We Are': An Indian Critique of Seventeenth-Century Christian
Missions," *William and Mary Quarterly*, 3 ser. XXXIV (1977), 66–82.
See also Gary B. Nash, "Notes on the History of Seventeenth-Century
Missionization in Colonial America," *American Indian Culture and Re-
search Journal*, II, no. 2 (1978), 3–8.

rectly encouraged Philip's retaliation. In short, while acknowledging the threat that Puritan missionaries and Puritan educators posed to Indian culture, I do not subscribe to the view that Eliot and his fellow proselytizers were a quasi-militaristic arm of Puritan aggression. Such an interpretation misreads the clergy's motives and methods.

Other aspects of Puritan-Indian relations that have generated interest or debate in recent years include New England's theories and procedures of land acquisition, the reasons for Thomas Morton's expulsion from New England, Roger Williams's relations with the Indians, the impact of European diseases on the native population, and the role of Puritan theology in shaping early Indian policy.[29] Recent writings either substantially support my interpretations of these matters or seem largely unconvincing. Some issues, of course, will forever remain controversial. Historians—like jurists, theologians, physicians, and everyone else—evaluate evidence in the light of their predilections and assumptions. On those there is seldom unanimity.

*   *   *

[29] On land acquisition see Francis Jennings, "Virgin Land and Savage People," *American Quarterly*, XXIII (1971), 519–541, which in slightly revised form appears in *Invasion of America*, ch. 8: "The Deed Game"; and Ruth Barnes Moynihan, "The Patent and the Indians: The Problem of Jurisdiction in Seventeenth-Century New England," *American Indian Culture and Research Journal*, II no. 1 (1977), 8–18. I have several fundamental disagreements with Jennings's interpretation but few with Moynihan's, despite her use of *New England Frontier* as a foil. I agree that the Puritans' claim to jurisdiction over the Indians was a crucial matter throughout the seventeenth century (as I thought I had made clear); in fact it was probably more important than the acquisition of land in arousing Indian hostility.

On Thomas Morton see Slotkin, *Regeneration through Violence*, 58–60; Michael Zuckerman, "Pilgrims in the Wilderness: Community,

The original edition of *New England Frontier* suggested
that the Puritan record before 1675 merits grudging respect
from two perspectives: in comparison with the stereotypes
to which most historians and the general public have subscribed (discussed earlier), and in comparison with other
seventeenth-century colonizing ventures.

Little serious comparative work has been done on colonization.[30] Many recent studies, however, analyze Indian pol-

---

Modernity, and the Maypole at Merry Mount," *New England Quarterly*,
L (1977), 255–277; and Karen Ordahl Kupperman, "Thomas Morton,
Historian," *ibid.*, 660–664. All three authors, I believe, misread the
evidence, and Kupperman grossly underestimates the significance of
firearms to the English and Indians alike. The already substantial
literature on Roger Williams continues to grow. Works that give
particular attention to Williams and the Indians include Moynihan "The
Patent and the Indians"; and Jack L. Davis, "Roger Williams among the
Narragansett Indians," *New England Quarterly*, XLIII (1970), 593–604.
The most important work on New England's Indian population was
done by the late Sherburne F. Cook. See his "Interracial Warfare and
Population Decline among the New England Indians"; "The Significance
of Disease in the Extinction of the New England Indians," *Human
Biology*, XLV (1973), 485–508; and *The Indian Population of New
England in the Seventeenth Century* (Berkeley, Calif., 1976). The best
study of Indian population loss from disease in Plymouth Colony, and
of its implications, is Alfred W. Crosby, "God . . . Would Destroy
Them, and Give Their Country to Another People . . . ," *American
Heritage*, XXIX, no. 6 (Oct./Nov. 1978) 38–43. On the role of Puritan
theology see Segal and Stineback, *Puritans, Indians and Manifest Destiny*,
and David C. Stineback, "The Status of Puritan-Indian Scholarship,"
New England Quarterly, LI (1978), 80–90. Aspects of the Indian side
of the religious equation can be found in Ronda, " 'We Are Well As We
Are';" Frank Shuffelton, "Indian Devils and the Pilgrim Fathers:
Squanto, Hobomok, and the English Conception of Indian Religion,"
New England Quarterly, XLIX (1976), 108–116; and William S. Simmons, "Southern New England Indian Shamanism: An Ethnographic
Reconstruction," in William Cowan, ed., *Papers of the Seventh Algon-
quian Conference, 1975* (Ottawa, 1976), 217–256.

[30] Most attempts are either multi-authored volumes in which each
contributor is conversant with only one area (see, for example, Howard
Peckham and Charles Gibson, eds., *Attitudes of Colonial Powers toward*

icy in the areas settled by the Spanish, Portuguese, French, Dutch, and English. And it is increasingly evident that the several English colonies did not act the same toward their Indian neighbors. In the broadest sense, of course, Indians were victims in every area of European settlement: they suffered discrimination, exploitation, and wholesale destruction—by disease and demoralization if not by sword and bullet. But there were differences of degree in treatment and differences of emphasis in attitude among the colonizing groups.

One need not, for example, wholly subscribe to the "Black Legend" of extreme Spanish cruelty or accept uncritically every charge by the Dominican bishop Bartolomé de las Casas to conclude that early Spanish treatment of the Indians was deplorable. Las Casas's claim that in forty years the Spanish slaughtered as many as twenty million natives "by making bloody, unjust, and cruel wars against them" may be hyperbolic, but only the staunchest defenders of Spanish policy deny the ruthlessness of the conquistadors and the inability of both crown and clergy to ameliorate appreciably the Indians' plight. When the Indians rejected Spain's civil and ecclesiastical authority, the *requerimiento* (read to the Indians in Spanish) warned them that "we shall take you and your wives and children and make slaves

---

the *American Indian* [Salt Lake City, 1969]), or the efforts of a single scholar whose expertise is weighted heavily in favor of one region at the expense of others (e.g., James Lang, *Conquest and Commerce: Spain and England in the America* [New York, 1975], which is far better on New Spain than on British America). Whatever their shortcomings, such studies have at least begun to provide a basis for historical comparisons. Because of my own unfamiliarity with many of the primary sources on non-English colonization, I offer my comparative judgments tentatively.

of them . . . and do to you all the harm and damage that we can . . . ; and we protest that the deaths and losses which shall accrue from this are your fault." Although Las Casas and many of his fellow missionaries objected vehemently to such tactics, colonial officials ignored the clerics with impunity. Moreover, the missionaries' goal was to convert and "Spanishize" the Indians, not to preserve their cultural identity.[31]

---

[31] Even Lewis Hanke, the most articulate defender of Spain's Indian policy, presents abundant evidence that the humanitarian views of Las Casas did not prevail in sixteenth-century America. See especially his *Spanish Struggle for Justice in the Conquest of America* (Washington, 1949) and *Aristotle and the American Indians: A Study in Race Prejudice in the Modern World* (Bloomington, Ind., 1959). In each work Hanke offers a comparative judgment of his own; in the former, for example, he asserts, that "No European nation with the possible exception of Portugal, took her Christian duty toward native peoples so seriously as did Spain" (p. 175). He sees this concern for "Christian duty" reflected in Spain's general treatment of the natives as well as in missionary efforts. Hanke singles out the Puritans as the Spaniards' antithesis, but offers in support only a quote, badly wrenched from context, from Theodore Parker, a nineteenth-century clergyman. In the published debate between Hanke and Benjamin Keen on the Spanish conquest, in the *Hispanic American Historical Review*, XLIX-LI (1969–1971), the overwhelming bulk of the evidence, in my opinion, is on Keen's side. See especially Keen's "The White Legend Revisited . . . ," *ibid.*, LI (1971), 336–355. The case for Spanish cruelty and forced conversion does not, as some critics of Las Casas forget, depend exclusively or even primarily on his testimony. Las Casas was one voice among many, though he was certainly the most persistent, articulate, and morally outraged. See also Las Casas, *In Defense of the Indians*, translated by Stafford Poole (DeKalb, Ill., 1974). For a convenient and reliable summary of Spanish treatment of the Indians see Charles Gibson, *Spain in America* (New York, 1966), especially chs. 2, 3, and 7. Important works that have appeared since Gibson's synthesis include J. H. Parry, *The Spanish Seaborne Empire* (New York, 1972); Juan Friede and Benjamin Keen, eds., *Bartolome de las Casas in History* (1972); Sherburne F. Cook and Woodrow Borah, *Essays in Population History: Mexico and the Caribbean*, 2 vols. (Berkeley, Calif., 1971–1974); Robert G. Keith, *Conquest and Agrarian Change: The Emergence of the Hacienda Sys-*

Studies of the Dutch in New Netherland and South America and of the Portuguese in Brazil reveal less wholesale destruction but little concern for Indian pròperty, culture, or lives in those areas. As in Spanish America, some voices were raised in defense of the Indians and some government regulations attempted to restrain the settlers' aggression, but usually the curbs were honored in the breach. Interracial wars were common, and the vanquished tribes either moved inland or endured flagrant discrimination and exploitation within the European spheres.[32]

New France is frequently cited as an area of friendly and equitable race relations. There is evidence to support the claim, although the paucity of French settlers and the relative abundance of Indians make comparison with other

---

tem on the Peruvian Coast (Cambridge, Mass., 1977); Nathan Wachtel, *The Vision of the Vanquished: The Spanish Conquest of Peru through Indian Eyes, 1530–1570* (first pub., France, 1971; English trans., Hassocks, Eng., 1977); Gibson, "Conquest, Capitulation, and Indian Treaties," *American Historical Review*, LXXXIII (1978), 1-15; and William L. Sherman, *Forced Native Labor in Sixteenth-Century America* (Lincoln, Neb., 1979). A convenient selection of primary sources is Charles Gibson, ed., *The Spanish Tradition in America* (New York, 1968); the quote from Las Casas is on p. 107, the quote from the *requerimiento* on p. 60.

[32] On the Dutch see Allen W. Trelease, *Indian Affairs in Colonial New York: The Seventeenth Century* (Ithaca, N.Y., 1960); Charles R. Boxer, *The Dutch Seaborne Empire, 1600–1800* (New York, 1964); and Trelease, "Dutch Treatment of the American Indian . . . ," in Peckham and Gibson, *Attitudes of Colonial Powers*. On the Portuguese see Dauriel Alden, "Black Robes versus White Settlers: The Struggle for 'Freedom of the Indians' in Colonial Brazil," in *ibid.;* Charles R. Boxer, *The Portuguese Seaborne Empire, 1415–1825* (New York, 1970); Stuart B. Schwartz, "Indian Labor and New World Plantations: European Demands and Indian Responses in Northeastern Brazil," *American Historical Review*, LXXXIII (1978), 43–79; and especially John Hemming, *Red Gold: The Conquest of the Brazilian Indians, 1500–1760* (Cambridge, Mass., 1978).

colonies difficult.[33] Too often French frontiersmen, who—
much like the Englishmen at Wessagusett and Merrymount
—consorted freely with the Indians, are compared with Puritan townspeople, who did not. The situations were radically different. The former were single men living in the
forests; the latter came, in most cases, as families and settled
in tightly knit communities. In New France, as in New
England, European immigrants in family-centered communities rarely mixed with Indian society or welcomed the
natives into the new settlements except as traders or converts. In general, the attitudes and policies of French settlers and missionaries seem to have closely approximated
those of the English, with a parallel determination to
"Frenchify" the Indians and to reduce as much as possible
the power and influence of Indian culture. From the outset,

---

[33] The literature on Indian-European relations in New France is en-
joying a boom. Some important recent contributions are Bruce G.
Trigger, "The French Presence in Huronia: The Structure of Franco-
Huron Relations in the First Half of the Seventeenth Century,"
Canadian Historical Review, XLIX (1968), 107–141; same author, *The
Children of Aetaentsic: A History of the Huron People to 1660*, 2 vols.
(Montreal, 1976); Conrad Heidenreich, *Huronia: A History and Geog-
raphy of the Huron Indians, 1600–1650* (Toronto, 1971); James P.
Ronda, "The European Indian: Jesuit Civilization Planning in New
France," *Church History*, XLI (1972), 385–395; W. J. Eccles, *The
Canadian Frontier, 1534–1760* (New York, 1969); same author, *France
in America* (New York, 1973); Cornelius J. Jaenen, "The Frenchifica-
tion and Evangelization of the Amerindians in the Seventeenth Century
New France," *Canadian Catholic Historical Association, Study Sessions,
1968*, XXXV (1969), 57–71; and same author, *Friend and Foe: Aspects
of French-Amerindian Cultural Contact in the Sixteenth and Seventeenth
Centuries* (New York, 1976). For additional citations see the excellent
bibliographies in the two books by Eccles cited above, and Robert F.
Berkhofer, Jr., *The White Man's Indian: Images of the American Indian
from Columbus to the Present* (New York, 1978), 231.

the French as well as the English found that the Indian was sometimes a ruthless enemy, often an essential ally, and occasionally an enthusiastic convert. He was not, however, esteemed as a cultural equal, and he was seldom integrated fully into the European community. Nor was he left alone. In the seventeenth century all Christian denominations sought to save the Indian from himself.

A more valid measure of Puritan policy toward the Indians comes from a comparison with the record in other English colonies, for there the variables are fewer and the evidence clearer. A case in point is Jamestown, founded only thirteen years before Plymouth and beset by similar problems of inadequate supply, inept financing, and high mortality. Virginia's record in Indian relations contrasts sharply with New England's; hostility characterized the Chesapeake colony's relations from the outset. By 1613, scores—perhaps hundreds—had been slain on each side. From then until 1622 the colony and neighboring tribes enjoyed a fragile peace, inaugurated by the kidnapping of Pocahontas and her marriage to John Rolfe and capped by efforts to build a college at Henrico for Indian youths. But the massacre of nearly 350 Virginia settlers in 1622, and the ensuing decade of warfare, ended interracial amity. For the remainder of the century the races stood apart: few conversions took place, few educational institutions admitted Indian students, and extremely few interracial marriages occurred. Nothing in the Virginia experience matched Puritan educational efforts on both the secondary and collegiate levels; no Virginia missionary achieved a substantial fraction of Eliot's or Mayhew's conversions; no Virginia court imposed the death sentence on Europeans for killing

Indians, as did courts in both Plymouth and Massachusetts. There are numerous other examples of a more amicable and integrative policy in New England than in Virginia.[34]

Several circumstances help to explain the contrasts between Anglo-Indian relations in Virginia and in New England. To some extent they reflect differences in the size and character of the native population: Virginians faced a far larger and more powerful array of Indians than did New Englanders. To some extent they reflect differences in colonial demography: the relatively transient Virginians were predominantly young adult males, in contrast to the men, women, and children of all ages who settled permanently in New England. To a considerable extent, however, the settlers' motives determined colonial policy. In both areas the English held Indian culture in low regard and assumed, as an article of faith, that Christianity and "civilization" would prove so attractive to the Indians that they would readily accept both religious and social conversion. But the Virginians' almost exclusive concern with profits, and eventually with a cash crop, encouraged an aggressive and generally exploitive policy. During the first seven years of

---

[34] On attitudes and policies in seventeenth-century Virginia see Wesley Frank Craven, "Indian Policy in Early Virginia," *William and Mary Quarterly*, 3 ser. I (1944), 65–82; W. Stitt Robinson, "The Indian Policy of Colonial Virginia" (Ph.D. dissertation, University of Virginia, 1950); Gary B. Nash, "The Image of the Indian in the Southern Colonial Mind," *William and Mary Quarterly*, 3 ser. XXIX (1972), 197–230; Alden T. Vaughan, *American Genesis: Captain John Smith and the Founding of Virginia* (Boston, 1975); same author, " 'Expulsion of the Salvages': English Policy and the Virginia Massacre of 1622," *William and Mary Quarterly*, 3 ser. XXXV (1978), 57–84; Edmund S. Morgan, *American Slavery, American Freedom: The Ordeal of Colonial Virginia* (New York, 1975); and J. Frederick Fausz, "The Powhatan Uprising of 1622: A Historical Study of Ethnocentrism and Culture Conflict" (Ph.D. dissertation, College of William and Mary, 1977).

settlement, the colonists traded mostly at sword's point; they also exacted tribute in goods and labor from many neighboring tribes. Even during the calm years from 1614 to 1622, tribute payments continued and many Indians were hired for menial labor. The result was a heightened mutual resentment and distrust, as early Virginia writings attest. After the 1622 uprising, English authorities advocated extermination or enslavement of the Indians. Only the difficulty of enforcing wholesale bondage preserved the surviving Indians from perpetual labor. By contrast, the New England colonists, and especially their leaders, expected their New World experience to justify their removal from England; not only must they create a godly society but they must bring the Gospel to the heathen.

The Puritan missionary impulse did not affect every New Englander. Some openly scoffed at exhortations to convert the Indians—by example as well as action—and many were simply indifferent to the natives. The ethos proved strong enough among the leaders and many of the followers, however, to shape a relatively benign Indian policy that was reflected in a multitude of regulations concerning conduct toward the Indians. To some extent the laws were self-protective, and to a considerable extent they were paternalistic. But they aimed, for whatever reasons, at an orderly and integrated frontier, where treatment of the Indians would be less callous and arbitrary than in Spanish America or English Virginia.

Puritan leaders did more than promulgate laws. With a few exceptions they sought peaceful solutions to interracial tensions. In war the Puritans could be as ruthless as any seventeenth-century mortals, as they demonstrated in 1637 and 1675. They preferred, however, to avoid force. Most of the civil leaders had strong commitments to a tranquil society. They had virtually no military experience, and they did not even accompany the few expeditions before 1675. Moreover, in times of crisis they turned to the clergy for guidance. Decisions on war and peace therefore usually reflected a ministerial mentality: in a "just war" the Lord wanted His enemies crushed, but war was to be a last resort and had to be clearly supported by moral and Biblical precept. Nearly all the leaders of early Virginia, on the other hand, were professional militarists. John Smith, Thomas Gates, Thomas Dale, Samuel Argall, and other hardened veterans set the tone of their colony's race relations. As Captain Smith boasted, "The Warres in *Europe, Asia,* and *Africa* taught me how to subdue the wilde Salvages in *Virginia.*"[35] Virginia's early leaders had lived by the sword; they were not reluctant to wield it against recalcitrant natives.

Another comparison may be instructive. Maryland was first settled in 1634, by Englishmen who also hoped to create a haven for themselves and their followers and to convert and civilize their Indian neighbors. The colony initially enjoyed amicable race relations. Within less than a decade, however, several incidents cast doubt on the colonists' ability to treat the Indians fairly. For example, in

---

[35] Edward Arber and A. G. Bradley, eds., *Travels and Works of Captain John Smith,* 2 vols. (Edinburgh, 1910), II, 925. A comparison of the Indian vocabularies compiled by Smith and by New Englanders such as William Wood and Roger Williams is instructive. Far more of Smith's words suggest conflict, and his sample sentences are highly aggressive in tone. For Smith's vocabulary see *ibid.,* 43–46; for Wood's see Alden T. Vaughan, ed., *New England's Prospect* (Amherst, Mass., 1977), 117–124; for Williams's see John J. Teunissen and Evelyn J. Hinz, eds., *A Key into the Language of America* (Detroit, 1973), *passim.*

February 1643, a Maryland planter, John Elkin, killed "a certaine Indian commonly called the king of Yowocomoco." Despite Elkin's confession, the twelve-man jury found him not guilty "because the party was a pagan, & because they had no president [precedent] in the neighbour colony of virginea to make such facts murther."[36] Governor Leonard Calvert ordered a new trial on the grounds that English laws rather than Virginia precedent should prevail, and Elkin was eventually convicted of manslaughter, but the case contrasts significantly with New England's reaction to colonists who killed Indians. I have, in fact, found no evidence of the execution of a European for the murder of an Indian in any seventeenth-century British colony outside of New England.

Among Britain's colonies in North America, Pennsylvania has long been acknowledged to have had the most peaceful and equitable dealings with the Indians.[37] On the whole the record supports this view, and the Quakers deserve much of the praise they have received. It should

---

[36] William Hand Browne et al., eds., *Maryland Archives* (Baltimore, 1883–), IV, 177, 180.

[37] There is need for a modern study of Pennsylvania's Indian-European relations. Useful but inadequate are Thomas E. Drake, "William Penn's Experiment in Race Relations," *Pennsylvania Magazine of History and Biography*, LXVIII (1944), 372–387; Frederick B. Tolles, "Nonviolent Contact: The Quakers and the Indians," *American Philosophical Society Proceedings*, CVII (1963), 93–101; Paul A. W. Wallace, *Indians in Pennsylvania* (Harrisburg, Pa., 1961); Francis Jennings, "Miquon's Passing: Indian-European Relations in Colonial Pennsylvania, 1674 to 1755" (Ph.D. dissertation, University of Pennsylvania, 1965); several articles by Jennings (for titles see the bibliography by Francis Paul Prucha cited in note 40); and C. A. Weslager, *The Delaware Indians: A History* (New Brunswick, N.J., 1972). The best work on early Indian-European relations in Pennsylvania, especially good in its portrayal of the Indian side, is Anthony F. C. Wallace, *King of the Delawares: Teedyuscung, 1700–1763* (Philadelphia, 1949).

be borne in mind, however, that the Quakers, like the other European colonists, held Indian culture in low esteem and sought its eventual demise. Moreover, Iroquois raids against the Susquehannocks, and subsequent European encroachments, had cleared most of eastern Pennsylvania of Indian inhabitants before William Penn arrived. When Quaker settlement began in earnest in the 1680s, the remaining Indians were largely peaceful Leni Lenapis (Delawares), who already enjoyed stable relations with the local Dutch, Swedish, and English settlers. Yet even this sparse and docile native population retreated westward before inexorable colonial expansion. And by mid-eighteenth century, when Pennsylvania's majority had become heavily non-Quaker, the colony's pacifist heritage was increasingly ignored; thereafter, Pennsylvania's Indian relations resembled the patterns established elsewhere. Even under Quaker dominance, the infamous "Walking Purchase," in which the Indians were defrauded of thousands of acres of valuable land, revealed that in Pennsylvania too the natives were not free from exploitation or swindle.[38]

*   *   *

What then can be claimed for the Puritans of seventeenth-century New England? Not success, certainly, for they clearly failed by both their criterion (assimilation) and ours (cultural pluralism). Not nobility of attitude either, for they exhibited as little appreciation of Indian ways as did other European settlers and were as insistent as any

---

[38] Francis Jennings, "The Scandalous Indian Policy of William Penn's Sons: Deeds and Documents of the Walking Purchase," *Pennsylvania History*, XXXVII (1970), 19–39. An important forthcoming collection of Pennsylvania Indian treaties and related documents, edited by Donald H. Kent, should encourage new monographic studies.

that the Indians commit cultural suicide. Perhaps the best that can be said for them—as I originally argued in *New England Frontier* and still maintain—is that the Puritans made a brief but notable effort to avoid the violent confrontations that characterized most other seventeenth-century European colonies and to incorporate the native population peacefully and voluntarily into their version of a holy commonwealth. The Puritans failed, partly because they would not or could not shed their ethnocentricity, partly because they did not always live up to their own ideals of equity, and chiefly because they presented the Indians with an unreasonable demand and impossible expectation, which predictably (from the hindsight of the twentieth century) most Indians rejected. When it became clear, in 1675 or perhaps earlier, that the Indians would never fulfill Puritan hopes and that their refusal was both a rebuke to the godly and an obstacle to English expansion, Puritan policy changed. Thereafter, New England's relations with the Indians were barely distinguishable from those of the other British American outposts: intermittent warfare along an advancing frontier, confinement to reservations for tribes which submitted or were defeated, and debasement or even enslavement for individual Indians within the European sphere.[39]

The study of Puritan-Indian contact deserves a respite from exculpation or polemical criticisms of the colonists.

---

[39] There has been relatively little attention to post-1675 Anglo-Indian relations in New England. Two important recent exceptions are John A. Sainsbury, "Indian Labor in Early Rhode Island," *New England Quarterly*, XLVIII (1975), 378–393; and Richard R. Johnson, "The Search for a Usable Indian: An Aspect of the Defense of Colonial New England," *Journal of American History*, LXIV (1977–1978), 623–651.

More promising are interdisciplinary analyses of the interplay of diverse cultures, European and Indian, and their
numerous subcultures. Studies that treat a limited aspect
of the subject will still be useful; contributions to scholarship always come in assorted packages. But the best hope
for a comprehensive and sophisticated understanding of
interracial or intercultural contact lies in a wide-ranging
ethnohistorical approach. Stimulated by anthropological
concepts and methods, especially as they relate to Indian
culture, yet firmly rooted in the historian's view of the
past as an ever-changing tapestry, ethnohistory sees culture
contact from both sides of the frontier. Ethnohistorians
have already made important contributions to our understanding of early race relations; more are in progress.[40]

---

[40] The vast outpouring of important books and articles during the last
fifteen years has, on the whole, improved our understanding of early
Indian-European contact. For reviews of some of that literature and
for articulate pleas for ethnohistory as the most promising approach to
future studies, see James Axtell, "The Ethnohistory of Early America:
A Review Essay," *William and Mary Quarterly*, 3 ser. XXXV (1978),
110–144; Calvin Martin, "Ethnohistory: A Better Way to Write Indian
History," *Western Historical Quarterly*, IX (1978), 41–56. Jennings,
Invasion of America, stridently purports to be ethnohistorical, and to
some extent it is—as, to a greater or lesser degree, are most studies of
Indian-European relations that have appeared in the last two decades.
But if ethnohistory attempts to understand European as well as Indian
culture, and if it encompasses an attitude as well as a method, some
recent studies fall far short of the mark.

Among recent guides to the abundant literature on Indian-European
contact, the most useful is Francis Paul Prucha, *A Bibliographical Guide
to the History of Indian-White Relations in the United States* (Chicago,
1977), which lists almost ten thousand books and articles. Also helpful
are the bibliographic essays on a variety of topics being published by
Indiana University Press for the Newberry Library's Center for the
History of the American Indian. Of those already issued, the most
pertinent to early New England are James P. Ronda and James Axtell,
Indian Missions: A Critical Bibliography (Bloomington, Ind., 1978); and

And their value may not be exclusively academic. Future relations among Americans—Indian, European, African, and Asian—may become more tolerant and hopeful as we better comprehend our nation's anguished prologue.

*   *   *

For perceptive critiques of the original edition of this book and helpful comments on a preliminary draft of this introduction, I am indebted to numerous students and friends. Especially generous were James Axtell, Barry W. Bienstock, Francis J. Bremer, Jr., and David C. Stineback. None will be entirely satisfied with the final version, but each, I hope, will find evidence of his judicious advice.

Elizabeth Tooker, *The Indians of the Northeast: A Critical Bibliography* (Bloomington, Ind., 1978).
   Probably the most important publishing project of the century for early-American ethnohistory is the Smithsonian Institution's twenty-volume *Handbook of North American Indians*, which will replace Frederick Webb Hodge's *Handbook of American Indians North of Mexico* (2 vols., Washington, 1907). Under the general editorship of William C. Sturtevant, volumes VIII (*California*) and XV (*Northeast*) have already appeared. Future volumes will cover all of the major geographical areas; topical volumes will include *History of Indian-White Relations*, edited by Wilcomb E. Washburn, and two volumes of biographical sketches. *Northeast*, edited by Bruce G. Trigger, is especially pertinent.

Introduction to the Third Edition

IN THE FIFTEEN years since the second edition of this book appeared, in 1979, scholarly and popular writings on the interaction of Native Americans and New England Puritans match—in quantity and intensity of interpretation—the fertile 1960s and 1970s. Nor is the end in sight. Who would have predicted in 1965 that Puritan-Indian studies would become one of American history's liveliest cottage industries?

Who would have predicted either (not I) that *New England Frontier* would survive three decades of historiographical battles? It bears some bruises, to be sure, but thanks to a cluster of loyal readers and sanguine publishers, this book begins its third incarnation. In the best of all worlds, I would have rewritten *New England Frontier* entirely, incorporating new research, rephrasing many passages, and rebutting several misguided works on Puritan-Indian relations that have appeared since the first edition. Although the resulting book surely would improve on the 1965 and 1979 versions, its basic argument would remain largely intact. (That argument is stated most baldly—and in terminology I would not use today—in the conclusion to the first edition and, somewhat modified, in the introduction to the second edition.) Instead, the University of Oklahoma Press kindly has invited me to update *New England Frontier* in this new introduction.[1] I welcome the opportunity to reassess

---

[1]This edition incorporates a few corrections, mostly of typographical

several aspects of Puritan-Indian relations while presenting
my gloss and strictures on some of the recent literature,
most of it published since I wrote the introduction to the
second edition in the late 1970s.

*   *   *

Scholarship in the past fifteen years has reflected a
curious interpretive disjunction. On the one hand, wide-
ranging assessments of Indian-white relations throughout
North America are more critical than ever of the Puritans'
attitudes and actions toward their Indian neighbors. On the
other hand, specialists on seventeenth-century New England, especially those who study missionary activity, warfare, and law, have rendered more favorable judgments than
have the generalists and—on balance—the specialists of the
1960s and 1970s. The gulf that now divides the Puritans'
harsh critics from their cautious defenders is not, as it often
was in the past, primarily a matter of the interpreters'
geographical origins (non-New England debunkers versus
New England-bred or -based apologists) but rather is between synthetic generalists and research specialists.[2]

General studies of Europe's "invasion of America"—to

---

errors, in the introduction to the second edition. For improving this new
introduction, I am grateful to Francis J. Bremer, Richard W. Cogley, and
Virginia M. Vaughan.
    [2]In the seventeenth through nineteenth centuries, the geographic align-
ment generally held fast, despite an occasional Adams family apostate (most
notably Brooks Adams). Even in the twentieth century the pattern held fairly
firm, with most writings sympathetic to the Puritans (whether on Indian-
white relations or on other aspects of New England culture) emerging from
the faculties of Harvard and Yale. For reviews of the historiographical literature from a variety of perspectives, see Francis J. Bremer, "From the Old
World to the New, 1620–1689," in *A Guide to the History of Massachusetts*, ed.
Martin Kaufman, John W. Ifkovic, and Joseph Carvalho III, (Westport,
Conn., 1988), 3–22.

borrow Francis Jennings's provocative but reductionist title—have been both abundant and strident in recent years,
spurred partly perhaps by the Columbian quincentennial.
Earlier condemnations of the New Englanders' treatment of
the Indians are tame indeed compared to the assaults in
Richard Drinnon's *Facing West* (1980), Forrest Wood's *Arrogance of Faith* (1990), and David Stannard's *American Holocaust* (1992).[3] These sweeping accounts invariably reflect,
and often cite, Jennings's book of 1975, which may be
explanation enough for their scathing assessments of Puritan attitudes and policies; synthetic studies have to rely in
large part on secondary sources, and the most recent and
self-assured work on a subject usually seizes the day.[4] With

---

[3]Richard Drinnon, *Facing West: The Metaphysics of Indian-Hating and Em-
pire-Building* (Minneapolis, 1980), part one; Forrest G. Wood, *The Arrogance of
Faith: Christianity and Race in America from the Colonial Era to the Twentieth
Century* (New York, 1990), 20–21, 95–96, 259–76; and David E. Stannard,
American Holocaust: Columbus and the Conquest of the New World (New York,
1992), esp. 108–18, 230–39. Another wide-ranging book that excoriates the
Puritans' attitudes and actions toward the Indians is Ronald Takaki, *A
Different Mirror: A History of Multicultural America* (Boston, 1993), 37–44.
Most of that section is borrowed verbatim from Takaki's article of a few
months earlier: "*The Tempest* in the Wilderness: The Racialization of Savagery," *Journal of American History*, LXXIX (1992–93), 892–912. For some of my
objections to Takaki's research and interpretations, see my letter to the editor
in *Journal of American History*, LXXX (1993–94), 764–67.
[4]Francis Jennings, *The Invasion of America: Indians, Colonialism, and the Cant
of Conquest* (Chapel Hill, N.C., 1975), part two. In addition to the works cited
in note 3, the following post–1979 studies explicitly or implicitly rely heavily
on Jennings: Neal E. Salisbury, *Manitou and Providence: Indians, Europeans,
and the Making of New England, 1500–1643* (New York, 1982); Alvin Josephy,
Jr., *Now That the Buffalo's Gone: A Study of Today's American Indians* (New York,
1982); and Ann Kibbey, *The Interpretation of Material Shapes in Puritanism: A
Study of Rhetoric, Prejudice, and Violence* (Cambridge, 1986). For my earlier
critique of Jennings's book see *Western Historical Quarterly*, VII (1976), 421–22;
and on Salisbury's book, see my review in *New England Quarterly*, LVI (1983),
129–32. Jennings's recent overview of Indian-white relations in North America, *The Founders of America: How the Indians Discovered the Land, Pioneered It, and
Created Great Classical Civilizations; How They Were Plunged into a Dark Age*

the exception of Neal Salisbury's *Manitou and Providence,* which ends in 1643, Jennings's book has been not only "the latest word" but also the most critical of Puritan sources, thus making all previous histories of early New England appear tainted.[5] Moreover, Jennings was saying what many historians and readers in the 1970s, 1980s and early 1990s wanted to hear: that our nation's modern foibles stemmed from a national character flaw which began in 1607 and grew inexorably worse as the centuries wore on. And because Christianity, ancient and modern, was often the megahistorians' ultimate villain, the pious, Bible-quoting Puritans were an obvious target.[6]

In contrast to many generalists' contention that the Puritans were unusually vicious and blatantly hypocritical toward their Indian neighbors, many specialists have viewed more benignly the New England colonies' relations with Indians in the half century before King Philip's War. Most notably in studies of Puritan missionary endeavors, recent commentators have judged John Eliot and his proselytizing contemporaries within the context of their times and the theological framework of evangelical Christianity. Whereas Jennings charged that "[f]ew historical records show more

---

by Invasion and Conquest; and How They Are Reviving (New York, 1993) includes interpretations of early New England that condense his earlier accounts.

[5]In *Invasion of America,* Jennings had charged the Puritan gentry with "excruciating cant and masterful guile" in their recording and preservation of evidence (p. 185), but recent specialist scholars of Puritan writings have rejected that assessment. On Jennings's admitted bias against Puritan gentry (*Invasion of America,* preface and ch. 1), see the postscript to my essay on the causes of the Pequot War in *Roots of American Racism: Essays on the Colonial Experience* (New York, 1995).

[6]For explicit condemnation of Christianity as the root of American racism, see especially Wood, preface to *Arrogance of Faith;* and Stannard, epilogue to *American Holocaust.*

sanctimonious piety in words [than the New England missionaries'] with less piety in performance," recent students of proselytizing in New England document Jennings's distortion of missionary motives and achievements and his indifference to religion as a historical force. Specialists have similarly assessed Indian responses to the missionaries in light of varied Indian needs, initiatives, and beliefs.[7]

Unlike almost all earlier historians, Jennings excoriated Eliot, the Roxbury, Massachusetts, pastor and "apostle," charging that he forced Indian conversions, armed Christian Indians to attack other Indians, and lied about his own and other missionaries' accomplishments.[8] A new generation of scholars, many of them with training in religion as well as history, sharply challenge Jennings's interpretation. While admitting that the missionaries undermined Indian culture, Richard Cogley, Timothy Sehr, and others have stressed Eliot's millennialist theology and its centrality in his missionary program.[9] In Sehr's words:

> The conversion of Indians would be proof [to the Puritans] of the outpouring of grace that is the prelude to the millenni-

---

[7]Jennings, *Founders of America*, 191. For a review of the literature on Puritan missionaries, especially John Eliot, see Richard W. Cogley, "John Eliot in Recent Scholarship," *American Indian Culture and Research Journal*, XIV, no. 2 (1990), 77–92.

[8]Francis Jennings, "Goals and Functions of Puritan Missions to the Indians," *Ethnohistory*, XVIII (1971), 197–212; Jennings, *Invasion of America*, ch. 14; and Jennings, *Founders of America*, 191–92. In the last work listed, Jennings not only summarizes his earlier critiques of Eliot but implies that Eliot sexually exploited Indian women at the Natick praying town.

[9]See especially Timothy J. Sehr, "John Eliot, Millennialist and Missionary," *The Historian*, XLVI (1983–84), 187–203; James Holstun, *A Rational Millennium: Puritan Utopias of Seventeenth-Century England and America* (New York, 1987), ch. 3; Richard W. Cogley, "John Eliot and the Millennium," *Religion and American Culture*, I (1991), 227–50; and Cogley, "Idealism vs.

um. God's kingdom would include all nations, and therefore the regenerate among the Indians would begin to feel the movement of saving grace within them if the last days had begun. For some commentators conversions among the Indians were particularly important. These men saw the Indians as Jews, descendants of the Lost Tribes of Israel [who] . . . must be converted before most of the Gentiles could be.[10]

Cogley's several articles expand on this theme and explicitly rebut the distorted version of Eliot and his work that appeared in *Invasion of America* and implicitly rebut Jennings's recent synthesis, *The Founders of America*. "A fuller appreciation of Eliot's millenarianism reveals the inadequacy of Jennings's materialistic interpretation," Cogley insisted, partly because Jennings's "misunderstanding of Eliot derives from his misunderstanding of religion." Even on issues that did not require a knowledge of religious thought and practice, Cogley demonstrated that Jennings often misrepresented the missionary through "contrived accounts" based on selective quotations, strategic omissions, and innuendo. "Yet for twenty years they have remained unchallenged in the historical literature."[11] Cogley's several articles and book-in-progress should go a long way toward setting the record straight.

Materialism in the Study of Puritan Missions to the Indians," *Method and Theory in the Study of Religion*, III (1991), 165–82.

[10]Sehr, "John Eliot," 190. Eliot's attachment to the Lost Tribes origin of the Indians has received considerable recent attention. See, for example, David S. Katz, *Philo-Semitism and the Readmission of Jews into England* (London, 1982); Richard W. Cogley, "John Eliot and the Origins of the American Indians," *Early American Literature*, XXI (1986–87), 210–25; and Alden T. Vaughan, "Early English Paradigms for New World Natives," *American Antiquarian Society Proceedings*, CII, part one (1992), 33–67, esp. 56–65.

[11]Cogley, "Idealism vs. Materialism," esp. 169, 165–66, 180.

Other historians have focused on the Indian side of missionary contact, demonstrating the significance of conversion for many Indians and the sincerity of most such cultural adaptations. Several of James Axtell's works make this case, especially his reassessment of Puritan (and Jesuit) missionary effectiveness, as do recent publications by Robert James Naeher and Charles Cohen.[12] Naeher emphasized the appeal to potential converts of the Puritans' emphasis on prayer:

> Destruction and displacement caused by English disease and settlement utterly disrupted traditional Indian culture. A tremendous need for order and stability was thereby created, for which the Puritan gospel was then offered as a solution. To say . . . that the Praying Indians were coerced into accepting Eliot's message, whether that coercion was overt or covert, is not to hear the Indians' voice in the dialogue conducted with Eliot. . . . Prayer was . . . the central motif of their Christianity, for it met, in a meaningful and emotionally satisfying way, deep human needs that the Indians shared with the New England Puritans.

---

[12] James Axtell, *The Invasion Within: The Contest of Cultures in Colonial North America* (New York, 1985), esp. 138–50; Axtell, "Some Thoughts on the Ethnohistory of Missions," in Axtell, *After Columbus: Essays in the Ethnohistory of Colonial North America* (New York, 1988), 47–57; Axtell, "Were Indian Conversions *Bona Fide?*" in *After Columbus*, 100–121; Robert James Naeher, "Dialogue in the Wilderness: John Eliot and the Indian Exploration of Puritanism as a Source of Meaning, Comfort, and Ethnic Survival," *New England Quarterly*, LXII (1989), 346–68; and Charles L. Cohen, "Conversion Among Puritans and Amerindians: A Theological and Cultural Perspective," in *Puritanism: Transatlantic Perspectives on a Seventeenth-Century Anglo-American Faith*, ed. Francis J. Bremer (Boston, 1993), 233–56. Cohen is primarily interested in the Indian converts' grasp of Puritan theology, but implicit in his analysis is the sincerity of Eliot's efforts and of the converts' intentions.

Missionary institutions also served vital Indian needs.

> Praying Church congregations were surrogates for frac-
> tured Indian kinship networks, and Praying Towns pro-
> vided supportive communities for a disoriented population.
> Carved from territories formerly theirs and now free from
> European encroachment, Praying Towns thus offered Indi-
> ans an opportunity to preserve their ethnic identity on
> [quoting James Axtell] "familiar pieces of land that carried
> their inner history."[13]

Axtell has argued that "[a]t the cost of a certain amount of
material and spiritual continuity with the past, [the converts'] acceptance of Christianity . . . allowed them not
only to survive in the present but gave them a long lease on
life when many of their colonial landlords threatened to
foreclose all future options." Physical and psychological
survival was the Indians' objective; conversion was valid,
even honorable, if it contributed to the goal. Axtell chided
"the new debunking" by Jennings, Salisbury, and others for
being "essentially polemical and [factually] incorrect."[14]

Another scholar of the missionary movement, Harold
Van Lonkhuyzen, emphasized "the social context of conversion." He discerned numerous and substantial reasons why
some Indians found Natick appealing, although in contrast

---

[13]Naeher, "Dialogue in the Wilderness," 367, 365.
[14]Axtell, "Ethnohistory of Missions," 51; Axtell, "Indian Conversions,"
108. Axtell takes issue with a number of histories of early New England and
Canada; among the former, his principal targets are Jennings, "Goals and
Functions" and *Invasion of America*, ch. 14; and Neal Salisbury, "Red Puritans:
The 'Praying Indians' of Massachusetts Bay and John Eliot," *William and
Mary Quarterly*, 3d ser. XXXI (1974), 27–54.

to Axtell's interpretation, preservation of native identity was not, in the long run, among them. But before 1675 at least, Eliot's converts borrowed English culture selectively and for a variety of reasons: "The Indians, seeking to enhance rather than abandon their traditional order, tried to take only what they wanted of the missionary program." In so doing, many of them—nearly one quarter of the Indians of southeastern New England in the three decades before King Philip's War—became "praying Indians," and a significant number in the older praying towns (about the same ratio as in the Bay Colony's English towns) became full church members under the day-to-day leadership of American Indian preachers and magistrates.[15]

The interpretive gulf that separates the generalists from the Puritan-Indian specialists is illustrated emphatically by their differing approaches to warfare in seventeenth-century New England. In generalists' eyes, the Puritans provoked every clash and intended—indeed sometimes accomplished—genocide. Specialists, whether of military history or of related topics, viewed the causes of the English-Indian wars as less simple, less unilateral, and the outcomes, though appallingly lethal, never genocidal. This difference of interpretations applies especially to the

---

[15]Harold W. Van Lonkhuyzen, "A Reappraisal of the Praying Indians: Acculturation, Conversion, and Identity at Natick, Massachusetts, 1646–1730," *New England Quarterly*, LXIII (1990), 396–428, quotations from pp. 404–5. See also Elise Brenner, "To Pray or Be Prey; That is the Question: Strategies for Cultural Autonomy of Massachusetts Praying Town Indians," *Ethnohistory*, XXVII (1980), 135–52; James P. Ronda, "Generations of Faith: The Christian Indians of Martha's Vineyard," *William and Mary Quarterly*, 3d ser. XXXVIII (1981), 369–94; and J. William T. Youngs, Jr., "The Indian Saints of New England," *Early American Literature*, XVI (1981–82), 241–56. On the number of converts to Christianity, several scholars have countered Jennings's effort to minimize the figures. For a more accurate estimate, see Axtell, "Ethnohistory of Missions," 49–50.

Pequot War of 1636–37, which has long been the litmus test of the Puritans' military methods and intentions.[16]

Here again Jennings's 1975 paradigm dominates the generalists' accounts. *The Invasion of America* portrays the clash between the colonies and the Pequot tribe as "the First Puritan Conquest," in which the fault lay wholly with the English, whose brutality marked a new low in savagery. Drinnon's version is equally pejorative but with additional sexual and racist accusations: at the Mystic Fort massacre "the Saints' suppressed sexuality at last broke out and found vent in an orgy of violence"; afterwards "the loud and clear answer of the war was that the Indians were truly animals that could be killed or enslaved at will." Stannard's account blends bloodlust with theology: at Block Island "[t]he colonists simply wanted to kill Indians," and later on, "[i]n killing the Indians in massive numbers . . . the English were only doing their sacred duty, working hand in hand with the God who was protecting them." Jennings's latest version of the Pequot War is comparably selective: "In 1636, Massachusetts Bay picked a fight with the Pequot Indians to acquire their tribute and territory. Connecticut forestalled Massachusetts by burning the Pequot women and children in a lightly defended 'fort.'"[17]

---

[16]Although the conflict of 1675–76—traditionally known as King Philip's War but labeled by Jennings "the Second Puritan Conquest" and by others as "Metacom's War"—was far more destructive of life and property than the Pequot War, and far more a historical turning point, it has generated considerably less historiographical heat. Most megahistories give more space to the earlier conflict. For recent studies that do address King Philip's War extensively, see Stephen Saunders Webb, *1676: The End of American Independence* (Cambridge, Mass., 1984); Russell Bourne, *The Red King's Rebellion: Racial Politics in New England, 1675–1678* (New York, 1990); and Philip Ranlet, "Another Look at the Causes of King Philip's War," *New England Quarterly*, LXI (1988), 79–100.

[17]Drinnon, *Facing West*, 56, 50; Stannard, *American Holocaust*, 112, 238; and Jennings, *Founders of America*, 210.

More thoroughly researched and sophisticated assessments of the Pequot War have appeared recently in scholarly journals. In 1988 Adam Hirsch contrasted Puritan and Pequot (or, more broadly, English and northeastern Indian) "military cultures"—their fighting traditions, their diplomatic and military strategies, and especially their expectations of an opponent's response in precombat situations. Neither side understood the other; neither responded as expected. Hirsch's conclusion that the war was a mutually unwanted tragic mistake was soon echoed by Stephen Katz, except that Katz emphasized the conflict's initial defensive character, for "both sides acted to defend what they perceived as rightly theirs." And in several articles (and a forthcoming book), Alfred Cave examined in unprecedented detail the events and attitudes that led up to the war. His conclusions stand in stark contrast to those of Jennings, Drinnon, and Stannard.[18]

A third realm of Puritan-Indian relations that has drawn new attention from specialists (but little from generalists) is the law, especially property law—an obvious concern to both cultures in a colonial context. Occasionally the subject appears in a synthetic work, usually to berate the colonists for disregarding Indian ownership of land and other natural resources. Stannard, for example, explained the doctrine of

---

[18]Adam J. Hirsch, "The Collision of Military Cultures in Seventeenth-Century New England," *Journal of American History*, LXXIV (1988), 1187–212; Stephen T. Katz, "The Pequot War Reconsidered," *New England Quarterly*, LXIV (1991), 206–24, quote on p. 212 (Katz takes Jennings to task on pp. 213–18); and Alfred A. Cave, "Who Killed John Stone? A Note on the Origins of the Pequot War," *William and Mary Quarterly*, 3d ser. XLIX (1992), 509–21. See also Harold E. Selesky, *War and Society in Colonial Connecticut* (New Haven, 1990), 4–10. For an expanded version of my thoughts on recent Pequot War historiography, see my *Roots of American Racism*, ch. 8. For the debate over genocide, see Katz, "Pequot War Reconsidered," esp. 222–23; and Stannard, *American Holocaust*, 318n, which rebuts (and misrepresents) Katz's position.

vacuum domicilium, whereby Puritan leaders assumed that unoccupied or underutilized land was free for the taking, and concluded that "the British colonists in New England appealed to it enthusiastically as they seized the shared common lands of the Indians."[19]

A more thorough and balanced account of the Puritans' position on land ownership and acquisition appeared in Yasuhide Kawashima's *Puritan Justice and the Indian.* After a brief period of land purchases in which the Indians misunderstood the colonists' assumption that ownership was permanent and exclusive, Massachusetts legislated a modus vivendi, which the other Puritan colonies quickly emulated:

> Those Indians who came into English communities were entitled to have "allotments amongst the English, according to the custom of the English," and a group of Indians who were qualified to form a township were, upon request, to be granted undisposed land. The law further guaranteed the Indians full enjoyment of the improved lands, hunting grounds, and fishing-places and protection from all encroachments on their land. Finally and most important, a provision on land transactions from Indians to whites simply stated that no person was . . . allowed to buy land without the General Court's approval and that all land bought illegally was to be forfeited.[20]

Such laws did not end all misunderstandings, of course, nor did they wholly prevent fraudulent purchases. But the force

---

[19]Stannard, *American Holocaust,* 234–36.
[20]Yasuhide Kawashima, *Puritan Justice and the Indian: White Man's Law in Massachusetts, 1630–1763* (Middletown, Conn., 1986), ch. 2, quotation from p. 48.

of law favored Indian land rights and voluntary sales. Moreover, as James Springer demonstrated several years ago, Puritan leaders reassessed the premigration notion of *vacuum domicilium* almost immediately on arrival in New England, where they recognized the reality and justice of Indian territorial claims. Not only did several prominent spokesmen repudiate *vacuum domicilium,* but—more tellingly—the Puritan courts generally upheld the Indian side of land disputes.[21]

*   *   *

Limitations of space preclude discussion here of recent work on other topics addressed in *New England Frontier:* Puritan perceptions of Indian character and culture, the fur trade, the manufacture and use of wampum, and the missionaries' efforts to make the Indians literate and (by Puritan norms) learned. Nor is there space to consider aspects of Puritan-Indian relations that the book touched on scarcely, if at all: the effects of colonization on New England's ecology, for example, or the particulars of demographic change among the Indians. But such subjects, despite their lively scholarly interest, have (with the exception of Puritan perceptions of the Indians) generated little controversy; knowledge accumulates, interpretations blend. According-

---

[21] James Warren Springer, "American Indians and the Law of Real Property in Colonial New England," *American Journal of Legal History,* XXX (1986), 25–58. Compare to Edgar J. McManus, *Law and Liberty in Early New England: Criminal Justice and Due Process, 1620–1692* (Amherst, Mass., 1993), 123–29. McManus's account is initially ambivalent about which of the main versions of Indian-white relations applies better to the legal situation ("[t]he reality . . . probably lies somewhere in between"), but on Puritan acquisition of land it sides with Jennings, citing him on this point. But McManus's notes and bibliography show no awareness of Springer's article nor of several other relevant writings, and his interpretation of the primary sources is quixotic.

ly, this brief introduction passes silently over several important topics, with only a footnote nod at a small portion of the
recent, and often significant, literature.[22] The three categories discussed in the previous pages must serve to illustrate
the current trends in the historiography of Puritan-Indian
relations, at the risk of implying that its practitioners are
perpetually at loggerheads.

I like to think instead that the overall trend among serious
students of early New England is away from the harsh

---

[22]What follows is a highly selective list of works since 1979. On Puritan
perceptions of Indians: Karen Ordahl Kupperman, *Settling with the Indians:
The Meeting of English and Indian Cultures in America, 1580–1640* (Totowa, N.J.,
1980); Alden T. Vaughan and Daniel K. Richter, "Crossing the Cultural
Divide: Indians and New Englanders, 1605–1763," *American Antiquarian
Society Proceedings*, XC (1980) 23–99; William S. Simmons, "Cultural Bias in
the New England Puritans' Perception of Indians," *William and Mary Quar-
terly*, 3d ser. XXXVIII (1981), 56–72; and Alfred A. Cave, "Indian Shamans
and English Witches in Seventeenth-Century New England," *Essex Institute
Historical Collections*, CXXVIII (1992), 239–54. On trade: Christopher L.
Miller and George R. Hamell, "A New Perspective on Indian-White Contact:
Cultural Symbols and Colonial Trade," *Journal of American History*, LXXIII
(1986–87), 311–28; and James Axtell, "The First Consumer Revolution," in
Axtell, *Beyond 1492: Encounters in Colonial North America* (New York, 1992),
125–51, which (like the Miller and Hamell piece) is not primarily about New
England but is suggestive. On ecology: William Cronon, *Changes in the Land:
Indians, Colonists, and the Ecology of New England* (New York, 1983), which errs
in accepting Jennings's accuracy but is otherwise solid and significant; and
Carolyn Merchant, *Ecological Revolutions: Nature, Gender, and Science in New
England* (Chapel Hill, N.C., 1989). On education: Axtell, *Invasion Within*,
passim; and Margaret Connell Szasz, *Indian Education in the American Colo-
nies, 1607–1783* (Albuquerque, N.M., 1988). On Indian warfare: Patrick M.
Malone, *The Skulking Way of War: Technology and Tactics among the New England
Indians* (Baltimore, 1991). On Indian-white relations along the outer edge of
Puritan settlement: Kenneth M. Morrison, *The Embattled Northeast: The
Elusive Ideal of Alliance in Abenaki-Euramerican Relations* (Berkeley and Los
Angeles, 1984); Richard I. Melvoin, *New England Outpost: War and Society in
Colonial Deerfield* (New York, 1989); and Colin G. Calloway, *The Western
Abenakis of Vermont, 1600–1800: War, Migration, and the Survival of an Indian
People* (Norman, Okla., 1990). On demography: Dean R. Snow and Kim M.
Lanphear, "European Contact and Indian Depopulation in the Northeast:
The Timing of the First Epidemics," *Ethnohistory*, XXXV (1988), 15–33.

revisionism of the 1970s and 1980s, that postrevisionism has finally arrived and is here to stay. That expectation may be overly optimistic, especially in light of the generalists' relentless Puritan-bashing, but from the vantage point of the mid-1990s a reverse swing in the pendulum seems plausible to me and, in the interests of historical accuracy, highly desirable. In any event I hope this new edition of *New England Frontier* serves effectively as a basic overview of Indian-white relations in early New England (whatever the reader's interpretive stance may be) as well as a corrective to the shrill insistence by nearly a generation of writers that the early colonists sought to destroy the natives and appropriate their lands in blatant violation of Puritan calls for Indian conversion and education, and for impartial justice. I trust this book makes clear that the Puritans' record before 1675 was mixed but far from the sordid story that has dominated the literature for nearly twenty years. The New Englanders' manifold shortcomings *after* 1675 are another, sadder story.

Preface

AMONG THE familiar events of early New England history, only two involve encounters between Indians and whites. Well remembered is Squanto's help to the Pilgrim fathers in their first years at Plymouth. Well remembered also is King Philip's War of 1675, which pitted certain Indian tribes against the Puritan colonies and their native allies in one of the bloodiest wars in American history. But even most specialists on seventeenth century America know little about the innumerable relationships of the intervening years — years in which colonists and Indians met sometimes in friendly intercourse, sometimes in respectful disputation, and occasionally in mortal combat.

This book attempts to reconstruct that portion of seventeenth century New England history — the story of the Puritan and the American Indian. In part it is a narrative of the significant contacts between natives and New Englanders; in part it is an examination of Puritan ideals and institutions and how they adjusted to the practical exigencies of the Indian frontier; and finally, to a lesser extent, it is an attempt to gauge the impact of Puritan colonization on native society.

That the histories of the Puritans and the Indians in New England from 1620 to 1675 are closely interwoven is readily discernible from the writings of almost any seventeenth century New Englander. The works of William Bradford,

John Winthrop, Edward Johnson, and Cotton Mather are laden with information about the Puritans' native neighbors, although each of these authors was primarily concerned with telling the story of his own people's venture in the New World. Other writers focused directly on the Indian and his response to English settlement: John Eliot and Daniel Gookin described the missionary work of the New England colonies; John Mason, William Hubbard, and Increase Mather told of wars involving native tribes; while Edward Winslow wrote detailed accounts of early diplomatic relations.

Even more revealing than the conscious histories are the sources which catch the colonists off guard. The amount of Puritan correspondence that survives is impressive, as is the accumulation of private diaries, journals, and notebooks that were not intended for publication. Here too the Indian plays a conspicuous role, appearing again and again in the writings of men who are not remembered by the present generation for their connection with Indian affairs. Finally, the official records of the New England colonies offer abundant evidence on the attitudes and actions of the Puritan toward the American Indian.

While these materials obviously reflect a Puritan bias, such a handicap for a study of this kind is not as restricting as might appear. In the first place, Puritan sources are voluminous and permit extensive comparison; rarely does our knowledge of any event rest on the testimony of only one chronicler. Moreover, the Puritans were usually content to record the facts, both favorable and adverse, confident that in the end the evidence would reveal that God's chosen people had overcome the obstacles Satan had placed in their path. While the New England Puritans may have seen cause to prevaricate when accounting for their treatment of religious dissenters, they had no reason to conceal their attitudes or actions toward the Indians. In fact, they have rarely been accused of doing so. Even the most hostile critics of the New England Puritans have themselves relied on Puritan accounts, basing their arguments on a particular selection and presentation of Puritan statements.

And other sources exist as a basis of corroboration. French, Dutch, and non-Puritan English material is often pertinent, and almost invariably it verifies the evidence found in Puritan writings.

The most serious gap in the documentation lies, of course, in the total absence of Indian sources. The native of New England had no written language, nor even a partial substitute for one. The materials, therefore, do not exist for a detailed account of acculturation in seventeenth century New England; by necessity, as well as by inclination, I have concentrated on the acts and attitudes of the Puritans toward the Indians and have not, for the most part, attempted to account for the actions and reactions of the natives. At times, however, Puritan and other European authors reliably report the views of a substantial portion of the Indians, as will be demonstrated in the chapters that follow.

What emerges from my investigation of the sources is a conviction that the New England Puritans followed a relatively humane, considerate, and just policy in their dealings with the Indians. In matters of commerce, religious conversion, and judicial procedure, the Puritans had surprisingly high regard for the interests of a people who were less powerful, less "civilized", less sophisticated, and—in the eyes of the New England colonists—less godly. Not every Puritan was mindful of the welfare of every Indian, to be sure, but the history of interracial relations from the arrival of the Pilgrims to the outbreak of King Philip's War is a more peaceful chronicle than that of most frontier confrontations.

During this period the Puritan colonies did not follow any clear-cut "Indian policy," largely because they seldom thought of the Indians as a race apart, in the modern sense of the term "race." Rather, the early settlers of New England were convinced that the American aborigine was a white man, darkened by the weather and skin dyes, and they strongly suspected that he was descended from the ten lost tribes of Israel. Thus while the New England colonists considered the Indian "barbarian" and "heathen"—as did all Europeans—they attributed his debasement to the environment or the Devil, not to color or heredity or divine judgment. The Puritans' task was therefore not to exterminate, enslave, or abuse the native, but to "civilize" and convert him as quickly as possible. That proved more of a challenge than the Saints had expected, and of course in the long run they failed. But their failure stemmed primarily from cultural myopia, not racism or indifference. The Puritans were determined to de-Indianize the native; they never intended a blending of English and native American cultures. They simultaneously underestimated the stamina of Indian society and overestimated their own powers to persuade. This attempt at the impossible generated many misunderstandings and injustices. But in the context of the seventeenth century, an especially intolerant era, and in comparison with colonizing ventures the world over, from the earliest times to the present, the Puritan record is impressive—in a negative sense for its restraint, and in a positive sense for its sincere attempt to harmonize the deeds and desires of two interdependent but radically different societies. In his dealings with the Indians, as in so many other aspects of his venture in New England, the Puritan is entitled to a more favorable judgment than he has often been accorded.

* * *

A study of this kind involves certain problems in terminology. Some words have taken on a pejorative tone with the passage of time. Other words have one connotation in the social sciences but another in popular usage. Accordingly, I have eschewed "savage" and "barbarian" and employed the word "race" only in contexts in which it is clearly intended to distinguish Europeans from Indians — nothing more, nothing less. Also, to reduce the monotonous repetition of "Indians" and "natives," I have occasionally employed the synonym "red man." While some scholars do not like it, the term is fully as accurate for the American Indian as is "white man" for the European or "black man" for the Negro. The last two are widely used by members of those groups, as well as by outsiders, and "red man" merits equal acceptance. [Note to Second edition: Such terminology did not become common until the late eighteenth century; by then the Indians were perceived as a separate race. I regret my use of color terminology herein.]

I have taken a few liberties with seventeenth century orthography as a convenience to the reader. The letters *u* and *v* of colonial documents have been interchanged wherever modern usage would dictate; the same has been done with *i* and *j*. Abbreviations have been expanded except when they appear in works originally published in the seventeenth century (and therefore were intended to appear in abbreviated form) or when they have been left as abbreviations by such eminent modern editors as Allyn B.

Forbes and Worthington C. Ford. In a few instances I have removed italics from quoted passages where their use reflected idiosyncrasy rather than emphasis.

The spelling of Indian names, always a problem for early colonial studies, has been made to conform, where appropriate, with the preferences of Frederick W. Hodge or Samuel G. Drake, though not, of course, where the names appear in direct quotations.

Dates have been left in Old Style unless otherwise indicated. The beginning of the year, however, has been changed to January 1 from March 25, so that the period between those dates will fall into the first part of the new year rather than into the last part of the old.

*   *   *

It is a pleasure to give thanks here to the many friends and acquaintances who have generously shared their time and knowledge, especially to Richard Strattner of Loyola University, Chicago, and David Burner of Oakland University for reading parts of early drafts; to Henry Graff, Sigmund Diamond, and Charles Wagley, all of Columbia University, and Douglas Leach of Vanderbilt University for their criticisms of the text at a later stage; to my students Barbara Bennett and Ralph Scott for assistance in preparing the final draft; and to Richard Morris and Robert Cross of Columbia University for encouragement and guidance throughout.

My thanks go as well to the staffs of several research libraries, cited in my bibliography, for their quiet help; to the many librarians of Columbia University for frequently enduring with good humor my importunities; to the administrators of the William A. Dunning Fund of the Columbia

University Department of History for financial aid; to the Institute of Early American History and Culture, Williamsburg, Virginia, and the *New England Quarterly* for permission to reprint portions of Chapters v and vii that previously appeared as articles; and to Alexander Williams of Little, Brown and Company, whose assistance exceeded that of the customary author-editor collaboration. And I wish particularly to acknowledge my indebtedness to Thomas West of Washington, D.C., for the keenness of his interest in my manuscript and for the patience with which he labored to make it better.

Finally, I am grateful to my wife and children, who — each in his own way — helped to make this book possible.

A.T.V.

Columbia University
New York City

New England Frontier

Puritans and Indians

1620-1675

The third edition
is dedicated to
my colleagues and students
at Columbia University

CHAPTER I

Antecedents

O F ALL the inhabitants of England in the summer of
1605, none had more reason to feel the religious and
political excitement of the early seventeenth century than
those who lived in the port town of Plymouth. Like their
countrymen, the people of Plymouth buzzed with daily
news of the rift between Archbishop Bancroft and the nonconformist clergy, for, only the year before, religious controversy had reawakened with King James's declaration of
war on the Puritan movement. In many towns, such as
Scrooby to the north, clandestine services were being held
in defiance of the royal will, and signs of the impending
clash between Anglican and Puritan theologies could be
seen in the Plymouth area as well.

But Plymouth had other news. The *Archangel*, commanded by Captain George Waymouth, had docked in the
harbor on July 18 after six months in America, and on board
were five American Indians.[1] Soon all of southern England
would be astir over the presence of the red men, the first to
grace the British Isles since one of Walter Raleigh's captains
brought two natives from Roanoke Island eighteen years
before.[2]

The year 1605 thus marks not only a new phase of the

English religious struggle that would soon force thousands of Puritans to emigrate to New England, but it marks as well the moment when many Puritans caught their first glimpse of an American native and perhaps began to form their first tentative opinions as to the origin, nature, and significance of the Indians. While contacts between England and "the Northern Parte of Virginia," as New England was then called, had become increasingly frequent since the turn of the century, the arrival of Waymouth's captives stimulated a fresh wave of interest in the New World. Sir Ferdinando Gorges, commander of Plymouth harbor and sometimes called the father of New England colonization, credited the five Indians brought by Waymouth with being "the means under God of putting on foot and giving life to all our plantations." [3] In addition to whetting the curiosity of the English and bringing them valuable information, these Indians and others who came later would give a helping hand to subsequent expeditions. After 1605 voyages to New England usually carried one or more Indians as guides and interpreters.

There had been, to be sure, some contact between Englishmen and American Indians for more than a century before Waymouth's voyage. Fishermen of many nations had long frequented the American coast in search of herring, haddock, and cod, and voyages of exploration had become increasingly common in the late sixteenth century. But whatever interracial meetings took place prior to the seventeenth century probably formed no precedent for future relations. The European fishermen turned homeward when winter approached: fish was their concern, they cared little for furs, land, or converts. Only when England began to take a more active interest in her North American claim as a land for settlement did an awareness of the nature and significance of the American Indian begin to dawn on the English mind. In the meantime, Elizabethan England was more concerned with finding stability at home, a stability that was temporarily reached by the end of the sixteenth century.

After 1600, then, England began to shift some of her attention from the problems of the Old World to the possibilities of the New. Riches from America offered a lure that could not be ignored for long. Once Spain's sea power had been devastated by the fortuitous alliance of Elizabethan sea dogs and North Atlantic tempest, Englishmen might violate with relative impunity the possessions of His Most Catholic Majesty.[4] New trading companies soon appeared with surplus capital to invest in enterprises across the sea, while the shifting fortunes of the rival religious sects gave thousands of Englishmen new reason to look to America. In short, political, commercial, and religious forces combined in the early seventeenth century to stimulate extensive overseas ventures.[5] And from the first, contact with New England as a haven or as an investment brought contact with its native inhabitants.

*   *   *

ALTHOUGH the first Puritan settlers did not arrive in New England until 1620, encounters between early explorers and natives were certain to affect the eventual relationships of the English colonists and their American Indian neighbors. The natives would form their first impressions of the white man not from William Bradford or John Winthrop but from such transient visitors as George Waymouth and John Smith. At the same time, knowledge of the aborigines gained by the early English explorers provided guidelines for the subsequent conduct of permanent settlers. The events of the period between Waymouth's voyage and the landing of the Pilgrims were therefore an important anteced-ent to the Puritan experience.

Important too were a few of the voyages that had pre-ceded the arrival of Waymouth's human cargo. At least two expeditions before 1605 had had extensive contact with the natives of New England and had helped to establish the pattern of relations that lasted until 1620 — a pattern pre-dominantly friendly but one that was occasionally blotted by armed conflict.

The first of those pre-1605 voyages had been com-manded by Bartholomew Gosnold, a veteran of Raleigh's ill-fated enterprise at Roanoke; his voyage to New England in 1602 was the first to bring back extensive information on the people and products of that area. Financed by the Earl of Southampton and other noblemen, Gosnold sailed from Falmouth in the *Concord* for the northern fishing banks where he was to investigate the natural riches of the New World — especially cedar logs and sassafras ("a plant of sovereigne vertue for the French Poxe . . . Plague and many other Maladies"). The natives along the coast will-ingly helped Gosnold find the products he sought, and they exhibited a lively interest in trade. Copper pipes, tobacco, deerskins, furs, turtles, and hemp were offered to the Euro-peans for knives, hatchets, and various ornamental trifles. When Gosnold established temporary headquarters on an uninhabited island, half a hundred natives paddled over from the mainland and "fell a bartering." John Brereton, chief chronicler of the expedition, found that the Indians would give vast quantities of valuable beaver, marten, otter, and seal for the most trivial English products; in fact, he recalled, "they misliked nothing but our mustard, whereat they made many a soure face." [6]

Unfortunately, friction between natives and explorers soon appeared. As so often in episodes of violence that attended the early relations of Europeans and American aborigines, the cause of the trouble is now obscure, and perhaps was obscure even to the participants. Possibly a gesture was misinterpreted or a thoughtless act magnified out of its true proportions; criminal acts may have been committed by irresponsible men of either race. In any event, occasional enmity was probably inevitable between two peoples of such dissimilar cultures and with such inadequate means of communication. So it was with the Gosnold expedition. One Indian who spent a night aboard the *Concord* stole — or borrowed — some pothooks, which immediately made the Englishmen suspicious of all their new acquaintances. Later several Indians attacked two of Gosnold's crew on a hunting party, and the sailors barely escaped with their lives. Seeds had been sown for conflict as well as for commerce.[7]

Captain Gosnold headed back to England in July 1602, laden with American merchandise. The value of his expedition, however, lay less in its financial returns than in its influence upon other promoters. While Gosnold praised the New World's natural resources and asserted that the size and strength of the natives proved the country's healthfulness, a companion hailed America as "the goodliest continent that ever we saw." And late in 1602 John Brereton published *A Briefe and True Relation* of the voyage. This pamphlet — dedicated to Sir Walter Raleigh, who then held a royal patent to explore and settle British North America — was the earliest English book relating to New England.[8] Richard Hakluyt and a large number of English merchants now revived dormant interest in the New World. Hakluyt and his successor as principal compiler of explorers' narratives, Samuel Purchas, kept a steady stream of descriptive accounts flowing to the English public, and in many of them the American Indian loomed large.[9]

The year after Gosnold's expedition, a group of Bristol merchants sent Captain Martin Pring to northern Virginia in search of sassafras and furs. As in the case of the previous voyage, trade with the Indians was brisk. But Pring's expedition, like Gosnold's, had its share of trouble with the natives and might even have been exterminated had not two mastiffs, brought for protection, routed a force of Indian warriors that had surrounded the explorers' encampment.[10] It was becoming evident that contact with the Indians of America involved danger as well as profit.

As far as English promoters were concerned, however, tales of the New World's hazards were less impressive than good reports on the climate, fertility, and material abundance of northern Virginia. The Earl of Southampton and his Roman Catholic son-in-law, Sir Thomas Arundel, soon conceived of a Catholic refuge in America, and it was they who sent Captain George Waymouth in 1605 to explore and map the area previously visited by Gosnold and Pring.[11]

Waymouth, in the *Archangel*, spent a month exploring the Maine coast. He was accompanied by James Rosier, who had been with Gosnold, and who later wrote the most complete account of Waymouth's voyage. Some ancillary trade with the red men did take place, for the English wished to "bring [the Indians] to an understanding of exchange," so that "they might conceive the intent of our comming to them to be for no other end." But since the Englishmen's real interest was in the eventual settlement of a colony, they made every effort to treat the natives "with as great kindness as we could devise," without regard for profit. Waymouth invited several of the Indians to dine aboard ship, and they were given extra food to carry home.

The natives in turn offered gifts of their "excellent sweet and strong" tobacco, for which the English insisted on paying.[12]

Despite the initial cordiality of the Indians, the Englishmen soon suspected them of planning an ambush and decided that these natives belonged "in the ranke of other Salvages, who have beene by travellers in most discoveries found very trecherous." According to Rosier, it became necessary "to take some of them, before they should suspect we had discovered their plot, . . . so the first that ever after came into the ship were three which we kept, and two we tooke on shore with much adoe, with two Canowes, their bows and arrowes." This brazen act of kidnapping undoubtedly heightened the natives' distrust of white men in general and of Englishmen in particular. Waymouth's men, however, justified their action on the grounds that the captives could provide useful information to prospective colonizers, and it was, as they saw it, in the interests of the "publique good, and a true zeale of promulgating Gods holy Church." Fortunately the prisoners proved cooperative once it became apparent that they would not be maltreated. They taught their captors the rudiments of their own dialect and in turn acquired a fair command of English.[13]

Sir Ferdinando Gorges immediately recognized the importance of Waymouth's captives:

And so it pleased our great God that there happened to come into the harbor of Plymouth (where I then commanded) one Captain Weymouth . . . [who] brought five of the natives, three of whose names were Manida, Skettawarroes, and Tasquantum, whom I seized upon. They were all of one nation, but of several parts and several families. This accident must be acknowledged the means under God of putting on foot and giving life to all our plantations.[14]

The two Indians not kept by Gorges were placed in the custody of Sir John Popham, Lord Chief Justice of England, who was also involved in New World projects. It was not long before Gorges and Popham discovered that their tawny guests were marvelous propaganda agents. Less than a year after the Indians' arrival, the Spanish ambassador in England reported to his monarch that the English were "teaching and training them to say how good that country is for people to go there and inhabit it." [15] The natives even seem to have encouraged rumors of gold and other riches in America, and they may have dropped hints of a lucrative commerce between the aborigines and China. As late as 1647 Gorges reported Indian claims of trade with Cathay.[16]

What Ferdinando Gorges and John Popham heard from the natives increased their interest in the New World. Within a few months both men had taken leading roles in petitioning the crown for the creation of two companies for the colonization of Virginia. In April 1606, patents were issued to the Plymouth and London companies, and in August Sir Ferdinando dispatched Captain Henry Challons, "a gentleman of a good family, industrious, and of fair condition," to form the nucleus of a colony in northern Virginia. Unfortunately, Challons disobeyed Gorges's instructions to travel the northern route and was taken by a Spanish fleet in the West Indies. The loss of the ship and crew was a severe blow to the promoters, but equally disturbing was the loss of two natives, Manedo and Sassacomit, who had been sent as interpreters and guides. Gorges, in particular, had had high expectations of the captives' assistance and strove to secure their release from the Spaniards.[17] Meanwhile, Popham sent out a ship under Thomas Hanham and Martin Pring which made a "perfect discovery" of the rivers and harbors along the Maine coast. The Indian Tahanedo went with this expedition but did not return; later expeditions found him reinstated as a local chieftain and somewhat ambivalent toward his former hosts.[18]

* * *

BEFORE 1607, all English voyages to the area later called New England were intended to be transient. But with the chartering of the London and Plymouth companies in 1606, major colonization projects began, and a year later two incipient colonies had precarious footholds on American soil. Within another year the London Company's settlement at Jamestown, though beset with troubles, held fast; its sister colony in Maine had already expired. In each case, relations with Indian tribes contributed to the fate of the colony.

In many ways the expedition to the northern coast dispatched by the Plymouth Company had seemed more promising than its southern counterpart. Behind it lay the years of exploration and planning in which Gosnold, Pring, and Waymouth had been particularly prominent. Guiding the Plymouth expedition from England were the experienced hands of Sir Ferdinando Gorges and Chief Justice Popham, while leadership of the expedition was assigned to George Popham, a nephew of the Chief Justice and seasoned in New World exploration. Furthermore, the northern expedition, unlike the Jamestown venture, had Indian guides to insure a friendly reception at its destination. On board the *Mary and John* was the Indian Skidowares, whose two years in the Gorges household had made him a competent interpreter, and on the other side of the Atlantic Tahanedo was expected to play host to the colonists.[19] The cooperation and friendship of these two natives would be invaluable in the establishment of trade and comity with the local tribes. There was every reason to believe that success would crown this first attempt under the charter of King James at permanent settlement in northern Virginia.

The first contact between the expedition and the natives gave grounds for hope. In early August 1607, shortly after the *Mary and John*, Captain Raleigh Gilbert, and the *Gift of God*, Captain George Popham, arrived near the mouth of the Sagadahoc River, Skidowares led Gilbert to a neighboring Indian town where Tahanedo "came unto them and imbraced them, and made them much welcome." This cordial welcome proved somewhat misleading, however, as the bulk of the natives remained suspicious of the white men. Moreover, Skidowares, despite his overt acquiescence in English life, now decided to rejoin his people, leaving the Popham expedition shorn of its guide and interpreter. Although Skidowares assured the colonists that he would return to the ship later on, "he heald not his promysse." But even without an interpreter, the colonists had no serious quarrels with the natives for the present.[20]

Seventeenth century colonies could not survive for long without obtaining some of their supplies from the natives, and Sagadahoc was no exception. While the planters, 120 in number, spent the first several months constructing Fort St. George on the west bank of the Sagadahoc River, hastily erecting a church, a storehouse, and some fifteen dwellings in preparation for the approaching winter, they also gave attention to commercial relations. Shortly after the colonists' arrival the local sachem sent his son to President Popham "to beat a trade with him for furs." This was a good beginning, but it did not last. Competition from French explorers and fishermen to the north undermined the settlers' market. Goods became scarce and prices high. Early in February 1608, Gorges complained to the Earl of Salisbury that the Indians had taken to hiding all commodities sought by the colonists. Gorges attributed this to the colonists' "devidinge themselves into factions, each disgracing the other, even to the Savages . . . whose conversation and familiarity they have most frequented." [21]

Other relations between the immigrants and the natives deteriorated rapidly after the first summer. On several occasions the outbreak of hostilities seemed imminent, and at one point it took a timely visit to Fort St. George by Skidowares and Tahanedo to temporarily revive cordiality. Late in 1607 Popham wrote optimistically to King James that Tahanedo had spread word of the greatness of the English sovereign and his God.[22] But at bottom, relations with the Indians remained precarious.

Then in the spring of 1608 a series of mishaps brought an end to the brief career of the Sagadahoc colony. Early that year George Popham died, and news soon arrived from England that Chief Justice Popham, the colony's leading promoter, had also passed away. Then a fire consumed most of the supplies and lodgings and left the colonists "wonderously distressed." Finally, Raleigh Gilbert, the new president of the colony, learned of the death of his brother and returned to England to assume the inheritance. These misfortunes, combined with the colonists' failure to discover gold mines — which they had "expected to uphold the Charge of this Plantation" — and the increasing hostility of the natives, led to the abandonment of Fort St. George. The remaining colonists sailed for England. Had the settlers been of unusual stamina they might have overcome the disasters, but Ferdinando Gorges would have us believe that too many of the men were unsuited to the experiment.[23]

Perhaps the most significant shortcoming of the Sagadahoc colonists had been their inability, after the demise of Popham, to treat the natives of the area with justice and good will, and the resulting hostility may have been more crucial in causing the downfall of the colony than the English chroniclers admitted. According to Father Pierre Biard, a Jesuit missionary in Canada, the first English leader had been "a very honest man, who got along remarkably well with the natives of the country. . . . But the second year . . . the English, under another captain, changed their tactics. They drove the Savages away without ceremony; they beat, maltreated and misused them outrageously. . . ." The Indians, therefore, determined "to kill the whelp ere its teeth and claws became stronger," and slew several of the settlers. The remaining colonists lost heart, according to the priest, and departed in fear of further native depredations.[24] Clearly the first English colony in New England had not followed King James's injunction that "kind and charitable courses shall be holden with such [natives] as shall conforme themselves to any good and sociable traffic and dealing with the subjects of us." [25] The experience at Sagadahoc showed that friction with the natives could be expected until the English provided exceptional leadership and considerate followers. These were not to appear in combination until 1620.

*   *   *

THE failure of the Sagadahoc settlement dealt a severe blow to plans for colonizing New England. "There was no more speech of settling any other plantation in those parts for a long time after," Gorges remembered, although Sir Francis

Popham, heir of the late chief justice, occasionally sent ships to New England for trading and fishing. This did not mean that England was forfeiting her claims to northern Virginia. On the contrary, when French traders and missionaries (including Father Biard) moved within the bounds of the Plymouth patent, Captain Samuel Argall sailed up from Jamestown to clear the area of foreign encroachment, and English vessels continued to dominate the coastline between Cape Cod and Nova Scotia.

To the extent that they maintained England's claim to the northern coast, these transient voyages were all to the good, but in their effect upon Indian relations they were decidedly unfortunate. Lacking the supervision and stability of colonizing expeditions, parties of traders and fishers gave little thought to the long-range result of their treatment of the natives. The fishermen were often blasphemous, drunken, and licentious, according to Ferdinando Gorges, who was then financing some of the expeditions and keeping in close touch with developments in New England. Worse still, they frequently cheated the Indians in commerce or more seriously abused them. And the natives were not long in finding means to even the score. From other traders they soon acquired muskets, fowling pieces, and additional items of European armament which they turned against their molesters.[26]

Adding to the hostility of the Indians toward the white man were fresh incidents of kidnapping. Captain Edward Harlow, on a voyage sent out by the Earl of Southampton in 1608, captured several natives along the coast and on Martha's Vineyard, five of whom he brought back to England. One of these was subsequently acquired by Ferdinando Gorges, who, dazzled by the Indian's tales of a gold mine, sent him back with Captain Thomas Hobson to

Martha's Vineyard. There the native escaped and did his best to slay his captors before they could leave the island. According to Gorges, the sole achievement of Hobson's voyage had been "a war now new began between the inhabitants of those parts, and us." [27]

While Hobson was stirring up trouble on Martha's Vineyard, Thomas Hunt — "a worthless fellow of our nation," according to Sir Ferdinando — was antagonizing the Indians on the mainland. In 1614 Hunt sailed on a commercial voyage to New England; there he seized twenty-four unsuspecting natives and carried them to Malago, where, reported Captain John Smith, he "sold those silly Salvages for Rials of eight." Most of the captives were eventually rescued from servitude by Spanish friars, and the opprobrium heaped on Captain Hunt prevented his ever again being employed in America.[28] But Hunt's treachery had created an intense distrust among the natives of New England that lingered for several years. One explorer lamented that "they presently contracted such an hatred against our whole nation as they immediately studied how to be revenged." [29]

Not all Englishmen who explored the Atlantic coast were so unscrupulous as Harlow and Hunt, nor did they leave such unsavory legacies to subsequent expeditions. In fact, the damage done by the troublemakers was partly offset by the brief presence in northern Virginia of the intrepid John Smith. Sent out by a group of London merchants in 1614, Smith had orders to catch whales, seek gold and copper mines, and as a last resort, take on fish and furs. The whales proved elusive and the gold mines turned out to be "the masters device to get a voyage," but the fish and fur did not disappoint, and Smith returned with a full cargo of skins acquired in amicable trade with the natives of New England.

With support from Ferdinando Gorges and others, Smith tried to return the following year to start a new plantation. His "main assistance next God," the Captain expected, would be the friendship he had promoted with the Indians, especially with a chieftain called Dohoday, who had lived for a time in England (he may have been the Tahanedo of the Sagadahoc region), and one Tantum, whom Smith had previously transported from England to Cape Cod. Smith had reason to expect the friendship and trade of the Indians, for he had already promised to help Dohoday's tribe against the Tarrantines, "whose tyrannie did inforce them to embrace my offer with no small devotion." Thus the Indians of New England, as early as 1614, were seeking to employ the Englishmen in their intertribal conflicts, and the white man was not reluctant to use the situation to his own advantage.

Thwarted by storms and French pirates, John Smith failed to reach America again, and the itinerant captain's colonizing adventures finally ended. However, his mark upon the new continent was permanent. From his brief contact with northern Virginia came the appellation "New England," officially designated as such by Prince Charles in 1616 on the basis of Smith's map of 1614. This map also gave English names to several locations along the coast, including Plymouth. And the captain might henceforth be considered New England's first press agent; for the remainder of his life he wrote enthusiastically of the area and its possibilities for settlement.[30] Still, no further attempts at colonization were made until 1620, and the Indians' hostility to the white man remained undiminished in several areas of New England.

*   *   *

INFLUENCED in part by the writings of Smith, in part by the
Stuart regime's growing hostility toward Protestant dissenters, English Puritans — most notably the Separatists —
gradually began to think of the New World as a possible
haven from persecution. But like other Englishmen, the Puritans were deeply loyal to their homeland and deeply imbued with its past. For all that has been written of their
uniqueness, which was real, and of their legacy, which has
been profound, the fact remains that the Puritans were as
truly products of the English heritage as were the orthodox
Anglicans. But by the third and fourth decades of the
seventeenth century, the rent in the Church of England
that had been widened by the first two Stuarts and was becoming permanent under William Laud had encouraged
the Puritan to see the New World and its denizens in a
somewhat different light from that of other Englishmen.

Puritans and orthodox Anglicans, to be sure, shared most
of the prejudices and ignorances of the day concerning
America. They differed, however, in the role they saw for
the New World and in the part they expected its natives to
play. As the government of England became increasingly
unsympathetic to Puritan dissenters, they increasingly
found solace in the thought of establishing a New World
Zion where they would be unmolested by the Archbishop,
and where they could show the Old World how God rewarded those who lived by His word. There was much of
this in the thinking of the Pilgrims; there was an abundance
of it in the leaders of the Massachusetts Bay Colony.[31] With
the Old Testament as their guidebook, Israel as their example, William Bradford and John Winthrop as their
Moses, the Puritans launched their "errand into the wilderness."

And the Indians? They, in the Puritan outlook, would be

one of the glories of the new Zion, for their conversion*
would be the first step in the extension of true Christianity
from His new community of the faithful.³² The Puritans
therefore gave far more rhetorical attention to the necessity
for converting the natives than did their Anglican contemporaries.

As they prepared for the long trek to America, then, the
Puritans did not think of the American Indian as an enemy
to be rooted out, but as an unfortunate heathen who deserved the saving grace of the Gospel. While they shud-
dered at the native's uncouth nakedness and primitive habits, they saw in the red man a potential Christian in custom
and in conscience, capable of education and civilization as
well as conversion. Satan had a hold on the Indians from
which they must be freed. (He also had a hold on the Spanish and the Irish; the Puritans were generally less contemptuous of the Indians' ignorance of God's truth — as the Puritans interpreted it — than they were of the papists' or,
later on, the Quakers'.) The later American frontier conviction that "the only good Indian is a dead one" never held
a dominant place in Puritan thinking; on the contrary, such
an outlook violated the basic concepts of Puritan theology.
Of course when pitted against a hostile tribe the Puritans,
like every other people in history, found theological justification for wielding a bloody sword. The Old Testament
provided convenient examples and ample vindication.³³

The Puritans' reliance on the Bible had another important effect on their attitude toward the Indians. Almost
without exception the Puritans of the seventeenth century
— at least those who recorded their opinions — believed
that the red man was descended from the ten lost tribes of

---

* See also Chapter IX, especially pages 235-236.

Israel and therefore was especially in need of the Gospel of Christ. This was the opinion of such influential clergymen as Roger Williams, John Eliot, and John Davenport, and of such lay leaders as Edward Winslow.[34] Even in Old England, the Puritans encouraged this view. Rev. Thomas Thorowgood, for example, argued it in his *Jewes in America, or Probabilities that the Americans are of that Race*, published in London in 1650. Among the evidences he offered were similarities between Jews and Indians in speech, customs, and ease of childbirth, and Thorowgood included in a sequent volume in 1660 two letters from John Eliot to corroborate the thesis. By Cotton Mather's day the Puritans would be less sure of the origin of the natives, but no less certain of their place in the scheme of things. "Though we know not *when* or *how* these Indians first became inhabitants of this mighty continent," Mather wrote in *Magnalia Christi Americana*, "yet we may guess that probably the devil decoyed those miserable salvages hither, in hopes that the gospel of the Lord Jesus Christ would never come here to destroy or disturb his *absolute empire* over them." [35]

In some respects Mather's attitude toward the Indians reflected a shift in Puritan outlook. By 1700 the New Englanders were more inclined than they had been eighty years before to consider the Indians as a race apart. But from the days of earliest colonization to King Philip's War, the Puritan remained convinced that the Indians were probably Jews and that all Indians were born white;* [36] there was no doctrine of racial inferiority to blind the Puritans to the desirability of civilizing and Christianizing the American aborigines. To be sure, the Englishman looked on the red man

---

* See also Chapter II, page 42.

as culturally inferior, but this could be overcome by exposing the native to the benefits of European civilization. Furthermore, as soon as the native accepted the Gospel he would be freed from Satan's grasp. Since the Puritans assumed that their efforts at civilizing and Christianizing would meet with little resistance, they did not spend much time, prior to their migration to New England, pondering their attitudes or planning their actions toward the red men of America. God, the future New Englanders assumed, would show the way in His own good time.

*   *   *

WHILE the Puritans looked upon the Indians as men to be helped rather than destroyed, they did not question the righteousness of what seemed to be God's judgment against the heathen. This was particularly true when the great plague of 1616-1617 struck down thousands of New England Indians. The Puritans did not gloat over the destruction of the red men but took it instead as a sure sign of God's favor to His elect. Clearly the Lord was making room for His people.[37] Given their Old Testament outlook, the Puritans could hardly have avoided such an interpretation, for the epidemic that swept through the New England tribes was the most deadly in recorded history to visit that section of the continent. Its path was strewn with the wreckage of tribes that had once been proud masters of their territories; it left them weak, unprotected, and frightened.

The cause of the plague is unknown. It probably was introduced by the English; at least they seemed immune to it, while it was most prevalent in the regions frequented by English explorers and traders.[38] Modern authorities are reluctant to diagnose the disease, for the scraps of historical evidence that have survived are vague and contradictory, but there is general agreement on what it was not: yellow fever, smallpox, jaundice, or typhoid fever. It may have been measles, bubonic plague, or even, perhaps, a combination of diseases that hit various tribes simultaneously. Seventeenth century writers usually referred to it simply as "the plague" or "pestilential sickness." [39]

Whatever the disease, its effect on southern New England was overwhelming. The living were too few to bury the dead, and when Thomas Morton traveled through the affected regions five years later he found "the bones and skulls . . . made such a spectacle . . . that, as I travailed in that Forrest nere the Massachusetts, it seemed to mee a new found Golgotha." A third, perhaps more, of the Indians between Narragansett Bay and the Penobscot River lost their lives.[40] This violent depopulation not only opened the coast for Puritan settlement but upset the intertribal balance of power as well. This, in turn, led to fresh native wars throughout New England. But of the plague's impact on Indian politics the Puritan was largely ignorant. It was enough to know that "divine providence made way for the quiet and peaceable settlement of the English in those nations." [41]

*   *   *

MAKING room for His people was an impressive sign of God's favor, but it was not the only one. He also provided a guide to the promised land for the first wave of Puritans. The contributions of Squanto to the early success of the Plymouth Colony were immeasurable, and there was no doubt in the minds of the Pilgrims that he "was a spetiall instrument sent of God for their good." [42] For two years he lived with the colonists, teaching them many useful things and, more important, acting as their interpreter and guide. A large part of the Pilgrims' success in establishing friendly relations with neighboring tribes must be attributed to this well-traveled Wampanoag.

The details and even the number of Squanto's journeys to Europe and back defy unraveling. Late in life Ferdinando Gorges listed Squanto among the five Indians brought to England by Waymouth in 1605. It seems hard to believe that Sir Ferdinando would have been mistaken as to the identity of so prominent a figure in the history of New England colonization, yet there is little corroborative evidence for his statement, and it has been rejected by most authorities. It is certain, at least, that Squanto was one of the natives abducted by Thomas Hunt in 1614. Sold in Spain, he escaped to England, where he lived for a time with John Slany, treasurer of the Newfoundland Company. Slany apparently sent him to Newfoundland in 1617, but the following year the Indian returned to England with Captain Thomas Dermer. He rejoined Dermer in 1619 for a final voyage back to Cape Cod. There he found that his tribe, the Patuxet band of the Wampanoags, had been exterminated by the plague. Thus Squanto survived to greet the Pilgrims and form a living link between the early years, with their scattered contacts between Indians and Englishmen, and the era of permanent colonization that began in 1620.[43]

*   *   *

FIFTEEN years after Captain Waymouth's *Archangel* dropped anchor in Plymouth, England, the *Mayflower* sailed into that city's New World namesake. In the period between those events, the Pilgrims had had some opportunity to learn about and to think about the American Indian.

They were therefore not completely unprepared for their initial encounter with the red man on American soil.

On the one hand, the Pilgrims knew that as Christians they had certain obligations toward the heathen. They must introduce the Indian to the glory of God and His true faith and work for the salvation of his soul. They could neither brush the Indian aside, nor treat him with distant respect and courtesy; their relations toward him must be positive, constant, and loving. But should he prove impervious to the teachings of Christian morality and charity, or pose a threat to Zion, he might be dealt with as the children of the Old Testament dealt with the foes of Israel.

On the other hand, the Pilgrims could draw upon a considerable amount of practical information — scattered, it is true, and often gathered at third or fourth hand. In the decade and a half since the homecoming of the *Archangel,* several natives, some of them from New England, had been displayed in various English cities where a number of the Pilgrims who were not of the Leyden group must have caught a glimpse of the captive Americans. Some of the Indians, like the one who later escaped from Hobson at Martha's Vineyard, "had been shown in London for a wonder." [44] Crowds followed every appearance of an American Indian. One of Shakespeare's characters in *The Tempest* voices disgust at the faddists who would "not give a doit to relieve a lame beggar, but will lay out ten to see a dead Indian." [45] By 1616 when Pocahontas came to meet the king — and be buried — in England, she could barely escape the mobs of curious followers who dogged her every step.[46] Such spectacles, of course, were of little importance in themselves, but they did whet the curiosity of the English and led to increased interest in the American Indian.

More to the point were the things that had been learned

by the explorers, traders, fishermen, and transient colonists in their contact with the New England natives. The first Puritan settlers might expect their new neighbors to be suspicious of white men in general, but for the most part to be friendly if treated with respect. At the same time, minor misunderstandings could easily arouse the natives to open hostility, and the enmity of the Indians — as the Sagadahoc colonists had discovered — could bring the downfall of the settlement. European weapons and watchdogs might prevent annihilation, but the long-run success of a colony was at least partly dependent upon amicable relations with the natives.

The Pilgrims and other early Puritans must also have recognized the potential value of the Indians' desire for European goods. While the early settlers of New England were not lured by hopes of wealth, they were not averse to reasonable profit, nor were they ignorant of the need of obtaining certain commodities from the natives during the infancy of the new settlements. It is, in fact, surprising that the Pilgrims did not come better prepared for trade with the Indians.

Finally, the first permanent English colonists undoubtedly recognized that not all Indians were alike. Some would prove friendly and faithful, others would cheat and steal. The wise observer in 1620 could hardly have missed this lesson in the contacts of the previous two decades. And he must also have noticed that the Indians were not universally friendly to each other. Individual and tribal animosities might therefore have a bearing on the Puritans' adjustment to the New World.

But whatever conclusions the prospective colonists might have drawn were probably not as obvious then as they seem now. The sailors' narratives collected and published by the

Puritan Richard Hakluyt and by his successor, Samuel
Purchas, told much that was conflicting and more that was
untrue. Furthermore, many of the earliest New England
Puritans had spent more than a decade in Leyden and thus
were probably more ignorant than most Englishmen of the
American Indian in general and those of New England in
particular. The second wave of migrants was far better
equipped to understand the native, for it could profit by the
accounts of Edward Winslow and others written from
Plymouth, and from the many works of John Smith that
appeared in the 1620's.[47] Even then, the Puritan would
know very little about the Indian until he had a chance to
view him in his New World setting. Eventually the writings of men such as William Wood, Roger Williams, and
John Eliot began to provide an intelligible basis for understanding the red man, and it is primarily from these accounts that we must reconstruct a picture of the New England Indians.

CHAPTER II

The Indians of New England

"I HAVE observed," wrote a Jesuit missionary at Quebec in 1633,

> that, after seeing two or three Savages do the same thing, it is at once reported to be a custom of the whole Tribe. . . . There are many tribes in these countries who agree in a number of things and differ in many others; so that, when it is said that certain practices are common to the Savages, it may be true of one tribe and not true of another.[1]

The priest's warning against hasty generalizations pertained as well to the natives of New England as to those of southern Canada, and his caution must be borne in mind when one is trying to reconstruct the life and customs of the Indians of New England from accounts left by the early explorers and settlers.

Unfortunately the Puritan chroniclers of the seventeenth century had little flair for anthropology. The records they left give a far less thorough description of the natives than today's readers would like, and a rounded picture of Algonquian society must therefore rely in part on the writings of the Puritans' European contemporaries and in part on the findings of modern social scientists. Still, the focus of this chapter will be on the American Indians as the Puritan understood them, for the attitudes and actions of the colonist towards the aboriginal inhabitants of New England were in large part determined by his conception of Indian character and society.

*   *   *

DESPITE an abundance of seventeenth century reports on the red men of New England, the size of the Indian population at the time of Puritan settlement can only be estimated. The best surmise sets it at about 25,000 in 1600.[2] That, however, was before the epidemic of 1616-1617, when at least a third of the natives succumbed to disease, leaving perhaps from 15,000 to 18,000 in all New England. They were concentrated in the river valleys and along the coast, while vast interior sections remained almost deserted. From the Piscataqua River to the eastern shore of Narragansett Bay, the plague had left only a thin remnant of the earlier population; it was into this area that Puritan migration first took place.

Even before the devastation of 1616, the native population of New England had been relatively small and dispersed. The largest tribes of the area, the Abnaki, Massachusetts, Narragansett, and Wampanoag, had memberships far inferior to many of the tribes to the south and west of New England. If the Narragansetts and Eastern Niantics be considered as a single tribe, their combined population of 4000 was twenty-five per cent greater than that of the next largest in New England. During the same period the Iroquois of New York could muster 5500, the Powhatan Confederacy of Virginia totaled 9000, the Choctaw of Mississippi numbered some 15,000, and the Cherokee of Georgia were estimated at 22,000. Midwestern tribes such as the Ojibway may have reached 35,000. In fact, most of the tribes that subsequently became famous in American history had populations greater than the two largest in New England combined, and some boasted more members than could be found in all that region. The forests of New England were not teeming with wild savages as so many Englishmen feared; on the eve of Puritan colonization the population density was probably less than .22 per square mile.[3]

* * *

ALTHOUGH divided into several distinct tribes, the New England Indians shared, in part, a common heritage. All were of the Algonquian family of tribes, and all had at some earlier time migrated into the area, probably from lands to the northwest. The first to arrive had come at least a century before the Puritans, and had spilled over the Hudson River into New York and on down the Atlantic coast as far as Tennessee and the Carolinas. Then the Iroquois pushed in from the southwest, splitting the Algonquians into northern and southern groups and forcing those in the area of New York and Pennsylvania to move further south or to recede north of the Hudson River.[4] While archeological evidence on the early movements of the New England tribes is annoyingly incomplete, the theory that they were pushed back into that area from New York finds corroboration in the mythology of the New England Algonquians: their legends invariably traced tribal origins to the southwest, the last direction from which the tribes had come before finally settling on the lands where the Puritans found them.[5]

What most readily distinguished the Algonquian from other Indian stocks was language. The Algonquian tongue was sufficiently homogeneous to permit a general but very imperfect communication between the tribes of New England — John Eliot asserted that the Massachusetts' dialect was readily understood from Cape Cod to Canada — although some authorities insist that local dialect differences were as pronounced as are the national distinctions within the Romance languages. Four major subdivisions of the New England Algonquian language have been distinguished; communication was facile within each, but extremely limited between the four subdivisions themselves. There was very little in common between the linguistic pattern of the Algonquians and that of the Iroquois of New York State or other neighboring Indian groups.[6]

In other things as well, the Algonquian tribes were culturally related. Though local variations were often pronounced, it is possible to make a number of valid generalizations on the economics, the politics, the society and customs of the New England Indians as they lived in the early seventeenth century.

All of the New England tribes were essentially stationary, inhabiting generally recognized tribal lands within which they shifted their dwelling places several times each year in accordance with the demands of weather and sources of food. This constant moving led some early observers to conclude that the Indians had no permanent abodes.[7] This was not so; they had several: one for summer, one for winter, and one or more for autumn hunting, but each site was fairly permanent and was in no sense abandoned when the occupants made their seasonal removes.[8]

These periodic migrations tell much of the story of the Indian economy. In the winter the Indians usually camped in the shelter of interior valleys, where they subsisted on fish and game, supplemented by corn and other vegetables which had been dried and stored the previous autumn. Having no salt or vinegar, the New England Indians had to get by without preserved meat for the most part. But game was always plentiful in the seventeenth century, and the basic agricultural diet was readily complemented by the flesh of deer, moose, beaver, bear, and other woodland vertebrates, as well as by such fowl as turkeys (weighing as much as forty pounds), ducks, geese, and pigeons in the "millions of millions." Turkeys were so copious, Thomas Morton wrote in the early 1630's, that "divers times in great flocks [they] have sailed by our doores; and then a gunne, being commonly in redinesse, salutes them with such a courtesie, as makes them take a turne in the Cooke roome." Summer found the Indians at the seashore enjoying the abundant seafood: cod, sturgeon, bass, mackerel, and salmon were easily taken by Indian men with line, spear, or net. The women and children added to the larder by patrolling the shores for lobsters, crabs, clams, and other shellfish. In the late fall part of the tribe moved to still another area for a few weeks or months of hunting.[9] Forest and ocean thus offered the Indian an affluence of fish and meat.

But the staple of the Indian diet was corn. In the spring of each year the squaws picked up the tribe's few belongings, including its portable wigwams, and trudged off to a site close to its planting fields. The spring months were devoted to hoeing (with bone or clam-shell tools) and planting — both female occupations. Some members of the tribe remained all summer to tend the crops. Fish was commonly used as manure for the corn; as a result, the fertility of the soil was not impaired and there was little need to scout for new farmland.[10]

There is strong evidence that all the Indians south of

Maine grew abundant corn and were rarely in want. Surplus corn was stored in underground caches against the needs of the winter months. And while corn was the staple crop, various other vegetables added to the Algonquians' agricultural supply. One food economist has recently computed that the Indians of southern New England consumed proportionally more vegetables and less meat than do modern Americans. These natives, then, looked to their cultivated fields for the bulk of their sustenance — not to the forests, to which romantic fiction has consigned them. Only in the region north of the Kennebec River in Maine did climate force the New England Indian to roam the woods for deer, moose, and beaver as a necessity of life.[11]

In their political organization as in their economic pattern, the Algonquian tribes were basically similar but varied widely in particulars. All were essentially "monarchial" — in the eyes of the Puritans — usually having a single ruler whose authority, like that of his European counterpart, rested in part on family descent and in part on satisfying the leadership needs of his people.[12] The title of the chief was sachem or sagamore; the two terms had identical meaning throughout most of New England.[13] Chiefs were usually men, but occasionally a squaw sachem ruled. Below the sachems were a variety of subordinate officials: sub-sachems who ruled over subdivisions of the tribe, war captains, powwows (medicine men), and many others. The remaining members of the tribe were simply subjects, though below them were often servant-slaves who had been captured in war. These were sometimes adopted into the tribe.[14]

The sachemship ordinarily was divided into bands — groups of related families which owned a particular portion of the tribal land by tradition and usage, and which lived in one or more villages in fairly close proximity. Each

band was ruled over by an under sachem, though most of
the colonists designated them merely as sagamore or sachem
and their followers as a nation.[15] This overlap of terms obfus-
cated the relationship between local rulers and the sachem
of a whole tribe. And to further confuse matters, the Europeans applied the term sachem to what they interpreted as
Indian princes, dukes, and other officials of a sachem's
court. Little wonder that the political and territorial structure of the New England Indians is perhaps less clearly com-
prehended today than it was by the Puritans themselves.

Sachems, like European kings, were never really omnipotent. Most native chiefs, however, enjoyed enough power
and prestige to rule without democratic trappings; they
were executive, judiciary, and legislature simultaneously.
Since no written constitutional checks limited the sachem's
authority, the tribe expected its chief to pronounce rules,
administer punishments, and make major decisions for all
his subjects. An annual tour of his country and the periodic
exaction of tribute from all subordinate sachems and sub-
tribes served as tokens of the chief's authority. Tribute also
provided his main source of revenue, though it was frequently supplemented by the spoils of war. But despite "the
chief sachem or sagamore's will being their law," the petty
sagamores had to be kept in good humor or there was danger of secession or palace revolution.[16] Such revolts did in
fact happen so often that tribal affiliations and tribal boundaries are impossible to reconstruct with accuracy.

Ownership of land and other possessions was usually
based on the family unit, although individual and tribal
ownership were also recognized. Private property was hereditary through the male line, though descent of property
— and even of office — through the female line may have
been practiced by some of the New England tribes. The

sachem usually had the final right to determine sale of tribal
land, yet the actual inhabitants customarily had to agree to
any alienation of territory. Both sachem and resident usually put their mark to land sale treaties. Other forms of material wealth, such as tools, weapons, clothing, wigwams,
and wampum (bead-money), were individually owned.
The sachems seem to have had some claim even here, however. John Eliot, Puritan missionary and close student of
Indian life, believed that few natives sought material prosperity because it would inevitably go to a covetous sachem
as "gift" or tribute.[17] This helps to explain the appeal that
English ways had for some of the natives: not only did the
white man's customs make it easier to accumulate wealth,
they also promised a better chance of keeping it.

If the sachem did not engross the Indians' possessions, the
medicine man or powwow often did. No group in the Algonquian society was more respected, feared, and pam-
pered. A rough parallel, in fact, existed between the Indian
and Puritan priesthoods, for both the New England clergyman and his native counterpart were forces to be reckoned
with in temporal as well as spiritual matters. They differed
sharply, however, in the order of their duties. The Puritan
minister was primarily a religious teacher who found time
to meddle in other affairs, while the powwow seems to have
divided his time almost equally among political, medical,
and religious roles.

But it was as a medicine man that the powwow enjoyed
his greatest prestige. The Indians used many effective herbs
and other natural curatives, but they also depended on the
powwow to expel the evil spirits from their suffering bodies.
While most of the New England Indians eventually realized
that the white man's medicine was more effective, it is not
surprising that the native was often reluctant to leave his

"family doctor" for the white specialist. (Considering the primitive state of European medical knowledge in the seventeenth century — bleeding was still a standard treatment — the gap between the red man's medicine and the white man's may not have been very impressive in any event.) The Indian, brought up to believe in the efficacy of pow-wowing, saw no quackery in a treatment such as William Wood described in 1634:

> The parties that are sick or lame being brought before them, the Pow-wow sitting downe, the rest of the *Indians* giving attentive audience to his imprecations and invocations, and after the violent expression of many a hideous bellowing and groaning, he makes a stop, and then all the auditors with one voice utter a short *Canto;* which done, the Pow-wow still proceeds in his invocations, somtimes roaring like a Beare, other times groaning like a dying horse, foaming at the mouth like a chased bore, smiting on his naked brest and thighs with such violence, as if he were madde. Thus will hee continue somtimes halfe a day, spending his lungs, sweating out his fat, and tormenting his body in this diabolicall worship.

Not only did the Indians believe that the powwow could cure, they also believed he could kill. Here again, contact with Englishmen — Puritan or otherwise — would not have encouraged the natives to alter their view: virtually every New England commentator insisted that the powwow was a witch and in league with Satan. Roger Williams, in fact, refused to endanger his soul by watching the devil's agents at work.[18] The Indians' belief in the supernatural powers of their medicine men thus found ready support from their white neighbors.

The powwow's religious function seems to have been the

least significant of his duties. Indian religion was largely amorphous; it possessed neither scriptures nor universal dogma, and it lacked a priesthood in the European sense. The powwows were holy men only to the extent that they seemed to be in especially close touch with divine spirits. Their ordination consisted of nothing more rigorous than the recital of an unusual dream experience followed by a two-day celebration. Although women could have these "Diabolical Dreams" too, female powwows were rare.[19]

Algonquian theology, according to the Puritans, was polytheistic and anthropomorphic. Some observers maintained that the Indians worshipped two gods, deities of good and evil, while others believed the native religion recognized a dozen or more. The elder Thomas Mayhew encountered a native of Martha's Vineyard who acknowledged thirty-seven gods, and Roger Williams recorded the names of thirty-eight deities revered by the Narragansetts. Most New England natives attributed divinity to the sun, moon, water, and various animals. In his *Key into the Languages of America*, Roger Williams noted with better philosophy than poetry that

> *The Indians find the Sun so sweet,*
> *He is a God they say;*
> *Giving them Light, and Heat, and Fruit,*
> *And guidance all the day.*

Where a few early commentators thought they saw signs of a dormant monotheism at the center of Algonquian theology, the wish seems to have been father to the thought.[20]

The Algonquian religion called for few rituals and little in the way of speculation on after-life. Thomas Morton perhaps came as close to the truth as any observer when he suggested that the Indians had a concept of God and after-life, but no real systematized religion. Occasional powwows were held to implore the deities for rain or other aid. These gatherings often lasted for days, sometimes for weeks. Similar ceremonies served to offer thanks for kindnesses received. Individuals sometimes offered prayer to their gods, particularly after experiencing a bad dream, which they believed to be a threat from a god. That prayer played a lesser role in Algonquian religion than it did in the Puritan faith is demonstrated by the custom among both Indians and whites of referring to native converts as "praying Indians." Of an after-life the New England Algonquians had vague notions. Both Roger Williams and John Eliot reported that the Indians believed the soul was immortal but did not comprehend resurrection in the Christian sense. Rather, the individual's ethical merits and demerits determined whether his soul went to the southwest or was destined to "wander restlesse abroad." [21] It is quite possible, of course, that the Algonquian tribes were as far from a consensus on their theology as were the Christians of England. These scattered and often hostile tribes, with dialect differences, no written language, and no discernible tradition of oral doctrine, could scarcely have shared a single set of beliefs.

The wars of the Algonquians, like their religion, bore certain definable characteristics, but here also the details varied widely. Long before the white man introduced new weapons and new rivalries, the Indians of New England had often engaged in war to settle boundary disputes, avenge insults, and extend or resist tribal authority. The first settlers soon discovered that intertribal rivalries were ancient and bitter, and their roots obscure.[22] These animosities were to play an important role in Indian-white relations throughout the seventeenth century, for the red man was not slow to make use of the colonist as an ally or defender if it suited his purpose, or to resist his presence if it threatened to upset a favorable power balance.

Unless his white allies had provided him with muskets and swords, the New England Indian was armed with an assortment of primitive — but decidedly lethal — weapons as he set out to meet his enemy. His bow had been carefully fashioned from young witch hazel trees and strung with animal gut. His eighteen-inch arrows were tipped with brass, stone, or eagles' claws. Leadership in battle came from war captains, variously called pinesses or mugwumps, who carried long spears — equally handy for fighting and for carrying home the heads of the enemy. Some warriors also carried tomahawks made by embedding smoothly chiseled stones, tapered at the ends and grooved in the middle, in the roots of young trees. In two or three years the roots had firmly entwined the stones; they were then ready for trimming and testing. Other war clubs resembled those of the Mohawks: thirty-inch wooden clubs with "a knob at one end as round and bigge as a footeball." The New England natives carried no armor except a skin or bark shield, although their dread enemies, the Mohawks of upper New York, wore suits and headpieces of bark which were impenetrable to Indian weapons.[23]

To secure themselves against attack by the Mohawks and other enemies, the Indians of New England built fortified towns. These were villages (usually the winter residences of a band) enclosed in a circular stockade of upright logs. Such a barrier often reached a height of ten to twelve feet, while the bottom three feet of the logs were buried in the ground. Earth was thrown up against the inner side of the timbers for greater protection; gaps were filled with small trees and branches, leaving only enough apertures for the bowmen inside. Entrance and exit were limited to narrow openings at opposite sides of the enclosure, and in time of war these were encumbered with piles of brush. From such crude fortresses the inhabitants could withstand the attacks of Indian enemies, who, as an early chronicler observed, "wanting butting Rammes and battering Ordinances to command at distance, lose their lives by their too neare approachments." [24] Against white men armed with guns the forts proved far less effective, which helps to explain the Indians' incessant craving for firearms.

Although the Indians of New England did show some ingenuity in devising lethal weapons and in constructing clever defenses, war among these natives was seldom costly in lives or property. Roger Williams maintained that the Indians' wars were far less bloody than the Europeans', and in respect to total casualties he was undoubtedly right. The forest provided natural protection, and native weapons were far less destructive than those of the European. As a result, a tribe seldom lost as many as twenty men in a single battle. Even an encounter in an open field was accompanied by so much leaping, dancing, and random shooting that few casualties were inflicted. An occasional ambush or direct assault might take a dozen lives, but it more often than not also ended the campaign.[25]

English chroniclers who observed war among the Indians were unanimous in their contempt for the lackadaisical method with which it was conducted. William Wood commented on the Indians' total absence of military tactics and their unwillingness to engage in hand-to-hand combat. "Their artillery being spent," he noted, "he that hath no armes to fight, findes legges to run away." After watching a clash between tribes in southern Connecticut a few years later, one Puritan captain reported that they came not near one another, but shot remote, and not point-blank, as we often do with our bullets, but at rovers, and then they gaze up in the sky to see where the arrow falls, and not until it is fallen do they shoot again. This fight is more for pastime, than to conquer and subdue enemies. . . . They might fight seven years and not kill seven men.[26]

It may be that war among the New England tribes served more of a symbolic role than did European warfare. Various reasons for fighting — petty grievances, revenge, defense of honor, and saving face — could perhaps be met by a show of courage without the wholesale slaughter that would only lead to prolonged and costly warfare. And since each tribe was small in membership, it had strategic as well as humanitarian reasons to avoid heavy casualties; this undoubtedly encouraged the Indians to wage the cautious kind of battle that the Puritans found so ludicrous. While it is not true that the white man introduced the Indians to the art of war, it may well be that he taught the red man how to practice it more energetically.[27]

In contrast to the mildness of Indian warfare was the fury with which the red men destroyed many of their captives. In fact, the relative tameness of group battles may have increased the need for symbolic destruction of the enemy through torment and mutilation of single enemy tribesmen. Male captives were often tortured to death in ways more fiendish than any inquisitor ever devised. The victim usually endured it with supreme stoicism, partly no doubt because he had been trained from birth to expect no better from his enemies.[28]

Scalping, not common until late in the century, may have been an invention of the white man, but it was more likely a practical modification of the ancient Indian custom of bringing home the head and hands of a vanquished foe.[29] It should be borne in mind, however, that the English were addicted to a similar butchering of the dead: drawing and quartering were still customary in England, as was the displaying of heads on London Bridge and other prominent landmarks. The Puritans brought the latter unsavory practice to New England, where it blended easily with the prevailing native custom. The seventeenth century had its share of barbarity on both sides of the Atlantic. Only in refinements of torture did the American Indian outdo the European.

*   *   *

IN personal appearance and in character, the New England Indians at first seemed to their European observers to possess that uniformity which every people ascribes to an alien group. In point of fact, the natives of New England were probably as varied in appearance and character as the colonists who settled near them. While no single physical type prevailed among the Indians, to the newcomers they all looked marvelously large and robust. Take, for example, William Wood's graphic if somewhat puzzling description, published in 1634:

> Of their Stature, most of them being betweene five or six foote high, straight bodied, strongly composed, smooth skinned, merry countenanced, of complexion something more swarthy than *Spaniards*, black hair'd, high foreheaded, blacke ey'd, out-nosed, broad shouldred, brawny arm'd, long and slender handed, out brested, small wasted, lanke bellied, well thighed, flat kneed, handsome growne leggs, and small feete: In a word, take them when the blood briskes in their veines, when the flesh is on their backs, and marrow in their bones, when they frolick in

their antique deportments and *Indian* postures; and they are more amiable to behold (though onely in *Adams* livery) than many a compounded phantasticke in the newest fashion.

Most other European observers agreed that the native of New England was a handsome physical specimen.[30]

While the term red man is commonly used to designate the American Indian and was employed at least as early as the seventeenth century, the actual skin color of most northeastern Algonquians was more bronze than red — with many variations of tone and shade. The New England Indians' natural skin color was rather light, but it was darkened considerably by exposure to weather and by the stains so frequently applied to their faces and bodies. In fact, most of the early chroniclers, including such reliable observers as Roger Williams and William Wood, believed the Indians were born white and were darkened "by the Sunne and their annoyntings." [31] This was undoubtedly true in part, for the New England native was fair-skinned enough to be amazed at the complexion of the Negro. In the early 1630's a lost blackamoor who had climbed a tree to find his bearings was taken for the devil by some Massachusetts tribesmen.[32]

Further disguising their natural skin color, the Indians of New England painted their faces with lurid colors, the exact choice depending on both whim and custom. Women painted their faces regularly for the beauty of it; the men usually did so only for special events. Red was often used for war or celebrations. Black was employed in mourning, when the natives smeared their faces with lead or soot and accompanied their lugubrious appearance with "Irish-like howlings." The natives also often tattooed and scarified their bodies.[33]

Far less ascertainable than the Indian's appearance was his character, and while "national character" is at best a questionable concept — especially for such a fragmented society — it should be possible to give some general ideas as to the common traits of the Algonquians of New England. The necessity of working almost entirely from Puritan sources makes such an undertaking hazardous, and the partial corrective that is found in French, Dutch, and other English records still does not give the Indian a chance to speak for himself. But at least we can obtain a picture of Indian character as the seventeenth century European measured it on his own scale of values.

What emerges from the contemporary accounts is not unflattering to the Indian. The impressions recorded by Roger Williams, William Wood, Thomas Morton, Daniel Gookin, and other prominent New England chroniclers are by no means uncritical, but neither are they fundamentally derogatory. All, for example, agreed that the Indians they knew were exceptionally hospitable to strangers, usually helpful to any in need, and about as pleasant as any people they had encountered. Roger Williams summed up the temperament of the Indians by noting that "the Natives are of two sorts, (as the English are). Some are Rude and Clownish . . . , the Generall, are *sober* and *grave*, and yet chearfull in a meane, and as ready to begin a Salutation as to Resalute." He added that "there is a favour of *civility* and courtesie even amongst these wild Americans, both amongst *themselves* and towards strangers." [34] This attitude on the part of the Indians would be important to the English colonists, for a persistently hostile native population might well have changed the character of Puritan settlement. As it was, most of the Indians were happy — though perhaps somewhat apprehensive — to see the white man arrive. Serious tensions later developed between some of the Indians and the Puritan community, but they did not grow from any innate hostility toward the newcomers.

Not only were the Indians generally courteous and hospitable, they also were quick to lend a hand to colonists in distress. The records of early New England reveal many examples of aid given to Englishmen lost in the woods, shipwrecked, or in need of shelter, food, and bodily care. Runaway servants, on the other hand, rarely found haven with the Algonquians, but were returned in good faith to the colonists. The Indians further served the English interest by disclosing the treacheries of the few who plotted against the colonists, and by acting as scouts and coastal lookouts in conflicts between the Puritans and their European foes.[35] Other Indians attached themselves to colonial settlements as interpreters and guides. The story of Squanto's assistance at Plymouth is only the most familiar example.

Although the Puritans deplored the Indian's lack of formal schooling, most of the chroniclers did not permit this deficiency to prejudice their view of the native's basic intelligence. Williams insisted that "they are intelligent, many very ingenious," and Edward Winslow considered them "ripe-witted." Thomas Morton was of similar mind but noted that many of his compatriots thought otherwise.[36]

Agreement was also far from universal as to the moral fiber of the Indians. Some observers believed that the natives were less prone to murder and theft than were Europeans; John Josselyn, on the other hand, found them "inconstant, crafty, . . . and so malicious that they seldom forget an injury, and barbarously cruel, witness their direful revenges upon one another." Also, he maintained, they were thievish, beggarly, and cannibalistic. Anglican clergyman William Morrell expressed a similar judgment in his verse history of New England:

> *They're wondrous cruell, strangely base and vile,*
> *Quickly displeased, and hardly reconciled.*

But few other New England writers were so critical; most of them could find only minor flaws in the Indian character. They recognized, however, that an occasional individual was thoroughly corrupt and treacherous.[37]

On only two counts did the New Englanders condemn the native without reserve: his indolence and his drunkenness. The former was presumed to be either an inherited defect or the work of the Devil; in either case it was regrettable to all Englishmen. (The Indians' violation of the work-ethic was as offensive to such non-Puritan New Englanders as Thomas Lechford and William Morrell as it was to those of the Puritan persuasion.) Nor did conversion to Christianity and adoption of Puritan clothes and customs necessarily instill in the Indian the habit of diligence, as the frequent complaints of John Eliot and Daniel Gookin testify.[38] In terms of the Protestant work-ethic, the Indian men were perhaps guilty as charged, but certainly the Indian women were not. Their lives were a dreary round of labor. And the indolence of the men was only intermittent; in hunting and fishing seasons, in wartime, and when special tasks challenged the family or tribe, Indian men showed more energy and stamina than most Englishmen could muster.

It is less easy to mitigate the charge of drunkenness, for it was voiced by Indian as well as by Puritan spokesmen. Within a short time after the arrival of the English, the Indians had become inordinately fond of alcohol. As early as 1637, Thomas Morton observed that "they will pawne their wits to purchase the acquaintance of it." In large part this weakness stemmed from unfamiliarity with intoxicants, for the Algonquians had no native equivalent to strong liquor. And no doubt the English were accessories to the crime, since the Indians obtained all their firewater from colonial or European sources until they eventually learned to make cider and brandy.[39] The Puritan authorities, of course, abhorred intemperance as much when committed by Indians as by settlers. Every New England colony passed strict rules against selling alcohol to the Indians, although such legislation was largely futile. Those Indians who craved intoxication had little difficulty in achieving it, and litigations involving drunkenness persistently marred relations between the Puritans and the Indians.

*   *   *

In their dwellings and in their methods of gathering food, in their clothing and in their recreations, the Indians of New England lived a primitive subsistence life, one that had not progressed beyond the Stone Age. Yet there was much in it that showed ingenuity and resourcefulness.

Indian houses in New England were neither the famous teepees of the prairies nor the well-known long-houses of the Iroquois, though one type closely resembled the latter. There was some diversity in size and shape, but the winter dwellings, the most substantial built by these Indians, were usually forty, fifty, or even one hundred feet long, and as much as thirty feet wide. Their frames were parallel rows of young trees anchored in the ground and bent over until they met in the middle. The junction point was tied with bark strips or hemp; the dome and sides were then covered with woven mats or bark. Doors were left at either end and were covered with hangings in inclement weather. A hole was left in the roof over each fire. Smaller huts, probably those used while hunting or fishing, were circular or oval in floor plan, "very little and homely." The great advantage of houses of this kind was their portability, which facilitated the peregrinations of their owners. Besides seasonal moves, the Indians occasionally changed their abode for spontaneous reasons: death in the family, disease in the neighborhood, or simply to escape the summer fleas. Often in seasonal removals, only the mats were taken, and the frames remained exposed until the occupants returned.[40]

The interior of an Algonquian wigwam was as simple as the exterior. An inside layer of mats, often decorated with embroidery, covered the walls and provided insulation as well as a touch of refinement. The huts contained almost no furniture, although some Indians had community beds of low platforms, twelve to eighteen inches off the ground. European visitors agreed that these abodes, often housing several families and without partitions, were filled with smoke and infested with vermin. In the absence of shelves, belongings were kept in hemp bags or baskets; skins for bedding were kept heaped on the ground or on the platform beds.[41]

What little clothing the Indians wore was fashioned from animal skins. The New England natives dressed skins expertly, and the women cut them into rough garments. Moose, deer, and bear skins were preferred, and were sometimes elaborately decorated. Summer clothing had the fur side out, winter clothing had it turned in. Shoes were made of deer or moose hide, as were the relatively uncommon leggings. For a touch of splendor, the women sometimes wove elaborate coats of turkey feathers. But generally the

Indians went almost naked, summer and winter alike, except when extremely cold weather made garments essential.[42] Aside from a deerskin loincloth held up by a snakeskin belt, and perhaps a pair of moccasins, the common covering was a liberal coating of vegetable or animal fat. William Wood reported that the Indians in Massachusetts greased their bodies regularly with fish oil or eagle or raccoon fat. Daniel Gookin added bear and pig grease to the list. The purpose was simply to protect the body from summer heat, winter cold, and mosquito bites, all without the inconvenience and expense of clothing. Needless to say, the habit of greasing met with some reproach from the Puritans, and it was one of the first customs an Indian convert was expected to abandon. At the same time, the colonists provided a new alternative, for their cotton and woolen cloth had qualities not found in animal skins. Yet an early chronicler noted that some Indian women found English clothes required excessive washing, and so shunned them; they "had rather goe naked than be lousie." [43]

Simplicity in dress did not mean lack of ornamentation. On the contrary, New England natives craved ornaments that seemed gaudy to the Puritans. Stone, shell, or bone pendants in their ears, wampum bracelets on their arms and waists and copper breastplating completed the elaborate makeup that tattoos, decorative scars, and paints had begun. As William Wood saw it,

A Sagamore, with a Humberd in his eare for a pendant, a black hawke on his *occiput* for his plume, . . . good store of Wampompeague begirting his loynes, his bow in his hand, his quiver at his back, with six naked *Indian* spatter lashes at his heels for his guard, thinkes himself little inferiour to the great *Cham;* hee will not stick to say, hee is all one with King *Charles.*[44]

Daily routine in an Indian village, on the other hand, had little enough ceremony. Women, the drudges of Algonquian society, had never-ending chores. They not only kept the home (and moved it when the time came), but tended the fields, prepared the food, and raised the children. Most of the Puritan chroniclers had high praise for the energy, ability, and loyalty of Indian women. As the tribe's gardeners they deserve high praise, for they provided the bulk of its food and did so without the aid of metal tools. The men rarely condescended to assist in any agricultural work except the tending of the tobacco crop.[45]

Indian men shared more equally with the women the manufacture of tools and utensils. Even here the women may have contributed the greater part, for they made most of the baskets, birch bark pails, and mats. But the men spent idle winter days carving wooden spoons and bowls and shaping clay pots, and they devoted long hours to making and mending their own war and hunting weapons. European observers were particularly impressed with their skill in building canoes. These were of two kinds. One was formed of a tree trunk, shaped on the outside with stone hatchets and hollowed on the inside by burning and scraping. Such vessels varied in size, holding from three to forty men. More familiar to later generations are the birch bark canoes, made by sewing sheets of bark to a light wooden frame. As these weighed far less than the hollowed logs. they were used more often by hunters and fishers who had to cope with frequent portages.[46] Occasionally the Indians used their canoes as war vessels: Roger Williams reported that some sea battles involved thirty to forty boats on each side.[47]

When not engaged in war or peaceful labors the men sat and smoked, played at traditional Algonquian sports, or searched for fish and game. Even hunting was often easy, for stalking and shooting in the best Hollywood tradition was probably less common than trapping, or driving the animals into a funnel of hedges and waiting for them to reach the narrow exit. Fishing was still less strenuous; nets and weirs were frequently used to catch small fish in quantity, while spear and line fishing were as much sport as necessity. The women were expected to gather shellfish and to dry a part of the surplus seafood for winter use.[48]

While the Indian women probably had little time for recreation, the men entertained themselves with a variety of sports and games. Individual contests in archery, running, and swimming absorbed their excess energy and helped keep them hardy. The only team sport of which there is record was a form of football, with goal posts a mile apart on a smooth beach. Players dressed in full war paint for these games, which sometimes lasted for days. Equally long were the gambling sessions to which the Algonquians seem to have been addicted. Even sachems were known to wager away all their possessions in a single day, though the chieftains could recoup by levying a new tribute. The Puritans, of course, frowned on both sorts of recreation. Roger Williams, a frequent guest of the Narragansetts, refused to attend their games, "that I might not countenance and partake of their folly, after once I saw the evill of them." [49] In their disparate attitudes toward recreation as toward religion, war, and industry, the Puritan and Indian possessed potential areas of misunderstanding.

*   *   *

WHAT has been said in the previous sections of this chapter pertained to the New England tribes in general. Yet distinctions between tribes must not be overlooked. Not only did they differ in location but in numbers, character, customs, and dialect. These and other features of the several tribes were often crucial in determining the relationships between the Indian nations and the Puritan colonies after English migration changed New England from a forest preserve into a frontier of western civilization.

Trying to make New England comprehensible to his readers in the mother country, William Wood wrote in 1634: "The country as it is in relation to the Indians is divided as it were into Shires, every severall division being swayde by a severall king." [50] These shires, or tribal holdings (colonial authors coined such words as "sachemdom" and "sachemship") are difficult to define geographically as their boundaries shifted from time to time and were never explicitly recorded in the first place. Wars, plagues, migrations, and transfers of allegiance all combined to make the territorial map of New England as fluid as that of eastern Europe. All tribes had subdivisions, frequently referred to as tribes but actually subordinate to one of the principal sachems. The pattern, however, is not always clear; authorities often disagree over important aspects of Indian polity, primary sources are sometimes infuriatingly vague, and the fact that each tribe had its own name for every other tribe adds further difficulty. But enough evidence survives to permit a general picture of tribal areas as they existed in the early seventeenth century.

At the time of the Pilgrims' arrival there were ten principal tribes or groups of sub-tribes in New England, while two tribes of New York had sizable holdings along the western border. [51] The northernmost tribe was the Abnaki (or Wabanaki), which inhabited western Maine, especially the valleys of the Kennebec, Androscoggin, and Saco rivers, and some adjacent parts of New Hampshire. [52] In many respects it was unlike the other tribes of New England, for its northern position forced the Abnaki to be hunters rather than farmers, their access to fur areas made them more commercially oriented, and their proximity to Canada made them pawns in the missionary struggles between Protestants and Catholics. They seem to have been one of the more warlike tribes as well, for the Indians in southern New England, especially the Massachusetts, lived in constant dread of raids by the Tarrantines (as they called the Abnaki), especially after the plagues of the early seventeenth century had weakened the southern tribes but left untouched the areas north of the Piscataqua River. With an estimated population of 3000 in 1600, the Abnaki vastly outnumbered the Massachusetts tribe by 1620. Among the English and their neighbors the Abnaki rapidly earned a reputation for cruelty and were even accused of cannibalism.[53] Part of their strength came from their early possession of firearms; since their region was abundant in fur and lay outside of effective Puritan control, they could easily barter for European weapons with the fishermen and traders of several nations whose urge for profit knew little restraint. Later in the century, the many sub-tribes of the Abnaki were welded into a loose confederacy, modeled after the Iroquois League.[54]

Southwest of the Abnaki lived the Pennacooks of southern and central New Hampshire, northeastern Massachusetts and southeastern Maine. Although they numbered about 2000 in 1600, they were decimated by the plague and were never again a significant tribe. Chief Passaconaway ruled many subordinate tribes including the Nashua, Piscataqua, Wamesit, and Winnepesaukee. The principal subdivision, also called Pennacook, was located near the present Concord, New Hampshire.[55]

Inhabiting eastern Massachusetts was the tribe of that

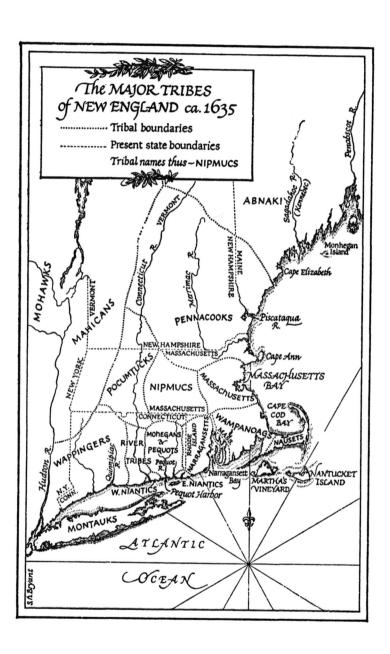

The MAJOR TRIBES
of NEW ENGLAND ca. 1635

················· Tribal boundaries
- - - - - - - - - Present state boundaries
Tribal names thus ~ NIPMUCS

name, once a power among the eastern Algonquians but devastated by plague and by wars with the Abnaki in the second decade of the seventeenth century. Between 1615 and 1630 the population may have dropped from 3000 to 500; this largely accounts for the cordiality with which the tribe received the Puritan immigrants, for any friendly neighbors, particularly if equipped with firearms, were a valuable shield against possible extermination. Among the important subdivisions of the Massachusetts, of which there may have been half a dozen or more, were the sagamore-ships ruled by Chickataubut and Cutshamekin, both of whom appeared often in early Puritan history.[56]

More famous to later generations was the Wampanoag tribe. This Indian nation played a crucial role in early inter-racial affairs because of its proximity to the Pilgrims, and its familiar figures include Squanto, Massasoit, and Metacom, better known as King Philip. Like the Massachusetts tribe, the Wampanoags suffered greatly from the epidemic of 1616-1617, so much so that part of their territory was completely abandoned. This was the area into which the Pilgrims moved in 1620. Anthropologists recognize nine subdivisions on the mainland, an additional four on Martha's Vineyard, and several others scattered throughout the offshore islands and coastal promontories. The mainland subtribes were generally quite cohesive, largely because of the strong leadership offered by Massasoit and his immediate heirs. The leading Wampanoag sachems kept their principal headquarters at Pokanoket (now Bristol, Rhode Island), which occasioned many observers to call the entire tribe Pokanokets.[57] The Wampanoags, led by King Philip, spearheaded the campaign against the colonists in 1675.

Prior to King Philip's War, the Wampanoags enjoyed amicable relations with the English but not with their Indian neighbors to the west. Every New England tribe, like every European nation, seemed to have a traditional enemy with whom it vied for power, border territory, and the support of potential allies; the Narragansetts fulfilled this role for Massasoit's people. Although Puritan chroniclers reported that the Narragansetts were the least warlike tribe in New England, the bulk of the evidence points to an opposite conclusion. During the half-century after the arrival of the Puritans, the Rhode Island tribe fought against almost every other major Indian power in New England, and it had been engaging in intertribal warfare long before the coming of the white man. This tribe of 4000 members (including the Eastern Niantics) escaped the ravages of the 1616 plague, and this may account for its more aggressive posture in the subsequent decades. Under chiefs Canonicus and Miantonomo, the tribe controlled the territory from Narragansett Bay on the east to the Pawcatuck River on the west. Situated in the southwest corner of that domain was the eastern wing of the Niantic tribe, sometimes subservient to the Narragansetts, sometimes allied to them, and at other times totally independent.[58]

The Narragansetts, in turn, had an enemy in its neighbor to the west. The Pequots, until their demise in 1637-1638, were the most fearsome tribe in New England, earning the enmity of white and red neighbors alike. The Pequots, in fact, were looked upon as intruders by most of the other tribes. Originally part of the Mahican group of the upper Hudson River, they had broken off from the larger body sometime in the late sixteenth century and begun a slow migration across to New England, then down the Connecticut Valley to the coast. The reasons for this move will probably remain obscure, but it may have had some connection with the formation of the Iroquois Confederacy, or it may merely have been a longing for new fields and forests. In any event, the Pequots' entry into New England did not go uncontested. But the tribes in its path were relatively weak, and the Pequots succeeded not only in carving out a new domain between the Pawcatuck and Connecticut rivers, but in acquiring an uneasy hegemony over the Indians in the southern Connecticut Valley. The feeble Niantic tribe that inhabited the coastal area was split in two, the western half acquiescing in Pequot control and the eastern half placing itself under the protective wing of the Narragansetts.[59] Originally known as Mohegan (a corruption of Mahican), the invading band's brutal tactics soon earned it the name Pequot, Algonquian for destroyer.[60] A successional struggle in 1636 led to the secession of part of the tribe under Chief Uncas; it revived the Mohegan name and succeeded to its prerogatives when the Pequots were destroyed in 1637.[61]

The four remaining tribes were less significant in the subsequent history of New England; they are also more difficult to delineate. The Nipmucs inhabited central Massachusetts but seem to have been too weak to prevent parts of their territory from being under foreign domination at various times. The Wampanoags, Narragansetts, Pennacooks, Pequots, and Massachusetts all occasionally controlled sections of Nipmuc territory and exacted tribute from its towns.[62] To the west of the Nipmucs, on the upper Connecticut River, dwelt the Pocumtucks, another loose association of bands of which the dominant one, located at the present Deerfield, Massachusetts, had the name of the entire tribe.[63] Directly below the Pocumtucks in the Connecticut Valley was a still less definable cluster of local tribes, often designated as "River Indians," which included the Podunks, Wongunks, and Siciaoggs. These are sometimes considered part of the Wappinger Confederacy of New York, but their historical association was with the New England tribes rather than with the Indians to the west. By the time the English encountered them, they were under the Pequot yoke; earlier (and perhaps as late as 1625) they may have had a considerable degree of autonomy and power under Chief Sequin.[64] Finally, the Nausets, a tribe of perhaps 1200 members, inhabited Cape Cod. They were closely related to the Wampanoags but acted independently of them on many important issues, especially after Plymouth Colony was settled.[65]

Two other tribes, both centered in New York, had footholds in New England, as previously mentioned. The Wappinger Confederacy inhabited the west bank of the Hudson River from Manhattan Island to present-day Poughkeepsie and extended eastward toward the Connecticut Valley. Because they controlled most of western Connecticut, the Wappingers were important to the Puritan settlements around New Haven. Further north another New York tribe, the Mahicans (parent tribe to the Pequots), claimed all the territory from their main location on the upper Hudson River through the western parts of Connecticut, Massachusetts, and Vermont. They rarely came into contact with the Puritan settlers.[66]

More important to the early history of New England than either the Wappingers or Mahicans were two other New York tribes, neither of which held title to any New England soil. The Montauks of Long Island, because of their geographical position, were closely involved in the affairs of the Puritan colonies. The eastern part of the island, in fact, was for a period considered to belong to Connecticut (and was thus a part of New England) while some of the Montauk bands were at times tributary to the Nian-

tics, Pequots, or Narragansetts. The consequent rivalries
led to an almost endless series of intertribal clashes along the
Sound that lasted throughout the seventeenth century.[67]

Still more formidable were the Mohawks, whose very
name struck terror into the hearts of New England natives.
Their ferocity in war, their early acquisition of firearms,
and their frequent raids to the east had given the Mohawks
an unsavory reputation long before the Puritans came. As
Father Druilletes, the Jesuit priest, remarked after his visit
to the Puritan colonies in 1650, "all the Nations of Savages
which are in New England hate the [Mohawk] and fear
lest . . . he will exterminate them. Indeed he has broken
the heads of many of their men, finding them hunting
Beaver, without making satisfaction." Both Puritans and Indians were especially appalled by the cannibalism of "these
inhuman homicides." [68] Fortunately for the colonists, the
Mohawks usually chose to molest New England's natives
rather than its white settlers.

*   *   *

IF the Puritan came to America largely ignorant of the true
nature of the American Indian, so too were the character
and customs of the newcomers a mystery to the red man. In
the first place, it was virtually impossible for the Indian to
distinguish between various nationalities of Europeans;
their languages were equally incomprehensible, their features all strange and indistinguishable, while the clothes,
customs, and goods of each revealed to the native eye none
of the national characteristics that a European would detect.

Few of the New England Indians had experienced any
close contact with the white man before 1620. Norsemen
may have ventured as far south as Cape Cod five centuries

earlier; Cabot, Verrazzano, and Gomez explored part of the
coastline late in the fifteenth and sixteenth centuries; and
fishermen of many nations had long frequented the coast of
New England. But none of this seems to have taught the
red man very much about the white, partly because the
visits were so brief, partly because the absence of a written
Indian language left each bit of information acquired by the
natives prey to the distortions of oral transmission. And
there is little evidence in the early writings of the settlers to
indicate any important tribal mythology in which the white
man had a role. Except for the fact that a race of light-
skinned, heavily bearded, elaborately clothed people made
occasional visits to his coast in great sailing ships, the red
man probably remained unenlightened about the Europeans
until the seventeenth century.

Then as the tempo of exploration increased, so did the
variety of contacts. Expeditions by Gosnold, Champlain,
Waymouth, Pring, Block, Smith, and others not only gave
the European a fuller knowledge of the New World, but
familiarized the New England natives with the white man
as trader, kidnapper, deceiver, murderer, and friend — in
no particular pattern or order. The Indians who were carried to England, of course, learned far more about their future neighbors. In short, the voyages that informed the
white man did the same for the Indian, though on a far
more limited scale because of the natives' primitive communications.

But by the time the first Puritans arrived in New England some tribes had particular reasons to question the
friendliness and integrity of Europeans. It is not hard to imagine the impact of Hunt's kidnapping excursion on the
wronged tribes (the Nausets and Wampanoags) in particular and on the coastal tribes in general. In 1620 some of the

Indians of southern New England still viewed the white man with suspicion if not with hatred.* [69] Fortunately for the Pilgrims, Squanto had apparently convinced his people that not all Englishmen were scoundrels, and the plague had left the Wampanoags in need of new allies.[70]

The Massachusetts Indians, like the Nausets and Wampanoags, harbored a distrust of the European before 1620, but their animosity had faded by the time of the Great Migration. About 1612 a shipload of French fur traders had clashed with natives in Massachusetts Bay; the red men were victorious, burned the ship, and made prisoners of five French survivors, who were distributed to five sachems of the bay area as slaves. Four of the Frenchmen died within the next few years, but the sole survivor managed to learn enough of the Indian dialect to "rebuke them for their bloudy deede: saying that God would be angry with them for it; and that hee would in his displeasure destroy them." The local sachem scoffed at the thought that any god could kill so many people; when the plague hit the bay area a little later and apparently fulfilled the prophecy, it created a new fear and respect for the power of the white man.[71] Partly for this reason the remnant of the Massachusetts tribe welcomed the Puritans to the bay. It also was the first group to accept the white man's religion.

By 1620 the Indians of the New England coast may have been able to distinguish Englishmen from the Dutch, French, and Spanish. Squanto and the other reprieved kidnap victims would have brought home a knowledge of the European nationalities, and accumulated contacts between representatives of the various European countries must have eventually made national distinctions apparent to the

---

* See also pages 64-65.

Indians. It is almost inconceivable, of course, that any of the natives could have fathomed the religious rifts within English society and could tell a Puritan from an Anglican, or either from a Roman Catholic. Further divide the Puritans into Presbyterians, Independents, and Separatists and even the European became lost in the doctrinal labyrinth. The Indian was doing well to know the subjects of King James from those of King Louis or those of the States-General. And in time the Indians of New England, except for the Abnaki of the north, succumbed to Puritan indoctrination and viewed Europeans of other nations and other faiths with additional suspicion. By 1634 William Wood was able to report that the Indians in his vicinity (Massachusetts) trusted the English far more than they did the French and Spanish.[72]

Meanwhile respect for the Puritan's God undoubtedly increased as more and more instances appeared of His power and generosity. By the 1640's the Narragansetts, while assiduously resisting Christianity, had begun to believe in the superiority of the Englishman's God over theirs, finding evidence in the Puritan's impressive material possessions if not in his theological contentions. To many Indians even the "laws" of the Puritan's God ceased to seem unreasonable, except for the stricture against polygamy.[73]

While the Indians' knowledge of the Puritan was slight, there is little doubt that many — perhaps most — of them welcomed the newcomer. The native was not so much concerned with *why* the Puritans came — the "errand into the wilderness" would not have been easy for the Indian to comprehend — nor even, it appears, how many would come. When some Narragansetts speculated on the reason for English settlement they concluded that the English must have burned all the firewood in their previous country and come to live where there was more.[74] This was one of the Indians' chief reasons for removal and they naturally projected it to the white man. They did not think of the settlers as invaders or usurpers until later.

When the early Puritans proved eager customers for furs, paid lavishly — by Indian standards — for land that had been deserted, provided the natives with iron hoes, knives, and other marvelously useful articles, and gave them protection against enemy tribes, the Indians' earlier doubts as to the desirability of the new neighbors rapidly vanished. Furthermore, as the Indians of New England differed sharply among themselves on many matters, so also did they fail to have a common outlook toward the Puritans' religion, government, and society. The Algonquian tribes had no feeling of racial or national unity, and they therefore carried no racial outlook into their dealings with the white man. Differences in skin color and differences in customs and culture of course made initial distinctions between Englishmen and Indians inescapable.[75] But as the events of the subsequent years clearly demonstrated, the New England natives based their loyalties on other criteria than racial affinity. It was the historian, not the Puritan or the aborigine, who insisted on making racial division the focal point of Puritan-Indian relations in New England.*

---

* The early Puritans, well aware that the Indians of New England were as divided in interest and policy as they were in social and cultural structure, did not portray relations with the Indians as determined by any fundamental distinction of race. Winthrop, Bradford, and their contemporaries treated the encounters of Europeans and Indians as though they were determined by all the complexities of human behavior. By 1675, however, when King Philip's War pitted a large portion of the Indians against the colonists, Puritan historians for the first time tended to represent the dealings of the two peoples as a confrontation of distinct races. Thus Increase Mather and William Hubbard, both of whom wrote their histories during the war years, bear some resemblance in approach to later historians who often began with the assumption that an expanding

colony necessarily finds all red men aligned against all whites in basic interests if not in actual combat. This simplistic view was well established by the middle of the nineteenth century. See for example, Peter Oliver, *The Puritan Commonwealth* (Boston, 1856), 100-153; and George E. Ellis, *The Red Man and the White Man in North America* (Boston, 1882), in which the section on Philip's War is entitled "War of the Races." Most writers in the twentieth century have continued the distortion, as can be seen in such works as William C. MacLeod, *The American Indian Frontier* (New York, 1928), *passim;* and Alvin M. Josephy, *The Patriot Chiefs* (New York, 1961), especially in the chapter on King Philip. The assumption that racial interests were fundamental and inherently incompatible is implicit in a work as recent as William T. Hagan, *The Indian in American History* (Service Center for Teachers of History, Publication #50 [New York, 1963]). Hagan (p. 3) recognizes the "bewildering cultural diversity and political fragmentation" of American Indian society, but concludes that the primary importance of these divisions lay in their "render[ing] the Indian incapable of withstanding the pressure of the whites. Unable to unite against the intruders, the Indians even permitted themselves to be pitted against each other. . . ." Today's historian, of course, deals with the problem of race from a moral standpoint the opposite of that which guided his nineteenth century predecessor. Whereas men like John Gorham Palfrey had little use for the Indians and could therefore think of them as an inferior race apart, most modern historians give full sympathy to the underdog. Yet in a manner slightly suggestive of the Black Muslim's racist rejection of white rascism, the contemporary historian is often led by moral indignation at the plight of the Indian to assume among the red men a community of interest and a racial cohesion that simply did not exist.

CHAPTER III

Pilgrim Precedents, 1620-1630

TO THE small band of Pilgrims huddled in the fetid closeness of the *Mayflower*, thoughts of the New World were not entirely hopeful. Few of the passengers had probably ever seen an American Indian, but all had undoubtedly heard the gruesome tales of Indian atrocities so familiar to Europeans. William Bradford, when recording his history of the Pilgrims a decade later, recalled how the decision to remove to the New World had been made in the face of what they fully expected to be the "continuall danger of the salvage people; who are cruell, barbarous, and most treacherous." The emigrants believed that they could expect no mercy from the red men, who

> delight to tormente men in the most bloodie manner that may be; fleaing some alive with the shells of fishes, cutting of[f] the members, and joynts of others by peesemeale and broiling on the coles, eate the collops of their flesh in their sight whilst they live, with other cruelties horrible to be related.

Such a prospect, Bradford added unnecessarily, was enough to make "the very bowels of men to grate within them, and make the weake to quake, and tremble." [1]

The fears of the Pilgrims were at least partly justified. The ship would soon discharge its human cargo where the natives were especially hostile to the white man; no less friendly landing place could have been selected by design. The prevailing animosity stemmed principally from the depredations of Captain Thomas Hunt, whose treacherous kidnappings have already been narrated,* and evidence of its intensity was all too obvious. The Nauset Indians had recently attacked English explorers on Cape Cod, and Captain Thomas Dermer would soon die of wounds inflicted by the natives of Martha's Vineyard. When the Pilgrims finally decided to build their village at Plymouth, they came within the bounds of the equally suspicious Wampanoags. Captain Dermer had explored the New England coast but a few months prior to the arrival of the Pilgrims and asserted that the Wampanoag tribe bore "an inveterate malice to the English, and are of more streingth than all the savages from thence to Penobscote." [2]

Under such circumstances, the rapid success of the Pilgrims in establishing cordial relations with the neighboring tribes is remarkable. Not only did the men of New Plymouth win the sincere friendship of most of the Indian leaders, but they managed within a few hectic years to set a model for interracial diplomacy that was followed, with varying success, by the later Puritan colonies. Justice, tolerance, decisiveness, and amity became the keynotes of Plymouth's Indian policy.

* * *

THE Pilgrims' first encounter with their native neighbors gave little promise of the harmony to come. In fact, for several weeks after the arrival of the *Mayflower* in Cape Cod

---

* See page 16.

Bay, Indian-white relations resembled a game of hide-and-seek, with the newcomers doing the searching. Not until November 15, four days after the Pilgrims began exploring the cape, did they catch even a distant glimpse of its Indian inhabitants. To the Pilgrims' relief, this meeting involved none of the torments they had imagined: the five or six Nausets took to their heels while still some distance away. The English followed their footprints for ten miles along the beach, but to no avail. The Indians, it appeared, were not so ferocious after all.[3]

The Pilgrims were certainly not looking for trouble with the Indians, and it was not in their nature to become overconfident, yet within a few days of their anchoring off Cape Cod the first Puritan settlers had given the red men cause for anger. When the Englishmen discovered some freshly concealed underground corn barns, they could not resist the urge to know what was inside. Once they knew, they could not pass up the chance to acquire food and planting seed. At the risk of jeopardizing the friendship of the natives, the Pilgrims carted off all the corn they could carry, vowing to repay the owners at the first opportunity. Bradford credited the stolen seed with saving the colony from possible starvation, but in the meantime it undoubtedly added to the prevailing hostility of the Nausets.[4]

More traces of the red men were encountered in November and early December, but still the Indians kept out of sight. The Englishmen discovered several canoes, uncovered more corn and a bag of beans, found and followed Indian trails, and William Bradford got himself caught in an Indian deer snare. But the only Indians the Pilgrims came upon were dead. The Englishmen found several burial mounds, one of which their curiosity drove them to uncover. Ironically, it turned out to be the tomb of a blond-haired European sailor, from whose grave they took "sundry of the prettiest things" before carefully recovering the corpse. Henceforth they scrupulously avoided molesting Indian graves, knowing "it would be odious unto them to ransack their sepulchres." The Pilgrims were less attentive to Indian property rights at two wigwams from which a selection of native craftware was taken back to the ship. The Englishmen intended to leave some trinkets of European manufacture in exchange, but the toil of exploration prevented them from returning to that area.[5] Another link in the chain of unfriendly relations had been forged.

Not until the eighth of December, 1620, did the Pilgrims come into direct contact with the Nausets, and the first meeting boded ill for future relations with that tribe. On the night of December seventh, a party of about twenty Pilgrims and sailors were camped on the inner shore of the cape within a barricade of logs and boughs. About midnight "a great and hideous cry" rudely interrupted their sleep, but a couple of musket shots quickly silenced it. Then at dawn the Indians launched a sudden attack, heralded by a shower of arrows. After a brief skirmish the English routed the Nausets, apparently without loss of life or serious injury to either side. The Pilgrims found eighteen arrows around their barricade, some of them lodged in the coats they had left hanging inside. These lethal instruments, some tipped with brass, others with eagles' claws, were sent back to England as souvenirs of the militant New World.[6]

A week after this clash the English entered Plymouth Harbor, and within another week they had selected a site for the construction of their village. The appeal of the gentle hillside lay only partly in its rivers of fresh water and its sheltered harbor; of equal importance were the cleared fields and signs of previous habitation. The soil invited planting with a minimum of effort, and there were no dense forests in the immediate vicinity to shelter hostile neighbors. Supply and defense were the two main considerations, and Plymouth met these needs admirably.[7] The English must have pondered the reasons why such a place had been deserted; they would later learn that they had settled at the Indian village of Patuxet, of which Squanto was the sole survivor.

Had the Indians chosen to attack New Plymouth that first winter, there is little doubt that the infant colony would have been easily exterminated. Although the Pilgrims labored with axe and hoe to provide the necessities of life, the chills from wading waist-deep in Cape Cod Bay during the explorations, the nutritional deficiencies of a sixty-five-day sea voyage, and the inadequacy of the food and shelter in Plymouth exacted a heavy toll among the immigrants. By springtime half of the one hundred and one colonists were dead, and of the remnant only six or seven were in full health. Pneumonia, scurvy, and constant fatigue left the English colony practically defenseless. It is little wonder that every trace of the Indians caused fear and alarm among the settlers.[8]

Many signs and sounds convinced the colonists that their presence was known and that they were probably under constant surveillance. On December 24 and 25 they heard savage cries, and a few days later they saw "great smokes of fire" a few miles away. Yet when Miles Standish led a small scouting party to the site of the smoke he found only empty wigwams. Toward the end of January Captain Christopher Jones and others aboard the *Mayflower* spotted two Indians in a canoe, but the natives fled precipitously on being discovered.[9] The Wampanoags, it appeared, were reluctant to commence relations of any kind.

As the months passed, however, the red men lost a little of their timidity. In mid-February 1621, a band of prowling Indians took some tools that had been left in the fields, and on another occasion two Indians appeared on a hilltop a quarter-mile from Plymouth and beckoned the English to approach. When Miles Standish and Stephen Hopkins went to meet them the Indians fled, but not before the sound of more Indians behind the hill aroused the Pilgrims' apprehension. "This caused us to plant our great ordinance in places most convenient," recorded Edward Winslow; two days later Captain Jones brought several cannon from the ship and helped station them on a hill that commanded the inland approaches to New Plymouth.[10]

*   *   *

IN spite of the ominous tone of the early encounters, the Pilgrims' first meeting with an Indian at New Plymouth was not only friendly but extremely helpful. The tale has often been told of how the Pilgrims gathered in mid-March to discuss military defense, only to be interrupted by "a certaine Indian [who] came bouldly amongst them, and spoke to them in broken English, which they could well understand, but marvelled at it." This was Samoset, Sagamore of Pemaquid (now Bristol) in eastern Maine. He had been carried to Cape Cod by Thomas Dermer some eight months before, had remained for a time with the Wampanoags, and now came to offer his linguistic talents to the English settlers. Samoset had learned a smattering of English from the fishermen who frequented the Maine coast, and he put it to good use as he talked long into the evening about the tribes of the vicinity — their names, numbers, strength, location, and leading men. This was priceless information to the settlers, and one can readily imagine the

Pilgrim Fathers sitting intently through the crisp March afternoon, carefully recording each bit of fact and straining to catch the meaning of Samoset's cryptic phrases. Red carpet treatment — or as close to it as the poor Pilgrims could come — was lavished on this naked guest: puddings, duck, biscuit and butter were brought forth, though "strong water" had to be substituted for the beer he requested. Before he left the next day, the colonists presented him with a knife, bracelet, and ring. Samoset promised to return later with members of the Wampanoag tribe and to bring beaver for trade.[11]

The appearance of Samoset marked the beginning of a relationship between New Plymouth and the Wampanoags that remained predominantly cordial until the 1670's. Within a few days of Samoset's arrival, the stolen tools were returned, a potentially lucrative fur trade was begun, and the several natives who visited the Pilgrims showed an eager friendliness.[12] All that was needed now was a more formal understanding with the dominant sachem of the area, and on March 22, 1621, that too was accomplished.

Chief Massasoit was by no means reluctant to befriend the colonists; his need for confederates against the Narragansetts had never been greater, and he seized with alacrity this chance to gain allies equipped with awesome weapons. Accompanied by his brother and sixty warriors, Massasoit soon arrived at Plymouth — so abruptly, in fact, that the Pilgrims were alarmed. The colonists dared not let so many possible enemies march into their town, yet at the same time they did not want to incur the wrath of the Wampanoag sachem.[13] A serious quandary was avoided by Squanto's arrival at this opportune moment.

Squanto had come with Massasoit, and he now took over the linguistic chores — and many of the diplomatic tasks as well. He arranged a parley between Edward Winslow and Massasoit at which Winslow (via Squanto) assured the sachem that the English wanted only peace, friendship, and trade, and emphasized his protestations with gifts. As evidence of the colonists' good faith Winslow offered himself as a hostage to the Indians; Massasoit and twenty unarmed followers then advanced to meet Governor John Carver. Determined to impress the natives with the power and dignity of Englishmen, the Pilgrims dispatched Captain Standish and a squad of musketeers to escort the visitors to the meeting place. The two delegations met at the town brook and exchanged salutes; Standish's honor guard conducted the native king to one of the partially completed houses, where a green rug and a few cushions provided symbolic luxury for the grand occasion. Then, with a flurry of drums and the blare of trumpets, Governor Carver made his own regal entrance, accompanied by another squad of musketeers. The pageantry over, serious negotiations began.[14]

No record exists of the verbal maneuvering that accompanied the drafting of the treaty. We do not know who proposed the specific terms or if there was any dispute over them. But what emerged was a remarkable document, extremely encouraging to the fledgling colony yet eminently fair to the Wampanoag tribe. The seven articles of the treaty embodied two main topics of agreement. First, Massasoit pledged that his people would neither harm nor rob the English, and that he would punish any of his men who perpetrated crimes against the colonists. Second, Carver and Massasoit each agreed to aid the other in the event "any did unjustly war against him." In addition, the Wampanoag chief was to inform his confederate tribes of the terms, that the treaty might encompass them also, and each party to the

treaty promised to refrain from carrying weapons when vis-
iting the other. The final article acknowledged that the
treaty with Plymouth was, in effect, a treaty with King
James; Massasoit and the Stuart monarch were now allies.[15]

Throughout the negotiations, the Pilgrim chroniclers recorded, Massasoit "trembled for fear." Perhaps this is true,
but it seems improbable. The colonists, few in number and
far from any military assistance (Jamestown was the only
other English settlement in America), were surrounded by
potential enemies. If the chieftain trembled, surely it was
from excitement or "strong water." In any event, we are
indebted to the same chroniclers for a vivid description of
Massasoit, portraying him as

> a very lusty man, in his best years, an able body, grave
> of countenance, and spare of speech. In his attire little or
> nothing differing from the rest of his followers, only in a
> great chain of white bone beads about his neck, and at it
> behind his neck hangs a little bag of tobacco, which he
> drank and gave us to drink; his face was painted with a
> sad [deep] red like murry [mulberry], and oiled both
> head and face, that he looked greasily.

A "great long knife" hanging on a string at his breast was
his only weapon.[16]

At the conclusion of the negotiations, Governor Carver
conducted his royal guest to the town brook where they
parted after an exchange of embraces.

The treaty of 1621 established a legal basis for Indian-
white relations, but mutual confidence could not be so
speedily achieved. The Pilgrims' knowledge that Massasoit
"hath a potent adversary, the Narragansetts, that are at war
with him, against whom he thinks we may be some strength
to him, for our pieces are terrible unto them," made the

colonists fear that their treaty was laid in shifting sands.[17] Actually, although both the Wampanoag sachem and the Pilgrim Fathers were guided as much by pragmatism as by altruism, throughout the remainder of Massasoit's life both signatories gave ample evidence of their sincerity.

For the next few months the colonists were too busy with the struggle against nature to devote much time to diplomacy. But by midsummer the major chores had been accomplished: crude but serviceable homes lined the narrow streets, corn and peas were ripening in the fields, and the defenses were well organized. Mercifully, the winter's sickness no longer held its death grip. Now, the Pilgrims saw, it was time to reaffirm the treaty of friendship and alliance. To let it lapse for lack of diplomatic niceties would be the height of folly. "It was thought meet," explained Governor Bradford (who had assumed the chief magistry on the death of Carver in April), "to see their new friend Massasoit and to bestow upon him some gratuity." Furthermore, there was a pressing need to end the frequent delegations of hungry braves who had been descending on Plymouth since the treaty and consuming the Pilgrims' scant provisions. The sachem himself or any envoys from him would be welcome, of course, but to keep every Indian in the area from claiming to be a "special friend" of Massasoit, the governor proposed to send a copper chain that the chief could give to his messengers as identification. Finally, the Pilgrims were curious: they longed to know the lay of the land, to see the native villages, and to acquire a firsthand acquaintance with the ways of their neighbors. Accordingly, Edward Winslow and Stephen Hopkins became New Plymouth's first ambassadors. In early July 1621, they set out for Massasoit's village of Sowamet, some forty miles to the southwest. Squanto accompanied them as guide and interpreter.[18]

Whatever doubts the Pilgrims may have had of Wampanoag friendship vanished with this first Puritan visit to Indian country. En route to Sowamet, the Plymouth envoys were treated with kindness and generosity — sometimes to the point of annoyance — by the sub-tribes they encountered. Chief Massasoit greeted the colonial ambassadors with even greater kindness, though much of it was wasted on men unaccustomed to Indian ways. The tedious Indian speeches, the "barbarous singing" with which the red men lulled themselves to sleep, and the honor of sharing a plank bed with the chief, his wife, and two braves were almost more than Winslow and Hopkins could endure. Winslow complained that "we were worse weary of our lodging than of our journey," and after two days he and Hopkins excused themselves from further agony by pleading the necessity of being home for the Sabbath.[19]

Despite such minor discomforts, the Pilgrim's first diplomatic mission was a total success. The Englishmen's gifts helped to set an amicable mood: bedecked in a new red coat and chain, Massasoit "was not a little proud to behold himself, and his men also to see their King so bravely attired." Massasoit graciously complied with the governor's suggestions. He also agreed to arrange for payment to the Nausets for the corn taken the previous fall. But most important was Massasoit's profession that he was "King James his man" and that the land belonged to the English monarch.[20] Perhaps Massasoit did not fully realize that he had voluntarily shifted his status from ally to subject of the Stuarts, but Squanto was there to translate and explain, and the subsequent history of Massasoit's relations with Plymouth gives no reason to question the willingness of his submission. It was, in any event, all the encouragement the Pilgrims needed to extend their judicial authority over the neighboring tribe whenever circumstances made it desirable.

The only neighboring Indians who now remained hostile to the English settlers were the Nausets of Cape Cod, and a relatively trivial event soon occurred to bring about peaceful relations with them also. Late in July a Plymouth youth wandered into the woods, soon lost his way, and eventually stumbled into the Indian village of Manomet. From there he was taken to Nauset. Governor Bradford received news of the boy's whereabouts from Chief Massasoit and a rescue party was immediately dispatched. It not only retrieved the lost youth but also concluded peace terms with the Cape Cod tribe. Reimbursement for the stolen corn, a matter on which Massasoit had apparently made little headway, was arranged, and the last obstacle to peace with the tribes in the Plymouth patent removed.[21]

*   *   *

WITHIN a few months the new harmony faced its first challenge. At the root of the trouble was the Narragansett tribe, ever ready to encourage lesions within Massasoit's domain. In the summer of 1621 the Narragansetts found a willing partner in Corbitant, sachem of a small Wampanoag band, who harbored no love for the English. Corbitant's followers railed at the recently concluded peace treaties; they also endeavored to intimidate those Indians who had most thoroughly befriended the English. There were then three such men: Squanto, Hobomock (a Wampanoag warrior), and Tockamahamon, about whom little is known except that he aided the Pilgrims for several months in 1621. All were then living at Plymouth.[22]

Corbitant's faction conspired with the Narragansetts to

upset both Massasoit and the English simultaneously. While the Narragansetts moved against Massasoit's village, Corbitant seized Squanto, Hobomock, and Tockamahamon; with them eliminated, "the English had lost their tongue." But Hobomock broke away from his captors and hurried to Plymouth with a tale of disaster: Massasoit routed and Squanto surely dead. Knowing that the mutual defense pact must now be observed or his allies would never trust the Plymouth colony again, Governor Bradford sent Miles Standish and fourteen men to rescue the survivors. If Squanto was dead, the soldiers were to return with Corbitant's head.[23]

The expedition against the conspirators accomplished its mission with little bloodshed. Squanto was found alive, Corbitant's faction fled, and the only casualties were three natives who were injured when they tried to escape Standish's surprise attack. The wounded were taken to Plymouth, where they received medical care from surgeon Samuel Fuller. Meanwhile Standish withdrew his men from Corbitant's village, but only after making it clear that Corbitant would be summarily punished if he persisted in conspiring against either the Wampanoag chief or the English of New Plymouth, and that immediate retribution would be meted out to any who harmed Squanto, Hobomock, "or any of Massasoit's subjects." [24]

The results of Plymouth's energetic stand were all that could have been desired. "They had gratulations from divers sachems," wrote Bradford, "and much firmer peace." Representatives from the Martha's Vineyard tribe came to Plymouth to proffer their friendship, and before long a contrite Corbitant sued for peace through Massasoit. On September 13, 1621, Corbitant and eight other minor sachems subscribed to "an Instrument of Submission to King

James." [25] Not only had peace been restored, but New Plymouth was now recognized from the eastern shore of Narragansett Bay to the western shore of Massachusetts Bay as agent for the King of England. By handling an awkward situation with dispatch and determination, the Pilgrims had set an important precedent and, at the same time, strengthened their own position.

The strange ambitions and machinations of Squanto also worked to the advantage of the Pilgrims. Because of his remarkable travels and his ability to converse with the white men, Squanto had gained considerable stature within the Indian community. His tales of the armed might of King James undoubtedly added to the military renown of the Pilgrims; friendship with Plymouth might lead to assistance from England in some future crisis. But Squanto was not content with his new prestige, and he saw the possibility of increasing it by playing on the credulity of his fellow red men. They feared nothing so much as a return of the plague, and great was their alarm when Squanto told them that the English had it buried under the floor of their storehouse. (The colonists had, in fact, buried some barrels of powder.) When Squanto hinted that he could influence the English to spring the killer from its lair, his stature rose to new heights, as did the Indians' fear of the colonists. Characteristically, the Pilgrims were too honest to perpetuate the hoax when they learned of it. They freely admitted that they had no such power, but added — with perfect sincerity — "that the God whom they served had Power to send that or any other Disease upon those that should doe any Wrong to his People." [26] To the Indians there was little substantive difference between the two interpretations. Puritan theology, then, coincided with fortuitous events to keep the bulk of the Indians in awe of the settlers.

The success of the Pilgrims' relations with the natives can also be attributed in part to a forthright integrity that encouraged the amity of the local tribes and made a lifelong impression on Chief Massasoit. It was as a trusting friend, we may be sure, that the Wampanoag king and ninety of his braves participated in America's first Thanksgiving celebration, to which the Indians contributed a supply of venison. Though the purpose of the event was to thank God for a plentiful harvest, the Pilgrims must surely have added a prayer of gratitude that "the Indians [were] very faithful in their covenant of peace with us, very loving and ready to pleasure us" — so much so, in fact, that the colonists could "walk as peaceably and safely in the wood as in the highways in England." [27]

While the Pilgrims were satisfied with the cordial bonds they had established with the Indians, they believed that they had improved intertribal relations as well. "There is now great peace amongst the Indians themselves," Edward Winslow wrote in December of 1621, which "would [not] have been but for us." The familiar charge that Europeans brought chaos to peaceful Indian tribes does not apply to the early years of New Plymouth. Evidence of Plymouth's just treatment of the Indians is, to be sure, primarily from Pilgrim accounts, but corroboration is offered by such diverse commentators as John Pory of Virginia, Increase Mather of Massachusetts, and Isaac de Rasieres of New Netherland. On a visit to Plymouth in 1628, Rasieres was impressed by the natives' high regard for the English, and he concluded that the Indians "better conducted" themselves because of the fine example of law and living set by the Pilgrim colony.[28]

Fortunately for the colonists, the harmony that had been established with the Wampanoags was extended, though not without some difficulty, to most of the adjacent tribes. In September 1621, Squanto guided a party of ten colonists to Massachusetts Bay. The Indians of the Massachusetts tribe were still suspicious of the English, and, according to Squanto, had often spoken ill of them. But the Pilgrims insisted on their policy of justice without timidity. When Squanto suggested that the English should seize the furs of the Massachusetts Indians, the Plymouth men assured him that they would do no harm to any tribe, no matter how much its members reviled the English, provided it did the Pilgrims no overt wrong. "But if once they attempted anything against us," the Pilgrims assured their guide, "then we would deal far worse than he desired." This policy seemed to bear fruit: the Indian women of Massachusetts traded the very furs from their backs, and they promised to collect more beaver for a future bartering session.[29]

Friendly relations were not so easily established with the Narragansetts to the southwest. The great plague of 1616-1617 had brought them to prominence by weakening their rivals. From the outset, the Narragansetts resented the Plymouth-Wampanoag alliance, while the failure of the Corbitant conspiracy of August 1621 rankled Narragansett pride. By January of the next year they "began to breathe forth many threats" against the English, and rumors reached Plymouth of a Narragansett plot to exterminate the colony. The tribe soon announced its hostility by sending to the colony a bundle of arrows tied in rattlesnake's skin, which Squanto explained as "a threatening and a challenge." Bradford was not cowed; he removed the arrows, stuffed the skin with powder and shot, and sent it back to Chief Canonicus of the Narragansetts. The Pilgrim leader also sent a verbal challenge: the English would not initiate war, but if the Narragansetts were determined to have it, "they might begin when they would." Meanwhile the colonists began construction of a palisade around the village and organized the able-bodied men into four squadrons with assigned emergency stations. If the Narragansetts chose to fight, this Puritan colony would not be caught unprepared. But the battle never came. Canonicus lost nerve at the sight of the returned snakeskin and would not allow the dread object in his house. The skin passed from village to village until it found its way back to Plymouth, still unopened.[30]

Not until the spring of 1622 did anything seriously jeopardize the amicable relations between Plymouth and the Wampanoags. But when a crisis did come, it left the colonists with an awkward dilemma: to preserve the treaty or to save Squanto's life. By a combination of circumstance, Puritan procrastination, and Massasoit's generosity, both objectives were achieved.

The cause of the trouble was Squanto's latest bid for power. He and Hobomock had departed in March for Massachusetts Bay with a new fur trading expedition. No sooner had the shallop departed than a relative of Squanto's, blood streaming from a fresh head wound, rushed breathlessly into Plymouth to report that attack was imminent: the Narragansetts, Corbitant, and Massasoit were in league to destroy the colony. A cannon shot recalled the shallop, which contained the irreplaceable Captain Standish and several men vital for the defense of the town. Hobomock flatly denied that Massasoit would be privy to any such scheme and sent his wife to Sowamet to investigate the rumor. Finding the plot pure fiction, she told Chief Massasoit of the furor in Plymouth. The Wampanoag sachem immediately sent reassurances of his good faith and friendship to Bradford. His conclusions as to Squanto's role, however, were much the same as Plymouth's. "They begane to see," mused Bradford, "that Squanto sought his owne ends, and plaied his owne game, by putting the Indians in fear, and drawing gifts from them to enrich him selfe, making them believe he could stir up warr against whom he would, and make peace for whom he would." Thus Squanto had "raised this false alarm, hoping, whilst things were hot in the heat of blood" to maneuver the English into attacking Massasoit and thus to remove the one Indian whose favor with the colonists and influence with the natives was greater than Squanto's.[31]

That Squanto emerged from this fracas alive was consistent with the *opéra bouffe* tone of the entire episode. Although Massasoit was reputed to be of a forgiving nature, he soon appeared in Plymouth and "inraged against TISQUANTUM." Bradford admitted that Squanto's treachery merited death, both for his attempted destruction of Massasoit and for the strife he would have caused the colonists. But the governor pleaded with the chief to spare Squanto for the practical reason that without him the English would have no competent interpreter. Massasoit was temporarily mollified but later had a change of heart and demanded custody of Squanto in accordance with the treaty of alliance. As an inducement, he sent the governor several beaver skins. One of the messengers who brought Massasoit's request also carried the sachem's own knife — with which he was to cut off the conspirator's head and hands.[32]

Bradford rejected the beaver: "It was not the manner of the English to sell men's lives at a price," yet he reluctantly decided to sacrifice the individual for the good of the colony. At that moment an unidentified ship appeared off Plymouth Harbor, and Bradford shrewdly used the emergency to save Squanto's life. With something less than perfect logic, the governor announced that he could not spare the services of Squanto when an unidentified and possibly hostile ship lay off Plymouth's shore. Disgusted at the governor's sophistry, Massasoit's messengers angrily withdrew. The emergency evaporated when the ship proved to be an English vessel, but Massasoit never again pressed the case. Still, Squanto was thereafter very careful "to stick close to the English, and never durst goe from them till he dyed." [33]

*   *   *

In the summer of 1622, some fifty or sixty men sent out by Thomas Weston, one of the principal "adventurers" of the Plymouth Company, arrived in New England to establish a new colony. Most of Weston's men had neither the sagacity nor the moral fiber of the Pilgrim Fathers; in the months to come the new arrivals seriously jeopardized New England's Indian-white relations and put the Pilgrims' Indian policy to its severest test.

For several weeks the new colonists lived at Plymouth while their leaders sought a place for permanent settlement. "The unjust and dishonest walking" of Weston's men and their "secret backbiting, revilings, etc." did little to endear them to the Pilgrims. And no sooner had Weston's men moved into their new quarters at Wessagusett, near the southern shore of Massachusetts Bay, than reports began to reach Plymouth that they were stealing corn and committing other abuses against the Massachusetts tribe. The Plymouth leaders reprimanded the newcomers, "advising them to better walking," but to no apparent effect. [34]

For a brief period the Wessagusett and Plymouth colonies combined efforts to procure corn from the tribes of southern New England, as both settlements were experiencing severe shortages. Perhaps the Pilgrims reasoned that Weston's men would be less likely to molest the Massachusetts Bay tribe if they could buy enough corn elsewhere, and therefore the joint expeditions promised both supply and a lessening of friction. The venture only partially achieved its end: enough corn was obtained to give both colonies minimum rations until midwinter. And even this limited success was not without its price; on a November excursion Squanto "fell sick of an Indean fever, bleeding much at the nose (which the Indeans take for a simptome of death)" and died within a few days. The loss to the English colonists was great; Squanto had done much to insure the success of New Plymouth, and his death undoubtedly gave encouragement to the latest conspirators against the colony.[35]

Hints of conspiracy began to appear in February 1623; by then the growing Indian disaffection toward Wessagusett had spread to include a distrust of Plymouth as well. Many of the Indians probably assumed that the Pilgrims condoned the actions of their English neighbors, and the sight of the two colonies working together in their search for corn must have promoted this assumption. The Pilgrims, however, remained largely unaware of the growing enmity and were hopeful that all was going moderately well — if only Wessagusett would conduct its Indian affairs with more integrity. In February a letter came to Governor Bradford from the Wessagusett leader, John Sanders, complaining of his inability to purchase corn from the natives and asking if he might not be justified in seizing enough to maintain life. Bradford vigorously objected, fearing that "all of us might smart for it," and advising his profligate neighbors to resort to shellfish and groundnuts as the Pilgrims were doing.[36] Pilgrim policy would not condone coercion so long as there remained a plausible alternative.

What saved the English colonies from the new conspiracy was not a reformation at Wessagusett, but a repetition of the earlier successful formula: timely information from friendly Indians and vigorous action by the colonists.

This time the informant was Massasoit, and again fortune smiled on the Pilgrims at the right moment — although lady luck (or the Puritan God) took a roundabout route. In mid-March 1623, news reached Plymouth that Massasoit was ill. According to the report, his condition was grave, and he would probably not survive the week. In keeping with Indian custom, the Plymouth authorities decided to send a representative to the invalid as a sign of friendship. Edward Winslow, by now somewhat adept at the Indian tongue and familiar with the trails to Sowamet, was given the assignment; he was accompanied by Hobomock and another Englishman. At Sowamet they found the chief alive, but his medicine men were "making such a hellish noise," observed Winslow, "as it distempered us that were well." [37]

Winslow at once became Massasoit's physician. The first dose of his "confection of many confortable conserves" restored the chief's failing eyesight; a liberal portion of English potage brought back his appetite; and a broth of corn flour, strawberry leaves, and sassafras — all strained through a pocket handkerchief — completed the cure. Massasoit was so impressed with Winslow's medical skill that he persuaded the colonist to treat all the other sick Indians in the village. Winslow's reputation for omniscience grew still greater when the chief glutted himself against his "doctor's" advice and suffered a frightening relapse. By the time medicines arrived from Plymouth, Massasoit was again clearly on the road to recovery and "brake forth into these speeches, 'Now I see the English are my friends, and love me: and whilst I live, I will never forget this kindness they have shewed me.' " [38]

The Wampanoag chief wasted no time in proving his sincerity, as Winslow found out a few days later. While the Plymouth envoys were plodding home, Hobomock revealed that Massasoit had told him of a plot to overthrow the English colonies. The Massachusetts, he testified, were the nucleus of the conspiracy, but they had been reinforced by the Nausets, Pamets, and several other tribes and subtribes in Plymouth's vicinity. Massasoit had been solicited but had refused. Now, heartened by Winslow's homemade remedies, Massasoit was ready to save the Pilgrims. He advised strong preventive action: "to kill the men of Massachuset' who were the authors of this intended mischief." Otherwise, Wessagusett was doomed and Plymouth's fate was dubious. [39]

The Pilgrims wasted no time in taking the Wampanoag's advice. Standish picked eight companions and prepared to sail for Massachusetts Bay, ostensibly to engage the Indians in beaver trade, but in fact to seize the ringleaders of the conspiracy. This decision had not been lightly made, for the Pilgrims knew that the Wessagusett settlers deserved little sympathy. The grievances of the Massachusetts against Wessagusett were mostly valid, and the tribe had not become hostile until severely provoked. Moreover, by their own actions the Wessagusett colony's leaders had acknowledged the justness of the accusations: the officers had publicly whipped and stocked some of the members for stealing from the natives, and one Wessagusett settler had been hanged in order to placate the Indians. Still, by the time Plymouth decided to act, the Wessagusett colony had almost disintegrated. Many of the colonists had sold all their possessions for food; others had hired themselves out as servants to the Indians. The settlement was dispersing gradually as individuals moved out of the palisaded village and foraged for themselves.[40] Clearly Weston's men were ill suited for their task and had ignored the example of diligence and foresight established by their Plymouth neighbors.

On the other hand, there was also no doubt as to the existence of a scheme to wipe out Plymouth as well as the offending Wessagusett. Massasoit's disclosure of the conspiracy was corroborated at this time by the brother of the Massachusetts' sachem, and overt unfriendliness on the part of some of the Indians lent further credence. Here were reasons enough for Plymouth's decision to take preventive action. But before Standish departed for Wessagusett, further evidence appeared. Learning of the cabal from a loquacious squaw, Phinehas Pratt, a Wessagusett settler, had slipped away to warn Plymouth of the impending attack. According to Pratt, the blow would fall as soon as the snow disappeared and the Indians had constructed enough canoes to assault the Wessagusett ship that lay in the harbor. Then the Wessagusett men "would all be knokt in the head." Pratt's tale undoubtedly stirred fresh memories of the recent horrendous massacre in Virginia that had taken the lives of more than three hundred colonists.[41]

The battle of Wessagusett, when it finally materialized, was a short but sanguine affair. Standish and his little army went to Wessagusett, but the Indians there immediately suspected his designs and would not congregate in the presence of the Pilgrim soldiers. Standish therefore decided to cut down the most obnoxious of the enemy and hoped that the rest would heed the lesson. His chance came in late March when Chief Witawamet, the leading conspirator, and three other Massachusetts braves came to Wessagusett. At a signal from Standish each Englishman attacked an Indian. All but one of the natives were slain on the spot; the lone survivor was Witawamet's eighteen-year-old brother, "whom the Captain caused to be hanged." Before the day was over, three more Massachusetts warriors paid with their lives the price of conspiracy. The Pilgrims carried Witawamet's head to Plymouth and triumphantly impaled it on their fort. While none of the Plymouth contingent was seriously injured, three of Weston's men who had previously moved out of the village were slain by the Massachusetts a few days later.[42]

The Wessagusett affair ended the cabal against the English colonies. Plymouth found it unnecessary to attack any of the other conspiring tribes; fear had thrown them into confusion. As Winslow wrote:

> This sudden and unexpected execution, together with the just judgement of GOD upon their guilty consciences, hath so terrified and amazed them as, in like manner, they forsook their houses, running to and fro like men distracted, living in swamps and other desert places: and so brought manifold diseases amongst themselves, where of very many are dead.

Among the dead were several of the sachems who had abetted the conspiracy. Members of the offending tribes who did not flee were too frightened to attend to spring planting, and so famine weakened them further.[43]

Much to the Pilgrims' relief, the cause of the conspiracy evaporated at the same time that its perpetrators did. Weston's men, discouraged by their sad experience, decided to abandon their plantation. Captain Standish gave them adequate provisions for a journey to Maine, where they could obtain passage to England on the fishing vessels. Once again Plymouth's bold action, with a generous assist from fortune, had restored interracial harmony.

*   *   *

ONCE the Pilgrim Fathers had achieved a stable and favorable relationship with the neighboring tribes, its perpetuation was the colony's chief diplomatic objective. During the remainder of the 1620's the greatest single threat to that happy condition was posed by fishermen and transient settlers who cared more for their own profits than for the welfare of the permanent colonists.

Since the first Europeans came to the New World, firearms had been coveted by the natives, and Indians along the Maine coast had acquired a few guns before 1620. English, Dutch, and French seamen were often willing to part with their highly valued weapons for large bundles of marketable beaver, from which a small fortune could be realized in a few months' time. By 1627 Governor Bradford was complaining to Sir Ferdinando Gorges that the illicit firearms trade "will be the overthrow of all, if it be not looked into." [44] The Indians, in fact, were becoming more expert in the use of firearms than the English themselves. Fear of the white man's weapons, which had at first been so great that "the very sight of one (though out of kilter) was a terrour unto them," had given way to admiration and then to acquisition. English colonists were shocked to encounter red men armed with muskets strolling through the woods and bagging game with remarkable proficiency. [45] There was little or nothing the Pilgrims could do about the fishermen, but when close neighbors engaged in the illicit commerce the Plymouth colonists took action in self defense. This was the situation that arose in the fall in 1626.

The story of Thomas Morton is a familiar one in the annals of early New England. In the spring of 1625 a Captain Wollaston — about whom little is known but his name — brought some thirty followers to Massachusetts Bay, where he established a colony a few miles from the abandoned village of Wessagusett. In the autumn of the following year Captain Wollaston and many of his settlers departed for the Virginia colony. No sooner had they left than Thomas Morton, a lawyer of dubious scruples and most un-Puritan morals, ousted Wollaston's appointed leader and made himself "head of a turbulent and seditious crew." Soon he was selling guns to the Indians and inviting them to his revelries at "Merrymount," his new and more appropriate name for Mount Wollaston. When Morton persisted in his unconventional behavior, lured indentured servants from their masters, and sent to England for more guns for barter, the Pilgrim Fathers took matters into their own hands. Miles Standish invaded the settlement, seized the drunken defenders, and brought "Mine Host of Merrymount" to Plymouth under armed guard. Morton was subsequently shipped back to England, accompanied by letters of grievance to Gorges and the Council.[46]

Historians who delight in censuring the drab morality of the Pilgrims and other Puritans have long found the Morton episode a choice example of moral bigotry.[47] They point out how shocked the Pilgrims were by the "lord of misrule" and his "schoole of Ath[e]isme." And they note Governor Bradford's condemnation of Morton for inviting Indian women to his nocturnal festivities and for "dancing and frisking togither, (like so many fairies, or furies rather,) and worse practises."[48]

There is no doubt that the social behavior of the Morton colonists offended the Pilgrim Fathers. But the documen-

tary record reveals that the Merrymount episode belongs
not in the realm of moral quibbling, but of interracial diplomacy. It is clear that Morton's selling of firearms (and possibly firewater) to the Indians was what ultimately brought
armed intervention by the Plymouth authorities. Had Morton been content with his "great licentiousness" he would
probably have been left alone; the Pilgrims would not have
condoned his behavior, but neither would they have presumed to interfere in matters outside their jurisdiction. But
the gun trade, centered in a growing settlement of lawless,
irresponsible, runaway servants, was a different matter.
"The savages," as Charles Francis Adams noted in his judicious study of the episode, "were as yet in pursuit only of
game and furs, but to men living in such absolute solitude as
those early planters, even the poor survivors of the Massachusetts tribe were a cause for apprehension; while behind
the impenetrable veil of the forest were the dreaded Narragansetts." [49]

By the fall of 1628 there were half a dozen small plantations in the Boston Bay area, and several others dotted the
New England coast. In most of these embryonic villages
lived women and children, as well as men. These people
would bear the brunt of the first Indian attacks; larger and
stronger Plymouth was relatively secure. It is not surprising, therefore, that the initiative for the overthrow of
Merrymount came from the outlying settlements. Sometime in the spring of 1628 these communities urged Governor Bradford to interfere before Morton's men triggered a
needless struggle. Seven settlements, besides Plymouth, contributed to the campaign chest, and the total of £12.7s was
used to raise a volunteer force. Still, the colonies resorted to
coercion only after Morton had insolently rejected two

written admonitions to observe King James's proclamation
against the gun trade. Morton insisted that "the Kings proclamation was no law" and that "the King was dead and his
displeasure with him." Although this may have been sound
law, it carried no conviction to men faced with the horrors
of wilderness warfare. And when at length the settlements
were forced to act, and they had shipped "this troublesome
planter" to the Council for New England "for remedy and
redress," they made it plain that their main concern had
been the very real threat to their security. Bradford's letter
to the Council asked help in curbing the firearms trade both
by settlers and fishermen, "otherwise we shall be forced to
quit the country, to our great grief, and dishonor to our
nation; for we shall be beaten with our own arms if we
abide." [50]

Though Morton escaped punishment and was soon back
in New England, the Pilgrims had averted another prospective clash with the natives, and peaceful relations continued
unabated. The Morton episode was strictly in keeping with
Plymouth's policy of decisive action in support of the general welfare.

        *   *   *

As the decade of the 1620's drew to a close, New Plymouth's role in Indian affairs began to be overshadowed by
those of her expanding neighbors. Each year more colonists
arrived to swell the tiny Boston Bay settlements into bus-
tling villages. In 1628 Plymouth contained more inhabitants
than the rest of New England combined; two years later
Plymouth was no longer even the largest Puritan colony.
The future would belong to the Massachusetts Bay settlement and its offshoots. But Plymouth had served New Eng-

land well: when Indian affairs in Massachusetts, Rhode Island, and Connecticut brought new problems, precedents established by the Pilgrims were put to use. Frequently they helped to make the early years of Puritan expansion successful and, for the most part, peaceful.

CHAPTER IV

The Expansion of New England, 1630-1636

THE SECOND major group of Puritans to seek haven in New England arrived in 1630. That year almost one thousand settlers swarmed into the area around Massachusetts Bay, turning the sparsely inhabited region north of Plymouth Colony into the center of New World Puritanism. And with this influx of colonists began a new phase in New England's Indian affairs.

In point of fact, the nucleus of the Massachusetts Bay Colony had been in the area since 1628, two years before the *Arbella* brought Governor John Winthrop and his followers to their wilderness Zion. By that time the Indian policy of the new colony had already taken on some distinctness of form. Some of the elements in that policy rested frankly on Plymouth precedents; others owed their origin to the experiences of the New England Company, the corporate predecessor of the Bay Company, which supported a small but thriving outpost at Salem, a few miles north of Massachusetts harbor. The Great Migration of the 1630's led to some shaping of new Indian policies and revising of old ones, for the Indian policy of Massachusetts Bay, like that of Plymouth, would be more the result of pragmatism than of planning. Yet so solid a base for the conduct of Indian affairs had been established in the late 1620's that within less than a decade after Winthrop's arrival, the Bay Colony had formulated a comprehensive Indian policy and had seen it carried to new frontiers in the Connecticut Valley and along the shores of Narragansett Bay.

*   *   *

By a stroke of fortune similar to that which aided the Pilgrim settlers at Plymouth, the colonists of the New England Company established their Puritan communities in an area almost void of natives. The Massachusetts tribe had been as devastated by the plague of 1616-1617 as had the Wampanoags. In 1628 the tribe probably numbered only a few hundred, scattered among half a dozen or more villages along the coast and river valleys near Massachusetts Bay.[1] Like the Wampanoags, too, the Massachusetts Indians confronted a deadly adversary, the Tarrantines, and were therefore in need of effective allies.[2] Not surprisingly, then, the settlers in Massachusetts Bay received a cordial welcome from most of the native inhabitants.

It fell to Captain John Endicott, resident agent of the New England Company, to perpetuate in Massachusetts Bay the atmosphere of mutual tolerance between natives and New Englanders that had been created by the Pilgrim Fathers in Plymouth. Endicott commanded several small settlements, including the principal one at Salem (or Naumkeag as it was then known), with a total population in 1628 of approximately three hundred persons. The communications between the agent and the corporation clearly demonstrate the importance of Indian affairs to both the settlers and the patentees. "We trust you will not be unmindful of the mayne end of our plantation," the company wrote to Endicott, "by indevoringe to bring the Indians to the knowledge of the gospell." Endicott's superiors did not expect him to effect immediate conversion through preaching — there were only two clergymen in the group — but rather to pave the way by insisting that the colonists "demeane themselves justly and curteous" toward the natives. The same instructions, however, grimly reminded the colonists of the Virginia massacre, the result of being "too confident of the ffidellitie of the salvages." [3]

Shortly after the royal charter creating the Massachusetts Bay Company had passed the seals in March 1629, fresh instructions were sent to Endicott from the new company, which now had full legal title to its corner of the New World and "ample power to govern and rule all his Majesty's subjects that reside within the limits of our plantation." Possessing a greater authority than that of the New England Company, the Bay Company (officially "The Governor and Company of the Massachusetts Bay in New England") could and did issue more specific regulations. Whereas the earlier instructions had merely invoked a word of caution, the new rules directed that all men must be "exercised in the use of armes," appointed a master gunner, and denied Indians access to the plantation except at specified times. A stiff directive prohibited traffic in arms with the natives. "Such of our nation," it read, "as sell munition, gunns, or other furniture, to arme the Indians against us, or teach them the use of armes, wee would have you to apprehend them and send them prisoners for England, where they will not excape severe punishment." But the greater emphasis on precaution did not alter the policy for everyday dealings with the Indians: no injury "in the least kinde" must be done to the heathen, and offending settlers must be punished. Captain Endicott was to post his regulations where both races could see them.[4]

The extent of Endicott's success in Indian affairs can only be estimated from scraps of evidence. Reverend Francis Higginson, one of the colony's clergymen, wrote that the Indians often visited the English and were treated kindly by them. As part of the program of good will, Lambert Wilson, the colony's physician, was directed to treat the illnesses of the Indians "from tyme to tyme," a policy that may have taken its lead from the deft work of Edward Winslow and Samuel Fuller at Plymouth. Yet all was not perfect harmony, for Higginson added that "we neither feare nor trust them." The lack of trust most likely stemmed from the Wessagusett affair, in which the Massachusetts tribe had been deeply involved. The absence of fear, on the other hand, clearly rested on the settlers' monopoly of firearms. As Higginson noted, "fourtie of our musketeeres will drive five hundred of them out of the Field."[5]

That Endicott was not altogether successful in promoting good relations between Indians and settlers is clear from an episode that occurred in the spring of 1630. The Charlestown Records relate that "there was a great design of the Indians, from the Narragansetts, and all round about us to the eastward in all parts, to cut off the English," including, it seems, those at Plymouth. This was probably another manifestation of Narragansett and Massachusetts hostility toward all friends of Chief Massasoit. At any rate, John Sagamore, a local chieftain "who always loved the English," revealed the plot. The Salem colonists announced their preparedness by firing several cannons, making "such a terrible Rattling among the Trees a far off, that the amazed *Indians* returned not a little afrighted." No more was heard of the conspiracy.[6]

*   *   *

IF the Massachusetts Indians had, in fact, wanted to oust the fledgling colony, their best opportunity was rapidly passing. So long as the English population remained sparse the Indians might conceivably have overcome their own inferiority in weapons by sheer weight of numbers. But within a year of the Salem episode that advantage had disappeared. At the end of 1629 there were about three hundred settlers at Salem and another hundred at Charlestown.[7] The next year seventeen vessels brought more than a thousand new colonists. By 1632 the English population of the Massachusetts Bay Colony totaled two thousand; it doubled in the next two years, and by 1637 had climbed to almost eight thousand.[8] Plymouth by that time had close to six hundred settlers,[9] while the grand total for New England may have been as high as 21,200.[10] In the meantime, an epidemic of smallpox killed off thousands of Indians so that their numbers shrank almost as rapidly as the white men's multiplied.

But from all accounts the tribes of eastern Massachusetts did not resent the sudden influx of Englishmen. A Massachusetts native greeted John Winthrop aboard the *Arbella* within hours of its arrival, and the sagamore of Agawam (later Ipswich) paid his respects to the new governor the next day. In the months that followed, according to William Hubbard, clergyman and historian, "their chief sagamores, both near by and more remote, made divers overtures of friendship." Among the supplicants was Chief Miantonomo of the powerful Narragansetts, who soon followed the precedent of the Massachusetts Indians. In the summer of 1632 he took the trail to Boston — the new capital of the Bay Colony — "to make peace or a league" with the English.[11] The reason for this voluntary acceptance of the intruders by the Indians of Massachusetts was many-sided: the red men had what they must have deemed a limit-less abundance of land, the English would make available the many items of trade that were rapidly becoming essen-tial to the Indians along the coast, and the presence of well-armed Europeans could only enhance the Massachusetts tribe's chance of survival against the attacks of its more nu-merous and powerful enemies — the Tarrantines to the northeast, the Pequots to the southwest. As John Eliot put it: "We are as walls to them, from theire bloody enemise, and they are sensible of it." [12]

Until 1636 there was little friction between the Massa-chusetts Bay Colony and the Indians of New England, and the few instances of hostility are more than offset by ges-tures of mutual friendship and trust. Colonial officials and Indian rulers frequently exchanged gifts, and on more than one occasion the natives aided shipwrecked Englishmen.[13] Furthermore, the suffering of the Massachusetts colonists during their first winter would have been far greater with-out the large quantities of corn that the natives supplied.[14] The Englishmen showed their gratitude, in part at least, by helping to secure the return of James Sagamore's squaw, abducted by the Tarrantines in a night assault.[15]

One of the main reasons for the good relations between the natives and the Bay Colony was the determination of the Puritan authorities to prevent their own subjects from mal-treating the natives. The first perpetrator to appear in the records was none other than Thomas Morton. He had re-turned to New England in 1629 and was soon at odds with the government of the new colony. According to Deputy-Governor Thomas Dudley, Morton fired a charge of "hail-shot" at a group of Indians who refused to bring him a ca-noe; one was hurt and several had their garments damaged before he appropriated the canoe for his own use. At the second meeting of the Court of Assistants, it was ordered that

> Thomas Morton of Mount Wolliston, shall presently be sett into the bilbowes, and after sent prisoner into England . . . ; that all his goods shalbe seazed upon to defray the charge of his transporation, payment of his debts, and to give satisfaction to the Indians for a cannoe hee unjustly tooke from them; and that his house, after the goods are taken out, shalbe burnt downe to the ground in the sight of the Indians, for their satisfaction, for many wrongs hee hath done them from tyme to tyme.

At last New England was rid of "Mine Host of Merrymount," though he was long remembered as "the Man that taught the *Indians* in these Parts *the Use of Gunns*." [16]

While Morton was the most notorious of those apprehended for maltreating the Indians, he was by no means the only one, nor the most harshly punished. John Dawe was led to the whipping post for "intiseing an Indian woman to lye with him"; Nicholas Frost was fined, whipped, branded on the hand, and banished, for stealing from the Indians and other crimes; Josias Plastowe was shorn of the title of "Master" and his servants whipped for stealing four baskets of corn; and Sir Richard Saltonstall had to make recompense on two different occasions for damage done to Indian property, in one instance by his servants, in the other by his cattle. And when the sagamore of Agawam in 1634 complained of damage to his corn by Charlestown's unfenced swine, the General Court ordered the town to make retribution.[17]

It is important to note, however, that the colony's government assumed that its authority applied to red men as well as white — and it pointed to the charter for legal support. Indians, particularly the sagamores, were held responsible for property violations and moral infractions. In most instances the native rulers apparently accepted with good grace this assertion of authority. Appearing before the General Court in May 1631, Chief Chickataubut and John Sagamore "promised unto the Court to make satisfaction for whatsoever wronge that any of their men shall doe to any of the Englishe, to their cattell or any other waies." A month later they were required to make recompense for "some injuries" done by their men to the settlers' cattle, and Chickataubut was fined a beaver skin for shooting one of Richard Saltonstall's swine. Other forms of punishment were also imposed on the sachems; in July 1631 the Court decreed that "the Saggamore of Aggawam is banished from coming into any Englishe mans howse for the space of a year, under penalty of 10 skins of beaver." In general the Puritan leaders seem to have dealt carefully and considerately with the native chieftains; their policy was in the spirit of an observation made in 1632 that "the more love and respect you shewe to the Sagamores and Sachems the more love and feare shall you gaine from the common natives." [18]

From the outset the government of the colony strictly enforced the principle, enunciated under Endicott, that the Indians must be prevented from acquiring firearms or even learning to use them. In September 1630, the Court made a law that "noe person whatsoever shall, either directly or indirectly, imploy, or cause to be imployed . . . any Indian to use any peece upon any occasion or pretence whatsoever." Stiff penalties were prescribed for noncompliance. A few years later this decree was modified to permit the employment of natives, but only with the expressed permission of the General Court. The privilege was sparingly granted; only the governor, deputy-governor, and one or two others were authorized to let their Indian servants "shoote at fowle." [19]

Though the laws were occasionally relaxed against allowing Indians the use of guns, there was no corresponding change in the laws against selling firearms to the Indians, and the penalties remained severe. In 1632 one Richard Hopkins was whipped and branded on the cheek for selling guns, powder, and shot to John Sagamore, and it was seriously questioned whether the death penalty might not be more appropriate. Hopkins was exposed by an Indian who had witnessed his transactions, but who (according to the colony records) insisted on anonymity "for otherwise he was sure to be killed" — but whether by Hopkins or by his fellow tribesmen the records do not reveal.[20]

At the same time that the Bay government was attempting to insure the colonists' monopoly on European weapons, it was providing a defensive network to guard against attack from land or sea. No doubt the need for an organized system of sentinels, forts, and militia companies was apparent from the beginning, but no systematic defense was implemented before the spring of 1631. Then one March night a Watertown settler fired a musket after dark to frighten the wolves away from a lost calf, and thereby spread a false alarm to every town in the colony. Drums were beat in Boston, and the colonists made hasty preparations for defense. Though the cause of the alarm became known by morning, the lesson hit home. Two weeks later the Court established nightly watches at the frontier towns of Dorchester and Watertown, set stringent penalties for shooting muskets after dark, and made Saturday drill mandatory for

each militia company.[21] Rigid application of punishments
for "negligence in watching" kept sentries alert, as the few
entries in the Court records clearly illustrate.[22]

During the summer of 1631 the military organization of
Massachusetts Bay took on a more professional appearance.
Besides the regular weekly training, one day each month
was designated as general training day. In order to impress
the neighboring red men, the captains of the several companies were to execute their military evolutions "att a
convenient place aboute the Indian wigwams." Should the
Indians fail to be intimated by this display of power, measures were taken to prevent dangerous gatherings of natives
in or near the plantations. When a large body of Indians,
including ten sagamores, assembled at Muddy River (later
Brookline) in late August, the governor sent Captain Underhill and twenty musketeers to disperse them. And partly
to prevent the Indians from staging a massacre under pre-
tense of trade, a law of June 5, 1632, required that each
town have a "trucking howse [trading post] . . . whither
the Indians may resorte to trade, to avoide there comeing to
severall howses."[23] Clearly the policy of Massachusetts
Bay envisoned preventive measures as the first line of defense.

As the colony expanded, the problems of adequate defense grew as well. The General Court continued to enlarge
and improve military installations and to insist on a well-
prepared militia. In 1634 each town appointed an "overseer
of powder and shott"; towns were authorized to impress
enough men to make carriages and wheels for ordnance,
and every trained soldier was required to be fully equipped
for battle. The following year a beacon was set up on a hill
in Boston (hence Beacon Hill) to be fired in the event of an

attack. While this was primarily a caution against attack by European enemies, it served as well to warn of Indian assault. Supreme direction of military affairs was assigned to the governor and a committee of ten (later reduced to five), with full authority over offensive and defensive war, appointment and removal of officers, enforcement of regulations, and punishments by "martiall tryall." [24] A reading of the proceedings of the General Court during its first five or six years reveals the extreme importance that Massachusetts attached to military preparations; no other issue received so much attention.

It was probably inevitable that the rapid expansion of the Bay Colony sooner or later would create some friction with the natives over boundaries, as, in fact, it did among the colonists themselves. The first such disputes did not appear until 1633, but no sooner had they arisen than, in the words of a Puritan chronicler, "God ended the Controversy by sending the Small-pox amongst the Indians." Between the fall of 1633 and the summer of 1634 several thousand New England natives succumbed to the worst epidemic since 1616-1617. Among the victims were such local chieftains as Chickataubut and John Sagamore. Seven hundred Narragansetts perished, and travelers to the Connecticut Valley reported that the disease had interrupted all trade there. To the east, all tribes were affected as far as the Piscataqua River in Maine.[25]

Although a few Puritan colonists gloated at this sudden destruction of their heathen neighbors, the majority responded with characteristic charity. When the Indians, panic-stricken by the horror of the epidemic, abandoned their sick and dying, the colonists lent generous assistance. The ill were given tender care, the dead were buried, and

orphaned children were taken into several English homes.
William Bradford related that "this mercie which they
shewed them was kindly taken, and thankfully acknowledged of all the Indeans that know or heard of the
same." [26]

By the time the epidemic had run its course, many Indian
villages had been exterminated and others had sustained
heavy losses, while only two English families had been
affected.[27] The implication of this disparity in casualties
was not lost on the Puritans. Surely this was proof positive
of the Lord's intention of making New England a haven for
His true church, for as Governor Winthrop put it, "if God
were not pleased with our inheriting these parts, why did he
drive out the natives before us? and why dothe he still make
roome for us, by deminishinge them as we increase?" And
besides revealing divine will, the epidemic helped solve the
practical problems of New England's expansion. The re-
corder of the Charlestown Records observed that "without
this remarkable and terrible stroke of God upon the natives,
[we] would with much more difficulty have found room,
and at far greater charge have obtained and purchased
land." [28]

*   *   *

ONE of the most persistent myths concerning the relations
between the Puritan settler and the American Indian asserts
that the colonist robbed the native of his land, either by
seizing it outright or by purchasing it in return for a handful of worthless trinkets. Such a view is no longer held by
those reasonably well acquainted with the history of early
New England, but its place has often been taken by a more
sophisticated though equally invalid explanation. The second theory holds that while the Indian willingly sold his

land to the white man, the native did not understand the implications of such transactions because of his unique concept of land tenure; he had meant only to sell a share in the use of the land, not to part with it forever.*

The disparity between English and Indian concepts of land tenure was actually rather slight. Edward Winslow, who among the Pilgrims was probably best informed on the practices of the Wampanoags, reported that "Every sachim knoweth how far the bounds and limits of his own country extendeth; and that is his own proper inheritance. Out of that, if any of his men desire land to set their corn, he giveth them as much as they can use, and sets them their bounds. . . . The great Sachims or kings know their own bounds or limits of land, as well as the rest." Basing his observations on an even wider acquaintance with Indian customs, Roger Williams maintained that "the Natives are very exact and punctuall in the bounds of their Lands, belonging to this or that Prince or People, (even to a River, Brook), etc. And I have knowne them make bargaine and sale amongst themselves for a small piece, or quantity of Ground." Anthropol-

---

* This view has been perpetuated by both social scientists and historians. For example, see Melvin R. Gilmore, "Some Indian Ideas of Property," in Museum of the American Indian, Heye Foundation, *Indian Notes* V (1928), 137-138, who states categorically that "the right of an individual to negotiate the purchase or sale of land as property [was] entirely alien to the Indian mind. . . . No Indians, of Manhattan or elsewhere, entertained at any time such an idea." Cf. *ibid.*, 143-144. More recently, L. F. Hallett, "The Colonial Invasion of Hereditary Lands," in *Bulletin of the Massachusetts Archeological Society*, XX (1959), 34, wrote of "two diametrically opposed concepts of land tenure." For an early statement of this approach by an historian, see George E. Ellis, "The Indians of Eastern Massachusetts," in Justin Winsor, ed., *The Memorial History of Boston* (4 vols., Boston, 1880), I, 249; for more recent repetitions see James Truslow Adams, *The Founding of New England* (Boston, 1921), 340-341; and George F. Willison, *Saints and Strangers* (New York, 1945), 391.

ogists now generally agree that most, perhaps all, of the New England tribes practiced some form of definite land ownership in the allotment of territory for residence and planting, and that ownership resided in the individual, the family, or some larger unit. Hunting land appears to have been subject to a similar system of allotment: specific areas were reserved for individuals, or larger groups, the exact arrangement varying somewhat from tribe to tribe. No instance has been documented of New England tribes which considered all land common property, or of several tribes sharing the ownership of any land. Even the Abnaki (Tarrantine) tribe of northern Maine, almost entirely dependent on hunting, seems to have had a family land ownership system. And the possessor of either farming or hunting land enjoyed full ownership, not merely rights of usufruct.[29] The later "typical" frontier transaction, in which the pioneer bought land from an Indian who, in fact, had no legal right to sell part of the tribal domain, did not occur in seventeenth century New England, where the tribes did not practice communal ownership.

There were, however, frequent cases of multiple claim. Often the Puritan purchaser had to make satisfaction to several Indian claimants — one or more of whom may have simply been taking advantage of the white man's determination to have an undisputed title. But most cases of overlapping claim were probably the result of honest confusion, stemming from the Indians' lack of a written record of land holdings. Rights of ownership based on oral agreements left an open door to conflicting titles — especially in areas where the plague had carried off the acknowledged owner.[30]

Only one step separates the rights of ownership from those of alienation: the approval of the prevailing political authority. As with European nations, an Indian government had a fundamental interest in the disposition or transfer of the property of any of its subjects, and it held sole title to land within its jurisdiction not claimed by any of its citizens. For that reason, sachems regularly participated in land transactions, sometimes as witnesses, sometimes as co-signers, and sometimes as sole venders. Native chiefs also seem to have exercised a primitive version of the right of eminent domain. Much like a European monarch, an Indian sachem had general authority over all the lands of his subjects, yet tribesmen held property under ancient rights of custom and possession.[31]

The Puritan governments also played an active role in matters of land acquisition. All New England colonies strictly limited the rights of their inhabitants to purchase land from the natives. Specific authority from the government was necessary as a rule, and most colonies required that purchases be made only by government agents.[32] Competent interpreters usually participated in land negotiations, and several witnesses of both races put their marks to the final document. Deeds were then recorded with the appropriate authorities. To forestall disputes over the validity of land sales, the colonists preferred to obtain signatures from the individual native claimant as well as one or more sachems. The Puritan settlers were also careful to make the provisions of their deeds as specific as possible in order to prevent later litigation.[33]

There is no doubt as to the willingness, often eagerness, of the Indian to sell land. It had always been a surplus commodity in New England, and after the epidemics of 1616-1617 and 1633-1634 there was even more to spare. In return the white man offered metal knives, hoes, and other implements of rare value to a neolithic society; in lieu of these the Indian might ask for cloth, clothing, jewelry, and other luxuries to brighten his life. The native often took the initiative in such transactions, for he coveted the white man's goods as keenly as the settler yearned for more land.[34]

Making the sale of land to the colonists especially palatable for the Indian was the knowledge that he could retain almost full use of the property he sold. The land was no longer his in the legal sense, but the thousands of land sale deeds that have survived the ravages of three centuries show unmistakably that the vender usually retained full rights of hunting, fishing, and sometimes even of planting. The English colonist was not much of a hunter. He raised cattle, sheep, swine, and fowl; when he had a yen for venison or wild turkey he usually purchased it from the natives. From them he also obtained the precious beaver skins that were such an important item in New England's early economy. It would have been foolhardy, therefore, to deny to the Indian the privilege of hunting on English-owned lands. Deed after deed included such phrases as those incorporated into the younger John Winthrop's contract for some Connecticut land in 1645; the Indian sachem agreed to part with all rights to the specified territory, "only Reserving for my selfe and people Liberty of Fishing and Hunting and convenient Planting in the said Grounds and Ponds and Rivers." The deed was signed "with the Consent of all the Indians of Tantiusques."[35]

Even when the deed did not specify the right to hunt, common law did. The public's right to hunt on unfenced land was an ancient European custom with full support in law, and the principle is still in force in the United States today. The Puritans were well aware of the English practice and they made no effort to curtail it in New England, except where religious considerations intervened. Hence the General Court of Connecticut in 1649 confirmed the

Indians' hunting and fishing rights on lands within its jurisdiction, "For no Indians are deprived of that libberty in any of our Townes, provided they doe it not uppon the Sabath day." [36] The only rights commonly forfeited by Indians who sold land to the settlers were those of habitation and setting traps, and exceptions to these were sometimes granted. It must be kept in mind that in the Indian's economy, hunting and fishing were subsidiary to agriculture.* The Indian therefore seldom sold his cultivated fields.

Throughout the seventeenth century, deeds of sale usually were so specific as to leave little room for misunderstanding. When disputes arose between Puritans and Indians over land sales, they most often involved questions of boundaries, not privileges. Colonial boundary designations were notoriously indefinite. Litigation frequently resulted, but boundary quarrels were as frequent over deeds involving only white men as in those in which a Puritan had bought land from an Indian.[37]

*   *   *

ALTHOUGH the Puritan scrupulously observed the niceties of purchase, he actually had three separate theoretical justifications for occupying the soil of New England; they were "pattent Purchase and possession." [38] For Englishmen who contemplated the righteousness of establishing colonies in America, patent and possession had equal stature with purchase.

The right of patent was simply the right that derived from discovery. According to prevailing European concepts, a Christian monarch had full authority over lands discovered in his name, so long as the inhabitants were not

---

* See pages 30-32.

themselves Christians. A patent issued by a Christian king to any individual or corporation, such as "the Governor and Company of the Massachusetts Bay in New England," permitted the grantees to act in his behalf. Since all land was the King's, patented land became the agent's. The Puritan therefore had every right, according to his own national law, simply to dispossess the heathen natives.

That, at least, was the theory. A few New England settlers — most notably Roger Williams — objected to it as bold presumption. Most Puritans, however, did not bother to refute it, for the realities of America rendered the patent theory in large part irrelevant. More precisely, the Puritan colonists dispensed with the part of the theory that would have given them property ownership of natives' land while keeping a firm grip on the part that vested the Christians with political jurisdiction. In short, the Puritan rapidly advanced from the abstractions of the Old World to the practical problems of the New, and at once saw that common justice required the recognition of the Indians as "the true proprietors" of the land.[39]

The Puritan's assumed but unexercised right by patent and his recognized right by purchase were supplemented by the third claim — right by possession. Bolstered by innumerable Old Testament citations, the New England Puritans tried to convince themselves and others that land not being used by the heathen was open to any who would make use of it.[40] John Winthrop had yet to see the New World when he stated in 1629 that

As for the Natives in New England, they inclose noe Land, neither have any setled habytation, nor any tame Cattle to improve the Land by, and soe have noe other but a Naturall Right to those Countries, soe as if we leave them sufficient for their use, we may lawfully take the rest, there being more than enough for them and us.

Winthrop was voicing a widely held theory of Indian land rights, although it lacked the Puritans' characteristic Biblical citations. These the Massachusetts General Court provided in its ruling of October 19, 1652, which declared that "what lands any of the Indians within this jurisdiction have by possession or improvement, by subduing of the same, they have just right thereunto, according to that in Genesis, 1 and 28, chapter 9:1, and Psalmes 115:16." As every good Puritan knew, in the book of Genesis God had expressly commanded His people to "Be fruitful, and multiply, and replenish the earth, and subdue it: and have dominion over the fish of the sea, and over the fowl of the air and over every living thing that moveth upon the earth." Psalms declared that "the earth hath he given to the children of men." On this ground, the Puritans based their theory of *vacuum domicilium*.[41]

At first glance this concept seems an open invitation to expulsion of the Indians from any desirable land. Apparently Roger Williams thought so, as did the Royal Commissioners sent in 1665 to investigate the loyalty and conformity of the Bay Colony. The Commissioners took one look at the land law of 1652 and threw up their hands in horror. To claim that the Indians forfeit title merely on the basis of those three Biblical passages, the Commissioners protested, "is both against the honor of God and the justice of the king."[42]

The Commissioners' mistake — and it is one that has been repeated often by critics of the Puritans — was to judge the New Englanders by their words alone.[43] Not that the Puritans were hypocrites; on the contrary they came as close to living by their pronouncements as did any other society of the seventeenth century, or any century, perhaps. But the fact is that *vacuum domicilium*, shorn of its religious rhetoric, was a theory that all European imperial nations followed.[44] It permitted the occupation of deserted or desolate lands, for which payment might be made if any native subsequently claimed ownership. Without such a theory as a supplement the right of discovery was meaningless, for any hostile native could deny the newcomer a foothold in otherwise unoccupied territory. Faced with this possibility, Christian nations evolved a doctrine that would permit an initial settlement to be made in unoccupied territory; whether additional land would be acquired by purchase depended upon the ethical tenets of the settlers. The Puritan needed Biblical justification for the acquisition of that first foothold, and he therefore cited chapter and verse in support of it. But at bottom the Puritan's argument was no different from that of his Dutch, French, and Swedish neighbors. It was, in fact, partly a pre-Lockean expression of the English theory of property rights in a state of nature.[45]

When the Puritans did make use of *vacuum domicilium*, they were actually applying a notion that had as much currency in Indian society as in English. The Indians, after all, observed a doctrine not dissimilar to it. While Algonquian tribal holdings were usually permanent, certain areas were sometimes totally abandoned by their owners. These regions could then be claimed by the first comers.[46] That is what happened at Patuxet after the plague of 1616-1617; even Squanto seems not to have advanced any claim to ownership of the land on which the Pilgrims settled. Of course Massasoit as the supreme sachem of the entire area retained indirect property rights and political jurisdiction. These he gladly relinquished, as has already been shown.

There is no evidence that any New England land for which a native claimant existed was taken under the guise of *vacuum domicilium*. A possible exception may have occurred on land which appeared to be deserted but to which an Indian later professed traditional title. Such matters appear to have been settled amicably, with the claimant invariably receiving a payment for something he had probably never intended to use.[47] For the natives of New England, it must have been a pleasant experience to be paid for land they had deserted to the wilderness.

Plymouth Colony set the pattern of Puritan land acquisition that was later observed by Massachusetts Bay and its offshoots. The Pilgrim Fathers did not question their right to settle at Plymouth even before they received Squanto's tacit approval and Massasoit's formal consent; here they exercised *vacuum domicilium*. After the spring of 1621, however, the Plymouth colonists scrupulously observed the property rights of the natives.[48] Even King Philip, who went to war against New Plymouth in 1675 ostensibly, in part, because of the encroachment of the white men on his ancient territory, sold considerable tracts of land to Plymouth residents as late as 1672.[49] After the war, Governor Josiah Winslow wrote to the Commissioners of the United Colonies:

> I think I can clearly say, that before these present Troubles broke out, the English did not possess one Foot of Land in this Colony but what was fairly obtained by honest Purchase of the Indian Proprietors: Nay, because some of our People are of a covetous Disposition, and the Indians are in Streights easily prevailed with to part with their

Lands, we first made a Law, that none should purchase
or receive of Gift any Land of the Indians without the
Knowledge and Allowance of our Court.[50]

The Massachusetts Bay Company proved equally mindful of native claims. In April 1629, the company advised
Governor Endicott that "if any of the salvages pretend
right of inheritance to all or any part of the lands
granted . . . in our pattent, wee pray you endeavor to
purchase their tytle, that we may avoid the least scrupple of
intrusion." There is no evidence that this policy was ever
violated. In later years some land was acquired by conquest,
but this was the result of declared war, not individual pil-
lage, and none of the New England Indian wars was fought
for the purpose of extinguishing native land claims.* [51]

During the first few years of its existence, Massachusetts
Bay imposed no restrictions on the purchase of land from
the natives; both towns and individuals freely contracted
for land. Then, in the spring of 1634, the General Court,
following a Plymouth precedent, decreed that no one could
buy Indian lands without the Court's permission. This regulation, undoubtedly aimed at preventing fraudulent and
wasteful purchases, was soon followed by a corollary re-
striction designed to insure efficient use of whatever lands
had been acquired: large individual holdings not built on or
improved within three years time became the property of
the Court, "to dispose of it to whome they please." A
month later the Court announced that it possessed the sole
right of granting land in the colony.[52] Thus Massachusetts
Bay, within five years of its founding, had developed a cen-

---

* See Chapter V for a discussion of the causes of the Pequot War;
Chapter XII on Philip's War.

tralized system of land distribution which promised a minimum of friction with its Indian neighbors.

*   *   *

By the early 1630's, the Puritans were beginning to probe
the interior regions of New England in search of fresh centers for settlement. This began a new phase of Puritan expansion, but before the end of the decade it was brought to
a sudden though temporary halt by the first important military conflict north of Virginia. There had been no major
friction between Indian tribes and English settlers in Plymouth or Massachusetts Bay, in part because those areas were
then lightly settled by the natives. The situation was somewhat different in the Connecticut Valley. There the Puritans came in contact with a numerous, powerful, and hostile
tribe; there they also found natives eager to enlist the white
man's aid against traditional enemies. The outcome was the
Pequot War of 1637.

It should be borne in mind that the first intruders into the
Connecticut Valley were not the English, but the Pequots
themselves.* No sooner had this tribe moved into southern
Connecticut and established undisputed authority over the
coastal area, than it endeavored to extend its authority inland. Led by Chief Wopigwooit, and later by his son Sassacus, the Pequots gradually subdued the small Connecticut
Valley tribes, most of which unwillingly accepted their
conquerors as overlords. By the time the Puritans arrived in
New England, the Pequots held sway over the entire southern Connecticut Valley.[53] Many of the subjected tribes,
however, were eager to throw off the Pequot yoke. Some

---

* See pages 55-56.

of them soon saw the expanding English plantations as a potential counterforce to Pequot hegemony; by the early 1630's they were encouraging English settlement in their valley.

Plymouth was the first of the English colonies to take advantage of Indian offers and gain a foothold on the banks of the "Long River," as it was known to the Indians. The Dutch, perhaps as early as 1630, had recommended the Connecticut Valley to the Pilgrims as a likely site for settlement and trade, but New Plymouth was then attempting to establish an outpost on the Kennebec and let the opportunity pass. But when in 1633 some Connecticut Valley Indians who had been ousted by the Pequots invited the Pilgrims to build a trading house there, the Plymouth colonists consented and erected a prefabricated trading house at Matianuck (now Windsor).[54] By purchasing land from the local inhabitants the Pilgrims met the moral requirements of acquiring new territory, but they also incurred the enmity of the Pequots.

A year later Massachusetts Bay followed Plymouth's lead. The newer colony had rejected a bid from the Connecticut Indians in 1631, and in 1632 Governor Winthrop declined William Bradford's suggestion of a joint trading venture. But by 1634 the Bay Colony was becoming crowded, and several towns petitioned the Court for permission to remove to more congenial sites. John Oldham, an "old planter" who had almost a decade of trading experience in New England, had already spent several weeks among the Connecticut Indians and had brought back samples of black lead and beaver. Clearly the Valley was the most promising area for expansion: the soil was fertile, the Indians friendly, and opportunities for trade excellent. A small vanguard spent the winter of 1634-1635 at Pyquag (later Wethersfield), and by 1636 three Massachusetts towns had transferred *in toto:* Dorchester occupied Matianuck — to the indignation of the Plymouth traders — and soon became Windsor; Newtowne migrated to Saukiog and changed its name to Hartford; and Wethersfield was settled by the former inhabitants of Watertown. In each case, title to the new settlements was purchased from the local tribes.[55]

While the settlement of Connecticut was primarily an episode in the expansion of the Puritan colonies, one important river community resulted from an attempt by certain English patentees to establish in New England a semi-feudal domain. In 1632 the Earl of Warwick, under authority of the Council for New England, had granted a section of land around the Connecticut River to several Puritan gentlemen, including Lord Say-and-Sele, Lord Brooke, and Sir Richard Saltonstall. The grantees seem to have done little about their rights until 1635, when they appointed John Winthrop, Jr., son of the ofttimes governor of Massachusetts, to construct a fort and settlement at the mouth of the river. Lion Gardiner, an experienced military engineer, was hired to emigrate to New England and see to the "ordering and making of a city, towns or forts of defence." * In 1635 Gardiner planned and supervised the construction of Fort Saybrook on the west bank of the mouth of the Connecticut.[56] This fort was destined to play a major role in securing English mastery of southern New England.

At about the same time that Thomas Hooker was leading

---

* At the time of his procurement by the Connecticut patentees, Gardiner was "Engineer and Master of works of Fortification in the legers of the Prince of Orange." Gardiner's son David was probably the first English child born in Connecticut, his daughter Elizabeth the first born in New York.

his congregation along the narrow Indian trails to Hartford, Roger Williams was establishing another colony to
the south. Long before his banishment in 1635, Williams
had befriended both Massasoit of the Wampanoags and
Canonicus of the Narragansetts. He may, in fact, have purchased land on Narragansett Bay the year before sentence
was passed against him by the Massachusetts magistrates.
When in January 1636 Governor Winthrop confidentially
warned him of his impending arrest, Williams knew where
he could find asylum. His first refuge was at Sowamet with
Massasoit, from whom he purchased a plot on the Seekonk
River (now Rehoboth). But Governor Winslow of Plymouth soon advised Williams to move to the west side of the
river, where he and his followers would be outside of the
Plymouth patent and thus "as free as themselves, and loving
neighbors together." This led to the founding of Providence in the spring or summer of 1636, on land given to
Williams by Canonicus.[57]

Roger Williams was one of the most complex men in
early New England history, and he remains one of the most
controversial figures of American historiography. One reason for the continuing interest in Williams is that he managed to be a part of the main stream of Puritanism and a
rebel against it. In most respects he was as much a Puritan as
John Winthrop or Increase Mather. He was certainly as de-
vout, as steeped in Scripture, as humorless, and as unbend-
ing as the other Puritan divines. At the same time, he was
more charitable, less sure of himself — in some matters at
least — and infinitely more willing to tolerate the views of
others within his New World colony.[58] Yet when it came
to Indian affairs he was not of so different a breed from his
New England neighbors as most of his biographers have
made him appear.[59]

From the outset, Roger Williams and the other Puritans differed very little in either their attitudes or their actions toward the natives of New England. True, the much cele-brated dispute over the validity of the King's patent helped cause Williams's expulsion from Massachusetts, and Wil-liams did challenge the right of the settlers to occupy land unless they had first "compounded with the natives." [60] To his way of thinking, neither *vacuum domicilium* nor the King's patent had any value; purchase alone justified occu-pation. On these matters he carried on a brief verbal battle with the elder Winthrop and a more extensive one with John Cotton. But the debates were without animus (both were lifelong friends of Williams), and the issues at stake were points of theory — in fact theology — not details of practice.[61]

In his *Key into the Language of America*, Williams con-demned the "sinfull opinion amongst many that Christians have a right to *Heathans* Lands." Cotton retorted in *The Bloudy Tenent, Washed, and Made White in the Bloud of the Lambe* that

> it was neither the Kings intendment, nor the English Planters to take possession of the Countrey by murther of the Natives, or by robbery: but either to take posses-sion of the voyd places of the Countrey by the Law of Nature, (for *Vacuum Domicilium credit occupanti:*) or if we tooke any Lands from the Natives, it was by way of purchase, and free consent.

And in *The Bloody Tenent Yet More Bloody, by Mr. Cot-ton's Efforts to Wash it in the Blood of the Lamb*, Williams sneered at "the sinne of the Pattents, wherein *Christian Kings* (so called) are invested with the Right by virtue of their *Christianitie*, to take and give away the Lands and

Countries of other men." Nowhere in the exchange does
Williams accuse his neighbors of evicting natives or stealing
their property; the whole argument centers on the theoretical justice of the doctrines.[62] Nor were Williams's opponents attempting, even in pure doctrine, to evolve an excuse
for expropriation of Indian lands. Rather, they were ex-
pounding theories that most Europeans believed, but which
they had tempered with common sense and humanitarian
justice.

When the theoretical question is laid aside, it can be seen
that Roger Williams and the Rhode Islanders treated the
Indian tribes within their limits very much as did the other
New England colonies — as the legislative and judicial records of the several colonies, the correspondence of their
leaders, and the reports of outsider observers all indicate.*
Religious and political squabbles kept Rhode Island from
joining the main stream of New England's development
throughout the seventeenth century. That Indian affairs
would prove a notable exception to this pattern appeared
within less than a year of Roger Williams's arrival at Narragansett Bay. Although the population of the new colony
was only a score or so at the outbreak of the Pequot War,
Rhode Island, mainly in the person of its founder, was to
play an important role in the outcome of that conflict.

*   *   *

** See especially Chapter VII. The one distinction of any significance
is that Williams obtained title to Providence *before* settling there; title
to Plymouth and Salem came *after* settlement. In these two later instances,
however, native claimants immediately gave their willing consent to English settlement. The Connecticut settlements, like Providence, were established on land that was first purchased. After the initial footholds had
been acquired, all New England colonies consistently purchased additional land.*

By the summer of 1636 New England could boast four colonies, though only Massachusetts Bay and Plymouth had achieved political and economic stability. All four had Indian policies based on consideration for native land rights, and all enjoyed the friendship and respect of their neighboring tribes. New England had expanded rapidly and, on the whole, peacefully in the sixteen years since the arrival of the Pilgrims. But armed conflict was not far in the future; the next phase of New England's aggrandizement would be a radical departure from the established pattern. As the English colonies spread into the interior they came into contact with new tribes and new problems of interracial adjustment. After a decade and a half of amicable relations, men and events conspired to submerge the years 1636-1637 in violence. A major turning point in the Puritans' Indian affairs had been reached.

CHAPTER V

The Pequot War, 1637

THE PEQUOT WAR, the first serious conflict in which Puritan military forces engaged, was one of the most important episodes in early New England history, possessing more drama and significance than it has usually been accorded. The war resulted in the extermination of the most powerful tribe in New England; it opened southern New England to rapid English colonization; and it witnessed one of the most sanguinary battles of the colonial period of American history when some five hundred Pequot men, women, and children lost their lives in the Puritan attack on Mystic Fort.

The war was not soon forgotten by the other tribes in the northeast, who from its conclusion until 1675 refrained from challenging Puritan power, nor by the English who memorialized their victory in prose and poetry.[1] The Pequot War even found its way into *Moby Dick* when Herman Melville chose the name of the vanquished tribe for his ill-fated whaling vessel.[2] The war also left a question of no little weight and complexity: the eternal question, attendant upon every military conflict, of the identity of the aggressor. The answer holds more than antiquarian interest; it inevitably sheds light upon the basic nature of the Puritan experiment, upon the whole problem of Indian-white relations during the first century of English settlement in New England, and upon the justice and humanity of the participants.

*   *   *

THE Pequot tribe, it will be recalled, had incurred by its forced intrusion into New England the enmity of its Indian neighbors, and it had won a notorious reputation for brutality. This notoriety had not diminished by the time the Puritan expansion brought the first contacts between English colonists and the tribe. According to William Bradford, the seven hundred Pequot warriors were by then, "puft up with many victories." Perhaps the Pequots did not purposely seek English victims, but to the Puritan mind the Pequots' crimes seemed premeditated. They were now, wrote William Hubbard, so "flushed with Victories over their Fellow-Indians [that] they began to thirst after the Blood of any Foreigners." The first white victims were Captains John Stone and Walter Norton and their crew of seven in the spring of 1634.[3] Their deaths set off a chain reaction that did not end until the Pequot tribe had been virtually exterminated.

There is considerable doubt as to how and why Stone and his shipmates were killed. It seems indisputable that the assassins belonged either to the Pequots or to a tribe subservient to them. But beyond that little is certain, for there are several conflicting versions of the encounter, all plausible but none corroborated. At any rate, Stone's previous career made it more than likely that he had got about what he deserved.

Captain Stone, a resident of Virginia, had piloted a shipload of cattle from there to Boston in 1634. At each stop along the way he managed so to embroil himself with the local authorities that he was soon *persona non grata* in every community north of the Hudson. His first escapade was in New Amsterdam, where he attempted to steal a Plymouth bark and was thwarted only at the last minute by some Dutch seamen. Later he almost stabbed Plymouth's Governor Thomas Prence. He acted little better in Massachusetts where he "spake contemptously of [the] magistrates, and carried it lewdly in his conversation," in particular calling Judge Ludlow "a just as[s]." On top of this he was charged with excessive drinking and adultery. Tried and acquitted for lack of evidence on the major charge, he earned by his lesser indiscretions a suspended fine of one hundred pounds and banishment from the colony under penalty of death. Stone was on his way back to Virginia, accompanied by Captain Walter Norton and crew, when he stopped off to explore the trading prospects of the Connecticut River.[4]

Of this much, history is certain. As to what followed, however, there are several incompatible versions. The Massachusetts authorities, despite their well-founded dislike for Stone, at first believed that the captain had been villainously assaulted while sleeping in his bunk, the rest of the crew slain, and the vessel plundered. Some of the English were content to wrap themselves in their piety and conclude with Roger Clap — a Massachusetts settler — that "thus did God destroy him that so proudly threatened to ruin us."[5] But for most it was enough that he was an Englishman; retribution was necessary.[6] And regardless of the justice of Stone's murder, his seven companions had also been slaughtered.

Up to this point there had been no direct contact between the New England colonists and the Pequots. But in

1634 the Pequots were at war with both the Dutch and the Narragansetts. And now the English were demanding revenge for the murder of John Stone. This was one enemy too many, and the Pequots soon made overtures of friendship to the Bay Colony. Late in October 1634, the tribe sent ambassadors to Massachusetts to treat for peace and commerce, reinforcing their appeal with gifts of wampum. The Puritan authorities were willing to negotiate but demanded Stone's assassins as a prelude to negotiations. The Pequots replied with an account of Stone's death that differed markedly from the colonists' version. Stone, the Indians contended, had seized and bound two braves who had boarded his ship to trade. Consequently when the captain later came ashore he was ambushed by several of the braves' friends. Furthermore, the sachem who had been responsible for this retaliation had later been killed by the Dutch and all but two of his henchmen had been victims of the pox.[7]

The Pequots' account was told with such "confidence and gravity" that the English were inclined to accept it in place of their earlier understanding of the event, and after several days of negotiations a treaty was signed on November 1, 1634, between the Pequots and the Bay Colony. By its terms the Indians agreed to hand over the two remaining assassins when sent for and "to yield up Connecticut" — which meant that the Pequots would no longer object to English purchases from the River tribes. In addition, the Pequots were to pay an indemnity of four hundred fathoms of wampum,* forty beaver and thirty otter skins. Commercial relations were projected by an agreement that Massachusetts Bay would send a trading vessel to the Pequots in the near future. Peace was thus maintained in New Eng-

---

* Wampum was usually strung on lengths of hemp or animal gut and measured in large quantity by the fathom — approximately six feet.

land. However, commerce between the Bay Colony and the
Pequots did not materialize; when John Oldham took his
trading ship into Pequot territory the next spring, he found
them "a very false people" and disinclined to amicable
trade.[8]

Though peace between the Bay Colony and the Pequots
lasted until the fall of 1636, there was little harmony. The
Pequots failed to surrender the remaining assassins of Stone,
they paid the indemnity only in part, and reports of further
Pequot disingenuousness began to drift into Boston. By midsummer of 1636, Massachusetts Bay had lost patience and
commissioned John Winthrop, Jr., then in the Connecticut
Valley, to demand that Sassacus surrender the murderers
of Captain Stone and reply to several other charges of bad
faith. Should the Pequots fail to meet these demands, the
Bay Colony threatened to terminate the league of amity
and to "revenge the blood of our Countrimen as occasion
shall serve."[9] But before Winthrop could fulfill his diplomatic mission an event occurred which put an end to peaceful dealings with the Pequot tribe.

Late in July, John Gallop, en route by sea to Long Island, spied John Oldham's pinnace near Block Island, the
deck crowded with Indians and not a white man in sight.
When no one answered his hail, Gallop tried to board and
investigate. A frenzied battle followed in which Gallop
routed the Indians. Most of them drowned; the two who
surrendered he bound and threw into the sea, an atrocity
reported without comment by seventeenth century chroniclers. On board Gallop found the naked and mutilated body
of John Oldham.[10]

At first glance it appeared that the Narragansetts were
responsible for Oldham's murder. The Indians of Block Island were subject to the Narragansetts, and, according to

one prisoner, all the Narrangansett sachems except Canonicus and Miantonomo had conspired with the Block Islanders against Oldham because of his attempts to trade with the Pequots the previous year. The Massachusetts Bay leaders contemplated war with the Narragansetts and warned Roger Williams "to look to himself" in the event. But Canonicus and Miantonomo speedily regained the confidence of the English by returning Oldham's two boys and his remaining goods from Block Island and by assuring the Bay Colony, through Roger Williams, that most of the culprits had been killed by Gallop. Meanwhile the few surviving assassins sought refuge with the Pequots.[11]

All threats of a rupture between Massachusetts Bay and the Narragansetts were removed a few weeks later when the colony sent an embassy to Canonicus and Miantonomo. The mission was ostensibly to settle the Oldham affair, but also to prevent a rumored Pequot-Narragansett alliance, which would have united the two most powerful tribes in New England against the Puritan colonies. Fortunately, the venerable Canonicus strongly favored peace with the English, partly because of his intense hatred for the Pequots and partly because of his respect for the weapons of the white man. He concluded that the Narragansetts would remain officially neutral in the dispute between the English and the Pequots, but would aid in avenging the murder of Oldham.[12]

Though Massachusetts Bay had dealt leniently with the Indians until the murder of Oldham, it now reversed its policy and launched a devastating reprisal. In late August, about a month after Oldham's death, ninety volunteers under John Endicott embarked for Block Island. Their instructions called for merciless revenge. Endicott was to put to death all the Indian men on Block Island, seize the women and children, and take possession of the island. He was then to proceed to the Pequot territory and demand the murderers of Stone and Oldham, one thousand fathoms of wampum, and some of their children as hostages. Should the Pequots refuse this ultimatum, the expedition was to impose it by force.[13]

Endicott vigorously complied with his instructions. He secured a beachhead on Block Island in the face of brief resistance and routed the defenders. While the Indians sought refuge in the swamps, the Massachusetts Bay troops burned wigwams, destroyed cornfields, and smashed canoes. Dissatisfied by the paucity of Indian casualties, the English soldiers heartlessly "destroyed some of their dogs instead of men." After two busy days of devastation the expedition set sail for Saybrook.[14]

Its reception at the Connecticut fort was not cordial. After scanning Endicott's commission and hearing a detailed account of the work at Block Island, Lieutenant Gardiner was far from pleased. "You come hither," he protested, "to raise these wasps about my ears, and then you will take wing and flee away." But finding that Endicott was determined to carry out his orders, Gardiner dispatched some of his own men to accompany the expedition to the Pequot country. He well knew that if negotiations failed his own cornfields would not long be standing and so instructed his men to gather Pequot corn in the event of hostilities.[15]

Four days later Endicott's fleet entered Pequot Harbor. The Indians met them with "doleful and woful cries," for it was obvious to the Pequots that this was no friendly mission. And whatever chance may have existed for peaceful negotiations rapidly vanished. The Pequot spokesmen obstinately refused to comply with Puritan demands, first offering a new version of the killing of Stone that attempted to absolve themselves of any blame, then claiming that their leading chiefs were on Long Island, and finally insisting that they were still trying to discover who the culprits were.[16]

The English became increasingly convinced that the Pequots' delay was a camouflage for ambush, particularly when they observed the Indians "convey away their wives and children and bury their chiefest goods." More Indian procrastination wore the Puritan patience thinner, and a final Pequot suggestion that both sides lay down their arms — interpreted by Endicott as a dastardly ruse — brought it to the breaking point. "We rather chose to beat up the drum and bid them battle," recorded Captain Underhill. A volley from the musketeers sent the Pequot warriors scurrying for shelter, and the pattern established on Block Island was repeated. The colonists spent the next two days in rampant destruction and looting. In deference to English firepower, the Indians kept a respectful distance.[17]

By the fourteenth of September, less than three weeks after their departure from Boston, the Massachusetts troops were back in the Bay Colony with but two casualties, neither fatal.[18] The Pequots were mourning somewhat greater losses: one or more killed and several wounded. Ironically, the first and perhaps only Pequot fatality may have been caused by Cutshamekin of the Massachusetts — who had joined Endicott as an interpreter and guide — for according to Lieutenant Gardiner, "The Bay-men killed not a man save that . . . Indian Sachem of the Bay, killed a Pequit; and thus began the war between the Indians and us in these parts." [19] In any event, the wasps' nest that Gardiner had feared would soon swarm over the Connecticut Valley.

Harsh "justice" had been imposed; harsh retaliation would follow.

The colonists did not have long to wait. No sooner had the Massachusetts ships set sail for Boston than the Pequots drew their first blood. The Saybrook contingent which had remained in the enemy harbor to gather more of the Pequots' corn was attacked by a horde of Pequot warriors, and two Englishmen were wounded before the shallop could escape to the protection of Fort Saybrook's guns. There Gardiner, realizing that the fort would soon be under siege, began to gather his own corn. Two of his harvesters were taken by ambush and tortured. A few days later five men from Saybrook were ambushed while gathering hay; three were slain outright, one was roasted alive, and "the other came down drowned to us . . . with an arrow shot into his eye through his head."[20]

The following February (1637) Gardiner himself came close to ending his days in an Indian torture ceremony. Taking ten companions and three dogs (the best protection against ambush), the lieutenant ventured half a mile from the fort to burn leaves and weeds, fell into an ambush, and barely escaped with his life. Two of his men were killed and several were wounded, as was Gardiner himself. A siege of the fort was prevented only by the arrival a few days later of seven men from the Connecticut plantations.[21] Thereafter the Indians shifted their attacks to the undefended banks of the river above the fort.

While these assaults were slowly whittling away the manpower of the Connecticut colony, diplomatic maneuvers proceeded on all sides. The Pequots had no desire to face the English alone; much less did they desire to see their Indian neighbors join forces with the white man. Two years earlier (1635) an intratribal rift had resulted in the secession of a large segment of the Pequots under the old tribal name of Mohegans. The wounds had not yet healed, and there was little chance of a reconciliation at present. However, Pequot relations with the Narragansetts had been reasonably cordial since 1634; there was every reason to believe that with proper persuasion a coalition against the English might be effected. Pequot ambassadors attempted to arouse the Narragansetts with stories that the English planned to exterminate the red man and seize his lands; if the English should conquer the Pequots, the Narragansetts' turn would come next. The Pequots did not ask for an all-out assault on the colonists, rather they proposed that the Narragansetts harass the English "by firing their Houses, and killing their Cattel, and lying in wait for them as they went about their ordinary Occasions." "Machiavel himself," protested William Hubbard, "could not have insinuated stronger Reasons." But the temptations presented by the Pequots were largely offset by the opportunity the Narragansetts saw to square accounts with a tribe they had long resented.[22]

When news of the Pequot delegation to the Narragansetts reached Boston, the Governor and Council of Massachusetts dispatched an urgent plea for assistance to Roger Williams in New Providence. No other Englishman was on so friendly a footing with the Narragansett leaders, nor so familiar with their language. Perhaps a less forgiving man would have been reluctant to help those who had so recently banished him from their seat of intolerance. But Williams bore no grudges, nor did he fail to see that the conduct of the Pequots endangered his own settlement as well as the other Puritan communities. Years later he described

his harrowing mission to Narragansett, where he vied with
a Pequot embassy for the allegiance of Miantonomo's warriors.

> . . . The Lord helped me [wrote Williams] immediately
> to put my life into my hand, and, scarce acquainting my
> wife, to ship myself, all alone, in a poor canoe, and to cut
> through a stormy wind, with great seas, every minute in
> hazard of life, to the Sachem's house.
>
> Three days and nights my business forced me to lodge
> and mix with the bloody Pequot ambassadors, whose
> hands and arms, methought, wreaked with the blood of
> my countrymen, murdered and massacred by them on
> Connecticut river, and from whom I could not but nightly
> look for their bloody knives at my own throat also.[23]

Williams succeeded brilliantly, and in October 1636,
Miantonomo and two of Canonicus's sons came to Boston
to negotiate with the magistrates of the Bay Colony. Miantonomo offered to enter into an offensive alliance against
the Pequots and to deliver a present to the English within
two months as a sign of his sincerity. The following day a
formal treaty was drafted, Miantonomo signifying his as-
sent with his mark, an arrow. The articles bound the two
parties into a close alliance; it called for perpetual peace and
friendship, free trade, and joint prosecution of the war
against the Pequots. The Narragansetts also promised to
execute or surrender any Indians convicted of murdering
white men. In order to protect the friendly Indians and
lessen alarms in the outlying communities, it was further
agreed that no Narragansetts should come near the English
plantations during the coming war unless accompanied by
an Englishman or an Indian known to the colonists. In
March of 1637 the Indian present arrived: forty fathoms of
wampum and a Pequot's hand.[24]

Meanwhile atrocities continued in the Connecticut Valley. Lion Gardiner imposed an inspection on all boats entering the Connecticut River and forbade any landings between Saybrook and Wethersfield. One John Tilley, however, chose to disobey these orders and soon paid the penalty. Shortly after Tilley set foot on shore, still within sight of the fort, he was ambushed, his hands cut off, and later his feet also. He lived three days after the loss of his hands and greatly impressed his captives "because he cried not in his torture." This is the mildest account of his fate; a more sanguine version laments that the savages "tied him to a stake, flayed his skin off, put hot embers between the flesh and skin, cut off his fingers and toes, and made hatbands of them." [25]

More of this sort of brutality could hardly be tolerated by the Connecticut plantations; to do nothing was to invite annihilation.[26] One more massacre, however, was needed to turn the scattered raids and counter raids into a full-scale war of extermination. And this time the blow came close to home. The Fort Saybrook area, reinforced by twenty troops from the Bay Colony, had become too dangerous for the Pequots; they decided to concentrate on the undefended plantations.[27] Early on the morning of April 23, 1637, two hundred howling Pequot warriors descended on a small group of colonists at work in a Wethersfield, Connecticut, meadow. Nine of the English, including a woman and child, were slain, and the Pequots carried off two young women whom they hoped would make gunpowder for the tribe's scanty stock of firearms. The raiding party later paddled past Fort Saybrook, hoisting on poles the shirts and skirts of the slain colonists in a mocking imitation of English sails. The total number of English fatalities had now reached thirty.[28] Peaceful expansion of the New England colonies was temporarily at an end; the next phase of Puritan aggrandizement would be by force of arms. The General Court of Massachusetts Bay convened on April 18, 1637, "for the speciall occation of prosecuting the warr against the Pecoits," and ordered the enlistment of 160 men, apportioned among the towns, for an expedition against the enemy. Two weeks later the Connecticut Court took similar action.[29] Scattered raids were about to give way to organized campaigns. New England's first major war had come.

*   *   *

THE causes of the Pequot War are not easily unraveled.* The reasons for the clash of the Puritan colonies, aided by the majority of the New England tribes, against the Pequots are legion: the restlessness of the River tribes under

---

* Interpretations of the causes have varied widely. Early nineteenth century historians such as Benjamin Trumbull (*History of Connecticut* [2 vols., New Haven, 1818] I, ch. 5) and John G. Palfrey (*History of New England* [5 vols., Boston, 1865-90] I, 456-470) sided with their ancestors, and with little qualification. A few writers in the nineteenth century — especially those whose roots were not in the Bay Colony — placed the blame on the Puritans, mostly because of the Endicott expedition. See Peter Oliver, *The Puritan Commonwealth* (Boston, 1856), 106-118; John Romeyn Brodhead, *History of the State of New York*, second edition (2 vols., New York, 1859), I, 237-273; and George E. Ellis, "The Indians of Eastern Massachusetts" in Justin Winsor, ed., *The Memorial History of Boston* (4 vols., Boston, 1888), I, 252-255. Most twentieth century authors find the Puritans at fault, either accusing them of land-grabbing or a combination of that and sheer viciousness, clad in hypocritical rhetoric. See, for example, William MacLeod's extremely inaccurate but still used *American Indian Frontier* (New York, 1928), 209-219; Roy Harvey Pearce, *The Savages of America: A Study of the Indian and the Idea of Civilization* (Baltimore, 1953), 19-35; and William T. Hagan, *American Indians* (Chicago, 1960), 12-13. For a brief analysis of the causes of the war which summarizes — with slight variations — the arguments presented in this chapter, see Alden T. Vaughan, "Pequots and Puritans: The Causes of the War of 1637," in *William and Mary Quarterly*, 3 ser. XXI (1964), 256-269.

Pequot hegemony; the murder of ten or more Englishmen between 1634 and 1636, most notably Stone and Oldham; the severity of the Endicott expedition; the vicious Pequot raids that followed it; the urge for revenge that moved the Narragansetts and Mohegans; and the uncompromising attitudes of both Pequots and Puritans. From a mere recitation of the causes, one fact is clear: there was no "Indian side" to the story. The outlook of the Narragansetts, Mohegans, Massachusetts, and River tribes differed radically from that of the Pequots. And since most of the tribes of New England were on the white man's side, the Pequot War cannot accurately be described as an "Indian war" in the usual sense. This was no racial conflict between white man and red, no clash of disparate cultures or alien civilizations.

What did propel New England into armed conflict was the attempt by the Puritan colonies — supported by the bulk of the Indians — to curb the militant Pequot tribe. The English had sought to live peacefully and equitably with their Indian neighbors; this they had been able to achieve until 1637. At the same time the Puritans were determined to prevent criminal acts against English subjects. Besides their strong devotion to English law and Biblical injunction, there was their own safety to consider: it made little sense to escape the clutches of Bishop Laud only to fall prey to an Indian tomahawk. The Pequots, by contrast, wanted to maintain their recently acquired dominion over the Connecticut Valley and its inhabitants; they also seem to have had little respect for the lives of either Englishmen or Indians who were not under their dominion. Given this disparity of underlying intentions, it is not surprising that minor irritants swelled to unmanageable proportions.

Some of the blame for the war must fall on the Pequots,

who, according to the testimony of all the whites and most of the Indians, were guilty of blatant and persistent aggression. Perhaps brilliant diplomacy could have prevented their bellicosity from provoking open warfare, but in the absence of a mutually recognized and respected arbiter, a peaceful solution was highly improbable. (Even Roger Williams, the most talented man for the role, had no influence with the Pequots.) Still, the Pequots did not resort to open warfare until the Puritans dispatched the impulsive Endicott to punish the Block Islanders and to browbeat the Pequots. To a substantial degree, therefore, the Bay Colony's punitive expedition served as the *casus belli.*

At first glance the Endicott mission appears to be simply an act of angry retaliation, the retaliation that any of the Indian tribes themselves might have visited upon an offender, and in some measure it was. Endicott had been given instructions not to effect unlimited revenge — except on the Block Islanders — but to obtain specific guarantees of good faith from the Pequots and to ensure the tribe's observance of an earlier treaty that it seemed to have forgotten. This was a policing action that had no designs on Pequot property or Pequot lives. To the New England mind, there was no choice but to accept the responsibility for maintaining law and order among the inhabitants of the area; the New World Zion must curb threats from without as well as from within. This, of course, was not a new Puritan policy. As the Indians at Wessagusett had discovered, it was not wise to threaten what the Pilgrim Fathers thought was their fundamental security. Massachusetts Bay had also taken action against Indian transgressors; and by 1637 the colony assumed the right to punish those who threatened its peace and security even though the offending tribe lay outside the Massachusetts Bay patent. The Bay Colony, in short, had taken over the chore of policing the frontier areas. While it may be argued that the Puritans had no right to extend their authority over the Pequots or anyone else, it is important to remember that many of the New England tribes had endorsed the principle of English jurisdiction, and most encouraged its imposition on the Pequots. In a frontier society, someone had to impose a semblance of justice and order. But in doing so, Endicott acted with such arrogance and harshness that Pequot retaliation was inevitable.

There is little doubt that the other Puritan colonies, although endorsing the principle of reprisal against Indian tribes that took the lives of Englishmen, did not approve of the specific application of that policy under Endicott. Spokesmen for Plymouth, Connecticut, and Fort Saybrook (then under separate government) all condemned the Endicott expedition, and even Governor Winthrop later tacitly admitted that Massachusetts Bay had provoked hostilities.[30]

Perhaps the explanation for the Bay Colony's severity in this instance lies in the character of its volatile commander, for Endicott's career shows him to have been the least temperate of the Puritan leaders. But since Endicott was following instructions that were themselves rather severe, it may be more appropriate to inquire into the conditions in Massachusetts Bay in the summer of 1636. In the first place, the Bay Colony could now afford to act more impulsively, since its expanding population and geographical position made it the least likely to bear the brunt of any retaliation. Secondly, Roger Williams had reported a heady boast of the Pequots that they could by witchcraft defeat any English expedition, a challenge hardly designed to soothe Puritan tempers.[31] Finally, and most important, Massachusetts was then in the throes of civil and religious controversy.

Roger Williams had been ousted but a few months earlier
for "divers dangerous opinions," the crown had recently instituted *quo warranto* proceedings against the colony's
charter, and the first rumblings of the Antinomian movement were faintly audible. If frustration is the cause of aggression, the Bay Colony was overripe for striking out at
what it now believed was Satan's horde.[32] While all of this
does not in any way exonerate Endicott and the Massachusetts leaders, it does help to account for their sudden severity. It was well for the Puritan colonies that most of the
Indian tribes were already convinced that the Pequots deserved no quarter.

*   *   *

UNFORTUNATELY for the new plantations in the Connecticut Valley, the brunt of the war which erupted in 1637 fell
on them. Although of all the colonies Massachusetts Bay
had been the most determined in opposing the Pequots and
had been responsible for the provocative Endicott expedition, Connecticut settlers were the victims of the Pequots'
campaign of revenge. This in itself would soon have pro-
pelled the fledgling colony into the conflict, but additional
pressure was brought to bear by the local tribes that had
welcomed the English to their valley, as much for protection as for commerce. "Though we feele nether the tyme
nor our strenght fitt for such a service," wrote Thomas
Hooker from Hartford, "yet the Indians here[,] our
frends[,] were so importunate with us to make warr presently that unlesse we had attempted some thing we had delivered our persons unto contempt of base feare and cow-
ardise, and caused them to turne enemyes agaynst us." [33]
And so, while the Bay Colony was first to declare war, Connecticut was first to launch an offensive campaign.

Like the other New England settlements, Connecticut was not totally unprepared for hostilities. The Connecticut Court in June 1636 had required each man to have his house in readiness with powder and lead; by November each plantation was conducting monthly drills, with heavy fines for nonattendance. At about the same time, the Plymouth Colony Court had directed that Captain Standish and Lieutenant William Holmes be "employed in teaching the use of armes" in Plymouth and Duxbury; it also directed all masters to provide servants with arms and ammunition at the expiration of indentures. The Bay Colony's military establishment was so large by 1636 that it had been divided into three regiments with Captains Traske, Patrick, and Underhill serving as paid "mustermasters." John Endicott was colonel of the Massachusetts forces, while the governor was automatically "chiefe generall." Lesser ranks were elected by the troops, with the approval of the Court of Assistants, but only freemen were eligible for captaincies. The Puritan colonies also adopted regulations to insure that every town established a watch and had its male residents ready for emergency action.[34]

Having decided at last on open war, the Connecticut Court heeded Hooker's admonition "not to do this work of the Lord's revenge slackly." Command of the Connecticut forces was assigned to Captain John Mason of Windsor, a veteran of warfare in the Low Countries and "full of Martial Bravery and Vigour," while Lieutenant Robert Seely was made second-in-command. Troops were levied from the three plantations. Hartford was required to contribute forty-two men, Windsor thirty, and Wethersfield eighteen. Provisions were also requisitioned from the plantations, and to quench the soldiers' thirst, "one hoggshead of good beare for the Captain and Master and sick men" was ordered.

Only one bottle of strong liquor was provided, but it must have been a priceless concoction, for "when it was empty, the very smelling to the Bottle would presently recover such as Fainted away." [35]

The best plan of operations against the Pequots would probably have been a joint campaign by the three English colonies, but intercolonial cooperation proved difficult to effect. On the day it declared war the Massachusetts Court directed the council to arrange alliances with Plymouth and Connecticut. Although the latter was more than happy to work in unison with its stronger neighbor, Plymouth chose this moment to air old grievances. The Pilgrims had long harbored a grudge against the Windsor settlement for its appropriation of the Plymouth trading post in 1635, and they also resented the Bay Colony's call for assistance.[36] After a tedious debate with the Massachusetts authorities, Plymouth finally succumbed and voted a force of thirty troops for land service and enough men to handle a bark. Lieutenant William Holmes was to lead the contingent. However the war was over before it could get under way. No hard feelings seem to have resulted, and William Hubbard later recorded, with more charity than accuracy, that the Pilgrims' slowness was "not to be imputed to any Backwardness in Their Minds, but to their too late Invitation to the Service." [37] In point of fact, Massachusetts Bay contributed her legions a bit tardily too,* for by the time a signifi-

---

* The Bay Colony may have been delayed by the theological disputes then raging in Boston. Apparently John Wheelwright and other so-called Antinomians convinced the Bostonians that Governor Winthrop was an enemy of Christ; accordingly Boston contributed but few soldiers and those "of the most refuse sort." [John Winthrop], *A Short Story of the . . . Antinomians, Familists, and Libertines . . . of New England* (London, 1692), 26-27.

cant number of her soldiers were on enemy soil, little Connecticut had already "given the main Stroak." [38]

That Connecticut was able to achieve a stunning victory, despite its limited manpower, was largely due to the assistance it received from the Mohegan tribe. Chief Uncas of the Mohegans had chosen the English cause, and when Captain Mason and his ninety soldiers sailed from Hartford on May 10, he was accompanied by Uncas and sixty Mohegans. Mason and the other English leaders were at first highly dubious of the loyalty of these Indians who had such strong blood ties to the Pequots; Mason's skepticism was considerably increased when the Mohegans parted company with the expedition shortly after its departure and proceeded to Fort Saybrook on foot. Since the Mohegans would reach the fort before his soldiers could, Mason feared lest his allies attack the fort rather than defend it.[39]

Uncas soon removed all doubt as to which side he favored. On reaching Saybrook he was challenged by Lieutenant Gardiner to demonstrate Mohegan loyalty by exterminating a small party of Pequots lurking near the fort. Uncas accepted the challenge, and within a short time the Mohegans presented the Saybrook commander with four Pequot heads and one prisoner. The captive, well known to the garrison as a former visitor at the fort and a spy for Sassacus, contemptuously predicted that his captors "durst not kill a Pequet." The English soldiers soon proved this a poor prophecy as they tied one of his legs to a post, put a rope on the other, and tore him limb from limb. Captain Underhill ended the victim's agony with a pistol shot. The body was roasted and eaten by the Mohegans.[40]

Glad tidings of Uncas's loyalty were conveyed by Underhill to Mason's little flotilla, then approaching the fort, at the precise moment its men were praying for some sign of Mohegan trustworthiness. Underhill's canoe slid up to the leading bark just as the Reverend Samuel Stone, chaplain of the expedition, was imploring the Lord to "manifest one pledge of thy love, that may confirm us the fidelity of these Indians towards us." [41]

Some reorganization of forces took place when Mason's army reached Saybrook. Twenty of the least fit Connecticut soldiers were replaced by Captain Underhill and his nineteen Massachusetts troops, which strengthened the expeditionary force and gave it an intercolonial character. At the same time precautions were taken to prevent the Pequots from obtaining more striking power: the Dutch, whose kettles could be made into good arrowheads, were forbidden to trade with the enemy. One Dutch ship, however, was given leave to enter Pequot territory and secure the release of the two English girls captured at Wethersfield. The Dutch effected this by capturing, under guise of trade, seven Pequot warriors and then demanding an exchange of prisoners. The Pequots complied, partly perhaps because they had lost interest in their captives as soon as they discovered that the girls could not make gunpowder. However, the released prisoners proved a valuable source of intelligence for Mason, as they had learned the extent of the Indians' weapons (sixteen guns and little powder) and could describe the layout of the Indian strongholds. [42]

Mason was now ready to proceed against the enemy, when a threat to the unity of the expedition unexpectedly arose. It did not originate in friction between the white and red allies but rather between two factions of the Connecticut forces. The Connecticut Court had ordered Mason to lead his troops in an amphibious frontal assault on the main Pequot village. A large segment of the expedition favored following these instructions to the letter. But Mason was endowed with enough military foresight to know that the plan was pure folly. In the first place, he argued, the Pequots were known to be keeping a close watch along the coast. Secondly, the enemy's vast superiority in numbers would make amphibious operations extremely hazardous. Mason offered an alternate plan that would surmount these obstacles.[43]

His scheme called for a flanking movement. Since the Narragansetts were allied to the English they could be expected to provide guides and reinforcements for an overland invasion of Pequot territory, using the Narragansett lands as a base of operations. The drawback was that such a move would be a technical violation of the Connecticut commission, and to men who took covenants — with man or God — seriously, that was a critical consideration. Mason therefore directed Chaplain Stone to "commend our Condition to the Lord . . . to direct how and in what manner we should demean ourselves in that Respect." The chaplain spent the night on board ship; in the morning he came ashore with the verdict: the Narragansett route was approved.[44]

The army sailed from Saybrook on Friday, May 19. Late that afternoon it passed the entrance to Pequot Harbor; on Saturday evening the shore of Narragansett Bay loomed off the port bow. Three days later Mason led his troops into Miantonomo's village and explained his plan to the Narragansett sachem. The chief agreed to a request for guides, and several hundred of his followers eagerly joined the expedition, as did some of the Eastern Niantics. Most of these warriors deserted, however, before the time for battle arrived, fearing that Sassacus "was *all one God*, and nobody could kill him." [45]

Mason's first objective was the Pequot fort on the Mystic River, the easternmost of two strongholds. This was a change from his original plan to attack Sassacus's main fortress near Pequot Harbor, but the lameness of one of his men (interpreted as divine intervention), the desertion of most of the Narragansetts, and the increasing probability of detection as he advanced further into enemy territory convinced Mason to assail the nearer fort. By the evening of May 25, the invasion force, guided by a former Pequot sachem, had advanced to within a mile or two of the palisaded village. There Mason's army encamped for the night while the English sentries strained to hear the sounds of revelry coming from the enemy fort; from the "Burthen of their Song" it was apparent that the Pequots were convinced that the English did not dare to fight them. Heightening the Pequot celebrations were 150 braves who had just arrived at the fort in preparation for a major assault on the English settlements the following day.[46]

The Puritan forces attacked at dawn. They were not detected until within a few feet of the palisades, and the surprise was almost complete. The soldiers fired a hurried volley between the log walls, then charged into the village. Inside they found some seventy wigwams from which the startled Pequot warriors emerged to do battle. Soon the scene was total confusion as each side struggled to destroy the other. Fearing that the Pequot's numerical superiority would prove insurmountable, Captain Mason seized a firebrand from a wigwam and thrust it into its straw roof. Within minutes the entire village was an inferno. The English soldiers retreated to the outside of the palisades where they formed a tight circle around the fort and shot down the Pequots who tried to escape. A second circle of Mohegans and Narragansetts cut down the few who broke through the English cordon. So great was the confusion that some of the friendly Indians, perhaps as many as forty, were mistakenly wounded, a tragedy that Roger Williams later attributed to their lack of distinctive markings.[47]

The unfortunate Indians who chose to remain within the fort also perished — men, women, and children to the number of several hundred. Estimates vary as to the exact figure. Mason calculated six or seven hundred; Underhill thought only four hundred; but both agreed that not more than seven Indians had escaped and about as many had been captured. English losses were slight: two killed (one of whom was probably felled by a stray English musketball) and about twenty wounded.[48] The entire slaughter had taken little over half an hour.

Mason's victory was complete, but in true Puritan fashion he gave full credit to his God who had "laughed his Enemies and the Enemies of his People to Scorn, making them as a fiery Oven. . . . Thus did the Lord judge among the Heathen, filling the Place with dead Bodies." To those who gasped at the brutality of the slaughter, John Underhill provided the stock answer:* "I would refer you to David's war. When a people is grown to such a height of blood, and sin against God and man . . . there he hath no respect to persons, but harrows them, and saws them, and puts them to the sword. . . . We had sufficient light from the word of God for our proceedings." [49]

---

* Since the late nineteenth century a key element in the anti-Puritan syndrome has been an indictment of the colonists for reveling in the destruction of the Pequots. Rather than reflecting sadistic pleasure, Puritan writings show how deeply they believed in God's direct manipulation of history. This outlook remained unchanged when the course of events turned against them; they described their own trials and misfortunes in identical rhetoric. It is worth remembering that modern nations have not been reluctant to equate victory with divine will, though their choice of words is usually more subtle.

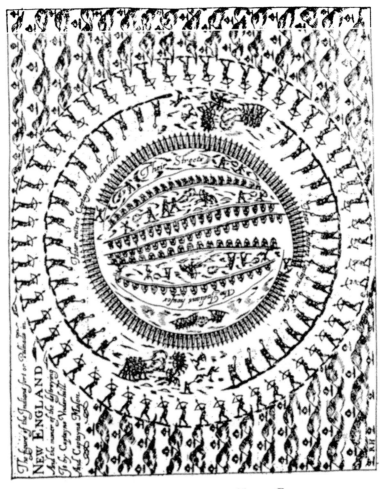

DIAGRAM OF THE ATTACK ON MYSTIC FORT

The totality of the English victory seemed to break the spirit of the Pequots. Although almost one-third of his English soldiers were wounded and his supplies of powder and shot were perilously low, Mason was able to march his forces from Mystic Fort to Pequot Harbor, a distance of about seven miles; there he hoped to rendezvous with his fleet. This was the heart of enemy country, and though he was constantly surrounded by Pequot warriors who had flocked to the scene of the battle from their other fort, Mason met little serious opposition. A few well-placed musketballs "taught them a little more manners than to disturb us," the Captain boasted. After putting his wounded aboard ship and receiving reinforcement from Captain Patrick and forty Bay Colony soldiers who had arrived in time to accompany the Connecticut boats, Mason proceeded overland with his Indian allies, scattering the Western Niantics on the way. The following day the Puritan army reached Saybrook where it was "nobly Entertained by Lieutenant Gardiner with many great Guns." When news of the victory reached the English colonies it was doubly welcome, as it had been preceded by rumors of a great disaster to the colonial forces. The Massachusetts General Court set aside June 15 as a day of thanksgiving.[50]

*   *   *

THE Pequots were left in utter confusion. Many of the tribe's leaders blamed Sassacus for the defeat, and only special pleading by his councilors persuaded them to spare his life. Most of the Pequots agreed, however, that safety lay only in flight. The majority headed for Mohawk country, where they hoped to find asylum, while a few sought refuge with neighboring tribes. Soon Roger Williams was able to report to Governor Winthrop that Sassacus was "gone or hid in the swampes, [and] not a Pequt is to be found." [51]

The task of finding the enemy sachem and exterminating the remnant of his followers fell to fresh colonial troops under the command of Captain Israel Stoughton. Stoughton arrived in Pequot Harbor with over one hundred Massachusetts Bay soldiers, while Underhill departed for the Bay Colony with his veterans. The new troops had an easier time of it. Their first assignment was to round up those luckless Pequots who had not taken to their heels, a task that was facilitated by the Narragansetts, who kept them "couped up as in a Pound" until the English arrived. Over one hundred Pequots were captured in that manner. Women and children were parceled out among the captors, thirty going to the Narragansetts, three to the Massachusetts Indians, and the rest to the Bay Colony. The captured braves, however, fared less well: twenty-two of twenty-four were executed; two sachems were spared on condition that they lead the way to Sassacus. [52]

In ferreting out the escaping Pequots, the colonists received a valuable assist from the Indians of Long Island. Three days after the Mystic Fort battle, a Long Island sachem called on Lieutenant Gardiner at Saybrook to know if the English were at war with all Indians. Gardiner made it clear that only the Pequots were enemies, but warned that if any Englishman trading on Long Island should be slain by fugitive Pequots, "I shall think you of Long Island have done it, and so we may kill of you for the Pequits." Gardiner suggested that to avoid an unpleasant mistake, the Long Islanders might destroy any Pequots who entered their territory and send the heads to him as evidence. Within the next few days a dozen Pequot heads arrived at Saybrook. [53]

Meanwhile Sassacus and the main body of Pequots

pushed westward toward New Netherland. The Puritan leaders, including Roger Williams, urged hasty pursuit lest the Pequot warriors escape to fight another day.[54] Fortunately for the colonial troops, the fugitives' trail proved easy to follow, for this was more of an exodus than a military retreat. Women and children slowed the fugitives' pace, and by clinging to the shore where food was abundant, the Pequots left a conspicuous trail. Part of the colonial force went by land, the greater part by sea, closely hugging the coastline. The land force, accompanied by a band of Mohegans and Narragansetts, slew or captured several enemy stragglers. The place where a Pequot sachem was beheaded is known still as "Sachem's Head," now in Guilford, Connecticut.[55]

The chase ended on the outskirts of modern Southport. Informed of the location of the main body of fugitives by one of the captives, the Puritan troops soon had them cornered in a "hideous swamp." Women, children, and old men were allowed to come out peacefully; about eighty fighting men chose to remain within. Shortly before dawn on July 14, the Pequots made a break for freedom; twenty or thirty succeeded, the rest retreated into the swamp or were slain. When the soldiers entered the swamp that morning they found groups of Indians huddled close together on the ground awaiting their fate. They received it with dispatch: muskets packed with ten or twelve balls were fired at them from close range. Sassacus, however, was nowhere to be found. He had apparently been warned of the English approach and had fled before the swamp fight began.[56]

By mid-July there was little left of the Pequot tribe. Over seven hundred Pequots, according to conservative estimates, had been killed or captured, and the other New England Indians trembled at the thoroughness of the English victory. Several tribes sent representatives to colonial officials with proffers of friendship and promises of tribute. As evidence of their good intentions all tribes now vied for the honor of slaying the remaining Pequots and, as Captain Mason observed, "happy were they that could bring in their Heads to the English: Of which there came almost daily to Winsor, or Hartford." [57] And in early August, there arrived in Hartford, as a gift from the Mohawks, the greatest prize of all: the scalp of Sassacus. Afraid of the Englishman's "hot-mouthed weapons," the Mohawks had seized Sassacus and forty of his warriors when they sought asylum, cut off their heads and hands, and confiscated their five hundred pounds of wampum.[58]

No semblance of Pequot organization remained. The scattered survivors now began to surrender voluntarily to the Connecticut plantations rather than be hunted down by the vengeful Mohegans and Narragansetts. Toward the end of 1637 the few remaining sachems begged for an end to the war, promising vassalage in return for their lives.[59] A peace convention was arranged for the following September.

With the Treaty of Hartford, signed on September 21, 1638, the Pequots ceased to exist as an independent polity.[60] The abolition of the defeated tribe was demanded as the price of peace by an allied tribunal in which Connecticut was represented by its magistrates, the Mohegans by Uncas, and the Narragansetts by Miantonomo. The treaty specifically forbade any of the former followers of Sassacus to be called Pequots and denied them habitation on the old tribal lands. The Pequot men who survived were assigned, with their families, to the Indian allies: eighty to Uncas and eighty to Miantonomo. Both chiefs agreed to pay annual tribute to the English for these captives. According to Captain Mason, another twenty Pequots were assigned to Chief Ninigret of the Eastern Niantics "when he should satisfy for a Mare of Edward Pomroye's killed by his men." [61] Henceforth all Pequot captives were to be known by the name of their new tribal affiliation.

Also included in the Treaty of Hartford were provisions for maintaining peace and equity among the victors. The tripartite agreement stipulated that the Mohegans and Narragansetts would not resort to arms against each other without the approval of the English.[62] Though this provision was frequently violated, it did mark the first attempt at regulating intertribal relations through colonial controls. This principle was to be carried a step further in 1643 with the formation of the Confederation of New England.

Relocation of the Pequots in the months that followed the Hartford settlement proved to be no simple matter. Some of the survivors willingly went to their new masters, a few fled to Long Island or the New England interior, but a large group returned to their former lands in violation of the agreement.[63] The Connecticut Court sent John Mason and forty men, assisted by Uncas and one hundred Mohegans, to dislodge them. Some of the squatters turned out to be Narragansetts, and the beginning of friction between the English colonies and Miantonomo's tribe may date from Mason's rough handling of them.[64]

Keeping the Pequots faithful to the treaty was but one of Connecticut's difficulties. Equally serious were the problems of providing enough food for the struggling plantations and paying the relatively heavy war debt. Large quantities of provisions had been requisitioned for the army, and the absence of all able-bodied men had left the fields only partially tilled and new crops unplanted. When food shortages became critical in 1638, the General Court commissioned

Captain Mason to purchase emergency rations of corn from the Indians at Pocumtuck (later Deerfield, Massachusetts). In addition the Pocumtucks were requested to contribute one and one-quarter fathoms of wampum per tribesman. Similiar levies were made against other Valley tribes.[65]

Although the war had not been fought to wrest land from the Pequots, most of the conquered territory was annexed by the English as the spoils of war. A Connecticut army of occupation had been sent into Pequot country shortly after Captain Stoughton's Massachusetts forces had quit the area in August 1637. Jurisdictional disputes between the Connecticut and Massachusetts colonies soon followed, for Miantonomo had previously given title to the Pequot country to Massachusetts Bay (although it had not really been his to give).[66] Friction over rival claims continued to plague this territory for decades until the Crown finally awarded it to Connecticut. In the meantime, much of the Pequot country was parceled out to Connecticut veterans; by the 1650's there were extensive settlements along the coast. New London was founded on the shore of Pequot Harbor and named in "memory of that renowned citty of London," while the adjacent river was appropriately renamed the Thames.[67]

*   *   *

THE effect of the Pequot War on Indian affairs was profound. Overnight the balance of power had shifted from the populous but unorganized natives to the English colonies. Henceforth there was no combination of Indian tribes that could seriously threaten the New England Puritans; only in 1675 when King Philip led half of the entire Indian population of New England against the colonists did they waver, and then only for a few months. The destruction of the Pequots cleared away the only major obstacle to Puritan expansion. And the thoroughness of that destruction made a deep impression on the other tribes.

Immediate ramifications of the victory were most obvious in Connecticut where the elimination of the Indian menace spurred immigration and expansion. Four years after the Treaty of Hartford the colony boasted 3000 souls. Another 2500 lived in New Haven, which had been founded on the Quinnipiac River in 1638.[68] Towns such as Farmington, Fairfield, Stratford, and Middletown soon dotted the countryside where the Pequots had roamed but a few years before. Massachusetts Bay and Rhode Island also took advantage of the peaceful interlude between the wars to extend their settlements. To claim that all this could not eventually have happened without the defeat of the Pequots would be a distortion of the case, but there is little doubt that the process of settlement was significantly speeded by the elimination of the only hostile tribe in southern New England.

Another benefit to the English of the Pequot War was the experience it afforded them in intercolonial cooperation. The informal wartime military alliance, while not without some misunderstandings and jealousies, did function effectively and did pave the way for the more comprehensive Confederation of New England in the next decade.

The colonies profited, too, from the lesson in military tactics and strategy. As this was the Puritans' first real clash with an Indian tribe, it gave them a chance to try out European methods on American terrain. Mason, for instance, found encirclement tactics successful. He also learned not to count on his Indian allies for much more than scouting duty, and at the same time discovered that this could be a crucial element in forest warfare. The plantations further

learned to keep emergency supplies on hand and to maintain permanent guardposts. Henceforth military training
was routine procedure in peace as well as in war. The ease
of their victory over the highly touted Pequots impressed
the English colonists with the importance of firearms, both
tactically and psychologically, and they did their best to
maintain a monopoly on European weapons. When they
lost it a few decades later, they had to enter a war with far
less initial advantage than they had enjoyed in 1637. And
most important of all, the Puritans discovered that intertribal rivalry could be counted on to provide native allies
against any Indian uprising.

Despite its brevity and limited scope, the Pequot War
marked a major turning point in the Puritans' relations with
the American Indian. Before 1637 there was some doubt as
to the ability of the colonists to exercise complete jurisdiction over the natives. After 1637, all New England tribes
south of the Piscataqua River acknowledged, if sometimes
unwillingly, the authority of the Puritan colonies. The next
step for the New Englanders was to systematize and perpetuate this authority through an intercolonial organization.

CHAPTER VI

Puritan Policy:
Confederation and the Indians, 1638-1675

URING THE late 1630's and early 1640's, many signs
pointed to the wisdom of establishing an intercolonial
league in New England. Foremost was the turbulent state
of English politics: the rift between King and Parliament
threatened to leave the American colonies without adequate
protection. Defenseless plantations would then become easy
prey to French, Dutch, or Indians.

Undoubtedly, certain Indian tribes posed a real threat to
the public peace of the New England colonies. The victory
over the Pequots had removed the principal native menace,
but intertribal frictions grew more ominous with each passing year. Most serious was the feud between Uncas of the
Mohegans and Miantonomo of the Narragansetts. Each of
these sachems commanded a large following and each
boasted of numerous allies. In the event of open warfare the
English colonies were certain to become involved. But in
trying to prevent hostilities the colonial governments faced
a new dilemma: both Uncas and Miantonomo had been
loyal allies during the Pequot campaign, and both were
bound to the English by solemn covenants.

Miantonomo's alliance with Massachusetts, it will be re-called, dated from October 1636, and provided for perpet-ual peace and friendship.* Uncas had made no treaty with the Bay Colony prior to the Pequot War, but once it was over he hastened to perform his obeisance to the dominant English colony. In June 1638, he led thirty-seven of his men to Boston where he offered a gift of wampum to Gov-ernor Winthrop and promised to accept English authority over his disputes with Miantonomo and over the disposition of his captive Pequots. He further ingratiated himself with the Governor by professing (with hand on heart),

> This heart . . . is not mine, but yours; I have no men, they are all yours; command me any difficult thing, I will do it; I will not believe any Indians' words against the English; if any man shall kill an Englishman, I will put him to death, were he never so dear to me.

Adorned in a new red coat from the Governor, and well supplied with corn for the homeward journey, Uncas left Boston "very joyful." [1] Then in September 1638, both the Mohegan and Narragansett sachems entered into a solemn covenant with Connecticut.

From the outset, Uncas had a diplomatic advantage over his Narragansett enemy. The Mohegan chief commanded the sincere gratitude of the Connecticut leaders and settlers for his role in the war, and he now had a close alliance with Massachusetts. Miantonomo, on the other hand, having played a far more modest part in the Pequot War, had a more tenuous tie to Connecticut; his covenant with Massa-chusetts Bay stipulated only perpetual peace and friendship (in contrast to Uncas's more comprehensive submission), and his record of cordial relations with the Rhode Island

---

* See page 132.

heretics was a potential irritant. By 1640 rumors began to circulate among the colonists that told of a vast Indian conspiracy against the English, with the Narragansetts cast as prime instigators and organizers.[2] These rumors were an important impetus to the formation of the New England Confederation in 1643, and it was the persistence of these rumors during the next two decades that led the Puritan colonies to send several expeditions against the Narragansetts and their allies.

So persistent had these tales been in the years from the Pequot War to the formation of the confederation that Miantonomo was often called to Boston to demonstrate his innocence. But these attempts at peaceful conciliation actually may have brought about greater hostility on the part of the Narragansetts. Miantonomo agreed to go to Boston early in 1640, for example, but only if Roger Williams were permitted to act as his interpreter. Though Williams had given invaluable assistance to Massachusetts during the Pequot troubles, he was still under decree of banishment, and the request was denied. When Miantonomo finally acquiesced and came to Boston without Williams, Governor Dudley added insult to injury by insisting on using a Pequot interpreter. The Narragansett sachem stalked off in what seemed to John Winthrop "a rude manner, without showing any respect or sign of thankfulness to the governor for his entertainment." Dudley retaliated by refusing to let the chief dine at the magistrates' table until he "acknowledged his failing." Miantonomo eventually gave in, but nothing constructive was accomplished except a reaffirmation of the old treaty of peace. Miantonomo left Boston conspicuously annoyed.[3] The Bay Colony's Indian policy, under Dudley's inept leadership, was sacrificing its major objectives for the sake of petty procedural details.

It is difficult to explain the uncompromising attitude of the Massachusetts Colony, for it had usually shown better judgment. Perhaps the Bay Colony felt so secure that it could afford to be picayune in its diplomacy. Unlike the other Puritan colonies, Massachusetts by 1640 seemed relatively immune to the dangers of Indian attack. Its own Indian population, already devastated by the 1617 plague, had been further diminished by the epidemic of 1633-1634. This fact, along with the continuing immigration to Massachusetts, meant that by the late 1630's Massachusetts probably had a white population greater than the entire Indian population of southern New England.[4] Indeed, so complete was the colony's authority that the government was able to confiscate all the Massachusetts Indians' powder and shot whenever friction with the Narragansetts reached critical proportions.[5] And making its position still stronger, Massachusetts Bay by 1640 had buffer colonies along much of its southern and western frontiers: Rhode Island and Connecticut might present certain problems to the Bay Colony authorities from time to time, but their very presence was worth any concomitant inconvenience. In fact, Massachusetts was in the enviable position of having little to fear from the natives and at the same time receiving considerable amounts of tribute from them.[6]

It was not long, however, before the other New England colonies were forced to take a more belligerent stand themselves. In 1642 tales of a new conspiracy, complete with sudden massacre under the guise of friendship, came to the ears of Theophilus Eaton in New Haven, and Roger Ludlow and John Haynes in Connecticut. The informers were Indians of southern Connecticut, and the River Colony could not lightly ignore their warnings. Uncomfortable in her frontier location, Connecticut now favored preventive warfare against the ringleaders. The General Court of Connecticut wrote to Massachusetts for help in stamping out the conspiracy before it materialized.[7]

Now it was the Bay Colony's turn to be cautious. Massachusetts had no desire to commit its men and resources in a war against tribes which had done its own citizens no harm. Only if the tribes within the boundaries of the colony were involved could the conspiracy be a genuine menace, and precautions were immediately taken to preclude this possibility. Cutshamekin of the Massachusetts tribe was deprived of all armaments, even his bows, and lodged in the Boston jail for a night. Simultaneously, forty men from the northern towns attempted to disarm Passaconaway of the Pennacooks, and while they exceeded their instructions and almost caused a local crisis, the expedition fulfilled the intentions of the magistrates "to strike some terror into the Indians." But at the same time, the General Court voted against an offensive war, fearing that the present turmoil was but another aspect of the enmity between Uncas and Miantonomo. Should a war against the Narragansetts later prove to have been unjustified, noted Winthrop, it would surely "provoke God's displeasure, and blemish our wisdom and integrity before the heathen."[8] Connecticut reluctantly decided against unilateral action.

The importance of this episode was twofold: peace was maintained and the need for intercolonial organization was made more evident. Connecticut had been persuaded to refrain from hostilities partly on the argument, advanced by the Bay colonists, that the Indians did not recognize any political subdivisions among the Englishmen, assuming, wrote Winthrop, "that we were all as one."[9] An attack by Connecticut would be interpreted by the Indians as an attack by all Englishmen and would therefore involve the other New England colonies. Under these circumstances logic demanded that some intercolonial organ be established so that colonial actions would, in fact, reflect a single policy. It is ironic that part of the impetus for intercolonial cooperation thus came as a response to the natives' misconception of the English polity.

While the crisis of 1642 was an important stimulus to confederation, its role should not be exaggerated. Thoughts of a New England union had been under way for several years — at least since the events of 1637.[10] But that year had ended with encouraging solutions to New England's problems, both military and religious, and it was not until 1642 that intercolonial and international problems were great enough to prod the settlements into effective action. Of these, trouble with the Indians was the most urgent. Threats from the Dutch and French and the chaotic state of affairs in the mother country were significant also, but they had neither the immediacy nor potential brutality of the Indian menace.[11] Despite the obvious necessity of union the wheels of diplomacy moved slowly, and it was not until the late spring of 1643 that representatives from four colonies — Massachusetts Bay, Connecticut, Plymouth, and New Haven — signed the Articles of Confederation.

As befitted a people deeply motivated by religion, the Articles of Confederation began with a statement of the religious reasons for the settlement of New England. Subsequent phrases, however, pointed to the need for an intercolonial league as a protection against possible European and Indian enemies. In order to meet such threats, the Articles made provisions for joint defensive actions, including the raising and financing of troops. And to prevent the necessity of war, Article VIII authorized the Commissioners of the United Colonies "to frame and establish agree-

ments . . . how all the Jurisdictions may carry it towards
the Indians, that they neither grow insolent nor be injured
without due satisfaction." [12] In practice, the authority of the
Commissioners was not quite so great as might appear from
the wording of this article. Rather, a federal principle was
adopted: affairs within each colony were regulated by the
colonial governments; the Commissioners exercised authority only over matters of intercolonial scope.

From their first meeting, the Commissioners of the United
Colonies found Indian affairs the most time-consuming and
most important topic of discussion and action. The records
of the Commissioners reveal that two categories of Indian
relations dominated their proceedings: attempts to maintain
peace, and, after 1649, the administration of the missionary
activities of "The Society for the Propagation of the Gospel in New England" (supplanted in 1662 by "The Corporation for Propagation of the Gospel in New England
and the parts adjacent in America").* In these matters, the
Commissioners reflected the Indian policy of the New England Puritans.

*   *   *

By far the most pressing of the early problems facing the
Confederation was that posed by the bitter feud between
Miantonomo and Uncas. Their rivalry had already threatened to embroil the English colonies on several occasions
since 1638. Fortunately for the settlers of New England, it
did not reach its climax until the very year that the Confederation came into existence.

It is difficult to know which of the two sachems was in
the right — if either. Most nineteenth century historians

---

*The role of the Commissioners in Puritan missionary activities is
treated in Chapters IX-XI.

sympathized with the Narragansett chief, picturing him as the victim of a wily Mohegan who duped the English leaders into championing his side in the quarrel.[13] But nineteenth century authorities rarely considered the alternatives open to the colonial authorities. Of the two chiefs, Uncas had contributed more to the victory over the Pequots, and since that time he had been the more cooperative in paying tribute, controlling his subordinates, and observing the regulations of the United Colonies. The Commissioners were faced with the unpleasant necessity of backing either Uncas or his blood enemy, or of allowing the two to disturb the relative tranquillity of New England. Far from being deceived by Uncas, the Puritans were only too aware of his duplicity, and they were by no means blinded by his flattery, no matter how much they enjoyed it.[14] They supported him as the only plausible choice, not because they thought he was guiltless.

Any defense of Miantonomo's side of the quarrel must explain away the many charges against him. That all of them were groundless seems inconsistent with the general reliability of Puritan documents, and they are nearly unanimous in portraying the Narragansett chief as the aggressor. Perhaps he had justification that fails to appear in the records, but all available evidence confirms that the Narragansett violated his treaties with Massachusetts and Connecticut as well as the orders of the Commissioners of the United Colonies when he attacked Uncas.[15] The Puritans could not allow a major sachem to violate covenants with impunity.

The events that led to the downfall and death of Miantonomo began in 1643. In that year the Narragansett sachem, according to Uncas's testimony, hired one of the Mohegan's Pequot wards to assassinate Uncas. The plot failed when the arrow intended for the Mohegan chief merely nicked his arm, and the would-be assassin left the scene without being recognized. Shortly thereafter a Pequot brave was observed with an unusually large supply of wampum and was immediately suspected of being involved in the plot. When he fled to the Narragansetts for protection, his guilt was taken for granted. But instead of taking the warpath, Uncas adhered to his earlier agreements and lodged a complaint with the English authorities.[16]

Miantonomo and the suspected Pequot were called to Boston to acquit themselves. Stoutly denying the charge, the Pequot maintained that Uncas had purposely cut himself with a gun flint and had urged the accused to help implicate Miantonomo by spending lavishly and then seeking haven with the Narragansetts. The Pequot might have been believed had his testimony not radically changed when he was re-examined with Miantonomo absent. The English began to suspect that the Narragansett chief was conspiring not only against Uncas, but against the colonists as well. Old fears of a Narragansett plot reawakened. Nevertheless, the Puritan magistrates released both Miantonomo and the Pequot pending further investigation.[17]

At this point Miantonomo sacrificed whatever confidence the English may have retained in him. On the way back to Narragansett country he decapitated the Pequot, thereby eliminating the star witness. The Narragansett sachem then collected a thousand warriors and launched a major assault against the Mohegans.[18] The covenant had been broken; there remained little chance that the Narragansett chief would ever again receive impartial treatment from the Puritan statesmen.

According to Edward Johnson, Miantonomo had been

encouraged to do battle with Uncas by Samuel Gorton of Rhode Island, who reputedly lent him a steel corselet to enhance his chances of victory. If that is the case, the plan had disastrous results for the Narragansett chief. Weighted down with unwieldy armor, Miantonomo was captured when the Mohegans routed his forces.[19]

Again Uncas chose a course of action certain to ingratiate him with the Puritan leaders. With his victory complete, the Mohegan did not execute his captive as Indian custom prescribed but rather turned him over to the Connecticut magistrates; they put the prisoner in the Hartford jail and then handed the case to the Commissioners of the United Colonies, sitting at the Confederation's first session in Boston.[20]

How to dispose of Miantonomo was a conundrum not easily solved. Throughout the month of September 1643, the honored Commissioners, John Winthrop presiding, "did seriously consider Miantinimos course and carriage . . . and well remembred his ambitious designes to make himself universall Sagomore or Governor of all these parts." The essential charge against the Narragansett, however, was that he had violated the tripartite agreement of 1638,

> in which one of the Articles were, That though either of these Indian Sagamores should receive injuries from the other, yet they should not make warr one of them against the other till they had first complayned, and that the English had heard their greevances, and had declared and determyned what was just and right betwixt them: And that if either of them should attempt against the other without consulting with the English, the English might then assist against the Invader.

The Commissioners also considered the charge that Mian-tonomo had several times attempted to assassinate Uncas — first in the episode related above, then by poison, and finally "by sorcery." [21]

After long deliberation the Commissioners concluded that "Uncas cannot be safe while Myantenomo lives." In this decision the Commissioners had the comforting concurrence of some of the Bay Colony's church elders, whose advice was sought in the crisis. But having determined that Miantonomo must die, the English authorities were not willing to perform the execution; in fact they denied having such right. Rather, they handed Miantonomo over to the Mohegan chief to dispatch as he saw fit, requiring only that he perform the execution in his own jurisdiction and that "in the manner of his death all mercy and moderation be shewed." As a precaution, Uncas was promised English aid if the Narragansetts should attempt to retaliate. Should Uncas refuse this chance to dispose of his enemy, Miantonomo was to be incarcerated in Boston pending further disposition of the case. [22]

Uncas did not decline the opportunity. The Mohegan chief gladly took custody of his enemy and accompanied by several English musketeers led him away from Hartford. Somewhere between there and Windsor, Uncas's brother stepped behind the captive and "clave his head with a hatchet." [23] A persistent but unsupported legend purports that Uncas cut a slice of flesh from his enemy's body and devoured it raw. [24]

The Narragansetts, who had unsuccessfully tried to ransom their chief, "took it quietly at present," and some of the tribes that were subservient to the Narragansetts actually were pleased. And the Puritans, though not exuberant over the outcome, were convinced that they had averted a major war.[25] They had closed the career of the only Indian leader since Sassacus to pose a threat to the New England colonies.

Debate over the justice of the English decision has continued ever since. Perhaps the colonists expected this, for they took great pains to state explicitly the reasoning behind their action. The most complete statement comes not from the records of 1643, however, but from a declaration issued by the Commissioners of the United Colonies two years later. Trouble with the Narragansetts had not yet abated, and the declaration was an attempt to review the entire history of friction with that tribe in order to justify further action against it. In referring to the decision to permit Uncas to execute his "treacherous and blood thirsty enemie," the English showed that they had been fully convinced that Miantonomo was at the center of a conspiracy designed "to cutt of[f] the whole body of the English [in] these parts." It seems clear, then, that the English had a double motive in indirectly disposing of Miantonomo: to punish the violator of civil convenants, and to eliminate the ringleader of a general Indian conspiracy.[26] That the Puritans in seventeenth century New England resorted to drastic measures to destroy a conspiracy should not appear implausible to twentieth century Americans who have themselves succumbed to anti-conspiratorial hysteria.

*   *   *

THE Commissioners observed in their declaration of 1645 that Uncas had slain "an enemie but not the enmyty against him." Neither, they might have added, had the colonists lessened enmity against themselves. The years following the execution of Miantonomo saw no significant change in either the pattern or extent of friction with the Narragansetts. Hostility between the Narragansetts and Mohegans continued as the primary threat to peace in New England, rumors of a Narragansett-led conspiracy remained prevalent, and Indian affairs were almost constantly on the verge of explosion.

The Narragansetts, though shorn of their principal leader, were hardly contrite. Shortly after the execution of Miantonomo, Pessacus, a younger brother of the deceased chief, sent an otter skin coat and girdle of wampum to Governor Winthrop with a request that Massachusetts not interfere with the Narragansetts' plan for revenge. Winthrop declined both the gift and the proposition. But Pessacus and elderly chief Canonicus continued to protest the execution of Miantonomo, partly on the grounds that Uncas was an "inhumane and cruell adversary" and partly on the claim that Uncas had taken some of the ransom offered for his captive but killed him nonetheless.[27]

The Narragansetts did not base their case on personal grievance alone, but offered a constitutional argument as well. Since they had willingly subjected themselves, their lands, and their rights to the government of King Charles, they were subjects of the same King as were the Massachusetts colonists; in the event of any disagreement between the tribe and the colony, "then neither yourselves, nor wee are to be the judges; but both of us are to have recourse, and repair, unto that honorable and just government." There is no record of the colony's answer. Presumably the flaw in the Indians' logic, as far as the Puritans were concerned, was that although the natives were subjects of the same king as the colonists, Indian tribes were necessarily subservient to the authority of patented civil governments — a claim supported by the wording of the royal charters, and bolstered by the refusal of the Crown to acknowledge the Narragansetts' submission.[28] The Puritans did their scrupulous best to treat the natives kindly and justly, but we mistake their fundamental view of Christian society if we expect them to have shared ultimate political power with uncivilized and un-Christian sachems who had neither charters from the Crown nor a record of honorable behavior. If the Puritan experiment were to succeed it must not divide its civil authority with other subjects of the King, either English or Indian.

The best that the Commissioners of the United Colonies could do in this situation was to call Uncas and the Narragansett chiefs before the annual meetings and attempt to lessen their grievances. Uncas was careful to answer every summons, which further added to his influence with the colonial authorities. The Narragansetts came grudgingly, if at all, and were reluctant to pledge obedience. Yet the Commissioners, to their credit, made every attempt to assure the Narragansetts of an impartial hearing. Messengers to the sachems were ordered to take down the Indians' statements in writing and to read back the translations to them before reporting to the Commissioners. It was hoped that this would eliminate misunderstandings caused by the language barrier. (That barrier, of course, had already been substantially hurdled by several competent interpreters, especially Benedict Arnold, Roger Williams, and Thomas Stanton.) Even then the Commissioners hesitated to determine disputes unless the evidence was irrefutable.[29]

Such precautions did not guarantee peace. Although regular meetings were held in September, the Commissioners found it necessary to hold a "meetinge extraordinary" in July 1645 to discuss a new clash between Pessacus and Uncas. Since it again appeared that the Narragansetts, abetted by the Niantics,* were the aggressors, the Commissioners voted to raise a force of three hundred immediately; delay might cause Uncas "to be swallowed up." Forty men from Massachusetts Bay were dispatched to reinforce Uncas, while the remainder of the men — 150 from Massachusetts, 40 each from Plymouth and Connecticut, and 30 from New Haven — were to rendezvous at Rehoboth for an attack on the Narragansetts and Niantics. Major Edward Gibbons of the Bay Colony was appointed commander-in-chief of the expedition, and was to be assisted by a council of war that included John Mason of Connecticut and Miles Standish of Plymouth. Pastor Thompson of Braintree "was to sound the silver Trumpet along with this Army." According to Gibbons's instructions, he was to resort to coercion only if diplomacy, conducted under the threat of force, failed. In that event he was to "make fayre warrs without exercising cruelty." [30]

Fortunately for all concerned, Gibbons won his objective without firing a shot. Choosing the safer half of an ultimatum to negotiate or fight, the leading Narragansett sachems — Pessacus, his son Mexano, and Witowash — led a large band of followers to Boston to treat with the Commissioners. Though the envoys insisted that "nothing but Uncas his head should satisfye them," they finally capitulated to far less favorable terms. The Narragansetts and Niantics agreed to an indemnity of two thousand fathoms of

---

* Though the Narragansetts and Eastern Niantics were separate tribes, they had long, close ties. At the time of the first English settlements, the Eastern Niantics were apparently subservient to the Narragansetts. Continual intermarriage, the death of Canonicus, and the growing power of Ninigret had almost reversed this relationship by the late 1640's. There was never a complete merger of leadership, however, for the two tribes often acted independently of each other, most conspicuously during King Philip's War when the Niantics remained neutral while the Narragansetts were being crushed.

white wampum for the cost of Gibbons's expedition against
them, reparations to Uncas for damage he had sustained,
and the return of all Mohegan captives. Hostages were to
be left with the English until these terms were fulfilled. The
agreement was formalized in a treaty signed August 28,
1645.[31]

That document was intended to resolve all issues between
the Puritan colonies and the Narragansetts. It contained a
schedule of reparations payments, stretching over a two-
year period, and pledged the Indians to make annual payments for their Pequot wards in accordance with the Hartford Treaty of 1638.* It verified English title to the entire
Pequot country by right of conquest. And most important
of all, the signatories did "promise and covenant to keepe
and maytaine a firm and perpetuall peace" with the English,
Uncas, and all tribes in friendship with or subject to the
English. The Narragansetts and Niantics pledged themselves not to begin future wars without "liberty and allowance" from the Commissioners of the United Colonies.
Although the grievances between the Narragansetts and
Uncas were not resolved by the treaty, provision was made
for settling them within the next year. The treaty placed
these matters on the agenda for the 1646 meeting of the
Commissioners, and, to prevent negotiations from dragging
on indefinitely, it was provided that the four hostages (of
whom one was to be Pessacus's eldest son) would not be

---

* Tribute payments from the Mohegans, Narragansetts, and Niantics
were based on the assignment of Pequots to those tribes by the Hartford
Treaty of 1638. The new masters supposedly collected the specified
amounts of wampum from the Pequots, then turned it over to the Commissioners as reparations for the atrocities committed by the Pequots
prior to the war and the cost of the war itself. Tribute was to be paid
at the rate of one fathom of white wampum per Pequot man, one-half
fathom per male youth, and one hand-length per male child. The tribute
was not collected until 1650 and for only ten years thereafter.

released until the differences with Uncas were resolved.[32]

The 1645 negotiations also reflected the Puritans' growing caution in Indian diplomacy. The Commissioners that year refused to treat with any deputies or minor chieftains of the tribes; only the leading sachems would be accepted, and they must have authority to speak for all. Further, the hostages were not to be released until certain other sachems had ratified the agreement. To the Commissioners the Treaty of 1645 was a major step toward fulfilling their obligation to "provide for the safety and Welfare of the Countrey." They felt so satisfied with their accomplishment, in fact, that they voted one hundred fathoms of the reparations wampum to Uncas in the belief that much of his suffering had been from "want of tymely ayde from the Colonyes," an admission of fault that would have been remarkable in any governing body.[33]

But the Puritans' hopes for peace were soon shattered. Where the English viewed the treaty as a solemn covenant, the Indian participants viewed it as a contract signed under duress and therefore not binding.[34] Trouble started as soon as the Narragansett-Niantic spokesmen departed. Instead of the stipulated hostages, some "base Papooses" were delivered, and the installments of wampum rapidly fell in arrears. Compliance of the Narragansetts to the treaty was accomplished only by new threats of military action. On one occasion Captain Atherton of Dorchester secured cooperation from Chief Ninigret of the Niantics by shoving a pistol against his breast and holding him firmly by the hair. These and similar tactics were successful, at least superficially, and according to Increase Mather's later account, the natives were "terrified into better Obediance." [35]

By 1647 the situation was again critical. New rumors told of a Narragansett-Niantic scheme to hire the Mohawks to

dispose of Uncas.[36] Although the veracity of these reports
has never been established, it can well be imagined how uncomfortable such rumors made the colonists. A conflict
with any or all of the New England tribes would be serious;
war against the Mohawks threatened disaster.[37] The Commissioners responded to the new crisis with another emergency meeting. This time it was Ninigret of the Niantics
who spoke for the accused tribes. The outcome was predictable: an unqualified denial of all charges of conspiracy and
a promise to observe the schedule of wampum payments.
Within a year the Commissioners were repeating almost
identical accusations.[38]

Again Ninigret came to Boston; again he was charged
with delinquency on tribute payments and inveigling with
the Mohawks. The latter charge was supported by reports
from the Mohawks themselves, according to Thomas Stanton, and from Roger Williams, a staunch friend of the Narragansetts. And Uncas took this opportunity to lodge new
complaints of plots on his life. A final touch of terror was
added by talk of a marriage between Ninigret's daughter
and the brother of Sassacus, former leader of the Pequots.
The possibility of a revival of the Pequot tribe was not a
pleasant one for the Puritan colonies to consider; Ninigret
now inherited the reputation as the prime threat to peace
that had previously been Miantonomo's.[39]

Matters remained in a state of semi-crisis until the major
flare-up of 1654. Problems relating to the Narragansetts
and Niantics dominated every meeting of the Commissioners as complaints against Ninigret continued to deluge the
colonial leaders. In 1650 twenty armed men were sent to
Niantic to collect overdue tribute installments and to warn
Ninigret against trying to resurrect the Pequot tribe.[40]
Though no armed expeditions were sent for the next two

years, relations between the Commissioners and the tribes of eastern Connecticut remained precarious.

*   *   *

ALTHOUGH New England and New Netherland were out-posts of different European powers, relations between these Atlantic coast colonies had been remarkably cordial. Neither particularly coveted the land of the other, though both went through the motions of upholding their home governments' claims to the whole area. Only when the English moved into the Connecticut Valley, New Haven, and eastern Long Island did the colonies of the two nations come into uncomfortable proximity. As the Puritan colonies spread westward, the Dutch drafted messages of protest and proffered occasional threats, but numbers were on the side of the English, and the Dutch eventually yielded. There was, after all, enough land for both nations, and the Dutch enjoyed a far more lucrative economic position than the English, both as to interior and exterior trade.

But what if the mother countries were locked in war? Undoubtedly the colonies would become officially hostile, and probably each would seize the opportunity to enlarge its effective boundaries. And in such a contest, one or both might well employ, or at least supply, Indian allies. This was the prospect which faced the New England settlements after Lord Protector Cromwell declared war on the Netherlands in 1652.

Complaints against the Dutch for selling guns and ammunition to the Indians had been legion from the beginning of English settlement. There is little doubt that under Governor Stuyvesant the practice was condoned as a necessary expedient. In any event, the Puritans were firmly convinced that the Dutch were supplying the Indians of New England with firearms. In peacetime the motive could be profit, but with England and Holland at war a more sinister reason seemed plausible. Imagine, then, the consternation among the English colonies when Uncas reported that Ninigret had purchased twenty guns in New Amsterdam.[41]

Evidence of Dutch aid to the Narragansett-Niantic alliance mounted. A captured Narragansett confessed the existence of a plot between his tribe and Governor Stuyvesant. Further confirmation came from a squaw near Wethersfield, Connecticut, who warned that a massacre had been planned for election day. (There was good reason to have faith in this squaw's testimony: her warning in 1637 of an impending raid on Wethersfield had been ignored with disastrous results.) Finally, nine sagamores from southern New Netherland added their account of Dutch complicity. Rumor had it that the Dutch would attack by sea and the Indians by land in a sudden and concerted attempt to eliminate the New England colonies.[42]

As in past crises, the political leaders of the Puritan colonies turned to the church elders for advice. Though impressed by the evidence of Dutch guilt, the elders urged caution, and the Commissioners therefore dispatched a delegation to Stuyvesant to expound the charges and seek explanation. But so expectant of war were the Commissioners that they used the interval to make preliminary military plans. These came uncomfortably close to being used, too, for when negotiations with Stuyvesant collapsed into repetitious charges and countercharges, the Commissioners were on the verge of declaring offensive war against New Netherland.[43] But Massachusetts chose this moment to question the fundamental right of the United Colonies to declare offensive war over the objections of any General Court. Massachusetts was not about to be dragged into an international war by its three small and impetuous neighbors. When the delegates, after much wrangling, finally voted for a campaign against Ninigret, the Bay Colony refused to contribute any troops.[44] Thus war was avoided for the moment, but only at the cost of seriously disrupting the organization responsible for regulating Indian affairs, and without any concurrent amelioration of the crisis with the Narragansetts, Niantics, or Dutch.

A year later, however, Massachusetts, stung by charges that the Bay Colony had violated its covenant with its sister colonies, and goaded by the apparent unruliness of Ninigret, did cooperate in raising an army against the Niantic chief. Ninigret had perhaps made this inevitable by denying the jurisdiction of the United Colonies over him. This affront to the Commissioners' authority, added to new evidence of Narragansett and Niantic infidelity, caused the Commissioners in September 1654 to raise an army of 270 foot soldiers and 40 horsemen. Only Roger Williams objected. Both the Long Island sachem against whom Ninigret was then at war and the Niantic chief himself were "barbarians," asserted Williams, adding that "the former is proud and foolish; the latter is proud and fierce." Nonetheless, Williams believed that in the present case, Ninigret was in the right.[45]

Little heed was paid to the Rhode Island heretic, however, and an army was soon mustered. Since news of peace between the Netherlands and England had removed the threat of a Dutch-instigated conspiracy, the purpose of this force was simply to coerce Ninigret into observing his prior commitments. The soldiers of the United Colonies, under Major Simon Willard of the Bay Colony, had instructions to collect arrears in tribute or else confiscate Ninigret's Pequots and resettle them in southern Connecticut under

English supervision. As usual, the cost of the expedition was to be borne by the Indians, and new sureties of good behavior were to be extracted.[46]

Ninigret obviously resented English interference with his war against Long Island and certainly did not relish paying the costs of some three hundred English soldiers. But when Major Willard made it plain that the alternative was to have "his head sett up upon an English pole," the Niantic chief succumbed to the Commissioners' demands. A new covenant, dated October 18, 1654, provided that Ninigret would surrender his Pequot wards to the English within seven days; the Pequots in turn agreed that they would henceforth submit to English rather than Niantic jurisdiction.[47]

All of these negotiations really meant little, for Ninigret had long since ceased to observe covenants signed under threat of force — in fact the evidence is convincing that he had always ignored all covenants with the English — and within a few months the old troubles were as pressing as ever. Ninigret failed to relinquish his Pequots, and a delegation from Long Island appealed to the Commissioners for protection from the continued raids by Ninigret's warriors. An uneasy calm finally settled over New England in 1655 when the United Colonies commissioned a coastal patrol vessel to ply the waters of Long Island Sound and thwart any Niantic forays against the Island tribes.[48]

*   *   *

FROM 1655 until the outbreak of King Philip's War in 1675, the New England Confederation was a shadow organization. The constitutional issue raised by Massachusetts was resolved only at the cost of organizational strength. With the power of the Commissioners now subject to a veto by each colony, the Confederation ceased to exert a

dominant influence in colonial affairs.[49] Fortunately for relations between the Puritans and the natives, the Commissioners continued to give attention to Indian affairs; in fact
that was the one role left they could play with a minimum
of intercolonial friction. Although the bulk of these Indian
affairs increasingly involved the dissemination of the Gospel, the task of maintaining the peace and security of New
England continued persistently to occupy the Commissioners.

Here the Commissioners had three especially pressing re-
sponsibilities. The first was supervision of the Pequots,
many of whom were now under English control; a second
was the prevention of intertribal clashes; and the third involved punishment of individual Indians for infractions of
Puritan law.

The solution to the Pequot problem was quite simple and
moderately successful. Ninigret had forfeited control of his
Pequot wards, and many of Uncas's had deserted him and
had wandered back to their old territory. To cope with the
administration of the increasing Pequot community, the
Commissioners in the 1650's established four towns. To supervise these communities the Commissioners appointed
two Indian governors, each to have jurisdiction over two
towns. Casasinamon (better known as Robin) ruled at
Nemeacke and Naweake; Caushawashott (Harmon Garrett) at Panquatucke and Wequapauge. Both of these Indians were themselves Pequots. Of Harmon Garrett little is
known, but Robin had been freed of tribute payments and
subjection to any Indian tribe for aiding the English during
the expedition against Ninigret in 1654. Both operated under written commissions from the United Colonies. Although the authority conferred on the Indian governors
was almost absolute, they received from the Commissioners

periodic instructions which included prohibitions against
blasphemy, murder, adultery, drunkenness, theft, and
witchcraft. War without the permission of the Commissioners was proscribed, and "whosoever shall plot Mischiefe
against the English shall suffer death or such other punishment as the case may deserve." Tribute to the Commissioners as specified in the Tripartite Treaty of 1638 was to be
delivered each year to Thomas Stanton three months before
the annual meeting of the Commissioners.[50]

This limited reconstruction of the Pequot tribe was not
flawless. As early as 1656 reports indicated that many of the
Pequots were "stuburne and Reddy to mannifest theire dis-
obeidience" to the authority of the Commissioners, so much
so that Robin and Harmon Garrett requested English assistance in enforcing the laws and collecting tribute payments.
Accordingly, the Commissioners directed John Winthrop,
Jr., John Mason, and Daniel Denison to give aid when
needed.[51]

Robin and Harmon Garrett, their annual appointments
renewed for several years, tried to serve the United Colonies well, but the frequency with which their difficulties appear in the records of the Commissioners shows that theirs
was no easy task. The problems confronting the Pequot
governors also make more comprehensible Ninigret's earlier
failure to control these same Pequots. The Indian governors
proved as unsuccessful as the Indian sachems had been in
collecting tribute payments, some Pequots engaged in unau-
thorized warfare, and rumors of plots between the Pequots
and other tribes continued to be common.[52] In addition,
boundary disputes, both intertribal and interracial, provoked constant tension until finally settled in the 1660's.
Not until 1667 did Connecticut, after being chastised by

the Commissioners, finally assign permanent reservations to the Pequots.[53]

Preventing intertribal clashes proved even more of a problem than supervising the Pequots. Some of the large autonomous tribes still held ancient grudges against each other and sought revenge.[54] Furthermore, there was frequent strife between subordinate tribes, partly, it seems, because the sachems' control over individual warriors was often tenuous.[55] And adding to the already complicated pattern of intertribal control, Uncas began to assume more and more of the responsibility for initiating and perpetuating hostilities. At various times the Mohegan chief was involved in raids or counter raids on the Pocumtucks, Narragansetts, Niantics, and Nipmucs, raids which frequently threatened to involve the colonies as well.[56] Little wonder, then, that the Commissioners were only partly successful in their endeavor to maintain the peace and security of New England.

One positive measure that the Commissioners took to lessen the possibility of a general war was to control the Indians' supply and use of firearms. In addition to the long standing ordinances against the selling of arms and ammunition to natives, the Commissioners in 1657 forbade armed groups of Indians from coming within a mile of any English town either in wartime or in periods of crisis.[57] This policy may well have contributed to a reduction of frontier tensions; at any rate in the period from 1655 to 1675 the United Colonies had no occasion to send military expeditions against any tribe. Though the peace was always uneasy, it was peace nevertheless.

In the handling of crimes by individual natives, the Commissioners shared with the colonial governments the chores of trial and punishment. Certain matters were predominantly under the jurisdiction of the federal authorities. For example, the Pequots under Harmon Garrett and Robin submitted to the Commissioners' courts as well as to the Commissioners' regulations. At first all cases were decided by the Commissioners themselves; each case was adjudicated on its merits at the annual meeting, much as the colonial general courts had once administered all justice for the settlers. Although occasionally the Commissioners referred a case to the appropriate colonial government, too much of the delegates' time was being devoted to judicial duties. A partial remedy was instituted in 1662 — a court of appeals for the Pequots. Composed of Daniel Denison, Thomas Stanton, and James Averill, or any two of them, this court heard appeals from the decisions of the Indian governors. It had final jurisdiction over crimes less than capital and also exercised original jurisdiction over disputes between the Pequots and their English neighbors.[58]

At the same time the Commissioners attempted to reduce the probability of minor infractions by the Pequots by decreeing that all strong liquors were to be seized, turned over to the English, and sold. One-half of the sale price was to go to the informer, the other half to the authority (presumably the governor) effecting the seizure. No evidence exists as to how this early experiment in prohibition succeeded.[59]

*   *   *

IT would be a mistake to think that every aspect of Indian affairs under the Confederation involved stern coercion. Though such matters did consume a disproportionate amount of the Commissioners' time, at least a few moments of harmony and cooperation brightened the Commissioners' duties. Since good times are usually assumed to be normal times, they tend to be accorded little notice in diaries, official records, amateur histories, correspondence, and the like. Disturbances of the peace, however, get full attention. Thus documentary evidence of periods or episodes of "good feeling" may be proportionally more significant than they at first might seem.

Such evidence is to be found in most of the sources that remain. The records of the Commissioners of the United Colonies dwell extensively on matters of Indian education, humanitarian assistance to individuals and tribes, and material aid to the natives. There are frequent entries attesting to mutual trust and respect. And it seems probable that there was less warfare in New England during the quarter-century following the creation of the Confederation of New England than during the pre-Pilgrim decades, and certainly less than in the period from 1620 to 1643.

That the United Colonies did not solve all of the interracial and intertribal problems is obvious. The Confederation did, however, compile a commendable record. Despite recurring periods of high tension, open war between the colonies and hostile tribes was avoided, and the Indians' intertribal conflict was limited to scattered raids. This was no modest achievement for a small group of Commissioners who had other demands on their time and energy. And their achievements came in the face of considerable obstacles, especially the opposition of some tribal leaders. Miantonomo and Ninigret were the least cooperative sachems, but even the most loyal sagamore, Uncas, at times violated covenants, defaulted on tribute payments, and was almost constantly at odds with one or more tribes.[60] In the light of present day evidence, it seems unfair to conclude with Samuel Drake that "Indian History scarcely affords a parallel in perfidy to Uncas"; it is, however, important to remember that the colonists were dealing with human beings, not undefiled "noble savages." Even Cutshamekin of the Massachusetts tribe, who acted as interpreter and virtual ambassador at large for the Bay Colony, acted deviously on at least one occasion.[61]

At the time the Confederation was being formed, John Winthrop observed that frequent disturbances were "raised up by the opposite factions among the Indians." [62] New England, it will be recalled, was inhabited by tribes, subtribes, and quasi-independent bands with varying relationships, loyalties, and rivalries. Some had submitted to colonial jurisdiction, others had entered into treaties of peace and amity with the colonies, while a few Indian nations on the fringes of New England — such as the Wappingers and Mahicans — did not acknowledge any formal relationship with the New England colonies. It was therefore difficult to curb the murders, raids, counter raids — in addition to the lesser forms of friction — that were disturbingly common among the native population.

The Commissioners always had to consider the potential impact of their actions on the Indian population in general. One of the principal reasons for upholding Uncas in his dispute with Miantonomo had been the realization that other tribes, both friendly and hostile, watched "with strict observation" the Englishmen's adherence to treaties with the red men. During the crisis of 1653-1654 many colonists feared that the vacillating policy of the United Colonies would have a disastrous effect on the loyalty of subordinate tribes, and the indecision of the Puritan governments might lead to a general contempt for the English among New England Indians. Similar fears were expressed during the later years of the Confederation.[63]

In trying to solve their manifold problems, the Commissioners attempted to be prudent, lenient, and impartial. Both sides to any dispute always received a hearing,[64] and judgments did not always favor the individuals or tribes most friendly to the colonists.[65] Instructions to military commanders always stressed the primacy of securing peace rather than vindication.[66] On the whole, the Commissioners' record of achievement from 1643 to 1675 bears testimony to the effectiveness of the Puritans' management of Indian affairs on the intercolonial level.

One question remains. Time and again during the period from 1643 to 1675 the Puritan colonies, acting through the Commissioners, had assumed jurisdiction over tribes that either denied colonial authority altogether or objected to a specific application of it. Were the Puritans justified in imposing their decisions on recalcitrant tribes?

While no one will subscribe to the thesis that might makes right, it is undeniable that in troubled times the alternative to chaos is positive action on the part of the most mature and effective political authority. This has never been a flawless system of justice, but it has always operated in lieu of international tribunals and even exists among the major powers after tribunals of arbitration have been devised. Power demands responsibility, and in seventeenth century New England the Puritan colonies were the strongest single force; they alone had the political unity and military strength to impose order on the various groups, both Indian and white, in that part of the New World.

The Puritans would have argued that they were not only the most powerful force in New England but also the most peaceful—a debatable proposition at best. But in their determination to establish a model Christian community they were profoundly committed to political and social stability. And it may be true, as some European observers claimed, that the Puritan authorities reduced the frequency (though certainly not the intensity) of warfare in New England.

Finally, many of the Indian leaders welcomed the presence of the Confederation as a check to intertribal warfare. Some, such as Uncas, may have owed his survival to the protection of the Confederation, and he frequently called upon the Commissioners for aid. The Long Island tribes also had occasions to request the intercession of the colonial union, while the Pequot remnant preferred Puritan to Indian supervision. Only the Narragansetts and Niantics showed resentment of Puritan authority. The Commissioners certainly did not relish their frequent coercions of these two tribes, but in the absence of a plausible alternative, the Puritans did not evade what they believed to be their duty.

CHAPTER VII

Puritan Policy:
Laws and Litigation, 1620-1675

AS LONG as Indian tribes and English colonies shared the confines of New England, neither could live in complete isolation. The English population of the five colonies south of the Merrimac jumped rapidly from 35,000 in 1638 to 45,000 a decade later, and may have reached 75,000 before King Philip staged his desperate uprising in 1675. The Indian population, down to perhaps 10,000 after the epidemics of the early thirties, may have increased slightly during the same period.[1] It is not surprising, then, that contacts between natives and New Englanders proliferated and grew increasingly complex as time passed. The fur trade, land transactions, law suits, and missionary affairs all helped to narrow the gap between the world of the natives and that of the New England Puritans. Most of these interracial contacts did not come under the purview of the Commissioners of the United Colonies; their tasks were primarily those of maintaining peace and promoting certain intercolonial projects. The bulk of the relationships between Indians and colonists involved neither war nor the attention of more than one colony and were therefore regulated by the individual Puritan governments.

The five New England colonies showed considerable consistency in their management of internal Indian affairs. Each evolved policies for settling boundary disputes, purchasing land, resolving individual acts of trespass or assault, and each devised means to prevent the occurrence of episodes that might result in reprisals or open warfare. Within a few years of its founding, each colony succeeded in creating an orderly and just system for the control of interracial affairs. Not that every plaintiff and every defendant was perfectly satisfied — no system of jurisprudence has ever achieved that distinction. But there is good reason to believe that Indians received substantial justice in specific court cases. The entire system, however, served the interests of the Puritans rather than the natives.

*   *   *

As might be expected, the Puritan approached matters of law and litigation with certain ingrained premises. Some of these appear rather presumptuous in the perspective of the twentieth century, but they were part and parcel of the seventeenth century European mind. In the first place, the Puritan assumed that wherever practicable, Puritan laws, based on the word of God and English experience, should prevail over un-Christian and uncivilized native customs. Second, the Puritan believed that he bore the burden of responsibility for administering the law: rarely did he permit the Indian to serve as anything but plaintiff, defendant, or witness, and he rarely if ever consulted the native when drafting laws. Finally, as has already been seen, the Puritan took it for granted that he, as agent of the mother country, had jurisdiction over all of the people within his colony's patent. The King claimed the whole of New England, and a good Englishman — Puritan or otherwise — did not question the basic justice of this. While the Puritan did not choose to rely on patent rights as a basis for his ownership of the soil, he did consider the patent the foundation of his ultimate jurisdiction over the land's inhabitants.*

Fortunately for the Puritan colonies, the decade of the twenties witnessed few occasions to test the validity of these assumptions. The Pilgrims were few in number and the distance between Plymouth and the Wampanoag villages was sufficient to preclude any involvement of the Indians in Plymouth's system of jurisprudence. Massasoit proved a faithful friend and kept his followers in check. As a result, the only rules pertaining to the Indians that the Pilgrims instituted during their first decade were regulations to insure good behavior by the colonists toward the natives, and such restrictions were few and far between.[2] There was little if any litigation involving the natives; the early settlers of Plymouth lived with the Indian on almost the same basis as they did with the Dutch of New Netherland: friendly but distant and guided by diplomacy rather than by a code of laws.

Far different was the situation in Massachusetts Bay. From the moment of their founding, the Bay Colony settlements were interspersed with Indian bands and a scattering of individual native servants, laborers, and vagabonds. Accordingly, early Massachusetts laws often applied implicitly or explicitly to the natives, and litigation inevitably occurred. As early as 1630 Thomas Morton had been deported, partly for wronging the Indians, and several less notorious settlers suffered for their crimes against the natives.† Then

* See pages 109-110.
† See pages 98-99.

came the murders preceding the Pequot War, and new questions of jurisdiction and punishment arose. The solutions conformed to the premises that had underlain Puritan policy from the outset: the offending tribes were punished on the basis of Christian law and with the tacit assumption that the King's patent provided whatever legal authority was necessary. During the generation of peace that followed the Pequot War, a more systematic pattern of laws and litigation evolved.

By mid-century, three categories of Puritan jurisdiction over the Indians had become discernible. In the first class were the tribes that either asserted total independence, such as the Pequots had prior to 1638, or gave only nominal subjection to the English crown, as the Wampanoags and Narragansetts continued to do until 1675. Only when a member of one of these tribes committed a crime against a settler, or when the entire tribe was held guilty of a transgression, did Puritan justice come into play. Then the leading sachem was called to account. If he proved intransigent, he and his tribe could expect a visit from the colonial militia. Before 1643 an individual colony might take coercive action of this sort: the Massachusetts expedition against the Block Islanders and Pequots in 1636 is a noteworthy example. After the formation of the New England Confederation in 1643, the Commissioners handled most cases of this nature for dealings with tribes such as the Narragansetts, Wampanoags, Niantics, and Mohegans invariably affected all of the Puritan colonies. Thus the United Colonies sent expeditions against Pessacus in 1645 and Ninigret in 1654, as has already been shown.* But when an individual member of one of the autonomous tribes committed a crime

---

* See pages 168-170 and 175-176.

against an English colonist, the case came under the jurisdiction of the aggrieved colony. To that extent, tribes in the first category were subjected to Puritan laws and litigation. The accused Indian faced trial by a colonial court and could expect to be punished in accordance with Puritan law, but his sachem and his tribesmen need not become involved in the affair unless they chose to question the colony's jurisdiction. In that event, the Commissioners of the United Colonies would assume the burden of negotiations.

A second category of Puritan jurisdiction consisted of tribes that had clearly submitted to the authority of a particular colony, either by indicating a desire to abide by its laws or by virtue of its total subjugation. For example, several tribes submitted to the Bay Colony shortly after the Pequot War, including the Pennacook and Massachusetts tribes in 1644, while the remnant of the Pequot tribe came under Connecticut's jurisdiction at about the same time.[3] The colonial governments usually left the administration of justice in such tribes in the hands of the sachems, who were expected to enforce the pertinent colonial laws as well as such tribal regulations as did not conflict with Puritan morals and practice. This was the case in the late forties when the Massachusetts tribe was forbidden to violate the Sabbath or to blaspheme God. In passing restrictions of this sort, the General Court reasoned that the natives had voluntarily submitted to Bay Colony regulation and therefore should abide by the same basic laws as did the English settlers.[4]

The third type of Puritan jurisdiction over Indians encompassed those individual natives who had joined the white man's society, willingly or not. Indian servants, war captives held as slaves, native students at colonial schools, and the occasional craftsman or handy man who separated from his tribe and took up abode in a New England town, all fell under direct Puritan rule. For them, there was no more tribal law; they were now subject to the Puritan courts and were treated like any other residents of colonial society — or nearly so. Certain regulations — such as that prohibiting the sale of liquor to Indians — did accord them a special and inferior status.

*   *   *

THE administration of justice in cases involving Indians presented a difficult challenge to the Puritan colonies. Misunderstandings could easily spring from problems of language, of variant customs, and of the dissimilar systems of trial and punishment practiced by native and New Englander. The language barrier could be breached by skilled interpreters, and the differences in custom were partly overcome as the passage of time brought greater familiarity between settlers and Indians. So too, the strangeness of English court proceedings and punishments must have rapidly disappeared as the Indians became accustomed to the colonists' practices. But at best this took several decades and it is therefore not surprising that the Indians did not appear as jurors in colonial courts until the 1670's.

Administering justice to tribes specifically subject to the colonies posed fewer problems than might at first be supposed. For the most part, the sachems had free rein over their subjects unless they requested assistance from the colonial government. The subject tribes in Massachusetts, for example, were left to rule themselves after their submission in the 1640's. Yet the Indians repeatedly asked for closer supervision and the colony eventually implemented a system of modified autonomy. Minor disputes were settled by the local sachem or by elected officials as in the "praying towns" established for Christian natives by the Puritan missionaries.* Matters of major weight were decided by a special court composed of one English magistrate and the principal local ruler. Appeals could be taken to the Court of Assistants.[5] After 1656, the Bay Colony had a full-time Commissioner of Indian Affairs whose job it was to supervise the welfare and orderliness of the subject tribes. A similar arrangement was established in Plymouth Colony in 1665 to care for the Nauset Indians who had accepted Christianity and wished to abide by Christian law.[6]

The greatest potential for friction between the colonies and subject tribes came in the rare instances when a sachem refused to surrender to the colonial courts a tribesman wanted for trial. The colony usually won the dispute by seizing hostages until the desired suspect was delivered into its custody.[7]

Most Indians involved in Puritan court cases came from neither autonomous tribes nor subject tribes, but were unaffiliated Indians who resided within English communities. For these natives as for those in the other categories, the Puritans' administration of justice came close to modern standards of equity. The legal institutions of the colonies were open to red man and white man alike, and extralegal judgments and punishments were not permitted. As early as 1638, the Connecticut General Court ordered that "noe Commissioners or other person shall binde, imprison or restraine, correct or whipp any Indian . . . nor give them any menacing or threatning speeches," except in self-defense or upon finding a native in the act of theft or murder. Disputes were to be settled through the normal legal channels. There is no evidence that summary justice outside

---

* On the administration of the praying towns, see pages 293-295.

the courts was imposed on the Indians.[8] The records and chronicles of seventeenth century New England disclose no cases of lynch law or vigilantism between 1620 and 1675.[9] Moreover, the frequency with which Indians appear in the court cases of the Puritan colonies — as plaintiff, defendant, witness, or very occasionally as juror — gives a strong impression that the Indian found fair and impartial treatment within the Puritans' legal procedure.

Prior to the 1670's, cases involving Indians were administered exclusively by Puritan judges and juries. That the Indian was not invited to participate more fully in the Puritan legal system was probably the result not so much of a suspicion that he was basically unworthy, as a very real awareness that he was inadequately equipped to function in a strange procedure and in a strange language. But as the Indian gained experience in the white man's ways, the Puritans relaxed their restrictions on the Indian's participation and began to let him sit as juror in cases in which both principals were Indians. Rhode Island was first among the New England colonies to attempt this; in 1673 its General Assembly ordered the jury in a particular case to be composed of six colonists and six Indians, the latter to be selected by the sachems of the two litigants "provided, they appoint such Indians to serve as are amongst the English accounted as honest men." The next year the Bay Colony empaneled a mixed jury to decide the fate of an Indian accused of raping a squaw, and in 1675 Plymouth Colony did the same in the trial of the murderers of John Sassamon, a Christian Indian.[10]

From the earliest days of Puritan settlement, the New England governments accepted the testimony of natives in court. Undoubtedly some white jurors were unwilling to trust the veracity of any Indian, but this kind of bias seems not to have tainted New England justice to any appreciable extent. When prejudice against Indian testimony did threaten to interfere, the Puritan authorities were ready to combat it as best they could. For example, in 1673 the Rhode Island legislature charged its juries to give full credence to native testimony in all cases involving disputes between Indians and to "accept or refuse the evidence as it were the testimony of an Englishman." The next year Plymouth Colony made sure that testimony of Indians who did not take an oath on the Bible would nevertheless be accepted in disputes between Englishmen and Indians, for "the Indians would be greatly disadvantaged if noe Testimony should in such case be accepted but on oath." Henceforth, the Plymouth courts "shall not be strictly tyed up to such Testimonyes, on oath as the Common law requires but may therin acte and determine in a way of Chancery; vallueing Testimonies not sworne on bothsydes according to theire Judgment and Conscience." [11]

Even with the most impartial of juries and the best of interpreters, Puritan jurisprudence must have at times become incomprehensible to the natives and therefore incapable of working true justice. The New Englanders were not unaware of this problem, as a Rhode Island court demonstrated in 1670 when it turned a particularly knotty problem over to a committee "because the Indians could not understand the way of our proceedings." Puritan courts also frequently assigned one or more colonists to arbitrate minor causes, a procedure that was often applied as well to cases involving only white litigants.[12]

Despite the apparent impartiality of Puritan jurisprudence, there remains the possibility that the Indian did not always fare as well in a New England court as did his white contemporary. There are hints in the records that this may,

at times, have been true. For example, in 1674 a Massachusetts court acquitted an Indian of charges of theft but required him to pay court costs — for what reason the records do not say. Furthermore, the very necessity of some
courts to direct juries to give full credence to Indian testimony implies that not all Puritan jurors were inclined to
accept the word of a red man.[13] Finally, differences in language and differences in customs may have imposed subtle
but very real barriers between the Indian litigant and complete justice.

At the same time, it is clear that the Puritan colonies labored hard to achieve fairness for all. If at times an unconscious prejudice worked against the Indian, it was the prejudice shared by all western societies, and it appears to have
been more effectively subdued in New England than in
most other European colonies. Puritan laws — except for
the special proscriptions on guns, liquor, and other potentially dangerous items — made no distinction between red
man and white; sentences were meted out with fine impartiality; and the eventual admission of Indians to jury status
indicates that the Puritans respected the ability as well as
the interests of the natives. Only in the bitterness of King
Philip's War did the administration of justice to the Indians
run afoul of popular enmities. When that happened, the
Puritan authorities continued to strive for impartial justice,
and their failures were perhaps no greater than the failures
of the American system of justice during two World Wars.
At no time in seventeenth century New England, including
the bitter war years of 1675-1676, was accusation tanta-
mount to conviction for an Indian defendant, nor was an
Indian's suit against a colonist unlikely to succeed. Without
a reconstruction of the entire proceedings of every case it

would be impossible to know how often the Puritans' decisions were entirely equitable, and of course incomplete records preclude such a reconstruction. Yet the evidence that survives for the modern investigator speaks highly of Puritan justice.[14]

*   *   *

WHETHER it was a matter of regulating the independent tribes, the subject tribes, or the individuals who had cast their lot with the settlers, the most important type of colonial Indian laws were those aimed at preventing violence or warfare. Defense was always a major concern of the colonial governments, and they therefore acted individually, as well as through the Confederation of New England, to shield their inhabitants from Indian attack. The colonies did not assume that all Indians were treacherous; they did, however, realize that some tribes and some individual natives could not be trusted.

The Massachusetts Bay Colony had least to fear, for she had a relatively small native population, and most of it had submitted to Puritan jurisdiction soon after the Pequot War. In February 1644, Governor Winthrop recorded in his journal that "Cutshamekin, and Awawan, and Josias, Chickataubut his heir, came to the governor, and in their own name and the names of all the sachems of Watchusett, and all the Indians from Merrimac to Tecticutt [Taunton], tendered themselves to our government." Needless to say, their submission was readily accepted, though not until the chiefs had signed a covenant and acknowledged their willingness to abide by the Ten Commandments. Other Massachusetts sub-tribes followed suit. And later in 1644 Passaconaway of the Pennacooks requested that his tribe and lands come under the Bay Colony's jurisdiction. By mid-century most of the Nipmuc bands had also acknowledged Massachusetts authority.[15]

Still, the Massachusetts magistrates were alert to any possible trouble, even with subject tribes, and did not hesitate to take necessary precautions. For example, when the sagamore of Nashua died in the fall of 1654, the Bay Colony took pains to assure the accession of a chief of its liking. One of the candidates was "a very debaust, drunken fellow, and no friend to the English"; the other was friendly and had leanings toward Christianity. Massachusetts dispatched Increase Nowell and John Eliot to Nashua to insure that the tribe chose rightly, though the envoys were admonished not to use compulsion.[16]

The newer colonies had to make more positive efforts to protect themselves from assault. In 1638 Connecticut, still smarting from the massacres of the Pequot War, required that any company of Indians settling near an English community must identify its sachem to the colonial authorities; he was then held responsible for the actions of all his tribesmen. This rule was incorporated in the colony's code of laws of 1650. In 1660 the River Colony forbade natives to settle within one quarter-mile of any English town.[17] The other frontier colonies made similar restrictions on Indian habitation. They also followed the lead of the earlier colonies in forbidding the sale of firearms, ammunition, horses, and boats to the Indians,[18] though the frequency with which penalties for infractions were issued shows that these rules were often honored in the breach.[19] In 1647 Rhode Island took even more positive steps to maintain the colony's military supremacy. The laws of Providence jurisdiction ordered every male settler from seven to seventy years of age, with some exceptions, to become proficient with bow and arrow, "forasmuch as we are cast among the Archers, and know not how soone we may be deprived of Powder and Shott, without which our guns will advantage us nothing." Other regulations made it mandatory for residents to have military weapons in working order at all times.[20]

The maintenance of military supremacy was but part of the job of preserving peace and security in New England. It was equally important to promote an atmosphere of friendship and equity. In putting the purchase of Indian lands under government supervision, in placing limitations on trade with the natives, in providing adequate legal machinery for deciding disputes between Indians and whites, each colony was aiming at the perpetuation of good will and tranquillity. Of like purpose, of course, were the laws denying alcohol and firearms to the natives. Prosecutions for trading in guns, ammunition, and liquor were extremely common, but actions of this kind were ordinarily initiated by the government against colonists rather than against Indians. The laws prohibited sale, not purchase, and so the Indian rarely became involved in the litigation resulting from the laws designed to keep him sober and unarmed. A potential exception appeared in Connecticut's law of May 1675 which decreed that a drunk Indian "shall as a penalty for his offence therein worke twelve days with the person that complains and proves his drunkenness," with one-half of the labor going to benefit the community, the other half to the informer (a standard division of fines and services in Puritan New England). This was a drastic solution to the chronic problem of Indian inebriation, but since the burden of proof lay with the accuser, sober Indians had nothing to fear from the regulation so long as Puritan jurisprudence retained its integrity.[21] Until 1675 it usually did.

* * *

DESPITE all the preventive measures of the Puritan government, litigation between colonists and Indians, and occasionally between two or more Indians, was frequent. Fortunately for good relations among natives and New Englanders, the most commonly recorded disputes in which Indians became involved were nothing more serious than the damaging of Indian fields and crops by stray animals belonging to the settlers. Cases of this kind reflected no animosity on either side but did indicate the mundane problems of frontier society, in which animals were often untended and fencing was always inadequate. The colonist who owned the livestock could expect to be fined for damage done by his strays, and the Indians usually received full satisfaction. To prevent recurrence the Englishmen were warned to provide better control over their kine, while the Indians were advised to fence their fields.[22] There are few recorded instances of Indian animals injuring English property; not many natives kept domesticated animals.

Far more grim, and fortunately far more rare, were the cases of malicious property damage. Arson, for example, was a particularly serious crime, and there are some recorded trials in which Indians were found guilty of firing Englishmen's houses.[23] Here again, the colonies drafted preventive legislation. Most Puritan governments passed laws forbidding Indians to "hanker about" English homes, especially on the Sabbath when most Puritans would be at the meeting house.[24]

Regulations against Indian loitering were also aimed at reducing the opportunities for theft. That the Indian was more frequently the trespasser than the victim reflected no depravity in his character but rather the disparity between

MASSASOIT

SQUANTO

ALGONQUIAN CRAFTSMEN

ALGONQUIAN WIGWAMS

HARVARD'S INDIAN COLLEGE
(oblong building at lower left)

FORT SAYBROOK

PLYMOUTH FORT AND MEETINGHOUSE

WILLIAM PYNCHON

EDWARD WINSLOW

JOHN ENDICOTT

JOHN UNDERHILL

JOHN ELIOT

WUNAUNCHEMOOKAONK NASHPE

MATTHEVV.

CHAP. I.

Ppometuongane *a* book Jesus Christ, wunnaumonuh David, wunnaumonuh Abraham.

2 *b* Abraham wunnaumonieu Isaakoh, kah *c* Isaak wunnaumonieu Jakobuh, kah *d* Jakob wunnaumonieu Judasoh, kah weematoh.

3 Kah *e* Judas wunnaumonieu Pharesoh kah Zarahoh wutch Tamarhut, kah *f* Phares wunnaumonieu Ezromoh, kah Ezrom wunnaumonieu Aramoh.

4 Kah Aram wunnaumonieu Aminadaboh, kah Aminadab wunnaumonieu Naaßonoh, kah Naaßon wunnaumonieu Salmonoh.

5 Kah Salmon wunnaumonieu Boazoh wutch Rachab, kah Boaz wunnaumonieu Obeduh wutch Ruth, kah Obed wunnaumonieu Jeßeoh.

6 Kah *g* Jeße wunnaumonieu David ketaßootoh, kah *b* David ketaßoot wunnaumonieu Solomonoh wutch ummittamwußuh Uriah.

7 Kah *i* Solomon wunnaumonieu Rehoboamoh, kah Rehoboam wunnaumonieu Abiahoh, kah Abia wunnaumonieu Asahoh.

8 Kah Asa wunnaumonieu Josaphatoh, kah Josaphat wunnaumonieu Joramoh, kah Joram wunnaumonieu Oziasoh.

9 Kah Ozias wunnaumonieu Jothamoh, kah Jotham wunnaumonieu Achazoh, kah Achaz wunnaumonieu Ezekiasoh.

10 Kah *k* Ezekias wunnaumonieu Manaßes, kah Manaßes wunnaumonieu Ammonoh, kah Ammon wunnaumonieu Josiasoh.

11 Kah Josias wunnaumonieu Jechoniasoh, kah wematoh, ut papaume na uttooche maßinneohteamuk ut Babylon.

12 Kah mahche mißinneohteahettit ut Babylon, *l* Jechonias wunnaumonieu Sa'athieloh, kah Salathiel wunnaumonieu Zorobabeloh.

13 Kah Zorobabel wunnaumonieu Abiudoh, kah Abiud wunnaumonieu Eliakimoh, kah Eliakim wunnaumonieu Azoroh.

14 Kah Azor wunnaumonieu Sadokoh, kah Sadok wunnaumonieu Achimoh, kah Achim wunnaumonieu Eliudoh.

15 Kah Eliud wunnaumonieu Eleazaroh,

kah Eleazar wunnaumonieu Matthanoh, kah Matthan wunnaumonieu Jakoboh.

16 Kah Jakob wunnaumonieu Josephoh, weßukeh Mary noh mo wachegit Jeiue uttiyeuoh ahennit Christ.

17 Nemehkuh wame pometeongash wutch Abrahamut onk yean Davidut, nabo yauwudt pometeongash; neit wutch Davidut onk yean ummißinohkonauh ut Babylon, nabo yauwudt pometeongash: neit wutch ummißinohkonauh ut Babylon ne pajeh uppeyonat Jesus Christ, nabo yauwudt pometeongash.

18 Kah Jesus Christ *m* wunneetuonk yeu mo, nagum okaßoh Maryhoh kah Joseph quoßhodnettit (aßquam naneeßinhettikup) mißkauau wutche keteauonat nashpe Nathauanittooh.   *m* Luke 1.27.

19 Neit weßukeh Josephuh wunnomwaenuqoh, matta mo wuttenantamooun wutayimauoh mußißewautut, unnantam kemeu nuppogken yeuoh.

20 Webe natwontog yeußhog kußeh wutangelsumoh Lord wunneeihtunkquoh ut unnukquomuonganit, noowau, Joseph ken wußnaumonuh David, ahque wabeßiß nemunon Mary kummittamwoß, newtuche uttiyeuwoh wachegit, ne nashpe wunneetupanatamwe Naßhauanittoour.

21 Kah woh neechau wußaumon woh kuttißowen *n* Jesus, newtutche woh wadchanau ummißinninnumoh wutch ummatcheßeonganoowout.   *n* Luke 1.31.

22 Wame yeush *n* nihyeupash ne woh *n* nih toh anoowop Lord nashpeu manittoowompuh noowau.

23 *o* Kußeh peenomp piß wonpequau, kah piß neechau wannaumonuh, kah piß wuttißowenuoh Emanuel, yeu nauwuttamun, God kowetomukqun.   *o* Isaiah 7.14.

24 Neit Joseph omohket wutch koußnat, wutußen uttoh anukqut wutangelsumoh Lord, kah neemunau ummittamwußoh.

25 Kah matta oowaheuh ne pajeh wunneechanat mohtompineginitcheh wunnaumonuh, kah wuttißowenuh Jesus.

CHAP. II.

JESUS *a* neekit ut Bethlem ut Judea ukkeßukkodtumut Herod Sontим, kußeh waantamwaenaog wamohettit wutchepwoeiyeu Jerusalemwaut.   *a* Luke 2.6.

A 2   2 No-

A PAGE FROM ELIOT'S INDIAN BIBLE

CHIEF NINIGRET

his sparse possessions and the wealth of the white man. Some Indians were bound to succumb to temptation, and no New England colony went for more than a few months at a time without some of its residents charging theft against neighboring Indians. The stealing of pigs and other livestock was common, while money, utensils, and firearms also were occasionally pilfered.[25] At times theft seemed epidemic, and harsh measures were taken to root it out. Plymouth arrested one "Notoriouse theife," who had broken jail and was lurking dangerously about the colony, and sold him to Barbadoes "to satisfy his debts and to free the collonie from soe ill a member." In 1659 Rhode Island decided that Indians convicted of theft involving more than twenty shillings who could not make restitution might be sold into slavery "to any forraigne country of the English subjects." The plaintiff was to be reimbursed from the sale price.[26] Here was a drastic departure from the usual code of punishments. Fortunately it was very rarely employed, for the colonists viewed sale out of the country as only one step short of capital punishment.

Although the white man had less reason to steal the meager belongings of the Indian, there were a few occasions when some settler made off with native property and paid the usual penalty for his act. Massachusetts Bay, it will be recalled, had frequently punished colonists in the early thirties for stealing from the Indians.* [27]

One form of theft by the Indians presented unusual difficulty. Natives were frequently accused of slaughtering swine and cattle belonging to settlers and then selling the meat to the English. One wily red man, in fact, sold Harvard's President Dunster a stolen cow under the guise of

---

* See page 99.

moose meat. Sometimes the Indians may have accidentally caught domestic animals in traps set for wild game; at other times the evidence points to intentional seizure of livestock for resale purposes.[28] Rhode Island and Massachusetts attempted to cope with this form of theft by prohibiting the Indians in their jurisdictions from cutting ear markings — a common practice among the colonists — on their own hogs. Pigs offered for sale by the Indians were then required to have whole and unmarked ears as proof that they were not pilfered swine.[29]

More serious, if less common, than disputes over property damage were instances of individual assault and threats of violence. Cases involving assault by a white man upon an Indian appear from time to time in the records of each colony and usually resulted in a stiff punishment for the aggressor. For example, on a number of occasions Plymouth Colony levied a fine against a citizen for striking a native. In 1655 the Pilgrim magistrates also fined and stocked a colonist for attempting to collect a debt from an Indian by invading the Indian's house and seizing a native child and some goods as collateral. In a 1667 case Massachusetts extended its protection of Indians even to the deceased: for the "barbarous and inhuman act" of digging up the skull of a sagamore and carrying it about on a pole, a Bay Colony man was fined, stocked, imprisoned, and required to repair the grave and rebuild its stone marker.[30]

Indians found guilty of abusing settlers were also punished according to law with sentences the equivalent of or milder than those meted out to Englishmen found guilty of similar crimes. The usual punishment was a fine, whipping, or both, though in a case of assault that came before the Plymouth Court in which an Indian had threatened two

English women with a knife and twisted the neck of one victim, the criminal was branded on the shoulder.[31]

Of utmost seriousness for Indian-white relations were the few instances of murder. Here a miscarriage of justice, whether it involved the punishment of an innocent Indian or the acquittal of a white assassin, could have frightening results, and the courts did their best to be strict but impartial. As early as 1638 Plymouth Colony executed three of its residents for the murder of an Indian youth. Arthur Peach, a veteran of the Pequot War, and three renegade servants were the culprits. En route to New Netherland, where Peach's companions hoped to be free of their indentures, they stabbed a young Narragansett man, robbed him of his furs and wampum, and left him for dead near the path from Plymouth to Providence. There he was found, still alive, by some Indian travelers; before he died Roger Williams and others heard his testimony. The assassins were soon taken into custody by the Narragansetts, held at Rhode Island temporarily, and then turned over to the Plymouth authorities for trial. One escaped to northern Maine, but confronted with Williams's testimony the remaining three prisoners confessed their guilt and were sentenced to death. Despite objections from "some of the rude and ignorante sorte," Peach and his two accomplices were hanged in Plymouth in the presence of several Narragansetts, "which," observed Governor Bradford, "gave them and all the countrie good satisfaction." [32]

Only a few other reports of white men murdering Indians can be founds in the sources, and at least one other trial of white suspects led to their conviction and execution.*

---

* See pages 318-319.

Some crimes may, of course, have been concealed so thoroughly that word of them never reached the colonial officials, but in Puritan New England such secrecy was quite unlikely.

Stern impartiality also required capital punishment for Indians found guilty of killing colonists. Fortunately there were only a few cases of this kind before 1675. Prior to the Pequot War, the only colonists known to have lost their lives to Indian assailants in the settled areas of New England were those involved in the Wessagusett affair in 1623 and those associated with the preliminaries of the war of 1637. The total of English victims between 1620 and 1638 may have been as high as fifty, but all of the killings were committed by hostile tribes and no trials were held; military vengeance rather than legal action was the Puritan response. The force of that vengeance was felt by Chief Witawamet and his followers in 1623, the Block Islanders in 1636, and the Pequots in 1637.

Records for the period from 1638 to 1675 reveal that there were acquitals as well as convictions in cases where Indians stood accused of the murder of settlers.[33] There is some evidence of other killings, particularly along the Maine coast where the long arm of Puritan law seldom reached, which did not result in court actions.[34] Such episodes, however, did not directly involve the Puritan governments, for not until the latter part of the seventeenth century did the Massachusetts colony's authority extend to the northern section of New England.

In the colonies that were under Puritan jurisdiction, however, the courts carefully followed the time-honored procedures of Old England, occasionally modified by Biblical precedents. Juries insisted on adequate evidence and normal legal procedure whether the accused was native or New Englander.

*   *   *

THE most remarkable evidence of Puritan impartiality is to be found in an episode connected with the Pequot War. The massacre of nine settlers, including women and children, at Wethersfield, Connecticut, in 1637 had been the final atrocity before the River Colony's declaration of war. It later became known that the local Wongunk tribe, led by Chief Sequin, had invited the Pequots to make the raid and had thereby actively conspired against the English. Sequin and his tribe were guilty not only of abetting the enemy at the cost of many English lives, but they had violated their covenant with the Wethersfield settlers in doing so.[35] It would not have been surprising had Sequin and the Wongunks felt the full force of Puritan revenge when the truth became known. The logic of the situation would seem to demand that the Wongunks share the fate of the Pequots.

Had the Wethersfield settlers been free to act as they saw fit, Sequin and his followers would probably have suffered for their perfidy. But revenge could not be taken without the approval of the General Court, and when the issue was brought before it in the spring of 1638 the Wongunk sachem received a "full debate and hearinge." Sequin defended himself by claiming that he had acted against the English only after they had wronged him. He professed to have sold land to the original settlers in 1635 on the understanding that he and his tribesmen might remain in the area and receive protection from the English against the Pequots, for the Wongunks, like the other River tribes, had long resented the harsh hegemony of Sassacus and his followers. Unfortunately for Sequin, however, the settlers at Wethersfield either did not understand the terms of the purchase or chose to ignore them. When Sequin set up a wigwam at Wethersfield early in 1637, he was driven out by force.[36] In fury the Wongunk chief had turned to his former enemies, the Pequots, for assistance in redressing his grievance.

His argument threw the Connecticut magistrates into a quandary. In denying Sequin the right to settle within the bounds of Wethersfield, the settlers had been unjust. In return the Wongunk sachem had caused the death of nine of the English, a heavy destruction of property, and untold human suffering on the part of the two captives and the surviving families. Could such a violent crime be justified by the earlier and relatively milder English wrong? Uncertain themselves, the leaders of the River Colony wrote to Massachusetts for advice.

Whatever one may think of Puritan intolerance in matters of religious dissent, there is good reason to applaud the Bay Colony's restrained approach to this problem. Governor Winthrop called in "such magistrates and elders as could meet on the sudden" and presented the question to them. They answered that Sequin, having been the recipient of the first wrong, had been justified in retaliating "either by force or fraud." The magnitude of his revenge was irrelevant, they pointed out, for had he returned damages one-hundredfold he would have been acting in accordance with the "law of nations" and would therefore have been morally and legally right. Nor had he forfeited that right by not waiting for a peaceful adjustment of his complaint; he had objected to the injury done him and his pleas had been ignored. Sequin had observed his side of the covenant;

the Wethersfield English had violated theirs and must accept the ensuing horrors.[37]

This opinion of the Bay Colony spokesmen did not bind Connecticut. But at a meeting of the General Court on April 5, 1638, the Connecticut magistrates announced themselves in full agreement with their neighbors' advice. After a thorough hearing of the evidence, the Court decreed that while each party had inflicted injuries on the other, "yet because . . . the first breach was on the English parte, All former wronges whatsoever are remitted on both sides and the said Soheage [Sequin] is againe received in Amytie to the saide English." [38] Connecticut and Massachusetts thus joined Plymouth in giving dramatic demonstration that Puritan justice was disinterested and binding upon all.

*   *   *

MOST of the court cases involving crimes between natives and New Englanders saw the Indian as defendant. One type of offense, however, more often found colonists than Indians at fault: those involving illicit sexual relations. From the outset of Puritan settlement, there were always some colonists who failed to live up to the rigid moral code of New England, and each colony had to adjudicate occasional charges of seduction, attempted seduction, and rape. Testimony varies as to the extent of promiscuity among Indian women; in any event there seem to have been many a New Englander who tried to find out for himself. If held guilty, the culprit could expect to be whipped, stocked, imprisoned, or a combination of these — the same penalties that applied to sexual offenses against any woman, English or Indian.[39] There were very few cases in which New

England women were accused of encouraging sexual relations with Indian men, although in 1639 a Duxbury woman was convicted of sexual intercourse with an Indian. She was whipped through town at cart tail and required henceforth to wear a badge of shame on her left sleeve. The Indian was also to be "well whipt," but suffered no further penalty as the Englishwoman was believed to have been the enticer.[40]

There are only a few scattered cases in which Indian males were charged with making advances on white women, and as the law recognized no racial distinctions, the penalties were the same as those imposed upon white perpetrators. In fact, even the white victim of an Indian advance did not always escape punishment: a servant girl who received "some abusive and filthy carriages" from an Indian was herself lashed for concealing the fact from the proper authorities until it reached their ears through common gossip.[41] At times, Puritan courts also passed judgment in cases of illegal sexual relations between two Indians subject to colonial authority.[42]

*   *   *

In addition to the punishments inflicted on English and Indian prisoners alike, the New England colonies added a few penalties specifically for natives. These were usually modifications of ordinary Puritan practices, adapted to the circumstances of the frontier and to the nature of Indian society. Banishment and "warning out," for instance, were frequently employed against whites to rid the colony of undesirables.[43] (Except in the case of Quakers, such methods usually accomplished their design with a minimum of harshness.) But similar sentences would have had little effect on red men. Indians were difficult for Englishmen to identify, and they could easily be concealed by other Indians. Therefore the practice of selling Indians into slavery in the West Indies emerged as a drastic but effective method of eliminating chronic troublemakers. Yet aside from captives taken in the wars of 1637 and 1675-1676, the Puritan colonies sentenced very few natives to West Indian servitude.[44] The principal peacetime reason for which sale abroad might be authorized was failure to pay an unusually large fine or debt.[45]

The Puritan colonies also sentenced some Indians to a status often referred to — both then and now — as slavery, but which in fact bore little resemblance to slavery in the usual sense of the word. In practice, domestic slavery for Indians seems to have followed the pattern of long-term involuntary indentured servitude for whites; it was rarely if ever for life and it was not a hereditary status. And there is no evidence that Indian servants fared worse than their white counterparts. For example debtors — either white or Indian — were often required to serve their creditors until the obligation was satisfied, during which time the master had to provide food, shelter, clothing, and education.[46] During such servitude the servant had full rights of redress in the colonial courts.

War captives, usually youths or women, constituted the bulk of the Indians sentenced to domestic slavery. But like those sentenced for debt or other crimes, the captives taken in war were treated as servants and were eventually released. Few, in fact, remained in bondage for very long. The Pequot captives sent to Boston by Israel Stoughton in the summer of 1637 proved so intractable that several were branded on the shoulder for running away. Of the women and girls sent to Connecticut and Massachusetts after the Swamp Fight, Captain Mason observed that "they could not endure that Yoke; few of them continuing any considerable time with their masters." (As Roger Williams had pointed out, enslavement of Indians who surrendered voluntarily only encourage them to remain enemies "or turne wild Irish themselves." [47]) In the end, most of the Pequot captives were allotted to the Mohegans and Narragansetts, not to the English colonists. Of those who were assigned to white masters, at least one became prominent — as John Eliot's first interpreter and language teacher.* [48]

* See pages 246-247.

*   *   *

PURITAN efforts at regulation of Indians under their jurisdiction did not stop at the punishment of specific crimes; there were also attempts to control Indian-white relations on a broader scale. Since one of the avowed purposes of Puritan migration had been to bring the word of God to the heathen, and since this implied — to the Puritan mind — introducing the Indian to all the benefits of English civilization, the New Englanders continued to hope that the natives would cast off all semblance of their heathen ways. Accordingly, Indians were encouraged to forsake their tribes and join in Puritan society. In 1652 the Bay Colony promised that "if any of the Indians shalbe brought to civillitie, and shall come amongst the English to inhabite in any of theire plantations, . . . such Indians shall have allottment amongst the English according to the custome of the English." [49]

Englishmen on the other hand were forbidden to forsake advanced society for the lure of primitive life. Connecticut established many penalties, including three years in a house of correction, for any who "departe from amongst us, and take up their abode with the Indeans in prophane course of life." There were, however, no laws against intermarriage;

Puritan society attempted to prevent backsliding in both religion and civilization, but it did not erect legal barriers between the races.[50] Yet Englishmen in New England, like those in Britain's other colonial possesssions, did not often intermarry with the natives. Differences of religion, culture, and education raised their own barriers, especially in the Puritan communities. Furthermore, the settlers of New England enjoyed a fairly even balance of English men and women. Thus for the New Englander, unlike the Frenchman to the north, the alternative to celibacy was not miscegenation. Of course a few Englishmen did live in Indian towns, while others fished and traded in the remote northern areas of the coast, so that some miscegenation undoubtedly took place.[51] But of legal intermarriages between natives and New Englanders before 1676 there is no record; no parallel to John Rolfe and Pocahontas brightens the New England story. Puritan habits, not Puritan laws, postponed the merger of native and New Englander until the next century.

*   *   *

If between 1620 and 1675 New England came more and more completely under Puritan rule, the reason can be traced in large part to the backgrounds of the two peoples who increasingly needed to discover formulas by which both could live in peace and security. The Indians of New England had no unified code of laws nor any common system of administering justice. The Puritans, on the other hand, brought to the New World a highly ordered society in which the concepts and practices of English law were a major ingredient; by education, religion, and morals, the settlers who came to New England were among the most highly ordered and self-disciplined of Englishmen, fitted to bear into a wilderness the ideal of systematic law, impartially applied and binding even upon its executors. The Puritan might modify his jurisprudence to suit his particular theological convictions, and he might adjust it to the realities of his new environment, but he was not going to discard a system that had grown and prospered through centuries of English experience. Fortunately for the New England colonies, most of the tribes voluntarily subjected themselves to Puritan rule; only those with exceptional solidarity and strong leadership chose to remain aloof. Even then, some of the most important sachems, such as Uncas and Massasoit, willingly offered to obey the sanctions of colonial authority, although the physical isolation of their tribes made everyday observance of Puritan regulations impractical.

By 1675, when the war against King Philip disrupted the tranquillity of New England, the Puritan colonies and their Indian neighbors had enjoyed for over half a century an equitable system of laws and litigation. The Indians had discovered that the Puritan justice was often strict but rarely harsh, sometimes presumptuous but seldom partial. As much as any other feature of seventeenth century New England, a mutual recognition of Puritan jurisprudence helped keep Indian tribes and English colonies on a friendly footing.

CHAPTER VIII

Commercial Relations, 1620-1675

THE New England Puritans were not primarily motivated by economic considerations, but they soon found that commerce with the natives would play an important role in their adjustment to the New World. During the first year of each colony's existence, food supplies from the Indians were often the margin between survival and starvation; later years saw commercial relations grow into an important element in the prosperity of both the New England Englishmen and the New England Indians. Each coveted the other's products, and a fair exchange soon evolved. This exchange remained a significant aspect of the Puritans' relations with the Indians throughout the seventeenth century.

Before the coming of the Puritans, trade patterns had been established in New England that would reappear after 1620.* The voyages of Bartholomew Gosnold in 1602, Martin Pring in 1603, and George Waymouth in 1605 were predominantly mercantile in character. So, too, was the brief settlement at Sagadahoc in 1607-1608. Its demise had been followed by various expeditions sponsored by Ferdi-

---

* See Chapter I.

nando Gorges and certain London merchants, again seeking immediate commercial gain or exploring the New World for signs of future profit. At the same time, French explorers were establishing a lucrative trade with the tribes of northern New England and the interior of the St. Lawrence Valley.[1] The commercial value of these early contacts was undoubtedly small. More important were the implications for later settlement, for the experiences of the first two decades of the seventeenth century gave promise of a flourishing trade between natives and New Englanders.

The first European explorers of New England encountered inhabitants to whom at least some of the complexities of trade were not new. Prior to the arrival of the white man, intertribal trading had been practiced by most Indian nations of the northeast woodlands, although it was naturally limited by the absence of extensive native crafts. Yet some specialization of production did exist among Algonquians and their neighbors, and it formed the basis of a moderately active, if limited, pattern of commercial exchange between the tribes. The Indians of the northeast frequently bartered skins, seafood, meat, corn, and copper. When the white man offered new and, to the natives, highly desirable commodities, the red man was only too willing to revise his existing network of trade relations to accommodate the newcomers. Before long the Indian had largely discarded his old patterns. New commercial systems centering on trade with the colonists emerged, which in some instances created bitter intertribal rivalries[2] — an unexpected and unwanted byproduct of the new prosperity.

*   *   *

THE Pilgrims had been on New England soil for several years before they developed a highly lucrative trade with the natives. In the interval, however, scattered commerce, especially in food, proved a godsend in Plymouth's struggle for survival. From the earliest days of the colony the set- tlers bartered for corn, but in exchange they could offer only a few tools, miscellaneous trinkets, and beads. Then in the mid-1620's, Plymouth began to enjoy a more profitable exchange with the Indians. The colony was becoming self- sufficient in agriculture, and there was even a surplus of corn with which to launch a fur trade with the non- agricultural tribes to the north. The Pilgrims also imported from England increasing quantities of cloth and tools for barter with the natives of southern New England.* [3]

A major opportunity for Plymouth came in 1627. In that year the Secretary of New Netherland, Isaac de Rasieres, visited the Pilgrims and introduced them to the intricacies of Indian bead money, wampum.[4] For some years the Pil- grims had been plying the northern New England coast in search of furs for which they had offered corn and trinkets, without particular success. Now, armed with wampum, and backed by the colony's increasingly productive economy, Plymouth traders could expand their operations. The northern tribes rapidly learned to appreciate the strange new currency, and within the next few years the agents of Plymouth Colony lured the bulk of the northern coastal trade away from the fishermen and individual traders who had dominated commercial activity in this area for decades. In 1628 the Council for New England granted to the Pil- grims a patent for a sizable portion of the coast around the Kennebec River. Soon Plymouth men were carrying on an active trade with the Indians at two truck-houses, one on the Kennebec and the other on the Penobscot.[5]

---

* See Chapter III.

Aware now of the profits to be gained by exchanging Indian money for animal skins, the Pilgrims expanded their commercial operations into other areas of New England. In 1632 they added a truck-house near Sowamet (Barrington, Rhode Island) that, combined with an earlier post at Aptucxet (Manomet), secured for the Pilgrims dominance of the fur trade in the Buzzards Bay and Narragansett Bay areas. Two more years found them erecting a prefabricated trading house at Matianuck (Windsor) on the Connecticut River. Commercial relations with the Indians earned the Plymouth colony over £10,000 in the period from 1631 to 1638.[6] So complete was the Pilgrims' control of the fur trade that in 1634 Governor Winthrop of Massachusetts Bay complained that Plymouth had "engrossed all the Cheif places of trade in N:E:" [7]

Yet Plymouth's prosperous fur trade was to prove short-lived. The Maine posts fell to the French in 1633, migrations from Massachusetts rapidly changed the Connecticut Valley from a wilderness to a center of population by 1638, and the arrival of Roger Williams and his disciples at Providence brought an end to Plymouth's trade in Narragansett Bay. Henceforth, commerce with the Indians would play a negligible role in Plymouth's economy. Yet the colony owed its financial independence to those few prosperous years of trade with the natives. In 1633, the Pilgrims finally obtained release from their indebtedness to the London adventurers; most of the remittances that had made this possible had been in the form of furs acquired from Indian hunters.[8]

While the fur trade was solving Plymouth's economic problems, it was also helping to attract settlers for a new Puritan colony. The traders who explored Massachusetts during the 1620's found the commerce in beaver so profitable that, according to Edward Johnson, they made "their abode in these parts, whom this Army of Christ at their comming over found as fit helps to further their designe in planting the Churches of Christ."[9] By the time Endicott took command of the bay area in 1628, a small but profitable commerce with the Indians had been established within the New England Company's patent. Full development of the area's economic potential awaited only the influx of prosperous colonists.

From their first arrival in 1628, the Puritans of Massachusetts Bay engaged in the fur trade and to a lesser extent in other commercial dealings with the natives. Since food supplies could be readily purchased from New Plymouth, Bay Colony merchants largely bypassed the food-buying stage that the Separatist community to the south had experienced, and they concentrated instead on the more lucrative trade in furs. Several men, among whom John Winthrop, Jr., and William Pynchon were particularly prominent, immediately began importing trading goods and shipping beaver back to the mother country.[10]

Returns of the first few years of the Bay Colony's fur trade did fall below those of the Dutch and the Pilgrims, but the trade in eastern Massachusetts had sizable if not limitless potential. A friendly northern tribe, the Pennacooks, were eager for trade and had the lakes area of New Hampshire at their disposal. Several towns — such as Concord, Lancaster, Chelmsford — that were once on the frontier of the Bay Colony were established mainly because they gave access to the rivers of the interior and so to the furs that abounded inland. Simon Willard, who by the midthirties had become the dominant figure in the region, was instrumental in founding Concord in 1634 and Chelmsford fifteen years later; in both instances he was motivated largely by commercial interests. Lancaster's founder was John Prescott, who built a trading post there in 1645.[11]

As the sources of beaver receded into the interior, New England fur merchants had to venture farther and farther from the coast. The most obvious interior point for control of the furs of central Massachusetts was on the Connecticut River north of the infant settlements of Connecticut Colony. As early as 1631 the River Indians had invited Puritan settlement in their territory; although the Massachusetts authorities had declined the offer they had retained an interest in the commercial aspects of the area. In 1636 William Pynchon — one of the rare Puritans of the first generation who followed with almost equal devotion the ways of theology, politics, and business — founded his trading empire in the central Connecticut Valley. His post at Springfield was near the juncture of the overland Connecticut Path and the Connecticut River, which put him in close touch with the source of trading supplies, the good beaver grounds of the Valley, and the friendly Agawam and Woronoco bands. For more than a decade he reaped handsome profits. Then after William Pynchon's return to England in 1652, his son John continued the family's venture. The surviving records, though incomplete, reveal that the younger Pynchon shipped nearly 25,000 pounds of beaver plus considerable quantities of mink, otter, and other skins to England in the period from 1652 to 1674. And as in eastern Massachusetts, fur traders played key roles in founding frontier towns. Northampton (1654), Hadley (1659), and Deerfield (1669) were established partly as offshoots or rivals of Springfield.[12]

In the meantime, the newer New England colonies actively pursued commercial opportunities with their neighboring tribes, although Connecticut, New Haven, and

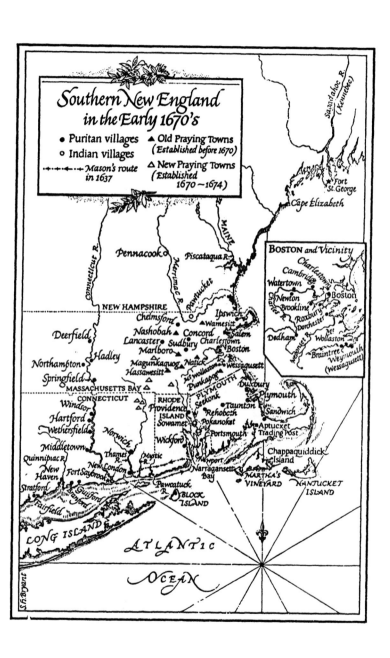

Southern New England in the Early 1670's

- ● Puritan villages
- ○ Indian villages
- ▲ Old Praying Towns (Established before 1670)
- △ New Praying Towns (Established 1670~1674)

+–+–+–+–+ Mason's route in 1637

Sandahoc R. (Kennebec)

Fort St. George

Cape Elizabeth

MAINE

Pennacook ○

Piscataqua R.

Merrimac R.

Pautucket

NEW HAMPSHIRE

Chelmsford ▲Wamesitt

Deerfield ●

Nashobah ▲ ●Concord Salem ▲
Lancaster ● Sudbury Charlestown
Marlboro ▲ ●Boston
Magunkaquog▲ ●Natick
Hassamesitt▲ ●Wessagusett
Mt.Wollaston

Northampton ●
Hadley ●

Springfield ●

MASSACHUSETTS BAY △

CONNECTICUT △ △ Punkapog

Windsor ● RHODE △Duxbury
ISLAND PLYMOUTH ●Plymouth
Hartford ● △Providence Sekonk
Wethersfield ● Rehoboth ●Taunton Sandwich
Sowams● ●Pokanoket
Middletown ● Norwich Wickford● ●Portsmouth Aptucket Trading Post

Quinnipiac R. Thames R. Mystic R. Chappaquiddick Island
New Haven ● Fort Saybrook New London Narragansett Bay
Stratford ● Guilford Pawcatuck R. MARTHA'S VINEYARD NANTUCKET ISLAND
Fairfield ● BLOCK ISLAND

LONG ISLAND

Connecticut R.

Ipswich ▲

BOSTON and Vicinity

Charlestown
Cambridge
Watertown
Newton ●Boston
Brookline
Roxbury
Dorchester
Dedham● Mt.Wollaston
Braintree Weymouth (Wessagusett)

ATLANTIC

OCEAN

J.G.Bryant

Rhode Island were never to know the kind of profits enjoyed by Plymouth and Massachusetts Bay.

The lower Connecticut Valley had first been tapped by the Dutch in the early 1630's, and the Pilgrims had been close on their heels. Not far behind came the ubiquitous John Oldham — representing the interests of those who would soon establish a separate colony there — who explored and traded in the vicinity of Wethersfield as early as 1633. He was back again the next year, and in 1635 he led a small group of settlers to the site of Wethersfield. Trade with local tribes was important in the early years of the Connecticut colony as it had been in Plymouth; after the Pequot War, for instance, the depleted food supplies of the colony could be replaced only by purchasing corn from the Indians at Pocumtuck (Deerfield). But the fur trade never became a major factor in Connecticut's economy. Thomas Stanton, the younger John Winthrop (who had moved to Fort Saybrook in 1635), and others did carry on a profitable trade, but the colony as a whole suffered from the competition of the Massachusetts truck-houses further up the river and of the Dutch to the west.[13]

Much the same was true of New Haven. Founded in 1638 at a spot deemed advantageous for commerce by land as well as by sea, the colony never during the seventeenth century fulfilled the economic prospects that had been projected for it. Competition from the Dutch, a none too friendly native population, and the relative paucity of fur-bearing animals in that area made commerce with the Indians a weak foundation on which to build prosperity. While the New Haven records tell of the appointment of Thomas Gregson in 1640 as "truck master," charged with the duty of obtaining venison from the Indians, there are remarkably few other references to commercial activity with the neigh-

boring tribes.¹⁴ In an imaginative if futile attempt to remedy
the situation, the New Haven merchants established a post
on the Delaware River in 1641 on land purchased from the
Indians. But the Dutch of New Netherland speedily put an
end to this intrusion into territory in which they had the
power to back their claims, and by destroying the Puritan
outpost they in some measure squared accounts with the
New Englanders for spoiling Dutch trade on the Connecti-
cut.¹⁵

In Rhode Island, Roger Williams dominated the early
commerce with the Indians as he did everything else in the
Narragansett Bay area. His knowledge of the Narragansett
tongue and his cordial relations with Canonicus gave him an
obvious advantage over his competitors. During his first
summer of exile, Williams established a trading house at
Wickford Harbor on the western shore of Narragansett
Bay. When by 1645 his manifold interests precluded his
giving full attention to commerce, he took on a partner, one
John Wilcox. Williams finally sold out in 1651 in order to
concentrate on the public affairs of the colony. He was
then netting £100 a year from his part-time operations,
and other Rhode Islanders seem to have been doing as well
or better. Richard Smith, who purchased Williams's business, had been engaged in trade with the Indians since the
late thirties; he and his son eventually became prosperous,
partly, it seems, by selling liquor to the thirsty natives.¹⁶

*   *   *

ALTHOUGH commercial relations between the Puritans and
Indians involved a wide variety of goods, during most of
the seventeenth century furs were at the heart of the New
England economy. Beaver, of course, was the most common of the New England long-haired animals and was the

easiest to capture. A good skin, if well cleaned, brought ten shillings during the first decade and somewhat less from that time on. Also common in the New England trade were otter, raccoon (increasingly so as beaver became more scarce), fox, muskrat, and bear. A choice item was black wolf, which Thomas Morton reported as being worth forty beaver skins, partly because the Indians valued it as a token of reconciliation between sachems. Deer, moose, and other short-haired skins were often used locally, but were never in great demand as export items.[17]

Many products of European manufacture tantalized the Indian into parting with his furs. Knives, combs, scissors, hatchets, needles, awls, looking glasses, and hoes were common items of barter. Most cherished by the Indians, aside from articles forbidden by the colonial governments, was cloth for clothing and blankets. Coarse woolen material, usually sold by the ell, found a ready market. As a rule, the natives preferred either "sadd Colours" or red, and alert New Englanders imported great quantities of those hues. Before long the colonists had branched into ready-made clothing and were placing orders with their English suppliers for coats, trousers, and stockings. Many of these goods were specially made for the Indian market, suiting the native taste in design and color. Merchant orders and inventories of the times include items such as "indin briches" and "papoose coats."[18]

By 1630 bead money had become the most cherished trade commodity for it could command all others. According to William Weeden, the economic historian of New England, "Wampum was the magnet which drew the beaver out of the interior forests."[19] This curious native coinage had probably been invented by the Narragansett tribes, perhaps those who lived on Block Island and along the northern shore of Long Island, and the Narragansett Bay area continued to be the primary source of shell money.[20] Wampum consisted of small white or blue-black beads, carved from the stems of seashells. White beads were made from periwinkle shells, blue-black ones from quahog shells; since the dark part of the latter was proportionally more scarce, the dark beads had a greater value — usually double that of the white.

The observations of Roger Williams indicate that there was no government monopoly, and any native could fashion wampum at will. During the summer the Narragansetts collected shells along the beach; long winter months were spent grinding, drilling, and stringing the beads. First the Indians cut the shells into small cylinders one-quarter inch long and one-eighth inch in diameter; then the beads were smoothed, polished, and drilled lengthwise for stringing on animal gut or hemp. Strung money was known as wampumpeage, or merely peage. It was customarily arranged in lengths of one fathom (six feet), which contained anywhere from 240 to 360 individual beads, depending not only on the size of the beads but on their current worth, for "fathom" soon came to denote a specific monetary value.[21] Individual strands were then worked into bands from one to five inches wide, to be worn on the wrist, waist, or over the shoulder, for wampum had ornamental as well as commercial value to the natives. Occasionally the Indians fashioned great belts containing over ten thousand beads. But throughout the seventeenth century the main function of wampum among the New England Indians remained economic. "With this wompompeague," noted Daniel Gookin, "they pay tribute, redeeme captives, Satisfy for murders and other Wrongs, purchase peace with their potent neighbors, as occasion requires; in a word it answers all occasions with them, as gold and silver doth with us." [22]

From the 1630's on through the end of the century, wampum was widely used by the Puritan settlers as well, not only in trade with the natives but among themselves. Each of the colonies accepted it as legal tender for both public and private debts, though the governments were constantly juggling the ceiling and exchange rates. For example, in 1641 Massachusetts Bay authorized wampum as legal tender for public and private debts on amounts under ten pounds. Two years later the amount was lowered to forty shillings, and in 1649 the colony abandoned the use of wampum for taxes but retained it for private debts. During the same period the official exchange value of white beads varied in the Bay Colony from four per penny to eight per penny. Despite such fluctuations in its value, wampum continued to serve a useful function; the alternative was to use such awkward commodities as wheat, peas, pork, Indian corn or bullets, all of which were tried at various times.[23] But the Puritan colonies were always uneasy about using Indian money, for it had neither the intrinsic value of foodstuffs or manufactured items, nor the universal value — universal within western society — of precious metals. Furthermore, its supply could not be regulated like that of gold and silver. Its volume and value were determined primarily by its appeal as ornamentation to the Indian, and it would become worthless the moment he ceased to covet it.

Another disadvantage of using wampum as currency was its susceptibility to counterfeiting or to shabby manufacture. A few individuals of both races sought fast fortunes by making shoddy or ersatz beads. Some tried to dye the white beads black (a simple way to double their value), while others manufactured them from glass, stone, or inferior shells. Roger Williams claimed that the Indians themselves were seldom deceived. It was the European who invariably lost out: once having accepted counterfeit wampum he could not retrade it to any native except at a ruinous discount. In self-defense the Puritan governments soon took legislative action, while the individual colonist learned to be more discerning.

By the time the Puritan governments stepped in, there was already a considerable amount of unsatisfactory wampum in circulation. In 1648 the Commissioners of the United Colonies heeded a petition from President Dunster of Harvard and ordered the destruction of "false badd and unfinished peage." The colonies accordingly passed regulations for the integrity of Indian currency. Connecticut, for example, ordered that "no Peage, white or black, bee paid or received, but what is strung and in some measure strung sutably, and not small and great, uncomely and disorderly mixt, as formerly it hath beene." Massachusetts provided that all wampum be strung in uniform units of one, three, and twelve pence in white, and in black at values of two pence, six pence, two shillings six, and ten shillings. As black was apparently easier to counterfeit because it could be achieved merely by dyeing, and because the darker color would help to disguise the nature of the material, the colonies increasingly insisted on the use of white only, despite its lower value per unit. In some areas blue-black wampum was so distrusted that it occasionally fell below the value of white.[24]

What brought about the eventual rejection of wampum was less the minor difficulties in its use than the coming of important changes in colonial trade patterns. The boom in wampum had coincided with the boom in furs; when the latter ceased to play a central role in New England commerce, Indian money suffered a sharp decline in value. Before 1627, wampum had little if any value in northeastern New England. After de Rasieres's trip of that year, the Pilgrims introduced it along the coast of Maine with such success that Plymouth and wampum both enjoyed new prosperity in the 1630's. Soon the Massachusetts colony entered the contest; by the late 1630's Connecticut and Rhode Island were also engaged in the competition for fur, and bead money flourished. But when the European demand for fur decreased, and the colonies began to develop more stable means of prosperity, wampum ceased to have its earlier status in intracolonial exchange. An influx of silver coin from the West Indies made bead money still less significant to the settlers.[25]

Although by the early 1660's the colonies had ceased to accept wampum as legal currency, it continued to be used on a private basis well into the next century. Since wampum had no basic value to the colonists, its continued use indicated a shortage of specie in the areas where bead money persisted. Silver from the West Indies began to appear in the commercial towns of the seaboard during the forties, and after 1652 the Pine Tree coins added to the hard money in circulation. But for a time, little of either reached the frontier areas; there the Indian beads continued to serve an important economic function.[26]

*   *   *

COMMERCIAL relations with the Indian did not always prove easy for the Puritans. According to Roger Williams, one had to have "wisdome, Patience, and Faithfulnesse," for frequently the Indian was a sharp bargainer and perpetually he was suspicious of the white trader. Often he accused the trader of lying or cheating, though it is clear that his distrust was often founded on simple ignorance of the workings of an international economy. For example, when the decline in English demand for fur led to a decline in the value of wampum, the persuasive powers of Roger Williams were taxed to explain to the Indian why he must pay greater amounts of bead money for English goods. Before the coming of the white man, the native had known only the modest and predictable trade among tribes. When there suddenly occurred a vast increase in the volume and variety of commercial goods largely dependent for their value upon markets three thousand miles away, the Indian was presented with an economic complexity beyond his comprehension.[27] That the American prairie farmer faced a similar situation more than two centuries later makes it plain that the Indian is not to be scorned for his economic bewilderment.

Besides being subject to remote economic forces, Puritan commerce with the Indian was under close governmental regulation. The General Court of Massachusetts expressed the prevailing view of the New England colonies toward the regulation of business relations with the natives when it declared in 1657 that "the trade of furres with the Indians in this jurisdiction doth propperly belong to the commonwealth, and not unto particcular person[s]."[28] From the outset, each of the colonies vested monopoly rights in the legal patent holders or limited Indian trade to persons licensed by the General Court. In practice, all New England colonies did a good deal of experimentation and rarely followed any one scheme for very long. Massachusetts first established a government monopoly in a subcorporation with a guarantee of fifty per cent of the trade. This method did not prove effective, and within a few years the fur trade was opened to anyone with a license from the General Court. Such licenses, however, were issued sparingly, so that local monopolies soon emerged. Connecticut farmed out the trade until 1662 when it became open to all, while New Haven usually retained Indian trade as a government monopoly. Rhode Island, more liberal in commercial regulations as in most else, removed restrictions sooner than the other colonies; as early as 1640 Newport made trade with the Indians "free to all men." Two years earlier, however, Newport had experimented with licensed monopoly when it granted four men exclusive right to the venison trade with the Indians. Each New England colony had a system of taxing the monopolists, either on the number or weight of skins, or by charging an annual fee. Thus the entire colony was ensured a benefit from trade with the natives.[29]

In placing the Indian trade under close governmental supervision, the Puritans apparently based their policy not so much on economic principle as on the politics of good Indian relations: a recognition that freedom of trade would inevitably lead to the kinds of fraud and deception that could endanger the colonies. It was safer to deny trading privileges to all but a few men who were of known integrity. Thus the early fur traders tended to be men of good repute, and, if the records tell the true story, they rarely dealt unjustly with their native customers.

One other condition characterized commercial relations between the races. While Governor Winthrop of Massachusetts might regret the placing of restrictions on trade with the Indians, "they being a free people," the colonial governments did most emphatically prohibit the barter or sale to the Indians of certain items. Undoubtedly commerce would have been far brisker had the colonies been willing to authorize the sale of the two commodities the Indians craved most: guns and liquor. The reason for the embargo on arms is obvious. In prohibiting the sale of alcohol to the natives, the Puritans were not only looking to their own safety but attempting, apparently quite sincerely, to protect the Indian against self-degradation. As in so many matters, Puritan policy on liquor trade fused elements of practical realism and idealistic morality. Considerations of peace, self-preservation, and the law of God took precedence over the urge to profit.[30]

Regulations against trade in weapons had been issued as early as 1622. In that year the Council for New England petitioned the crown for a prohibitive decree. Its request was granted and on November 1, 1622, the Royal Seal was affixed to "A Proclamation Prohibiting Interloping and Disorderly Trading in America." In it King James chastised fishermen, stragglers, and others for the "promiscuous trading" that was undermining the peace and stability of the legitimate plantations, and forbade anyone to trade with the natives without the permission of the Council for New England, or in violation of Privy Council regulations, "upon Paine of our high Indignation." The danger, it soon became evident, lay not with the inhabitants of Plymouth and the Bay Colony — though infractions did occasionally occur even there — but with the unattached rovers who continued to enjoy the freedom of an unpoliced coast. At the request of the magistrates of Massachusetts Bay, the Crown issued a second proclamation in 1630. The new decree forbade "Interlopers, Fisher men, or Mariners or any other of Our Subjects whatsoever . . . to Sell, Barter or any wayes deliver or convey unto any of the Salvages or Natives of America . . . any Weapons or Habiliments of Warre." Governors of the colonies were to initiate action against violators.[31]

It was one thing to issue a proclamation, but something else to enforce it. Even on the well-regulated frontiers of Puritan New England it was impossible to prevent the gun runner from having his day. As early as 1628, William Bradford complained to Sir Ferdinando Gorges that the natives were beginning to shun trinkets and knives; "There is now almost nothing vendible amongst them, but such munition," lamented the Plymouth governor, and he estimated that the New England Indians already had more than sixty pieces. The situation did not improve with time. In an awkward verse history of New England that he penned in the 1650's, Bradford emphasized the extent to which the colonies were losing the monopoly on firearms. "A most desperate mischief" had developed, wrote Bradford,

> *For these fierce natives, they are now so fill'd*
> *With guns and muskets, and in them so skilled,*
> *As that they may keep the English in awe*
> *And when they please give to them the law;*
>
> .   .   .   .
>
> *Thus like madmen we put them in a way,*
> *With our own weapons us to kill and slay:*

Nor could the culprits be apprehended, for

> *The Indians are nurtured so well*
> *As, by no means, you can get them to tell,*
> *Of whom they had their guns, or such supply,*
> *Or, if they do, they will feign some false lie:*
> *So as, if their testimony you take*
> *For evidence, little of it you can make.*[32]

Lawbreakers who were caught, of course, paid a heavy price. Thomas Morton was only the first of many settlers and transients who felt the wrath of Puritan justice. Most subsequent violators were fined, usually £ 10 for the first offense, but at least one fur merchant was sent back to England and pondered his accounts in the Fleet. The only defense the English traders might offer was a desire to offset the unfair competition of the Dutch and French, neighbors frequently suspected of bartering firearms to the New England Indians. In truth, since New France and New Netherland were faced with the same potential dangers as New England, and since all three had laws against arms trade, it seems probable that whatever violations did take place were more the result of individual infraction than of official conspiracy.[33] It is also true, however, that the tighter discipline and closer societal organization of the Puritan communities made it easier for them to enforce the prohibition on arms than it was for their European neighbors. To that extent, the New England colonists may have been justified in placing the burden of blame for the weapons trade on the Dutch and French.[34]

Whenever the military situation appeared to warrant, the English colonies did relax their strictures against bartering arms, ammunition, and military accoutrements. But the Puritans seldom felt secure enough to lift the arms embargo entirely, and unfortunately the period of greatest leniency culminated in King Philip's War. In 1668 the General Court of Massachusetts granted licensed traders to sell to "any Indian or Indians, not in hostility with us or any of the English in New England" such heretofore forbidden items as powder, shot, guns, and swords. But even then the government kept a close watch: the trader must submit to the colony treasurer an account of such transactions and he must also pay a steep tax on them. The treasurer, assisted by a special committee, was directed to supervise all trading.

Connecticut and Plymouth saw with dismay what the new policy of Massachusetts Bay would do to their trade; rather than let the Bay Colony divert their channels of commerce, Plymouth in 1669 permitted the sale of powder and shot to the natives, and the River Colony responded reluctantly with easements of its own. The new regulations remained in force until King Philip's uprising persuaded the New England colonies that in this case the old rules were the best.[35]

In their regulations against the sale of alcohol to the Indians, the Puritans enjoyed moderate and very incomplete success. Strict rules and fairly alert enforcement kept the transactions in liquor within bounds; and the incidents that are commonly associated with later frontier history, in which drink sometimes drove an Indian to frenzy against the whites, are hard to discover in the records of seventeenth century New England. If occasionally a well-placed jug of cider induced its befuddled victim to part recklessly with land or furs, the evidence is sparse. But since the sale of alcohol would not create for the colonies a menace as great as would the sale of weapons, frontier merchants who balked at the arms trade were more lax in their observance of the liquor regulations. Again and again the colonies legislated against commerce in alcoholic beverages but with far from satisfactory results. The Courts were seriously concerned, not only because of the danger to the colonies — and certainly not because the officials shared the prohibitionist sentiments of later moralists — but because they were concerned for the plight of the Indians who "in theire drunkeness . . . committ much horred wickedness, as murthering theire nearest relations." Still, the colonial laws did not become stable until the mid-fifties. It was then that Plymouth, Connecticut, New Haven, and Rhode Island all made their restrictions specific. Even that did not stem the "swinish drunknes" that so disturbed the Puritan conscience. Massachusetts, for example, authorized for a few years the sale to Indians of limited quantities of wine through licensed retailers, and liquor could be administered for medicinal purposes. Such loopholes were quickly exploited.[36] Moreover, in time the Indians learned to distill their own cider, brandy, and other intoxicants.

Arms and liquor were the two major forbidden items, but horses and boats were also proscribed in the 1650's. Occasional exceptions were made here, as they had been with weapons and alcohol, for diplomatic or missionary purposes. These exceptions were granted sparsely though, for the laws on horses and boats were primarily aimed at preventing the Indians from having the means "to disturb our peace and quiet." For example, when King Philip requested permission to purchase a horse in 1665, it was denied for fear of the precedent it might set, although the colony gave him one as an outright gift. At the same time, an Indian at Barnstable who had taken up farming and resided within an English community was allowed to purchase a horse to be used in his occupation.[37]

A number of miscellaneous regulations and prohibitions were also placed upon trade with the Indians. Trading on the Sabbath was forbidden, foreigners were denied trading privileges after 1650, and transactions in Connecticut had to be conducted in boats or English trading posts rather than wigwams.[38] At various times there were also strictures against letting the natives buy on credit. This last provision was the result of bitter experience. Too often the Indian who fell into debt with a fur trader simply had no means of repaying his obligations except to hunt for more furs, though occasionally an Indian might forfeit some land in settlement of debt.[39] Too often the indebted Indian had nei-

ther this nor any other escape from his burden. The colonial laws against indebtedness therefore benefited both
white man and red, and lessened the opportunities for dis-
cord between them.

*   *   *

THE fur trade, heart of New England's commercial relations between Puritans and Indians, hit its peak in the mid-
forties, then suffered a steady decline until the outbreak of
King Philip's War. Several unrelated factors came together
to undermine the trade. A decline in the fur supply played a
part; once the beaver had been taken from the New England streams and lakes the source of supply was at an end.
The beaver, kingpin of the New England trade, was an animal of low fertility, and the New Englanders were so
hemmed in by physical and political geography that they
could not probe the interior of the continent for new supplies. Needless to say, the beaver of New England did not
disappear suddenly or completely, as John Pynchon's account books make abundantly clear, but their number fell
steadily. Moreover, when the English civil war of the
1640's temporarily dampened commercial relations with the
mother country, New England merchants increasingly
turned to the West Indian trade, where there was no
market for furs, and to fishing.[40]

The decline of the fur trade meant in large part the decline of the Indian trade. First Plymouth, then Rhode Island, and finally the Bay Colony, saw their commerce with
the Indians dwindle down to a shadow of its 1640 dimen-
sions. The Puritans, too, contributed to the trend; through
an intelligent self-interest not unmingled with the Puritan
ethic, they had imposed costly restraints on themselves and
had refused to exploit the most enticing prospects for quick

profit. By 1647 Governor Winthrop complained that the New England restrictions on weapons were the "occasion whereof the greatest part of the beaver trade was drawn to the French and Dutch." And Roger Williams, in some respects the most thorough-going Puritan of them all, insisted on supplying the Indians only with goods that tended to civilize them.[41]

While it lasted the thriving commerce with the Indians had given the Puritan colonies a badly needed economic base. Of course the fur trade never proved large enough to offset the cost of incoming supplies, and New England had to suffer the unfavorable balance of trade that was typical of all the English colonies during their formative years. Most of the fur that the merchants acquired from the natives was shipped directly to England as remittance for colonial purchases. Still, the impact of Indian commerce on the New England colonies was considerable. Not only did the traffic in furs prove a tonic to the infant economy of New England, but Indian trade played an important part in settling the upper Connecticut Valley. To a somewhat lesser extent it also helped settle the interior sections of the Bay area. The early traders, in keeping with the Puritan ethos, were town builders as well as merchants.[42]

The most useful by-product of commerce with the Indians was wampum. This was no mean asset to a people, accustomed to an active internal commerce, who found themselves abruptly deprived of their familiar circulating currency. Some form of money was needed to permit a ready exchange of goods within the English colonies as well as between the colonists and their Indian neighbors. It was the red man who provided the solution. But for the curious polished beads, the wheels of New England's economy would have turned at a far slower pace.

What impact commercial relations with the white man had on the Indian is harder to measure. While today's needs and standards place little value on an iron hoe or a metal knife, these were items of overwhelming significance to a native. A durable hoe or an iron plow could vastly increase the yield of his cornfields, while a metal knife or hatchet could aid him in countless ways — peaceful and otherwise. And European cloth offered comfortable clothing at far less effort than finding and curing an animal skin. By the 1670's the New England Indian was dependent upon a continuing supply of certain European commodities; his everyday life had been changed more than the white man's by their commercial relations.[43]

Of this the Puritan was largely unaware. He had enjoyed the trade in furs and other goods as long as they had brought comfortable returns, but by the time King Philip's War put a temporary stop to interracial commerce, he had found other sources of profitable trade. Further, beginning at about the time that the fur trade was passing its crest, a new relationship with the Indians began to arouse keen interest in New England. For it was in 1646 that John Eliot and his associates first carried the Gospel to the natives. From then until the holocaust of 1675-1676, missionary activities would be the most significant aspect of Indian-white relations in New England.

CHAPTER IX

Early Missionary Activity, 1620-1650

AS THE Puritan went about the business of securing his New World refuge, he could never completely forget that he was under heavy obligation to spread to the heathen the comforts of the faith. Most seventeenth century Englishmen, whether Puritan or not, ranked conversion of the natives among the major justifications for establishing American colonies; so argued such men as Richard Hakluyt, Walter Raleigh, and John Smith. To be sure, William Bradford made little mention of proselytizing as a reason for the Pilgrims' migration to America, and a few other early settlers were similarly indifferent to missionary motives. But the bulk of the New England Puritans, while weighting the task of conversion as but one among many, deemed it particularly worthy. For example, Francis Higginson, the first minister of Salem, placed Christianizing the natives second on his list of motives for immigration, and Governor Winthrop included it as one of his "Particular Considerations" — though far from the most important. "It is a scandale to our Religion that we shewe not as much zeale in seekinge the conversion of the heathen, as the Papists doe," Winthrop lamented, but he, like many of his collaborators, was at first more deeply concerned with finding

a haven for his kind of English dissenters than with bringing the Gospel to the red man.[1]

Yet throughout the early years of settlement, conversion
of the natives remained an avowed purpose of the New
Englanders. The Charter of Massachusetts charged the
governor and company to "Wynn and incite the Natives . . . [to] the onlie true God and Saviour of Man-
kinde," while the Governor's oath, drafted by the members
of the corporation, required him to "doe your best endeavor to draw on the natives of this country . . . to the
true God." Similar professions and obligations were voiced
frequently during the subsequent decades. At first glance
they do not seem to have been accompanied by comparable
achievement in missionary endeavors; in the first twenty
years of Puritan settlement the number of converts was
negligible. This was partly because the natives were reluctant to accept the white man's initial efforts, partly because
the struggles of the first settlements demanded all of the Puritan's attention. Survival in the New World environment
proved more challenging than most Englishmen had expected, and for a time it precluded missionary efforts. In the
mid-forties a correspondent of the younger John Winthrop
placed conversion of the Indians a poor seventh in his enu-
meration of the reasons why God had brought His people
to New England. That was a far cry from King Charles's
assertion in 1628 that conversion was "the principall Ende
of this plantacion." [2]

There is, then, some justification in the customary charge
that the Puritans were slow to meet the challenge of propagating the Gospel among the Indians. Some Puritans themselves eventually admitted that the early record was not impressive.[3] But in fairness to those who remained faithful to
resolves of the early years, critics of the missionary effort

should consider the obstacles that confronted the first settlers, obstacles partly inherent in their theology and partly
inherent in native society.

The Puritan's measure of conversion differed markedly
from that of the Catholic and the orthodox Anglican, his
closest competitors for the soul of the heathen. What the
Puritan asked of the Indian was not symbolic allegiance or
regular attendance at services, but full church membership,
something a majority of white New Englanders were unable to achieve. At the heart of the matter was the "conversion experience," without which no applicant — regardless
of ethnic background or social influence — could be admitted as a communicant. The experience had to be based on a
deep knowledge of the Bible and a full awareness of the
Puritan creed, and no Indian was likely to meet these standards without rigorous and prolonged effort. Neither could
he fulfill the requirements without first being able to read
the Bible. For this he must learn to read English — until
John Eliot published an Algonquian edition in 1663 — or
else find a New England clergyman who had command of
the Algonquian tongue and enough time and patience to in-
struct the native in the mysteries of Puritan theology. Such
preachers were hard to come by.

Again and again, Puritan writings condemn the Jesuit
missionaries for claiming to convert the red man merely by
sprinkling him with water and gaining his permission to
raise a cross in the native village. The Puritan was proud of
the greater task he had set for himself; at the same time he
was disturbed by its practical implications. In particular, it
became increasingly evident to the Puritan that religious
conversion must be preceded, or at least accompanied, by
social conversion. It would not be enough to have the Indian accept the tenets of the faith, he must also live in ac-

cordance with its scriptural regulations: polygamy must be rejected; fornication, blasphemy, indolence, idolatry, and immodesty must be repudiated. As early as 1633, James Hopkins wrote to Governor Winthrop from England, "If you can first civill the natives, and then bringe some of them to know god . . . you shall have cause to rejoyce." [4] The native, in short, must live like the Puritan's image of a true Christian if he was to qualify for the consolations of God's church. As a result, Puritanism presented a rigorous intellectual and moral challenge to the potential convert and demanded that he change his ancient patterns of life. That relatively few Indians were able to make so drastic an adjustment should not evoke surprise.

To the hurdles of theology and custom, Puritan church polity added still another. The New England clergyman, it is true, was entirely free from ecclesiastical supervision. Within the rather vague confines of Puritan precepts, the pastor was free, as he set out upon his career, to preach where and when he pleased. However, once he entered a covenant with a church fellowship, he was bound by an extremely restricting commitment. By written agreement, he was obligated to serve the needs of the regenerate to the virtual exclusion of all others. The elect had chosen the pastor, and the elect expected the benefit of his talents. While any Puritan minister assumed that he should endeavor to uncover other saints — as befitted a doctrine of faith — his primary obligation was always to serve the visible elect. Thus Puritan church polity by its very decentralization tended to tie the pastor to his flock and to diminish the situations that might have led some clergymen into missionary work. There were no religious orders to appoint some of their members as missionaries; there were no presbyteries to channel the needs of the many through the energies of a

few; there was no hierarchy to decree that some should sacrifice for the good of all.[5] The result was that the only
missionaries the Indians saw in seventeenth century New
England were those who stole time from their parish duties.
For example, John Eliot, the greatest of the Puritan missionaries, was pastor of the First Church of Roxbury, Massachusetts, almost all of his adult life. That he was able to
dedicate so much of his time to the natives without losing
his popularity with his white parishioners is a tribute to
Eliot's remarkable energy and character.

Finally, there was the barrier of language. From the outset, New England could boast of a few Englishmen who
were expert in the Indian dialects and of many who knew
enough Algonquian to conduct simple business transactions
and the like. But conveying a theology is difficult with the
best of communications; when confronted by the necessity
of translating all ideas into a language that had no written
form, had few positive rules of grammar, and had no words
at all for a number of English concepts, the missionaries
were almost defeated from the start. Of the few New England colonists before the 1640's who could claim to be experts in the Algonquian tongue, only Roger Williams was a
clergyman. Thomas Stanton, Miles Standish, and Edward
Winslow did not qualify for missionary duties; in fact, of
those three, Winslow was probably the only church member.

Williams did not neglect his obligation to indoctrinate
the Indian. However, his own religious seekings did not
make him willing to proselytize in any but the vaguest
sense. Furthermore, the founder of Providence was in full
agreement with the more doctrinaire Puritans that superfi-
cial conversion was worse than useless. In his *Key into the
Language of America*, written in 1643, Williams testified

that he could have persuaded the Narragansetts to observe
the Sabbath, submit to baptism, and adopt other outward
forms of faith, but believed it would be meaningless without sincere repentance and "true turning to God." He expounded that theme more fully a year or two later in a brief
pamphlet entitled *Christenings make not Christians, A
Briefe Discourse concerning that name Heathen, commonly given to the Indians*, published in London in 1645. In
it he insisted that acceptance of Christianity involved "a
turning from Idols not only of *conversation* but of *worship*." He also chided his sanctimonious critics, reminding
them that the Indians were no more "Heathen" than most
Europeans.[6]

If the Puritan colonists faced impressive difficulties, they
also had to live with their own consciences. Satan must not
be permitted to win souls at their very doors, not while
God's elect had a chance to prevent it. The plague of 1616-
1617 had so reduced the native populations in the Plymouth
and Massachusets Bay areas that the problem could be
more easily ignored, but there was always a nagging doubt
that enough effort was being made. The seal of the Massachusetts Bay Company depicted an Indian pleading "Come
over and help us," and friends in England did not let the
emigrants forget this obligation. But the Puritans who remained behind in Holland and England never quite understood the problems confronting the colonists. It was one
thing for Pastor Robinson to admonish the Pilgrims in 1623
for killing some Indians before they had converted any, but
it was quite another thing to convey to the natives even the
rudiments of Puritan theology, a task the gentle Robinson
never had to face.[7]

*   *   *

DESPITE the many handicaps and despite the very real distractions of the early years, some missionary work did take place before John Eliot began his notable labors in 1646. The efforts of Plymouth Colony in the 1620's were largely informal attempts to explain Christianity to whatever natives were capable of understanding English; the hope was that example and explanation would combine to persuade the red man that the white man's religion was the higher faith. In this work the Pilgrim was greatly aided by circumstance: he had superior weapons, superior tools, bigger ships, and more impressive ornaments. He also seemed immune to most of the diseases that ravaged Indian tribes. Perhaps for these reasons, or perhaps for reasons that defy explanation, several of the Indians who had close contact with the Plymouth colony expressed an attachment to the white man's religion. Squanto departed this world, according to William Bradford, "desiring the Gov[erno]r to pray for him, that he might goe to the Englishmens God in heaven." Hobomock, the other Indian who lived out his life in Plymouth, was apparently well on his way to full conversion when he died in 1642. But Massasoit and the other Wampanoag sachems showed no inclination to overthrow their ancient deities.[8] And since the Pilgrims at no time during the first decade had a satisfactory preacher for their own congregation, it is little wonder that they had none to send to their Indian neighbors.

Missionary efforts made comparably modest progress in the Bay Colony during its first decade. As in the case of Plymouth, some natives showed signs of accepting the Puritan's religion. As early as 1632 James, sagamore of the Lynn and Marblehead region, appeared willing to be civilized and converted. The prospect of winning a petty ruler was encouraging to the Massachusetts colonists, but James succumbed to smallpox the following year, as did most of his tribe. At about the same time, John Sagamore of Watertown "began to harken after God and his ways." The scorn of his fellow Indians kept the chief from professing his new faith openly, but on his deathbed he left his only child to Reverend John Wilson of Boston. By the end of the 1630's several Indian children were living with Bay Colony families as apprentices or servants — some as a result of the Pequot War — a number of whom "use to weep and cry when detained by occasion from the sermon." By that time a few more minor sachems had begun to observe the rules of the Sabbath, at least to the extent of prohibiting work on that day, and several other sachems were not unfriendly to the spread of Christianity among their followers.[9] In Connecticut, Wequash Cook, a minor sachem, had not only converted to Christianity but had actively proselytized among the natives before his death in 1642.[10] The extent of missionary activity prior to 1646 was well summarized by the author of *The Glorious Progress of the Gospel, amongst the Indians in New England*, published in 1649: "the *English* were not wholly negligent this way, but had in sundry parts of the Countrey long before brought divers to a pretty competency of right understanding in the mystery of salvation, who lived orderly, and dyed hopefully."[11]

The most impressive of the early missionaries was Thomas Mayhew. He and his father arrived in New England in the 1630's, and in 1641 bought the island of Martha's Vineyard from Lord Stirling, who held it on a patent from the defunct Council for New England. The Mayhew families moved to the Vineyard the following year. That island and the neighboring ones were heavily populated with Indians, partly, no doubt, because their insular location had kept them relatively secluded from enemy attacks and from epidemics. In any event, the younger Mayhew, a Congregational preacher, quickly gave his attention to the religious state of the natives, though he apparently did not become proficient in their language until the end of the decade. Mayhew's influence soon spread to Nantucket and other islands, and before long he had several communities of Indians looking forward to his periodic visits.[12]

In 1650 the Reverend Henry Whitfield, en route back to Old England, was forced by contrary winds to put in at Martha's Vineyard. For ten days Whitfield observed the progress of the Gospel on the island, not only hearing of it from "Mr. Mahu," but from many of the Indians as well — by way of the preacher's translation. On his departure Whitfield asked Mayhew to describe in writing "the Story of Gods dealing with the Indians" on Martha's Vineyard since the arrival of the English. Mayhew's report was subsequently published along with some letters by Eliot as *The Light appearing more and more towards the perfect Day. Or, A farther Discovery of the present state of the Indians in New-England, Concerning the Progresse of the Gospel amongst them.*[13] From this work we can reconstruct the history of missionary activity on the islands off Cape Cod.

Several factors seem to have fused providentially to insure rapid conversion of the natives. First was the character of Mayhew, a man of unusual tact, superior skill, and abundant energy. Moreover, good fortune seems to have attended his efforts from the beginning. His first convert was Hiacoomes, "a man of a sad & a sober spirit," who proved a loyal and effective worker. Hiacoomes began his conversion in 1643; by 1649 he was delivering two sermons to the natives every Sunday. His progress toward Christianity seems to have been furthered when a local sagamore who had been his chief tormentor was hit by lightning in 1644;

and when a "universal sicknes" visited the island the next year, "they that did but give the hearing of good counsel, did not taste so deeply of it, [and] Hiacoomes and his family in a manner not at all." All this led the natives to serious second thoughts, and before long the ranks of the Christian Indians were swelled by new accessions. More converts followed when a local sagamore who had befriended the missionaries almost miraculously escaped death at the hands of an assassin. Other special providences included Mayhew's curing of an old man whom the powwows had given up for lost, and a similar revival of a sachem's son, who survived not only his illness but also the extensive bleeding that Mayhew applied as a remedy. In addition to these fortuitous events, Mayhew's efforts were undoubtedly aided by geography. The island setting gave him a captive audience: once he had converted the most influential Indians the rest fell into line with barely a murmur. By 1650 he claimed twenty-two converts to Christianity and many more in preparation.[14] His converts, however, were not church members in that they had not yet covenanted themselves into a holy congregation; that final step in the Puritan's theological progression did not come for another decade. In the meantime, Mayhew's Christian Indians continued to explore the mysteries of the Puritan faith.

*   *   *

WHILE Mayhew was busy on the island, the General Court of Massachusetts was beginning to reflect a new interest in missionary work on the mainland. Early in 1644 several sachems had gone to Governor Winthrop and "tendered themselves" to the government of Massachusetts Bay, agreeing at the same time to accept instruction in Christianity. The next year the Court asked the colony's church elders to formulate a plan for civilizing and converting the Indians; a year later the Court provided for the election of two clergymen each year to deliver sermons at the Indian towns.[15] The scheme was never implemented, partly because of the cost involved, but mainly because a more satisfactory solution appeared. The heart and head of that solution was John Eliot, "Apostle to the Indians."

Eliot's background had followed the familiar dissenting pattern. Born in Essex County, England, in 1604, he had been educated at Jesus College, Cambridge, where he became imbued with Puritan doctrines. Eliot then taught school for a year under Thomas Hooker — who undoubtedly furthered the young man's nonconformist commitment — before removing to America. Eliot arrived at Boston in November 1631 on the *Lyon,* the same ship that brought many of his former neighbors and Governor Winthrop's wife. Nothing in his Old World experience seemed to have particularly fitted him for his later work, unless his reputed proficiency at ancient languages indicates a flair for linguistics in general.[16] Certainly there was no close similarity of ancient languages, or modern either, to the Algonquian tongue.

His first position in New England was that of substitute for John Wilson — then in England — as teacher to the Boston congregation. When Wilson returned the next year, Eliot declined an invitation to remain as teaching elder and moved to Roxbury, where many of his friends and relatives had settled and where he had probably already agreed to begin his pastorship. There he was ordained in the New England fashion, with a simple laying on of hands. In this post he remained the rest of his life, for many years serving his parish without the aid of an assistant. At the same time, he sired a family of five sons and one daughter. No man in early New England was so universally appreciated and loved. This was not the result of an impressive intellect, for in this capacity he was undistinguished. Neither was it the result of any pliability of character, for Eliot could be stubborn at times, as his superiors in the missionary work discovered. Rather, Eliot seems to have won a devoted following largely from a single-hearted dedication to duty and service, coupled with a becoming modesty and sweetness. He was generous, thoughtful of others, forgiving. In sum, John Eliot was one of those rare men who anger none, irritate few, and earn love and respect by practicing those qualities themselves.[17]

It is not known exactly when or why John Eliot became interested in the Indian language. Sometime in the early 1640's he apparently took notice of the linguistic abilities of a Long Island native — Eliot called him "a pregnant-witted young man" — who had been taken captive in the Pequot War. When Eliot first met him, this talented native was a servant to Richard Calicott of Dorchester and had already learned to speak and read English. The Roxbury pastor taught him to write it also, and engaged him as teacher and interpreter. By 1646 Eliot was sufficiently fluent in Algonquian to converse on matters of theology with the natives of eastern Massachusetts. The Indian, Cochenoe, was at the same time preparing to join the Dorchester Church — thus the interchange between Eliot and his interpreter encompassed faith as well as works. There is no evidence to indicate whether or not the Indian satisfied the New England clergy of his conversion; that he would not have been denied church membership on the basis of race is evident from the admission of a Negro servant to the Dorchester congregation some years earlier. In any event, Cochenoe appears to have been released from his servitude at about that time, and he probably returned to Long Island before the end of the decade.[18]

Whether Eliot ever became fully expert in the language is open to some question. In 1647 he modestly professed that he could "but stammer out some pieces" in Algonquian. This was certainly an underestimate of his skill at that time, though undoubtedly his command of the native tongue was far less adequate in 1647 than it would become in the ensuing years. Added practice and the discipline of translating the Bible helped to expand Eliot's vocabulary and to sharpen his pronunciation.[19] The early struggle to master the elements of Algonquian must have been arduous even with Cochenoe's help, for in the absence of a written language there were no phonetic guides, and the only printed vocabularies in existence at that time were the primitive efforts of William Wood (appended to his *New England's Prospect*, 1634) and Roger Williams (*Key into the Language of America*, 1643). There is no evidence that Eliot had the use of either of these works.

Until the fall of 1646, Eliot had made intermittent visits to the neighboring tribes, aided at all times by his interpreter. On some Indian leaders he made little impression. Cutshamekin, for example, remained indifferent to his preachings. Others were more receptive, particularly Waban of the Nonantum (Newton) band, who welcomed the missionary into his wigwam and gave his eldest son to be trained and converted by the English. This lad was soon enrolled in the Puritan school at Dedham. Not surprisingly then, it was at Waban's village that Eliot conducted his first service in Algonquian. This memorable event took place on October 28, 1646, in the presence of Waban, his son (then home from school and clad in English clothes), and four Englishmen. One of the visitors, probably John Wilson, minister of the Boston Church, wrote a detailed account of the proceedings which was later printed in London as part of New England's propaganda for pecuniary assistance.[20]

Eliot was not sure enough of his language to attempt to use it for prayer in that first service; he offered a prayer in English and hoped that the Indians would be more impressed by the solemnity that they could not understand than they would have been by a prayer in their own language studded with errors. Next came a seventy-five-minute sermon in Algonquian that included an explanation of the Ten Commandments and a recounting of the punishments visited on those who violate "the least title of them," with particular application to the Indians present — all of which was presented "with much sweet affection." But Eliot did not stop there; he went on to explain the path to salvation through Christ, the fall of Adam, the nature of God, and the tortures of hell, but avoided "medling with matters more difficult, . . . which to such weake ones might at first seeme ridiculous." [21]

Catechism followed. First the Indians posed questions, each of which was answered by the English and translated by Eliot, usually with the aid of "some familiar similitude." Then the procedure was reversed, and the Indians tried to give suitable answers to the Puritans' interrogation. Through enthusiasm, or politeness, Waban and his people endured three hours of this and asked for more. "But wee resolved," a witness recalled, "to leave them with an appetite," and so brought the service to an end. With a mind to the more mundane aspects of winning the heathen to the Gospel, the Puritan delegation distributed apples to the children and tobacco to the men before departing.[22]

Eliot wasted no time in following up on his early success. Two weeks later he and his colleagues were back in Waban where they were met by a large crowd of natives. Again Eliot chose to open his service with a prayer in English, but to convince the Indians that Christ understood their language as well as his, he closed the meeting with a lengthy prayer in Algonquian. Whatever Eliot's doubts about his own proficiency in language may have been, his supplications conveyed enough emotion to bring one in his audience to tears. This so impressed the Puritan observers that after the meeting they spoke to the affected Indian, "and he there fell into a more abundant renewed weeping, like one deeply and inwardly affected indeed, which forced us also to such bowels of compassion that wee could not forebeare weeping over him also: and so wee parted greatly rejoycing for such sorrowing." This second service at Waban's wigwam also saw the first catechizing of the children, one of whom "powred out many teares and shewed much affliction." [23] All in all, it was a misty-eyed but encouraging sequel to the first service.

The pattern established by these early meetings was followed, with minor variations, for the next several years. Eliot made biweekly visits to Waban's village, usually on Thursdays. Soon the Roxbury preacher was spending alternate Thursdays at Cutshamekin's village of Neponset (Dorchester). Eliot's audiences steadily increased in number, and he also began to receive delegations of Indians at his home. Before long, there were abundant signs that the natives had sincere trust in Eliot and respect for his religion. One Indian proposed to let the English raise his own son and three other boys, aged four to nine. Two Indian men offered themselves as servants in return for the religious instruction they would receive in their masters' homes. The men were accepted, but the children were put off until adequate arrangements could be made. And after only four vis-

its from Eliot, the Indians at Nonantum ventured to submit
all of their children to Puritan education. At the same time,
the Indians who were being won over by Eliot's preaching
had voluntarily cut their hair in the English style.[24] The
difference between Christian Indians and their heathen
brethren thus became increasingly obvious to all. The missionaries rejoiced; the powwows sulked or threatened.

From Nonantum, Eliot's missionary influence spread.
The sachem of Concord heard of the apostle's services and
came to Waban's village to see for himself. "Hee was so
farre affected," observed Thomas Shepard, "that he desired
to become more like to the English, and to cast off those
Indian wild and sinful courses." After stemming some opposition among his tribesmen, the sachem invited Eliot to
preach in his town; he also requested that land be granted
him for a separate Indian village within the bounds of Concord, where proximity to the English would encourage his
people's adherence to their new faith. The Concord Indians
were apparently determined to live as well as believe like
white men. In February 1647 a set of rules drawn up by
Simon Willard of Concord was ratified "by divers Sachims
and other principall men amongst the Indians at Concord."
These curious regulations include prohibitions against
"Pawwowing" and body-greasing as well as against a number of more commonly recognized sins. Rule number fourteen decreed "that there shall not be allowance to *pick Lice*,
as formerly, and eate them, and whosoever shall offend in
this case shall pay for every louse a penny." [25] The Concord
Indians were taking much more from the white man than
his theology.

By the summer of 1647, Eliot was so confident of the
progress of his missionary efforts that he was ready to pub-
licize it with a master stroke of propaganda. When the lead-

ing clergy and laity of the Bay Colony held a synod at Cambridge that June, Eliot put his converts as well as his talents on display. "A great confluence of Indians" came to Cambridge to hear the apostle preach to them in the native language. The schedule of prayer, lecture, question period, and catechism was enacted with enough success "marvellously [to] affect all the wise and godly Ministers, Magistrates, & people." This demonstration not only encouraged greater support among the New Englanders, it also gave Thomas Shepard an opportunity to rebut the skeptics in Old England, "for what was done at *Cambridge* was not set under a Bushell, but in the open Sunne, that what *Thomas* would not beleeve by the reports of others, he might be forced to beleeve, by seeing with his own eyes and feeling Christ Jesus thus risen among them with his own hands." [26] Puritans on both sides of the Atlantic now began to take note of the progress of the Gospel in New England.

Not everything went smoothly for Eliot, but even the annoyances often turned to his ultimate advantage. A "malignant drunken Indian" who tried to embarrass the preacher by shouting "*who made sack* [wine]?" was effectively quieted by a dignified answer from Eliot and was "snib'd by the other *Indians*, calling it a *Papoose* question." Those who fled from his preaching fared no better, as the Pennacook sachem Passaconaway ("that old Witch and Powwaw") discovered. He escaped to the forests when Eliot came to proselytize him, but in their sachem's absence the people of Pennacook showed no aversion to hearing Eliot and his praying Indians. In fact they proved to be a most stimulating audience, asking such difficult questions that Eliot forbore answering some of them until he could consult with other Puritan clergymen. "Suppose a man before hee knew God," queried one, "hath had two wives, the first barren and childless, the second fruitful and bearing him many sweet children. . . . Which of these two wives [should the convert] put away?" Eliot's answer must have satisfied the Pennacooks, for many of them succumbed to his preachments; in fact, a year later Passaconaway himself solicited Eliot and Simon Willard to settle near his village.[27]

Eliot's efforts were also aided by the same kind of fortuitous circumstances that Mayhew had experienced. When the pox cut a mortal swath through Massachusetts in 1649-1650, the sorriest sufferers were "a company of wicked Indians"; the converts were relatively unscathed.[28]

*   *   *

ALTHOUGH many of the New England Indians now championed the Puritan theology, far too few of them — in the eyes of their white neighbors — were making corresponding improvements in their living habits. Not that the converts were unwilling: they requested schools, English-style government, English clothes, and tools.[29] But all of these would cost an amount of money that fledgling New England could scarcely afford. The colonists had spent their limited funds for the necessities of life; there was little surplus for propagation of the Gospel among the natives. Occasionally small sums were granted by individuals and by colonial governments for particular projects, but these could never be the basis for a flourishing missionary endeavor. Only one course held real promise to the missionaries, and they had pursued it since the early forties — this was simply to pry the necessary funds out of the pockets of Puritans, humanitarians, or anyone else in the mother country who could be induced to support the missionaries. Partly to this end the Bay Colony had sent three agents to England in 1641: Hugh Peter. Thomas Welde, and William Hibbins. They were admonished to avoid "begging or the like," yet begging was perhaps the only way they could hope to raise funds in an England then entering the most severe crisis of her domestic history. Under the circumstances, it is not surprising that the agents collected only scanty amounts. Several hundred pounds were realized, but little of it was earmarked for conversion of the Indians.[30]

To further the success of their solicitations the New Englanders and their friends tried to create a climate of opinion favorable to their efforts. In an attempt to offset the increasingly frequent jibes of English critics, Peter and Welde in 1643 published a miscellany of information provided mainly by President Dunster of Harvard. Their pamphlet, entitled *New England's First Fruits*, put the colonies' best foot forward, especially in respect to the progress already made in converting the Indians and in providing higher education for the colonists at Harvard.[31] The agents hoped that both the proselytizing and collegiate projects would benefit from a new surge of generosity. Although the response was not overwhelming, the pamphlet did lead to Harvard's first scholarship, and to some support for the missionaries. Lady Mary Armine, wealthy widow of a former member of Parliament, gave the largest single gift, a £20 annuity to support "the Preacher to the poore Indians in N. Engl." [32]

Encouraged by these beginnings, the New Englanders wrote more pamphlets. In 1647 one appeared — probably written by John Wilson — under the title *The Day-Breaking, if not The Sun-Rising of the Gospell With the Indians in New-England*. Unlike the earlier *First Fruits*, this tract made an open plea for aid. It narrated Eliot's achievements at Natick and elsewhere and stressed the need for financial support if this work was to be continued.

While boasting that "Hee that God hath raised up and enabled to preach unto them, is a man (you know) of a most sweet, humble, loving, gratious and enlarged spirit," the author made it clear that Eliot could not educate, clothe, and feed Indian children without material help from those at home. The following year, 1648, Shepard's *Clear Sun-shine* continued the narrative and repeated the plea.[33]

This second of the "Eliot Indian Tracts" opened with a dedicatory letter to Parliament. This was not mere courtesy: the promoters of missionary work were now aiming at a project far more impressive than the collection of random gifts. Edward Winslow had arrived in England as the Bay Colony's agent, and he was taking advantage of his diplomatic skill and considerable influence in Parliament to promote the creation of a private corporation for the support of New England's missionaries. Winslow had already contributed to the enterprise by seeing the two propaganda pamphlets through the press, and he had secured the signatures of several clergymen to a dedicatory epistle in *The Clear Sun-shine*, thus adding impressive emphasis to the needs and worthiness of the project.[34] While the public was reading the pamphlets, Winslow was buttonholing members of Parliament; both tactics yielded full return.

In March 1648, the House of Commons began to debate the chartering of a new eleemosynary corporation.[35] While Parliament hemmed and hawed, read and revised, Winslow busied himself with the preparation of still another tract. This one consisted of letters by Eliot and Thomas Mayhew and was entitled *The Glorious Progress of the Gospel, amongst the Indians in New England.*[36] Its appearance in May 1649, with a dedication to Parliament and the Council of State, may have been instrumental in pushing the bill for the corporation through its last stages. In any event, the final result was highly pleasing to Winslow and other friends of the missionaries. A charter created "The President and Society for Propagation of the Gospell in New-England," with authority vested in a president, a treasurer, and fourteen assistants. The society was to maintain residence in London where its primary function would be raising funds. The disbursing, however, was not to be done by the company itself but through the Commissioners of the United Colonies, the only body of men in New England who could claim to speak for more than one colony.[37] The Commissioners did not, of course, have the right to act for Rhode Island, but that did not bother them then or later. On the whole, the society was well planned and wisely constructed. It was fortunate for the New England Puritans that their brethren at home were now in political control; even the press of events in war-torn England could not prevent the English and American branches of the Puritan cause from cooperating in a long-desired project for the propagation of their common faith.

*   *   *

THE chartering of the society was the capstone to a decade of remarkable progress in the propagation of the Gospel in New England. In 1640 the Indian converts in the Puritan colonies could have been enumerated by name; they were so few that the well informed probably knew of them all. But Mayhew and Eliot worked a revolution. They gave order and purpose and momentum to the missionary movement; they turned it from an incidental effort into a major Puritan project. And from their early successes came the publicity that brought in the first trickle of funds; their continued achievements helped to bring about the creation in the mother country of a permanent fund-raising organi-

zation, solely for the support of the New England enterprise. All this had been accomplished in ten years' time, despite the chaos in England and despite the many obstacles
inherent in frontier living and in the peculiar demands of
the Puritan faith. Eliot and his colleagues could be proud of
their efforts.

Not all of the credit, however, should go to the men involved; the times were undoubtedly ripe for a shift in Indian sentiment. As Edward Winslow observed in *The Glorious Progress*, it had taken time for the natives to observe

> our conversation amongst our selves, and with our de-
> meanor towards them, as well in peace, as in such warres
> they had unavoidably drawn upon themselves; whereby
> they had such experience of the justice, prudence, valour,
> temperance, and righteousnesse of the *English*, as did not
> onely remove their former jealousies and feares concern-
> ing us, and convict them of their owne uneven walking;
> but begat a good opinion of our persons, and caused them
> to affect our Laws and Government.[38]

Winslow wrote, of course, with a Puritan bias, yet there is
probably a good deal of truth in his words. It was not until
the 1640's that the New England native was in a position to
weigh the records of the colonists on several matters: their
power, their justice, their respect for the red man's life and
property. On the whole, the Indian seems to have been favorably impressed. Gradually, then, some of his resistance
to the Puritan's theology subsided, and the missionaries began to number their native followers in scores and then in
hundreds.

Still, in 1650 most Indians in the five colonies remained
untouched by the missionary effort. Tribes that had es-

caped the decimation of the plagues, or that were separated physically from centers of English population, kept immune to the best efforts of the Puritan preachers. Almost no progress had been made among the Wampanoags, Narragansetts, Niantics, or Mohegans. In fact, when in 1647 Shepard, Wilson, and Eliot visited Yarmouth, in Plymouth Colony, the sachem showed his contempt by going fishing instead of attending the service.[39] Since the large autonomous tribes constituted the bulk of the New England Indians, it could be said that the 1640's had been a decade of transition, not a decade of fulfillment.

Even in those areas where the greatest success had been realized, the Puritan missionaries had made only a dent. From the outset opposition was bitter, particularly from the powwows. Their motives are obvious: they were the closest equivalent the natives knew to a priesthood, and the success of a rival faith meant their personal downfall. Every early convert had to face the wrath of the powwows of his tribe, and it is not surprising that some Indians were unable to resist the warning of their traditional holy men, especially when illness struck: then the powwows added the prestige of medicine to that of mysticism. Often the powwow won the battle of loyalties, even after an Indian had formally adopted Christianity, and most of the New England chroniclers were candid enough to admit that reversion to old ways was regrettably common. As Henry Whitfield put it in 1650, "it cannot be expected but that the Devil should be like himself . . . so as to cause many of them to totter, back slide, and fall away from what they have professed."[40]

In their resistance to the blandishments of the missionaries, the medicine men found formidable allies in many of the sachems. The tribal chiefs had much to lose also: prestige, power, and tribute. Some of the sachems friendly to the English admitted that their principal reservation against Christianity was its threat to their collection of tribute — and this became an increasingly common explanation in the period after 1650.* Since opposition from the chiefs inevitably meant opposition from the rank and file, Eliot and Mayhew made particular efforts to win over the leaders at the outset. Some, like Waban, became active missionaries themselves; others, like Cutshamekin, remained unconverted but generally cooperative. In most instances, when the sachem succumbed to the new faith, the entire tribe could be considered ripe for Christianity. As Eliot observed to the president of the New England Company: "There be two Great Sachems in the Country that are openly and professed enemies against praying to God namely Unkas and Nenecrot. And when ever the Lord removeth them, there will be a dore open for the preaching of the Gospel in those parts. . . ." The resistance of the major tribes is therefore partly explained by the obstinacy (as the Puritans viewed it) of Massasoit, Miantonomo, Ninigret, Uncas, and their successors.

The Puritan missionaries were well aware of their failures; they also knew that they had come a long way since the early 1630's. The scattered sub-tribes of Massachusetts had responded encouragingly to Eliot's overtures. By 1650, the apostle was making biweekly visits to Nonantum and Neponset, and less regular calls at Concord, Sudbury, Dedham, Pawtucket, and several Nipmuc towns in western Massachusetts.[42] If the number of Indian converts to Puritanism was not large — when measured by the standards of most other Christian denominations — it was simply that

* See Chapter XI.

the Puritan missionaries did not begin to count a man as a convert until he had demonstrated a deep devotion to the faith and discarded all practices that smacked of heathenism. The convert had to make profound adjustments in his private morals, in his relationship to his fellow Indians, and in his economic and political behavior. Yet some Indians were willing to undergo all this, and by the end of the forties several native villages in Massachusetts were observing Sabbath services, with or without the aid of a Puritan clergyman. On Martha's Vineyard, Thomas Mayhew, Jr., was enjoying similar success. With the prospect of a steady flow of pecuniary support from the mother country through the new society, the New England Puritans at mid-century looked forward with confidence and enthusiasm to the future progress of the Gospel among the Indians.

CHAPTER X

Missionary Efforts:
Years of Growth, 1650-1665

EARLY IN his missionary work, Eliot spelled out to some friendly natives what he believed to be the only fundamental differences between Englishmen and Indians: first, the English knew and served God, second "we labour and work in building, planting, clothing our selves, etc. and [you] doe not." The more Eliot observed the natives in their own villages the more convinced he became that elimination of the second distinction was vital to overcoming the first. By 1649 he was ready to state categorically that "I find it absolutely necessary to carry on civility with Religion." [1]

To Eliot's way of thinking, adherence to Christian theology was meaningless if not accompanied by Christian living. One could not worship God with sincerity and at the same time have several wives, associate with idol worshippers, and defy any of the rules of "right walking." The whole man must be Christianized. And this view was widely shared by Eliot's fellow New Englanders. Men such as Richard Mather, Dorchester clergyman and progenitor of the distinguished Mather clan, also hoped for a transformation of Indian character. "If there be any work of Grace amongst them," Mather advised his readers, "it would surely bring forth, and be accompanied with the Reformation of their disordered lives, as in other things, so in their neglect of Labor, and their living in idleness and pleasure." [2]

The Puritans did not find it easy to bring the natives of New England up to European definitions of civilization. Where they constituted the majority of a tribe, the praying Indians, as they had come to be known by both races, had already made major concessions to "civility." The code of Concord — already related — is testimony to this. At Nonantum, the Indians requested Eliot to institute a government modeled after the colony's. Eliot accordingly petitioned the General Court, which in 1647 approved a plan for establishing monthly courts administered by the Indians themselves and quarterly courts composed of Bay Colony magistrates. Fines collected by the courts were to be applied to the construction of meeting houses for the converts. Schools were also established at two of the Indian towns. In addition, the Puritans encouraged the Indian men to fence their land, tend to agriculture, and begin to manufacture salable goods for the New England market. As early as September Eliot reported that the praying Indians of Massachusetts "begin to grow industrious, and find something to sell at Market all yeer long: all winter they sell Brooms, Staves, Elepots, Baskets, Turkies." In the spring, summer, and fall, he continued, they sold fruit, fish, and meat. Some hired themselves out to nearby farmers in haying season. All this the Christian Indians did without material aid from the Puritans, save when Eliot provided some spinning wheels for the women, and "Shovels, Spades, Mattocks, Crows of Iron" for the men. [3]

Along with changes in economic customs went modifications in other habits of daily living. Most male converts cut
their hair short, and those who could adopted English
clothes — usually secondhand garments donated by friends
of the missionaries. To obtain a modicum of privacy and
modesty some families constructed partitions in their bark-
covered wigwams, though Reverend Eliot would have
much preferred to eliminate "Those dark and despicable
Tartarian Tents." [4]

Eliot found these gropings toward civilization to be
promising and a clear sign that the Lord was pleased with
the missionary work, but by 1650 he was becoming increasingly dissatisfied with the geographical dispersal of the
praying Indians. The Puritans vastly preferred well-
meaning churchgoers to heathens, but attendance at divine
worship was only a step in the evolution of the true Christian; the ultimate goal was full church membership. Church
membership, in turn, required a community of the elect, for
no man could be a church by himself. As early as 1648 Eliot
believed that there were enough Indian converts to form a
church, if they could only be settled together. In their present scattered condition, he argued, it was inevitable that
some would revert to "Pau-wauing," and many would fail
to live by the Gospel from too little contact with it. Eliot
and his colleagues could make only occasional visits to most
Indian villages; even Nonantum was dependent on the Puritan clergymen for its Christian services. Eliot's persistent
advice, therefore, was to create special villages "remote
from the English, where [the Indians] must have the word
constantly taught, and government constantly exercised,
meanes of good subsistence provided, [and] incourage-
ments for the industrious." But the drawback to this, as to

so many humanitarian projects, was only too plain: "I feare it will be too chargeable," Eliot concluded.[5]

And so it was until the chartering of the New England Company in 1649. Although large sums of money were not immediately forthcoming, the prospect of a sharp increase in operating funds encouraged the Commissioners of the United Colonies to back projects that would have seemed extravagant a few years earlier. The Commissioners had, however, some precedent on which to build: in 1646 the Massachusetts General Court had authorized the purchase of land for the settlement of Christian Indians, on the request of the natives themselves. The same year the Bay Colony appointed Eliot to a committee for encouraging the Indians to live more "orderly," and in 1647 Massachusetts voted the apostle a gratuity of £10 "in respect of his greate paines and charge in instructing the Indians in the knowledg of God."[6] By mid-century the Puritans of New England were ready to take a bold new step to promote their faith among the red men.

*   *   *

IN 1651 the first praying town became a reality at Natick, Massachusetts. In the face of the skepticism of many of the New Englanders and the outright hostility of most of the sachems, Eliot had sought rights to a parcel of land in eastern Massachusetts to which he could bring most of the converts from Nonantum. Waban, the Nonantum leader, had enlisted enthusiastically in the project, but Cutshamekin, the most influential chief in the Massachusetts tribe, was against it. He and the other sachems knew that levying tribute on tribesmen in a Christian village would be nearly impossible. While Eliot did not insist on ending tribute to

traditional leaders, he recognized that Cutshamekin predicted accurately. "The bottome of it lieth here," confessed
Eliot, "he [Cutshamekin] formerly had all or what he
would; now he hath but what they will." Nevertheless,
Eliot was sure he had God on his side and made it known
that the propagation of the Gospel would proceed despite
the disfavor of Cutshamekin or anyone else.[7]

Eliot's persistence was rewarded. After a frustrating
search for available land "the Lord did by his speciall providence, and answer of prayers, pitch us upon the place
where we are at Natick." The site occupied both banks of
the Charles River, some eighteen miles from Boston and
about the same distance from Roxbury. Title was acquired
in the summer of 1651 when the town of Dedham exchanged two thousand acres there for an equivalent amount
at Deerfield; that fall Waban's men broke ground for the
next spring's planting.[8] The converts also constructed a
sturdy eighty-foot bridge across the river. All the while,
Eliot hovered about, giving advice, offering prayer, and
lending a ready hand. But the bulk of the work was done
by the natives, even on the meeting house. One English car-
penter helped for a day or two with the final construction,
but the red men had cut and squared the timbers, sawed the
boards, mortised the joints, and wattled the chimneys. The
finished product was handsome and spacious, with a large
room fifty feet by twenty-five on the first floor, and a similar room on the second floor. The upper story also contained a separate corner room for Eliot, but was used as
well by the Indians for hanging their furs and other valu-
ables.[9]

By the time Governor Endicott and Reverend Wilson
visited Natick in October 1651, they were amazed to find a
neat and thriving village already completed. Three "fair

long streets" had been laid out, two on the north side of the river, a third on the south bank near the planting fields. House lots had been assigned along these streets after the English fashion, and in the center of the town was a palisade fort. Most of the inhabitants lived in Indian houses, but a start had been made on several English style buildings.[10]

In devising a civil organization for the first praying town, Eliot adhered as closely to Biblical precedent as any Puritan could. The Roxbury preacher had long pondered the kind of government his converts should have, and he had consulted John Cotton, the eminent Boston divine. The solution, Eliot finally decided, was to "fly to the Scripture, for every Law, Rule, Direction, Form, or what ever we do." In short, the first community of Christian Indians in New England must form the perfect Biblical community, "makeing the Word of God theire only magna charta." [11]

Organizing the Natick polity on Biblical patterns accorded well with Eliot's theology; it also promised relief from some of the duties with which he had been burdened since the founding of the village. Until August 1651, Eliot had decided disputes, ordered punishments, and played the role of judge, jury, and chief executive. This enlightened despotism was less onerous to the Indians than to Eliot, for while he was capable of handling the most touchy disputes with consummate tact, and the natives were content under his gentle hand, Eliot had found the demands on his time excessive. It was with some relief, then, that he held a meeting at Natick on August 6, open to all Christian Indians who could attend, to decide their future civil polity.[12] Eliot left the proselytes little choice when he read from the Book of Exodus the episode in which Jethro admonished Moses for being the sole judge over the people he had led out of Egypt. "The thing that thou doest is not good. Thou wilt surely wear away, both thou, and this people that is with thee: for this thing is too heavy for thee; thou art not able to perform it thyself alone." [13] Jethro had instructed Moses to select rulers of tens, fifties, hundreds, and thousands. As there were no thousands to rule at Natick, that aspect of the scriptural model was omitted, but the remainder of the Hebrew theocracy was put into effect. Cutshamekin, now resigned to the triumph of Christianity over his tribe, was chosen ruler of the hundred; two others were selected for fifties, and ten as rulers of tens. A month later, the residents of Natick entered into a solemn "Covenant with God, and each other, to be the Lords people." [14]

Only one step remained in the process of transforming the Natick flock into a truly Christian people, but it was the hardest of all. The town now had land, buildings, self-government, and economic support, but it did not have a church. The meeting house, to be sure, was the material shell in which a congregation might worship, but in Puritan theology the only real churches were convenanted bodies of regenerate Christians. Natick would not qualify for church status until a substantial number — eight or ten at least — of her citizens had proven the depth, as well as the sincerity, of their faith.* The formation of an Indian church became John Eliot's major missionary interest during the remainder of the decade. It would take that long to convince the outside world that Indian Christians were as truly saved as were Englishmen who had fled from Bishop Laud.

These proved frustrating years for the apostle. By 1652

---

* Although Puritan theology recognized the independence of congregations, a new church had to have the endorsement of some of those already acknowledged to be among the visible saints.

Eliot thought he had enough sincere believers to form a church. He had listened to their accounts of conversion and had kept a transcript of them. These he read to several of the neighboring elders, who were favorably impressed. In turn, the elders appointed a day for a public hearing of the confessions to be attended by several eminent Puritan clergymen. These pious gentlemen spent the better part of a day listening to professions of religious awakening, in most of which the Indians stressed the sinfulness of their former lives, the opposition they had met from sachems, powwows, and friends, and the joy they experienced in accepting Christ.[15]

But in the end, the "Magistrates, Elders, and Grave men" were not satisfied. As impressive as the occasion must have been, it failed to meet the rigorous standards for admission to Puritan fellowship. While professing to be pleased with the performance in general, the ministers feared haste in a matter of such importance. They recommended that formation of the church be postponed until more interpreters could be employed and more time allotted. Eliot was disappointed, but he soon persuaded himself that the decision was in accordance with God's wishes.[16]

The next year proved uncongenial for a similar experiment. Trouble with the Dutch was at a new peak, rumors of Dutch and Indian conspiracies ran rampant, and it was not long before some overactive Puritan minds imagined the praying Indians conspiring with the enemy in a grand master plot.[17] Under such circumstances, the missionary's best move was to keep his charges out of the public eye for the duration; besides, Eliot wanted to allow time for some of his recent propaganda to take effect. He had drafted an account of the 1652 public interrogation, accompanied by verbatim translations of many of the confessions. The following year these were published, along with a letter by Thomas Mayhew, as *Tears of Repentance: Or, a further Narrative of the Progress of the Gospel Amongst the Indians in New England*.[18] In time these accounts might encourage friends on both sides of the Atlantic to look more favorably on the formation of an Indian church. In the meantime, the general caution toward Indians that accompanied the possibility of a Dutch-Indian conspiracy convinced Eliot that "this businesse needeth a calmer season." [19]

A year later, in 1654, conditions seemed more promising, and Eliot's converts again submitted themselves to public display and cross-examination. This time the service was held in the sympathetic environment of Roxbury and was preceded by a fast day proclaimed in all the churches of the Bay Colony. The corps of interpreters had been doubled by the addition of Thomas Mayhew, who journeyed to Roxbury to assist his fellow missionary. But these good omens were deceptive. Shortly before the appointed day, the Natick schoolmaster fell ill and was unable to attend — and he had been one of Eliot's most articulate prospects. Then three praying Indians "of the unsound sort" seized an opportunity to purchase ten quarts of liquor; the three became thoroughly intoxicated and plied with alcohol the eleven-year-old son of one of Natick's rulers. Adding further embarrassment to the episode was the disclosure that among the culprits was Eliot's interpreter, Job Nesutan. Since the spree took place only ten days before the meeting, one can well believe that Eliot did not exaggerate when he recalled how "the Tidings sunk my spirit extreamly." The Indian rulers of Natick sentenced the adult defendants to a stretch in the stocks and twenty lashes apiece; the boy was condemned to a shorter time in the stocks, then was whipped by his father before the children at the village school.[20] Such was the penalty for those who succumbed to the white man's drink.

The drinking episode seriously damaged the prospects of the Roxbury meeting. Although Job Nesutan was temporarily dropped from his assignment as interpreter, and all the culprits were severely lectured by the Natick rulers, no amount of punishment or admonition could erase the unpleasant event from the minds of those who had to decide on the acceptability of the converts to church membership. Eight aspirants were examined that June 13, and the list of questions and answers, carefully preserved by the Roxbury pastor, are impressive testimony to the thorough training they had received. But again the Puritan sages decided against accepting the Indians into full communion, not from dissatisfaction with the catechization, but rather from a reluctance to let the Indians take so important a step without longer apprenticeship. Again Eliot professed to be content with the decision, even quoting Scripture in support of gradualism.[21]

The long delayed church covenant was finally consummated in 1660. A decade had passed since the founding of Natick; almost fifteen years had passed since Eliot's first Algonquian sermon. In view of the rigorous admission procedures of the churches of early New England, the waiting period of the Natick Indians was perhaps not unduly long; in any event the news that Eliot's native converts had finally been admitted to full church membership was cause for rejoicing among the missionaries and their supporters.

By 1660 a second praying town was in existence, largely formed by the Cohannet Indians. Eliot had originally tried to get land at Cohannet for his first town, but the English settlers there were unwilling to cooperate. Some of the Cohannet tribe, most notably their sachem Cutshamekin, had subsequently joined the Natick community. But others were jealous of Waban's people for dominating the first praying town and refused to join with them. This was particularly true after the death of Cutshamekin in the early 1650's. His position as ruler of the hundred had given his people some consolation for their minority status at Natick; this compensation, however, disappeared with the accession of Josias Chickataubut to the sachemship on his uncle's death, and the Cohannet group became increasingly anxious to establish a separate Christian community for themselves. In any event, there was need for another praying town since all of the house lots at Natick had been assigned by 1656, leaving no room for expansion. The result was the establishment of Punkapog in 1657. It eventually achieved church status and remained one of the principal praying towns until King Philip's War.[22]

*   *   *

BUILDING towns, dispensing tools, and providing direct assistance to actual and potential converts were expensive undertakings. Fortunately for the missionary interests of the New England Puritans, the corporation founded by the Rump Parliament in 1649 proved equal to the task. In the long run, it was the Puritan in Old England who paid the bill for converting and civilizing the Indians of New England.

The act of incorporation of "The President and Society for Propagation of the Gospell in New-England" had been drafted with full awareness of a charitable organization's need for publicity. Acting with considerable foresight, its authors had directed that the act itself should be read by every minister in England to his congregation on the first Sabbath after its delivery, and the clergymen were to "exhort the people to a chearful and liberal contribution." Furthermore, churchmen were encouraged to conduct a door-to-door solicitation on behalf of the society. The results of the appeal were gratifying. Within the first few years, over £500 came in from the army, almost £1000 from the parishes in London, and lesser amounts from the rural areas and from individual donors. Receipts to 1653 totaled more than £4,500; by the end of the first decade they exceeded £15,000. One-third of this sum was sent to New England in the form of cash or goods. Most of the rest was invested in English land in order to insure a steady income in future years.[23]

By the early 1650's, then, the American Puritans were at last in a position to expand their missionary efforts on a fairly stable basis. The act of incorporation had designated the Commissioners of the United Colonies as the society's dispersing agents, and these officials set to work to devise a comprehensive scheme for promoting Puritan Christianity among the natives. Yet they faced a number of handicaps that made their work exceedingly difficult. In the first place, the society usually insisted on sending goods — such as tools, cloth, firearms — rather than negotiable currency. Some of the goods, especially those sent on request of the Commissioners, were immediately distributed to the Indians. But other items the Commissioners were forced to sell on the local market in order to raise cash for necessary expenditures.[24] The resale system also was employed to meet salaries; Eliot, Mayhew, and several other clergymen drew regular payments for their missionary labors; others — both Indian and white — were paid for interpreting, carrying messages, serving as schoolmasters, and the like.

The society insisted on detailed accounts of expenditures, which soon prompted the Commissioners to hire Ed-

ward Rawson to do their bookkeeping. Although both
Rawson and the Commissioners seem to have performed
their duties well, the administrative side of the missionary
effort was subjected to constant criticism. The Massachusetts General Court complained that the Commissioners
were spending too much time on Indian affairs, other colonies protested that they were giving the bulk of the funds
to the Bay Colony, and the society pestered them for more
accurate accounts.[25] To top it off, John Eliot was always
asking for more money.

Eliot, in fact, was somewhat of a trial to the Commissioners. None of them questioned his selflessness nor the virtue
of his works, but all found him difficult to deal with at
times. While his impetuous generosity and his indifference
to his own needs never ceased to win admiration for the
apostle, such traits often created embarrassing situations for
the Commissioners. When Eliot wanted a raise in salary —
most of which would be spent on the Indians — he went
over the heads of the Commissioners and wrote directly to
the society; when he needed additional funds he wrote to
friends in England — such as Jonathan Hanmer, rector of
Barnstaple — who rarely failed to meet his requests. Worst
of all, Eliot seemed incapable of keeping a record of his expenditures. A sort of friendly warfare prevailed between
the Commissioners and the principal missionary which
lasted throughout the lifetimes of both.[26] He was always
after them for additional funds; they were always after him
for accounts.

Eliot, of course, won most of the battles. He was the
indispensable man, while the Commissioners were ex-
pendable administrators who increasingly found themselves
backing down under pressure from London. Eliot's salary,
as well as his independent sources of aid, continued to

grow. There is no indication that he became perceptibly better in bookkeeping, and eventually the Commissioners stopped trying to reform him.

The insistence on written evidence of disbursements had been no bureaucratic whim of the Commissioners. Their superiors, the members of the society, persistently requested better accounting, and the society in turn was pressured by its own critics into an obsession with detailed accounts. It was not an easy job to collect funds in England, and to make matters worse there were many cynics who thought the entire project a snare and a delusion. Some Englishmen were simply hostile to Puritan projects, though their voices were muted during the Cromwellian fifties, while others suspected that their earlier contributions to New England charities had been badly mismanaged. Finally there was the insidious carping of Hugh Peter, Thomas Welde, and other ex-New Englanders who vented their aggravations against the Bay Colony by belittling its missionary efforts. The society defended itself in two ways. One was to open its books to public scrutiny, which it did each Saturday morning at Cooper's Hall, London. The other was to publish what eventually became known as "Eliot Indian Tracts," short pamphlets comprised mainly of letters by Eliot, Mayhew, and others in New England, extolling the progress of the Gospel among the heathen. The society also published several pertinent letters and broadsides of English origin.[27]

As early as 1650, the society met the requests of the New England missionaries for purchases of long-range value to the Puritan missionary effort. The first entry in the society's ledger reports the purchase of Reverend Thomas Jenner's library, in response to a plea from Eliot that books be acquired for Thomas Mayhew. ("I will name no books," the apostle had added, "he needs all.") The society also bought Thomas Welde's library for Eliot.[28] A few years later, when Eliot was ready to publish his translation of the Bible, the English corporation purchased a printing press, type, paper, and the services of a skilled printer. On the whole, then, despite occasional dissensions, the society, the Commissioners, and the missionaries worked together toward a common goal with about as much efficiency as could be expected of such a hybrid creature with three thousand miles of ocean separating its head from its hands. By 1660 there was much for the Puritans on both sides of the Atlantic to be proud of.

The Restoration of Charles II brought an end to the brief career of the Society for the Propagation of the Gospel in New England. It did not, however, end the cooperation between Old and New England in missionary endeavors. In fact, as far as most Puritan missionaries were concerned, the fiscal arrangements actually improved somewhat after the Restoration.

By the Act of Oblivion and Indemnity the old corporation expired; its members, however, soon petitioned for a new charter. They also practiced a good deal of discretion in voluntarily purging their ranks of the more blatant anti-Royalists and by enlisting the aid of the influential Earl of Clarendon.[29] The Merry Monarch could hardly permit the continuation of a corporation chartered by his father's executioners, but he could authorize an almost identical organization. After some delays, occasioned both by routine governmental procedure and by the tactics of a few enemies of the project, a new charter was sealed on February 7, 1662. It created a corporation to be known as "The Company for Propagacion of the Gospell in New England and the parts adjacent in America." Most people were content to call it

the New England Company, and the New Englanders did
not bother to adjust their terminology at all, usually referring to both the old society and the new company as "the
corporation." Little wonder, for almost nothing had
changed but the number of members, now forty-five instead of sixteen. As nine of the members were carry-overs,
no real break in continuity occurred.[30]

What made the new corporation superior to the old one
was its governor, Robert Boyle. The distinguished scientist
was not a figurehead; no member of the New England
Company either before or after the Restoration labored
more actively for its success. Not only was he well
connected among high government agencies, but he also
was more closely in touch with American colonists than
most Englishmen of his day. In addition, Boyle had the advantage of being a moderate Anglican, thus shielding the
company from ecclesiastical attack, while he himself sympathized with what continued to be an essentially Puritan
enterprise. Finally, as a wealthy bachelor, he was often
able to refill the company's coffers.[31] All of this was heart-
ening to the New England Puritans.

Throughout the remainder of the century, in fact until
the American Revolution, "The Company for the Propagacion of the Gospell" continued to support the Puritan missionaries. The company's income became reasonably stable
once its right to property acquired during the Interregnum
was established and once the policies of the Restoration had
stabilized the economy. As before, the Commissioners of
the United Colonies acted as the company's agents in
America, though this time by free choice of the company
rather than by specific direction of the charter. Before long
the Commissioners gained an additional measure of control
over the company's funds, for after the fire and plague of

the late sixties made London a poor investment risk, an increasing amount of the corporation stock was transferred to New England to be invested as the Commissioners saw fit.[32] While this change did not cure all the ills of the missionary project, it did give the Puritan colonies a freer hand in applying the remedy.

*   *   *

REGARDLESS of who held the purse strings, first priority on missionary funds in the years between the founding of Natick and the outbreak of Philip's War went to the publication of "the Indian Library." At the heart of the Puritans' uplifting of the heathen was the conviction that he must read the Bible. For Indians who learned English, access to Scripture was no problem, but it became increasingly obvious that bilingual natives would remain a minority for a long time to come. In the meantime, the thousands of natives who remained ignorant of the white man's language would be denied the deepest consolations of the Gospel. The Roxbury pastor determined to give them a new chance.

As early as 1647, Eliot had contemplated making a translation of the Bible, and he seems to have started work on it a few years later. The task must have been arduous beyond description. He had not only to invent a written language — in itself an overwhelming task — but to do so for a tongue he himself understood imperfectly. In addition there were syntactic structures and vocabulary for which there were not always English equivalents. In the main, Eliot translated without major assistance, although he often tested his phonetics on Job Nesutan and others. When the Commissioners of the United Colonies suggested that Thomas Stanton, possibly the best linguist in New England, lend a hand, Eliot declined to accept him, probably concurring in the judgment of the New England Company that he was not godly enough "for the spirituall parte of this worke." [33]

Eliot's first published Indian translation, a primer or catechism intended to familiarize the Indians with his written version of their language, came off the press at Cambridge, Massachusetts, in 1654; it had been preceded only by some brief handwritten translations of religious tracts used in Indian schools and meeting houses as early as 1651. [34]

Convinced that Eliot's book would be incomprehensible to the Indians of Connecticut, Reverend Abraham Pierson of that colony immediately began a bilingual catechism of his own "to sute these southwest partes." Although Pierson was assisted by Thomas Stanton, his book was not completed until 1658. [35] When it finally appeared, Pierson's catechism must have given a jolt to Indians who thought they had mastered the white man's language. For example, the English version's explanation for the existence of one God read "Because singular things of the same kind when they are multiplied are differenced among themselves by their singular propertyes; but there cannot be found another God differenced from this, by any such like propertyes." [36] A glance at Pierson's book gives a broad hint as to why the Connecticut Indians remained in a state of catechumens far longer than the Massachusetts tribes. Pierson's proved to be the only work set in Algonquian during Eliot's lifetime to which the apostle had not contributed. [37]

But while Pierson toiled over his primer, Eliot had already shifted to his greatest work, a translation of the entire Bible into the Indian tongue. The translation was begun in 1650; by 1655 Genesis and Matthew were completed, with copies distributed for criticism and correction. Linguistic experts, both Puritan and Indian, found it acceptable, though Eliot humbly observed that "after times will find many infirmities in it." In any event, the work was continued enthusiastically, and late in 1658 Eliot wrote that the first draft of the whole Bible was nearly completed: "it wanteth but revising, transcribing, and printing." [38]

Printing facilities in seventeenth century New England were primitive at best, but the peculiarities of the task demanded that it be done there rather than in the mother country. Close supervision of the typesetting and close reading of the proofs would necessitate the constant presence of both Eliot and an Indian assistant. The company therefore agreed to send over at its own expense the requisite equipment and "some honest young man, who hath skill to compose." One Marmaduke Johnson agreed in April 1660 to accept a three-year renewable appointment. Not until he had the Bible well under way did the Puritans discover that his prime reason for leaving England had been to escape from his wife.[39]

Even before Johnson arrived, Samuel Green and an Indian helper, James Printer, had run off several pages of the Bible on the college press. Samples were sent to the company in 1659; enormously impressed, the members voted to raise the quota from 1000 to 1500 copies. With Johnson contributing another experienced hand, the presses were worked with commendable speed from mid-1660 to September 1661, when the New Testament was completed. Two hundred copies were distributed to the Indians, and several were shipped to the company. Two years later the Old Testament was also in print and bound with the New. About one hundred pages of psalms in meter and a brief catechism were inserted between the Testaments. Twenty copies of the finished work went to England for special binding; one was presented to Charles II, to whom the "Up-

Biblum God" was dedicated, and others were sent to various supporters of the missionary work. Eliot fully deserved the wide acclaim he soon received — and far more than the £50 honorarium from the company — for his was not only the first Bible published in a native tongue, it was also the first to be printed in any language in the New World.[40]

The Puritan missionaries and especially John Eliot were not content to rest on their laurels. A steady stream of Indian books flowed from the Cambridge Press during the next decade, and to all of them John Eliot lent a helping hand. A Psalter and Richard Baxter's *Call to the Unconverted* appeared in 1664, an abridgement of Bishop Bayly's *Practice of Piety* came out the next year, and a work entitled *The Indian Grammer Begun, or an Essay to bring the Indian Language into Rules, etc.* was published in 1666. A Primer in 1669, some Indian Dialogues in 1671, and a Logic-Primer in 1672 complete the list of publications prior to King Philip's War. The Cambridge Press also issued a number of works in English that were intended, in part at least, to benefit the missionary work. Small wonder the corporation called Eliot "the best of God's servants." [41]

The effect of the Indian library on the Puritans' missionary efforts is difficult to measure. The first edition of the Bible and most of the other books found eager readers; most were out of print by the 1680's, and all are either rare or nonexistent today. Enough of the surviving copies bear marginal notations and signs of heavy usage — presumably by either Indians or missionaries — to prove that at least some of the books served their intended purpose.[42] But better evidence, perhaps, is the increase in the number of converts in the sixties and early seventies, very few of whom could read English. The Indian library had been their chief contact with Puritan theology.

CHAPTER XI

Missionary Efforts:
Years of Harvest, 1665-1675

H AD A majority of the Indians in New England been able to read and write a language, the problems of the missionaries would have been far simpler. But since the Algonquian tongue had no written version until John Eliot contrived one in the 1650's and 1660's, the Puritans' Indian policy attached considerable importance to providing English schooling for the natives. The motive was not entirely religious. Education of the Indian, as of the white Puritan, was aimed at improvement of the whole man, in the course of which — the New Englanders believed — the interests of religion would also be served. Thus the ties between theology and pedagogy were always strong, and education for the Indians became a cherished objective of both laymen and clergy in seventeenth century New England. And most of them hoped that the early Indian graduates of the Puritan schools would become teachers or ministers to their fellow Indians. But should the educated red men decide to follow other pursuits, all would not have been in vain, for if nothing else an English education would "Reduse them to Civillitie." [1]

The most impressive evidence of the Puritans' determination to provide the Indian with a thorough education was the establishment of an Indian College at Harvard. The prime mover of the project was President Henry Dunster, who took seriously the statement in Harvard's charter of 1650 that the purpose of the institution was "the education of the English and Indian Youth of this Country." Dunster hoped "to make Harvard the Indian Oxford as well as the New-English Cambridge." [2] This was an ambitious goal, and it is not surprising that in the long run the Indian College fell far short of Dunster's intentions. Yet if judged by the sincerity and energy of the attempt rather than by the number of degrees awarded, this aspect of the Puritans' Indian policy is in many respects the most remarkable.

The evolution of a program for higher education of the Indians began with the preparation of special teachers who would serve the Harvard faculty as experts in the Algonquian tongue. In 1653 the Commissioners of the United Colonies voted to send two sons of Thomas Stanton to Harvard at the cost of the Society for the Propagation of the Gospel. From their father they had already acquired a proficiency in Algonquian — at least the Connecticut dialects — but unfortunately for the experiment, little in the way of academic inclination.[3] Nor do they seem to have had the missionary zeal necessary for lives dedicated to uplifting the heathen. Like their father, they were probably more akin to the later American frontier type than to the Puritan reformers. Neither lad appears to have completed his own undergraduate course or to have been employed as a tutor. Several other New England youths followed the Stanton boys to Harvard, partly or wholly subsidized by the corporation, but none of them really fulfilled the intentions of their sponsors.[4] In fact throughout the seventeenth century, a shortage of competent teachers remained a critical barrier to schooling the Indian.

If the Puritans had little success in preparing a bilingual faculty for Indian collegians, they could at least point with pride at Harvard's physical facilities. In the early 1650's, the Commissioners and the corporation agreed to finance a separate building in the Yard for Indian scholars. Completed in 1655 or 1656, the new house was, according to the specifications of the Commissioners, a substantial brick structure, designed to accommodate some twenty students.[5] Unfortunately, that many Indian scholars never came to Harvard. But for almost half a century, the building was available for "hopefull Indian youthes."

During that time several Indian boys — perhaps a total of six or eight — were exposed to the rigorous curriculum of seventeenth century Harvard. One can easily imagine that a four-year stint of logic, rhetoric, Greek and Hebrew had little appeal to sons of the New England forest; what concessions the curriculum made to the drastic differences in background and preparation of Indian students we do not know, but even a substantial compromise probably would have done little to entice Indian youths to Cambridge. Still, some seen to have overcome the obstacles, for the Commissioners informed Robert Boyle in September 1662 that two Indians were then at the college "where they have good commendations of the president and their tutors, for their proficiency in learning." [6]

In addition to problems of recruitment, Harvard's experiment in Indian education seems to have been burdened with an inordinate amount of ill fortune. Among the several Indians who are believed to have attended Harvard, most did not live long enough to exert a significant influence on the other natives. Of four Indian students whose existence has

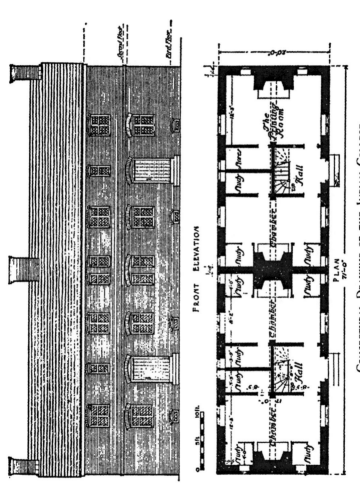

FRONT ELEVATION

PLAN

CONJECTURAL DRAWING OF THE INDIAN COLLEGE

been well established, three did not complete the course: one was killed while still an undergraduate — by Indians after he was shipwrecked at Nantucket Island; another died before graduation, presumably of disease; and the third appears to have attended college only briefly. This last Indian, John Wampus, was the only native to live a lengthy life after exposure to a Harvard education.[7] Two other Indians, both of whom died violent deaths in 1675, may have studied at the college. John Sassamon of the Massachusetts tribe perhaps attended Harvard for a time in the 1650's; his murder was one of the major events leading to the war against King Philip. And one of Philip's own Wampanoag counsellors, killed in battle by colonial forces in 1675, had apparently spent some time at the college.[8]

Only one Indian, Caleb Cheeshahteaumuck, class of 1665, completed the four-year program. This son of a minor sachem on Martha's Vineyard thereby attained a unique distinction, but he too shortly succumbed to disease, probably consumption, and died within a year after graduation.[9] Thus out of perhaps half a dozen New England natives who studied at Harvard's Indian College, only one graduated and only one lived for more than a decade or so following his brush with higher education. Since the Indian College failed to serve its intended function, the building was used for other purposes until its demolition in 1693. Still, education of Indians was not entirely abandoned, for when in 1695 the Commissioners of the corporation approved the construction of a new Harvard building from the bricks of the old Indian College, they stipulated "that in case any Indians should hereafter be sent to Colledge, they should enjoy their Studies rent free." [10]

Puritan attempts to educate the Indians of New England

were not confined to the Harvard experiment. Less dramatic but somewhat more successful were the efforts to
provide schooling on the primary and secondary levels. As
early as 1645, Governor Winthrop reported the establishment in Massachusetts of free common schools in which
young Puritans would learn to read, write, and cipher, and
"Indians' children were to be taught freely." [11] The colonial
records show that some Indians availed themselves of this
kind of instruction before 1650. This was the first step on
the educational ladder. In 1659 two Indian lads earned the
praise of President Chauncey for their proficiency in Latin,
demonstrated in a public exercise; by 1665 the Commissioners of the United Colonies had sent a score or more of
"hopeful young plants" to Elijah Corlet at the Cambridge
Grammar School and to Daniel Welde at Roxbury, who
were to prepare the budding Indian scholars for entrance to
Harvard. But again, the best of beginnings went awry. The
mortality rate among the Indian students was frightfully
high, partly, the Puritans believed, because of the radical
change in the boys' "diet, lodging, apparel, [and] studies."
And few, if any, of Corlet's and Welde's students went on
to Harvard, even if they survived the physical dangers of
Puritan society; yet some did return to teach and proclaim
the Gospel to their kinsmen. Others drifted into English
occupations such as seamanship and carpentry. One product
of Puritan schooling went to England, but he also rapidly
succumbed to the fatal effects of civilization.[12]

Aside from Massachusetts, no colony made any extensive
efforts toward formal education of the natives. Through
the activities of their missionaries, however, most colonies
did make some inroads on illiteracy. Plymouth and Connecticut were active in this respect, although prior to 1675 they

could not match the record of the Bay Colony, where by
1665 there were six praying towns, each with schools for
adolescents and adults.[13]

The reason for Massachusetts's leadership is not hard to
find; while most of the New England Puritans heartily endorsed the establishment of schools in the Indian villages,
again it was John Eliot who led the way. In 1649, he urged
that "we must have special care to have Schools for the instruction of the [Indian] youth in reading, that they may
be able to read the Scriptures at least." He also argued that
the only way to insure good instruction was to have annual
incomes for schoolmasters and dames. A year later he was
again insisting "that the care of their schooling may be
among the chiefest cares," and he soon broadened his goal to
include daily instruction in reading and writing for all Indian men, and even — he hoped — instruction in reading
for the women as well. By 1670 he wanted to begin teaching "some of the Liberal Arts and Sciences." [14] While far
too busy to give any of his own time to classroom instruction, the Roxbury pastor did assist the educational program
with translations of primers, grammars, and other aids.

Some progress was made. Eliot reported in 1651 that
many natives were learning to read and write at his Natick
school. Two Indians served as teachers under Eliot's "guidance, and inspection." The chief instructional material at
first was Eliot's Indian-language catechism, which he had
written in the teacher's lesson book. Instruction at the other
Massachusetts praying towns was even less elaborate, but
no less enthusiastically offered. In each of the Bay Colony's
Indian schools, some natives responded readily to their lessons and were sent to English institutions for further education. And on Martha's Vineyard, Thomas Mayhew was
conducting a school for the native youths of the islands; by

October 1652, he had about thirty children attending.[15] A case might even be made for the superiority of Mayhew's brand of education: the two natives who were most successful at Harvard, including the one who graduated, were both from his island.

There is no way to estimate accurately the total sum spent by the Puritans on Indian education. Not only are the records incomplete, but the payments to teachers and administrators often covered more than one kind of service. Still, there is evidence that a large proportion of the funds for missionary activities went into educational projects. The Acts of the Commissioners of the United Colonies are studded with disbursements for Indian teachers, Puritan teachers, interpreters, students' books, and maintenance of scholars as well as preachers. In the year 1662, for example, the Commissioners' accounts list salaries for eight Indian schoolmasters on Martha's Vineyard, three in Massachusetts proper, and two in Plymouth Colony. Among the colonists drawing pay that year, at least partly for educational duties, were Daniel Welde and the Eliots (father and son) of Roxbury, Daniel Gookin and Ezekiel Cheever of Cambridge, and such potential missionary-teachers as Matthew Mayhew and one of the Stanton boys. The total spent for education in 1662 was perhaps £300 out of a total budget of £728:8:6. By comparison, in the same year the Indian Bible, then in its final stages of printing, cost the Commissioners £237:5.[16]

Second only to Eliot as a champion of education for the Indians was Daniel Gookin. He had long been in favor of free schooling for the natives, and his extensive experience in Indian affairs had introduced him to its manifold difficulties. In 1674 he proposed to the Commissioners a plan that aimed at overcoming the vexing problem of cost. In the

center of the New England town of Marlboro was a plot of
150 acres owned by the praying Indians of that town. This,
Gookin suggested, should be furnished with enough houses
and barns to make an adequate farmstead, with additional
rooms for holding classes. A master could then be hired
with the free use of the farm as his only recompense. Income for books and supplies would come from tuition paid
by the white residents of Marlboro, who having less than
fifty families, had not established a school of their own;
they would now have one without having to bear the cost
of the teacher or the schoolhouse. The Indian scholars
would have to provide their own food and clothing (except
for a blue coat apiece), but the education would otherwise
be free for them. This scheme was not intended for Marlboro alone; Gookin hoped a similar arrangement could be
applied to other communities.[17] But before this promising
supplement to the Puritans' educational schemes could materialize, New England had been plunged into Philip's War.
Had that calamity been avoided, Gookin's plan might have
contributed significantly to better education for the Algonquian Indians.

*   *   *

THE decade before 1675 was the harvest time for Puritan
missionaries. The years before 1650 had been a planting
season, with only a handful of sowers in the field. But
others quickly followed the lead of Eliot and Mayhew, until by the 1660's an impressive number of helpers had taken
up the work. Soon the names of John Eliot, Jr., and the
younger John Cotton in Massachusetts, Richard Bourne
and William Leveridge in Plymouth, Abraham Pierson and
James Fitch in Connecticut, and Thomas James on Long

Island were commonly associated with conversion of the Indians.[18] Meanwhile William Bradford, Simon Bradstreet, Thomas Dudley, Theophilus Eaton, John Endicott, John Haynes, Roger Ludlow, John Mason, and John Winthrop, Jr., all served at one time or another as Commissioners for the United Colonies and were therefore closely involved in the missionary work, at least in its fiscal and administrative aspects.[19] Edward Rawson acted as agent for the Commissioners throughout this period. Among those actively involved in providing schooling for the Indians were presidents Dunster and Chauncey of Harvard, and such schoolmasters as Elijah Corlet, Daniel Welde, and Ezekiel Cheever. A combined roster of laborers in missionary and educational enterprises for the Indians would include almost every prominent name in Puritan New England.

Since their founding in the 1650's, the Bay Colony's praying towns had commanded the most attention and claimed the most achievement in the propagation of the Gospel. Natick, by virtue of its seniority and its relative proximity to Roxbury, remained the most prominent, though not always the most populous community of Christian Indians. In 1670, the chief ruler, Waban, lived there as did most of the Indian church members. In that year there were forty or fifty communicants and many others preparing for admission to full fellowship. Four years later the population of the town was calculated at twenty-nine families, or about 145 persons. In many respects Natick resembled any other Puritan town of that size: courts were kept, military training was held from time to time, most of the children attended school (though here both teachers and pupils were native), church services followed the standard

New England formula — to which most of the congregation sincerely subscribed, and the few who did not tried
hard to conceal their doubts. The preacher was one of their
own people, as were the elders and other officers of the
church and town. Moreover, Natick was producing an
abundance of Indian leadership, for it was from there that
Christian natives went out to other praying towns to promote education and the Gospel.[20]

By 1670 six more praying towns had been established in
the Bay Colony. All of them resembled Natick in general organization but differed from the first praying town and from
each other in numerous details. We are indebted to John
Eliot and Daniel Gookin for recording extensive descrip-
tions of each of the communities; Eliot's *Brief Narrative*
was written in 1670, Gookin's *Historical Collections* in
1674.[21] From these accounts it is apparent that the Puritans'
missionary program was meeting with considerable success
but always in the face of serious handicaps and occasional
setbacks.

All of the praying towns were plagued by the misfortunes attendant upon new communities. Some of the most
necessary leaders died at inopportune times, some of the followers lost their earlier enthusiasm, and funds were never so
plentiful as could be desired. In addition, there was human
hostility to contend with.

This came not so much from the white man as from the
red. There were, to be sure, occasional clashes of interest
between neighboring communities of Puritans and Christian Indians. Particularly at Marlboro, disputes arose with
disturbing frequency, but the evidence is strong that the
English settlers at Marlboro were far less responsible, tolerant, and honest than those in most other Puritan settlements, and that the troubles of the Marlboro converts re-

flected the peculiar circumstances of that community rather than a prevalent New England pattern.[22]

Far more damaging to the continued success of the propagation of the Gospel was the war between the New England tribes and the Mohawks that erupted in the 1660's. Marauders from the New York tribe had long molested the Christian Indians at Wamesit, a community of Massachusetts and Pennacook Indians located at the junction of the Concord and Merrimac rivers. In 1668 the Mohawks had slain the brother of the sachem, and on orders from Daniel Gookin Wamesit had established a garrison to prevent further encroachment by the enemy. But when other New England Indians took the warpath to Iroquois country the next year, the converts of Wamesit succumbed to the urge for revenge. In the subsequent route of the invaders, Wamesit suffered more casualties than any other praying town. For a while the future of the community looked bleak. By 1674, however, it had regained most of its former strength, largely because of the conversion of the eldest son of Chief Passaconaway of the Pennacooks.[23]

Wamesit was not the only praying town to suffer a set-back because of the Mohawk war. The town of Nashobah (Littleton), twenty-five miles west-northwest of Boston, was in Eliot's words "a place of much Affliction." For a time the community had progressed well under the leadership of a Christian sachem who also served as a ruler of fifty. Then ill fortune descended on Nashobah. When the sachem died, Eliot wrote, "a chief man in our *Israel* was taken from us." The sachem's son showed promise of following in his father's footsteps, but he, too, soon died. Then came the Mohawks, who killed the father of the pastor and caused the town to be deserted for a year. The combination of misfortune and intertribal warfare seemed to have destroyed one of the Puritans' achievements. Yet the nucleus of church members and baptized converts soon reunited the group, and by 1674 the town had fifty residents.[24]

Before 1670, most of the converts in Massachusetts Colony belonged to the Massachusetts tribe, although there were some Pennacooks at Wamesit and a town of Nipmucs had been formed at Magunkaquog (Hopkinton). With seven "old towns" now firmly established, Eliot and his colleagues began to seek new soil for promoting the Puritan faith. It was Nipmuc country, situated in central Massachusetts, that became the new frontier for Puritan missionaries in the early seventies.* Before Philip's War set all to naught, seven "new towns" had been carved out of the wilderness.

The Nipmucs had first shown some friendliness to Christianity in the 1650's, but it had waned in the sixties. However, their interest had revived by the time Daniel Gookin and John Eliot visited the Indians of the western area in the summer of 1673, "to encourage and exhort them to proceed in the ways of God." [25] The following year the missionaries returned to further the conversion of the Nipmucs, to establish civil governments for them, and to provide them with qualified clergymen. For this last purpose Eliot and Gookin took along "five or six godly persons, who we intended to present unto them for ministers." The response was encouraging, and the Nipmuc tribe seemed well on its way to the kind of reorganization into Christian communities that had taken place among the Massachusetts tribe. Much still remained to be done, however, as permanent land allotments had to be obtained from the General Court. There was also an impasse with Uncas to be settled: the

---

* Some of the towns are now within the boundaries of Connecticut. See map on p. 217.

Mohegan chieftain claimed jurisdiction over one of the towns and was "not well pleased" that the Puritan preachers were enticing his people to Christianity. In true Puritan fashion, Eliot replied that it was "his work to call upon all men every where . . . especially the Indians, to repent and embrace the gospel." At the same time he denied trying to subvert Uncas's civil jurisdiction, and Gookin assured Uncas's agent that it was not the intention of the Bay Colony "to abridge the Indian sachems of their just and ancient right over the Indians, in respect of paying tribute or any other dues." [26] Eliot and Gookin were not interested in tribute; they did want to create good Puritans out of red heathens.

By 1674 Gookin estimated at approximately eleven hundred the total number of Christian Indians distributed among the fourteen towns in the Bay Colony. Two additional towns in the Nipmuc country were approaching full Christian status, but Gookin declined to include them in his totals.[27] Only two *bona fide* churches existed in all the praying towns — one at Natick and the other at Hassawesitt (Grafton) — the remainder being in a state of catechumens until enough residents could convince the neighboring white and Indian churches that their knowledge of Scripture and depth of conviction met the Puritan standard. But most of the praying towns had at least a few church members; these attended services with one of the Indian congregations or with a neighboring English congregation. In short, while the number of converts increased fairly rapidly, the number of Indian churches remained small, in keeping with Puritan precepts.

Although the evolution of the Christian Indians' religious institutions proceeded slowly, the same could not be said of their civil counterparts. Shortly after the establishment of the first praying town, the government of Massachusetts Bay had sought to devise an efficient and just system of administration for the Indian tribes within its jurisdiction. In 1656 the General Court took an important step in that direction by appointing Daniel Gookin of Cambridge to be superintendent of all Indians who acknowledged the authority of Massachusetts. He therefore had jurisdiction over the praying towns as well as over the tribes that had submitted to the Bay Colony in the 1640's but had not accepted the Puritans' religion. Gookin continued to serve in this capacity until his death in 1687 except for the years 1658 to 1661, when he was out of the country. Major General Humphrey Atherton held the post during Gookin's absence.

The functions of the superintendent were never clearly defined, but they included sitting as a judge at the quarterly Indian courts, installing new town officials, as well as "making of orders, and giving instructions and directions, backed with penalties, for promoting and practising morality, civility, industry, and diligence in their particular callings." In addition, the superintendent was responsible for providing teachers for the Indians, distributing "encouragement" among the rulers, supervising the collection of tithes, and insuring that the Indians observed the Sabbath and attended religious services.[28]

On the local level, each praying town selected native rulers (whether always on Eliot's Biblical system is uncertain), including a number of public functionaries such as marshals and constables. The Indians' choice of officials was freely made but subject to veto by the quarterly court, an authority it exercised rarely if at all. The Indian rulers had judicial as well as executive powers, deciding alone on minor causes, and sitting with the English magistrate (Gookin or Atherton) in the quarterly court. In that body they did not enjoy complete equality with their white associate; he alone could appoint the time and place of the court, and no decision or sentence was valid without his concurrence. Still, the burden of administering justice fell largely on Indian shoulders. Only the most serious cases went to a court in which the Indians were not directly represented, for the Court of Assistants, in accordance with the colony's charter, was the final court of appeals.[29] Some Indians may have preferred their new polity. It gave them substantial self-rule and was, perhaps, less autocratic than some tribal governments.

*   *   *

It has long been customary for accounts of the Puritans' missionary effort to give almost exclusive attention to John Eliot and the Bay Colony, leaving the impression that the Puritan story and the Massachusetts story are synonymous. While John Eliot and his colleagues did make notable progress in propagating the Gospel in their colony, other missionaries contributed importantly to the spread of Christianity among the natives of New England. This was particularly true of the Mayhews on the offshore islands, and of Richard Bourne in Plymouth. Their historical reputations have suffered partly from comparison with the indefatigable Eliot, and partly from the paucity of literature that survives to sing their praises. Mayhew and Bourne, however, were as truly a part of the Puritan missionary effort as were the apostle and Daniel Gookin.

Although Martha's Vineyard was at times under the authority of Massachusetts and at times under New York during the quarter-century before Philip's War, the island enjoyed a virtually autonomous status.[30] It also experienced unparalleled success in its missionary efforts. By 1651, only about four years after Thomas Mayhew had begun exhorting the natives, he claimed 199 converts. The next year the figure was up to 283, not counting young children. He added, according to his own account (and his reputation for modesty makes exaggeration unlikely), fifty converts in one glorious day. So many professing natives wanted to attend religious services that Mayhew was forced to divide his attentions between two congregations, though each also had an Indian preacher of its own.[31] It appeared that nothing short of a disaster could keep Thomas Mayhew from converting the entire island population, then estimated at about 1500 persons, to the Puritan faith.

But in 1657 disaster did strike. Mayhew took ship for England in November of that year, accompanied by one of his most impressive converts. They and the vessel were never heard of again. The Puritan colonies received few setbacks more damaging to their missionary program. "The Lord hath given us this amazing blow to take away my brother Mayhew," John Eliot wrote sadly. But while others added their voices in mourning, another Mayhew was already taking up where the lost missionary had left off. This was Thomas Mayhew, senior, who until his son's death had lived on the island but had shown somewhat less interest in the missionary project than the younger Thomas — at least his name is rarely mentioned either in the writings of the other Puritans or in the records of the New England Company. Now with encouragement from Eliot and a stipend from the Commissioners of the United Colonies, the elder Mayhew carried on his son's work with exemplary energy, particularly for a man who was then sixty-five years old. As a layman, he was unable to act in exactly the same capacity that his son had, but the elder Mayhew nevertheless became the mainstay of the Puritan effort on the islands and proved a useful aid to the Indian clergy. Eliot paid him occasional visits, during which the Roxbury pastor assisted with baptism, the ordination of elders, and conversion. John Cotton, Jr., also preached on the island from time to time.[32]

The first church in Martha's Vineyard was established in 1659, and another was added a few years later. By 1674 the senior Mayhew could report that most of the natives on the island, including all the leading sachems, were at least nominally Christian and that some fifty of them were full communicants. They were ministered to by ten Indian preachers, who tended the two churches and several other congregations. Six services were held every Sabbath. The Indians on the nearby smaller islands of Chappaquiddick and Nantucket were equally Christianized, the latter, for example, having three hundred professing Christians, three praying towns, four native preachers, and one church of thirty communicants.[33] Thus in many respects the native population of the offshore islands resembled the religious demography of the Puritan communities of the mainland: few were full communicants, most were professing Christians, and all were more or less willing disciples of the New England way. And like the Puritans of the mainland, they also had to silence dissenters: in the early 1670's some English Anabaptists on Nantucket tried to prevent infant baptism among the Christian natives, "but now they are quiet, and meddle not with them." In fact, so thoroughly was the population of the island Christianized that on two occasions Eliot celebrated the Lord's Supper before combined Indian-white congregations — once in the English church, the other time in an Indian meeting house. The services were conducted in both English and Algonquian.[34]

Bilingual services would have been held more often had

not the language barrier made it impractical: on the eve of
King Philip's War, very few of the island's natives had any
command of English. Since only Mayhew and his two
grandsons, Matthew and John, among the Englishmen of
the island could speak the native tongue fluently, there was
no way of merging the white and Indian congregations
without great inconvenience to both.[35] An indication of the
problems facing the Puritan missionary program can be
seen here; in order to fully blend the Christian Indians with
their English brethren, far more than theological conversion was necessary. Barriers of custom and language also
had to be overcome.

If Plymouth Colony, located geographically midway between the Bay Colony and the offshore islands, did not quite
match the missionary success of its neighbors to the north
and south, its achievements were at least respectable. And
the record of the Plymouth missionaries would have been
far more impressive had it not been for the determined resistance of the Wampanoag tribe. Massasoit had befriended
the Pilgrims, but his friendship did not extend to matters of
religion. Neither did that of his heirs, Alexander and Philip.
The latter is reputed by Cotton Mather to have taken Eliot
by a coat button and boasted that he cared no more for
Christianity than he did for the button. (Mather consequently dubbed him a "blasphemous leviathan.") Daniel
Gookin, on the other hand, had some hopes for Philip's
conversion as late as 1674.[36] In any event, no missionary
claimed any success among the Wampanoags before the
bloodbath of 1675-1676.

Moreover, the Pilgrims never had missionaries of the cali-
ber of Mayhew and Eliot. William Leveridge of Sandwich
was the first of note, and oddly enough he turned to mis-

sionary work out of disgust with the progress of the Gospel among the white men of Plymouth Colony. As he saw it, dissension in the English churches was "the last but most pernicious plot of the Devill to undermine all Religion, and introduce all Atheisime and profanenesse." In a moment of pique he accepted the invitation of an Indian friend to preach to the natives, and he soon received encouragement from Eliot to continue his new course. But Leveridge never mastered the native tongue and, in any event, moved to Long Island in 1653.[37] Fortunately for Puritan interests in the Old Colony, Richard Bourne, who may have started his missionary efforts as early as 1640, took over Leveridge's former congregation. By August 1670, his converts at Maktopog (near Sandwich) were ready for church status; after a day of fasting and prayer, the church was covenanted in the presence of six Plymouth magistrates, many of the elders, and the ubiquitous Eliot.[38]

Bourne's success, like that of the other Plymouth missionaries, was achieved entirely among the Nauset tribe of Cape Cod. The Nausets proved far more susceptible than the Wampanoags, possibly because they had been a smaller, weaker, and less cohesive tribe from the earliest days of contact with the English. Like the Massachusetts and Nipmucs in the Bay Colony, the Nausets had no strong tribal attachment to serve as an alternative to the attractions of Christianity.

The missionary efforts of Leveridge, Cotton, and especially Bourne were certainly not wasted — if the number of converts is taken as the measure of success. Bourne reported to Gookin in 1674 that his colony contained eight centers of praying Indians with a total of 497 persons. One church (Maktopog) claimed twenty-seven communicants, and ninety more had been baptized. But problems remained. Most of the native converts in Plymouth lived in tribal lands that had not been specifically designated as Indian towns in perpetuity; these lands, therefore, were liable to piecemeal sale by the inhabitants. Bourne, with encouragement from Gookin, attempted to remedy the situation and soon found that the Plymouth government was eager to cooperate — "our honoured governor and magistrates being always very careful to preserve lands for them, so far as is in their power to do it." [39]

Bourne and Cotton also complained that a shortage of primers and Bibles prevented more rapid progress.[40] It may well be that Plymouth was handicapped in these and other missionary affairs by being allotted somewhat less than its due share of corporation funds.[41] Plymouth regularly received some appropriations, however, and since the colony selected two of the eight (six after 1664) Commissioners of the United Colonies, any serious skimping of the colony's allotment would have brought discernible protest.

The record of Puritan missionary achievement in Massachusetts, Martha's Vineyard, and Plymouth was not matched by the other New England colonies. Despite its large Indian population, Connecticut never rivaled either the energy or the success of its eastern neighbors. In part this can be explained by the resistance of one man, for Uncas, like Massasoit, while maintaining cordial relations with the civil authorities, persistently shunned the advances of the Puritan missionaries. Nevertheless Connecticut tried earnestly for a time. The General Court decreed in 1650 that Thomas Stanton and one church elder were to proselytize the neighboring tribes twice a year — but this had no appreciable effect. Neither did it matter that the royal charter of 1662 exhorted the inhabitants to live soe religiously, peaceably and civilly . . . [that you] may wynn and invite the Natives of the Country to the knowledge and obedience of the onely true God and Saviour of mankind, and the Christian faith, which in our Royall intentions and the Adventurers free profession is the onely and principall end of this Plantation.[42]

In the face of Uncas's opposition, this was inefficacious rhetoric. When Reverend James Fitch of Norwich began preaching to the Mohegans about 1670, he soon discovered "great obstruction" in Uncas, "an old and wicked, wilful man, a drunkard and otherwise very vitious." In 1674 Fitch reported only thirty converts.[43]

Meanwhile other Connecticut Puritans labored with equally discouraging results. As previously noted, in the late fifties Abraham Pierson of Branford — which was in New Haven's jurisdiction until that colony was absorbed by Connecticut in 1664 — had written a catechism primer. Pierson remained one of the few active missionaries in that area until his departure to New Jersey after the demise of New Haven's autonomy. He was on the Commissioners' payroll from 1654 to 1667, during which time he preached to the Indians — but with no discernible effect.[44]

Elsewhere in the colony the Puritan missionary program fared little better. The remnant of the Pequot tribe, residing in the vicinity of New London, offered some promise to the missionaries, since these Indians were entirely dependent on colonial authority and like the Nauset and Massachusetts tribes had little political solidarity. But no competent minister was willing to undertake the task of working with them. Thomas Mayhew declined the offer in 1648, and Thomas Blindman accepted it for only a brief period in the fifties. Missionary work was also undertaken among the River tribes of the Connecticut Valley, by Pierson and others, but there is no evidence that it met with any success.

If Connecticut's missionary record looked bleak, it was at least better than Rhode Island's — if we can believe the accounts from the other New England colonies. In his 1674 survey of missionary progress, Daniel Gookin asserted that he knew of no conversions in Rhode Island, which he attributed to the sachems' opposition and to the disreputable behavior of the English in that colony, "where civil government and religion . . . runs very low." Gookin considered Rhode Island's behavior doubly unfortunate, since he believed the Narragansett tribe to be among the most industrious in New England. Other Puritan spokesmen harped on the religious unorthodoxy of Roger Williams and his neighbors, and a few even took delight in their missionary failures. Thomas Shepard undoubtedly felt self-satisfied when he reported that a Narragansett sachem had discovered Williams working on a Sabbath and would therefore not listen to his preaching.[45] And Eliot recounted that two of his stellar catechumens visited Providence and Warwick where they ' heard their publike exercise, but did not understand what they meant." On their return to Massachusetts the Indians asked Eliot how such different talk could come from the same Bible.[46] This introduction to Christian schism must have been an upsetting experience to the young proselytes.

But to blame the paucity of conversions in Rhode Island on civil and religious dissension was hardly realistic. Roger Williams, after all, was a sincere Puritan in the broader sense of the word. No Bay Colony clergyman was more interested in saving souls than was Williams, and in most respects he shared the basic theology of his New England neighbors. It is not surprising, then, that Roger Williams did a good deal of preaching among the Narragansetts.[47] That he never formed a church was partly because the

Narragansetts were so intractable, partly because Rhode Island so often needed his services on other matters, and partly because his own religious convictions were for a long time unsettled. Furthermore, Rhode Island never enjoyed the beneficence of the New England Company. At a meeting in November 1657, the members of the corporation agreed "to consider of Mr. Williams and Mr. Blackstone for fitt persons to preach to the Indians in N:E:" but apparently decided in the negative as no further mention is made of the two Rhode Island ministers.[48] Since their colony was not represented in the New England Confederation, they had no Commissioners to insist on a share of the funds.

*   *   *

PURITAN achievement in spreading the Gospel among the Indians is difficult to measure. The eve of King Philip's War was the time of greatest success, and yet the total number of Indian converts probably did not exceed 2500. This represents perhaps 20 per cent of the native population of New England. The percentages for Massachusetts and the Mayhews' islands were extremely high and tend to mask the almost total lack of converts in Maine, New Hampshire, Rhode Island, and Connecticut. But at the same time it must be borne in mind that the criteria for Puritan conversion were not the same as those for some other faiths. The only Indians included in the missionaries' reports were those whose commitment to Christianity was overtly and frequently demonstrated.

That the figures are not higher can be attributed to several causes. In the first place, the Puritans got off to a slow start, in part because their attention was occupied by the arduous demands of frontier settlement and in part because they arrived largely ignorant of the problems involved in converting the natives. Before coming to New England, the Puritan had underestimated the reluctance of the natives to embrace the Gospel. As a result, the Puritan was not at first prepared for the extensive effort and expense of an elaborate missionary program. In the early years, therefore, the New England colonies left the job to the relative few who were willing and able to make a secondary career of it. One could hardly expect John Cotton, Richard Mather, and Thomas Shepard to desert their congregations in middle life, master a totally foreign language, and stride off into the forest. That a few like Eliot and Mayhew were competent for the task is more of a credit to them than a criticism of those who were not. In addition, the very nature of Puritanism made it difficult to develop an extensive corps of missionaries. So long as the individual congregation was the most important institution in Puritan polity, it would be difficult to develop a tradition of service outside the congregation.

Finally, the Puritan may have been trying to accomplish what was impossible from the outset. Unless one is ready to assume that the ultimate conversion of all peoples to Christianity is divinely ordained, there is no reason to believe that the Puritans *could* have made a Christian out of every Indian. What the New England missionary offered was not an easy package: it involved learning to read (illiteracy and Puritanism were wholly incompatible), accepting a complicated theology, and drastically changing the patterns of daily life. That is a lot to expect of anyone, especially of those on the other side of the language barrier.

In the long run, then, the Puritans stumbled over the improbable task of changing the religion and behavior patterns of 15,000 people who were scattered throughout the New England forests and who had little in common with the ways of the white man. In thwarting the Puritans' hopes, the sachems played a leading role. Massasoit, Canonicus, Uncas, and the other powerful chiefs of New England had no intention of diminishing their authority and wealth by allowing their people to succumb to a system of belief that had as one of its avowed purposes the subversion of part of the Indian complex of loyalties, customs, and mores. For example, it was all well and good for the missionaries to deny an intention of discouraging traditional tribute payments. No doubt they meant it. But their religious doctrine must ultimately have undermined the practice of tribute. Christian Indians, especially those in praying towns, ceased to rely on the sachem as a source of protection or leadership. If the sachem remained a heathen, he then appeared to the convert as Satan's henchman, and loyalty to the new faith required the Christian Indian to reject him altogether. If the tribal leader was himself a convert, he could no longer extract tribute payments merely on the grounds of hereditary position; his Christian subjects would not take kindly to payments to any leaders who did not apply the proceeds to projects condoned by their new religion. Only a sachem who had little to lose, in either power or tribute, was likely to embrace the Puritan gospel or to allow Puritan missionaries to preach to his tribesmen.

Certain characteristics that were deeply rooted in Indian society and culture also helped thwart the Puritan missionaries. There is abundant testimony that even the best of Indian converts rarely expended the kind of energy that was essential to fulfillment of the Puritan program.[49] The Indians simply would not consistently channel enough productive energy into their economic well-being to earn the surplus that would permit further refinements in living standards, bring further educational opportunities, and insure them a more integral role in the white man's society. Yet this, it must be remembered, was the society they had chosen and which they repeatedly professed to emulate.

Another native trait was far more damaging. As has been related earlier, both white and Indian spokesmen decried the susceptibility of the red man to alcoholic beverages. And the habit of excessive drinking often clung to Indians who had begun the process of Christianization. For example, Daniel Gookin deplored the number of heavy drinkers at the praying town of Nashobah. Their habit could not be blamed on unscrupulous white men, for the Indians manufactured the beverage themselves, "they having a native liberty to plant orchards and sow grain . . . of which they may and do make strong drink that doth inebriate them." [50] Perhaps the problem merely reflects the psychological unsettling that accompanied so profound an alteration in the convert's life, a change in which the influences vying for his loyalty continued to wage war in his mind long after his overt submission to the Puritan way had been completed.

Most frustrating of all to the Puritans must have been the high Indian mortality rate, which seemed to snatch away the most promising scholars and converts at the moment of greatest progress. Contact with new diseases undoubtedly provides the explanation. In that sense, the white men may have been innocent agents of destruction. Ironically, the first victims of disease were usually those the Puritans had most thoroughly converted and civilized.

Yet the Puritans kept at it doggedly. While John Eliot, the Mayhews, and Daniel Gookin were the most prominent figures in the early missionary effort, many others were equally dedicated, if perhaps less talented. Of those who served the missionary cause with distinction prior to 1675, Richard Bourne, Edward Rawson, John Cotton, Jr., and

John Eliot, Jr., deserve special mention. Others, too young to play an active role at this time, were learning from distinguished parents of the substantial work being done, and would eventually do their share in carrying it on. These included the second and third generations of Mathers, Increase and Cotton; the third generation of Winthrops, Wait-Still; the third generation of Masons, John of Norwich; the third generation of Cottons, Josiah; and innumerable progeny of the Eliot and Mayhew families.[51]

After the setback of 1675-1676 the men of the first and second generations who were still alive continued their work and were soon joined by younger hands. When in 1685 the Commissioners of the United Colonies terminated their federation, special Commissioners of Indian Affairs were selected by the colonies. Since the sole function of the new Commissioners was the administration of the missionary program, it can be assumed that the only men chosen were those who had a deep interest in the work. Among the outstanding Commissioners of the late seventeenth century were Simon Bradstreet, Joseph Dudley, Samuel Sewall, Wait Winthrop, Increase and Cotton Mather. The recent historian of the New England Company has especially high praise for the contributions of Samuel Sewall and Cotton Mather.[52]

The other side of the Puritan's missionary efforts, the attempt to "uplift" the Indian, merits more praise than it has usually received. The construction of the Indian College at Harvard, the establishment of schools in the praying towns, and the free schooling of Indian youths in the Bay Colony's village schools were more than token efforts at education. No other English colonies came close to matching it in the seventeenth century. Nor did the colonies of any other European power produce native language books and pamphlets on a scale comparable to New England's. Less successful were the efforts to change the Indian's economic habits, although the vast quantities of agricultural and construction tools, spinning wheels, and other domestic equipment give evidence of the Puritan's determination to encourage the Indian to try the Englishman's ways. Had war not intervened, much more would have been achieved.

At no time were any of these educational or economic offerings made compulsory. Rather, the Puritan saw them as an integral part of the whole process of conversion. The missionary program of the New England Puritans was intended to bring the Indians to high standards of education, industry, law and order, as well as to high standards of faith and public worship. It is little wonder that the Puritan, having set so demanding a goal, enjoyed only partial success in his missionary efforts.

CHAPTER XII

Epilogue and Conclusion

KING PHILIP'S WAR AND AFTER

IN THE spring of 1675 few Puritans had any idea that a holocaust was about to strike New England. Everything seemed to be going well in politics, in economics, in Indian affairs. To be sure, Puritan clergymen ranted from their pulpits that the new generation had lost sight of its mission and could not long escape God's wrath. But after each Sabbath service the younger generation only stretched contentedly and went home to covet its possessions and enjoy its liberties; it had heard the prophets of doom since birth and had long ago learned to treat the clergy with equal parts of respect and apathy. The signs of God's favor, decided the youth of New England, were too obvious to permit contradiction. So when the new Puritan — fast becoming a Yankee — gave a passing thought to his Indian neighbors, he took heart in the good work of Eliot and Gookin, and reflected that New England had enjoyed almost unbroken peace since the chastisement of the Pequots in 1637. Only the normal intertribal conflicts and an occasional rumor of something more serious had ruffled the tranquillity of the intervening years.

Few were still alive who could recall the Mystic Fort campaign and the Swamp Fight. Roger Williams remained, as did John Winthrop, Jr., and Lion Gardiner, but they were all far past their prime. Long since departed were the elder Winthrop, Bradford, Hooker, Mason, and the impetuous John Endicott. Of the new leaders of New England, Governor Josiah Winslow of Plymouth had been born in 1627, Fitz-John Winthrop and Increase Mather not until 1638. So out of touch with the realities of Indian war were the Puritan youth that many assumed a single colonist was fair match for any ten Indians.[1] Plymouth Colony was sufficiently confident of the prospects for continued peace that in 1674 it removed its embargo on the sale of ammunition to natives.[2]

Yet in an instant, a peaceful New England was at war — the terrible conflict that bears the name of King Philip, sachem of the Wampanoags.

It is not intended here to describe the causes and events of King Philip's War. The source materials for that topic are voluminous, and they deserve nothing less than separate and thorough treatment. This has recently been provided by Douglas E. Leach in his able *Flintlock and Tomahawk*.[3] All that will be attempted here are some suggestions of the relationship of this dramatic episode in Puritan-Indian relations to earlier Indian affairs, and some indication of later trends.

Traditional accounts of the war — aside from those of the early Puritan apologists — have clung tenaciously to a belief that the New England settlers, in an arrogant hunger for Indian lands, drove a desperate Wampanoag chief to take a final noble stand for Indian rights.[4] Even Professor Leach, who has brought much fresh interpretation to early New England history, adheres to the same explanation in a more sophisticated form. Although he assigns a large part of the responsibility for the immediate event to Philip himself, Professor Leach still finds the basic causes of the conflict in Puritan land avarice and the misunderstandings that accompanied land transactions between property-conscious Europeans and Indians innocent of the subtleties of ownership and alienation.[5]

Such a view of the causes of King Philip's War has some validity. As early as 1664 Roger Williams had expressed fear that "God Land will be (as it now is) as great a God with us English as God Gold was with the Spaniards," and the attempts of the Atherton Company — a group of New England land speculators that included the younger John Winthrop — seemed to bear out the prophecy.[6] When war came, King Philip himself attributed part of his anger at Plymouth Colony to its encroachment on his tribal holdings.

On the other hand, a careful review of New England land purchases, both in their general nature and in their specific application to the Wampanoag tribe, undermines the credibility of the land-grievance interpretation.* To be sure, the Puritan colonists did buy increasing quantities of land in the half-century after the arrival of the *Mayflower*, and as the white population swelled the urge to profit from rising land values tantalized many a New England settler. (It was this that Roger Williams feared, not any unscrupulousness in the manner of acquiring the land.) And the Indians continued to sell; even King Philip, despite his professed objections to the alienation of land to the colonists, continued to barter parts of his domain as late as 1672.[7] Meanwhile the Atherton Company was endeavoring to gain title to the Narragansetts' territory (not King Philip's), but the issue

---

* See pages 104-109.

that arose in this case was more intercolonial than inter-racial. At stake was the right of outsiders to own land in Rhode Island, and the resulting controversy between spokes-men for the colonies was as acrimonious as it was com-plex. But in point of fact, there is no substantial evidence that resentment over land transactions spurred any tribe, even the Narragansett whose grievances were the most per-sistent, into violent reprisal. Throughout the seventeenth century, Puritan institutions and Puritan officials kept most frontier dealings equitable as well as peaceful.

At bottom, Philip seems to have been moved to violence by a combination of growing Puritan influence and gradual realization of his own declining power. His father had sought out the Pilgrims as a counterforce against Narra-gansett attacks; the counterforce now far outweighed the ancient Indian enemy and was therefore no longer wel-come. It was not so much that the Plymouth Puritans now had title to more land than the Wampanoag tribe or that they had maltreated the Indians, but that they increasingly dominated the political, economic, and social life of Philip's section of New England. Sometime in the 1630's or 1640's, the white population overtook the red in Plymouth patent. The weight of numbers, combined with superior weapons, tools, and the other accoutrements of a more advanced civ-ilization, gave the old Wampanoag territory the stamp of the New Englander rather than that of the native. Most in-habitants of the territory — red and white together — now practiced the Englishman's religion, most now settled their disputes in the white man's courts, most wore English clothes, and most made their living, in part at least, in ac-cordance with the white man's economic pattern. When disputes were to be settled between the governments of New Plymouth and the Wampanoag tribe, it was the Indian chief who traveled to the Pilgrim capital. And always lurking behind the colonist's side of any debate — and tacitly recognized by both parties — was the knowledge that if mediation failed, a violent settlement would be decided ultimately in the white man's favor. Or would it . . . ?

*   *   *

WHEN war came in the early summer of 1675, the Wampanoags did not carry the fight alone. Philip had been trying for months — perhaps even years — to enroll the other New England tribes under his banner. In the end, however, he secured the assistance of only three major tribes — the Narragansetts, Nipmucs, and Pocumtucks — and of these the Narragansetts were reluctant and ineffective. That tribe, in fact, signed a treaty of amity with the colonies on July 15, 1675, when Captain Edward Hutchinson led an army of Massachusetts troops to Wickford, Rhode Island, where Roger Williams helped negotiate a treaty. In that contract the Rhode Island tribe agreed to remain loyal to the English and surrender any of Philip's followers who sought refuge in Narragansett country. When it later appeared that the tribe had failed to live up to this treaty, a force of soldiers was dispatched to obliterate the convenant-breakers before they could more openly aid the Wampanoags.[8]

The Nipmucs played a still less useful role for King Philip. They had never been a power in New England, as far back as history records, and their only contribution to Philip's cause was harassment of a few border towns in central Massachusetts. Equally ineffective was the Pocumtuck contribution. That tribe lent Philip all the support it could, but war with the Mohawks in the 1660's had shattered the Pocumtuck nation. It did, however, join with bands of Nipmucs and Narragansetts to raid Hadley, Northampton, Deerfield, and Springfield and leave the Puritan frontier a shambles.

While the Narragansetts, Nipmucs, and Pocumtucks gave assistance to King Philip, several other tribes sided with the Puritan colonies. Chief Uncas of the Mohegans sent an ambassador to the Bay Colony as early as July 1675 and offered immediate aid to the settlers. Other tribes also enlisted in the Puritan cause. The Pequots (who had either forgotten or forgiven an earlier New England fracas), the Massachusetts, the Nausets, and a considerable portion of the River tribes contributed to the final defeat of the Wampanoags. The Niantics remained neutral,[9] as did most of the Pennacooks and Abnakis, though the last two later took up their own quarrel with the New England Puritans in what Cotton Mather described as the "Decennium Luctuosum." In short, King Philip did not lead a united Indian race against alien encroachment. If such noncombatant allies of the English as those on Martha's Vineyard and Nantucket are added to those who actively aided the colonies, the division of Indian forces is perhaps almost equal. While population estimates are extremely tentative for this period, especially for native tribes, a fair estimate must acknowledge something between six and eight thousand supporters of King Philip, perhaps five thousand clearly favoring the English cause, and the remainder neutral. Once again, a New England war did not pit race against race but cause against cause. A good many Indians, for one reason or another, found the Puritan side more attractive. It is clearly inaccurate, then, to characterize Philip's resistance to Plymouth as a Pan-Indian crusade for freedom from white encroachment.

*   *   *

AMONG the Indians most loyal to the colonial cause were those who had adopted the religion of the settlers. Most of the praying Indians had endured a large measure of calumny in discarding their old ways and taking up the new, but before the war was over their allegiance was put to an even more severe test. The story of the Christian Indians in King Philip's War is one of great pathos and drama; and it sheds much light on Puritan attitudes and actions toward the Indian.

At the outset of the conflict, when each Indian had to make a choice of allegiance, the praying Indians of New England chose the English side by an overwhelming majority. The island tribes were far removed from the danger of Indian retaliation and could therefore choose without fear. The Nausets of Cape Cod had a somewhat more difficult choice to make, but they also had an English buffer between them and the Wampanoags. Only the Nipmucs and Massachusetts were in positions between the firing lines; the former, "being but raw and lately initated into the Christian profession," went with Philip, the latter adhered to the Puritan cause almost to a man. The defection of the Nipmucs was a blow, of course, but even some of them chose faith over race and attached themselves to the Massachusetts praying town at Marlboro.[10]

Puritan military strategy would have been served best by the formation of an outer ring of armed villages, from which patrols could range the woods between the stockades while one or more armies sought a showdown with the enemy. This is what Daniel Gookin and others proposed, but it never received either official or popular endorsement. Although the converts themselves wanted to form "a living wall to guard the English frontiers," once the war had begun many of the settlers came to equate "Indian" with "enemy." [11] The result was a series of grave injustices against the Christian Indians, a few of whom even lost their lives to the wartime hysteria. The whole episode lingers as an ugly blemish on the record of the New England Puritans.

There were, however, some extenuating circumstances. Many of the Nausets and a few of the Massachusetts had close ties of kinship with Philip's people and might decide to aid him from within the area of Puritan settlement. Should the praying Indians join Philip, overtly or covertly, the Puritan colonies might fall victim to a sudden frightful slaughter of the kind that had twice ravaged Virginia. Caution demanded some preventive measures, but in the end these gave way to cruel confinement. Yet if the hazards of 1675 are compared to those of 1917 and 1941, the observer will perhaps find less to condemn in the policy of the scattered settlements, threatened by an immediate antagonist, toward the praying Indians than in the policy of a mighty nation, relatively secure behind two oceans, toward its citizens of German and Japanese descent.

By proving their loyalty in early engagements with the enemy, the Nausets had been able to win the confidence of the settlers in Plymouth Colony. It was in Massachusetts Bay that the lot of the Christian natives was most harsh. Suspicious and at times belligerent toward them was a large part of the frightened and angry populace; in defense of fairness and moderation stood Puritan officialdom, the institutions of Puritan justice, and a group of determined men — among them Eliot, Gookin, and Simon Willard — who represented much that was finest in the Puritan society.

Gookin's *Historical Account of the Doings and Sufferings of the Christian Indians in New England*, written in 1677, tells the story in vivid detail and with poignant sympathy.

In early July of 1675, less than a month after hostilities had erupted, fifty-two Christian Indians from the Bay Colony took part in a campaign against Philip's stronghold at Mount Hope. Little damage was inflicted on King Philip's forces in that abortive expedition, but what there was came at the hands of Mohegan and Massachusetts Indians. The English commanders praised highly the work of the Christian natives. Still, prejudice died hard with the men in the ranks, some of whom spread rumors of cowardice and disloyalty on the part of the Indian allies. Those who took time to check the evidence saw good reason to rejoice in the steadfastness of the Indian converts, some of whom, like Job Nesutan who had done so much to make Eliot's Algonquian Bible possible, had sacrificed their lives.[12]

But the common people insisted that it was foolhardy to leave hundreds of armed and unwatched red men in the midst of English settlements. The Massachusetts Council of War finally gave way before public pressure (no omnipotent oligarchy here), and in late August restricted the praying Indians to five specified towns.[13] In self-defense the Indians pleaded for some of the English to live in their towns for the duration and observe the truth of their fidelity, but those Englishmen who carped the loudest proved the most reluctant to test their own assertions. Two New Englanders did reside at Natick for twelve weeks and gave unqualified testimonials to the civil and religious deportment of the Indians. One of the observers had formerly been skeptical of Indian loyalty; he was completely won over. But so strong was public calumny that the new champion of the Christian natives was roundly abused by some of his fellow Puritans.[14]

Before long the situation was out of control. A rough frontier captain named Samuel Mosely decided to take the law into his own hands and marched fifteen Marlboro Indians to Boston to be tried for murder. The Court of Assistants found most of the prisoners not guilty, but during the fever of the trial a mob tried to lynch the prisoners.[15] Faced with the impossibility of giving full freedom to the praying Indians without jeopardizing their lives, the General Court ordered them to be compounded on Deer Island. There some five hundred men, women, and children sat out the war. Others were later taken to an adjacent island. The praying Indians who managed to avoid this incarceration either deserted to the enemy or fled to the north. Most of those on the islands endured cold, hunger, and disease until the spring of 1677.[16]

Even in the midst of "the rude temper of those times" — Gookin's apt phrase — the Puritan government made a sincere effort to see justice done. In the hands of Puritan authorities the Indians fared well. The prisoners brought in by Mosely received an impartial trial and were given every physical and legal protection by the government against the hysteria of the masses. On another occasion several armed Indians were captured on the frontier but were released by the Massachusetts authorities when it became apparent that the captives were not fighting against the colonies.[17]

Complete protection, however, could not be provided in all instances. Before the removal to Deer Island, many praying Indians watched helplessly as lawless settlers confiscated their guns, cattle, and other possessions. So high were popular passions by September 1675 that one Indian was shot down in cold blood. The authorities arrested, imprisoned, and tried the murderer, but the jury refused to return a sentence of guilty. The accused pleaded that his gun had gone off by accident and according to Gookin, the "witnesses were mealy-mouthed in giving evidence." The magistrates sharply disapproved of this patent injustice, but the jury undoubtedly reflected popular sentiment.[18] On the other hand, for the brutal murder of three squaws and three Indian children in the summer of 1676, four men were tried by the Bay Colony courts; all were found guilty and two were executed.[19] But there were other crimes that never came to court.[20]

Before the end of the war public estimation of the praying Indians had shifted perceptibly. Philip's forces had met with frightening success throughout the first year: dozens of English towns had been deserted to the torch and tomahawk, and colonial armies had been ambushed and all but obliterated. Military necessity demanded a bolder policy. The men of Deer Island were therefore prevailed upon to bail the white man out of his dilemma. First as spies, then as emissaries for the ransom of Mrs. Rowlandson (author of the famous captivity narrative), and finally as a unit in the conclusive campaigns of the war, the Christian Indians helped win New England for their Puritan friends. Daniel Gookin estimated that during the summer of 1676 alone, the Bay Colony's praying Indians killed four hundred of the enemy. This may have turned the tide of battle. About ten of their own number lost their lives.[21]

The end of King Philip's War finally came in August 1676, when the Wampanoag chieftain, like so many of his warriors, fell at the hands of an Indian marksman. Soon the colonists and their red allies had subdued the remainder of the enemy. Philip's wife and son were sold into slavery in the West Indies. Male captives believed to have actively warred against the English were executed or sold in the Indies.[22]

The war and the related dispersal of the praying Indians cut deeply into the native population. Total Indian casualties cannot be measured with accuracy, but a figure of five thousand does not seem excessive. Surviving members of the Wampanoag, Narragansett, Nipmuc, and Pocumtuck tribes either submitted in abject surrender or fled to the relative safety of New York and Canada. Some of them later drifted back into New England, but most were absorbed by distant tribes. The Puritan colonies had suffered severely too. A higher percentage of the population suffered death or wounds in King Philip's War than in any subsequent American conflict. Battle deaths alone may have exceeded ten per cent of the forces engaged. More than a dozen towns had been totally destroyed and deserted; several more had suffered serious damage but managed to survive. The material cost to the United Colonies was estimated at £100,000.[23]

In the wake of King Philip's War, the colonies embarked upon new Indian policies designed to ensure their future safety. New England tribes were henceforth restricted to an early form of reservations, in effect the remaining tribal lands, now under close supervision from the colonial governments and hemmed in by English communities.

Fate had dealt harshly with the Indians of New England, but Puritan policy after 1676 continued to seek just treatment of them. John Eliot persisted in his missionary activities much as before, although the war had set back his work immeasurably. At the age of seventy-four the Roxbury pastor simply began again. A second edition of the "Up-Biblum God" was published in 1685, and several missionary tracts were printed in Algonquian during Eliot's lifetime and well into the eighteenth century.

Despite the best of efforts, the praying towns declined.

After the war Massachusetts reduced their number to four, which seemed sufficient for the Christian Indians of the colony. They enjoyed some prosperity and even a brief spurt in membership in the 1680's, but the death of Eliot in 1690 took away the guiding hand. Even the good reputation the Indians had so abundantly earned in the war added in the long run to their undoing. As John Eliot sadly recorded:

> The success of the Indians was highly accepted with the soldiers, and they were welcomed whenever they met them. They had them to the Ordinaries, made them drink and bred them by such an habit to love strong drink, that it proved a horrible snare unto us. They learned so to love strong drink that they would spend all their wages & pawn anything they had for *rumb* or strong drink. So drunkenness increased and quarrelling and fighting and more, the sad effects of strong drink. Praying to God was quenched, the younger generation being debauched & the good old generation of the first beginners was gathered home by death. So that Satan improved the opportunity to defile, to debase and bring into contempt the whole work of praying to God.[24]

By 1734 the names of Englishmen were beginning to appear as town officers in Natick; by 1764 the Indians were a minority there, and in 1781 Natick was incorporated as an English town.[25] The other Massachusetts praying towns had been absorbed even earlier. A few new Indian centers did appear in the western part of New England in the eighteenth century, most notably at Stockbridge where a sub-tribe of the Mahicans resided from 1736 to 1785 — with Jonathan Edwards as its clergyman for part of that time — but this did not indicate a reversal of the downward trend.[26] By 1750 the Indian population of New England was probably down to a few thousand. The perspective of the twentieth century confirms what was suspected at the time: King Philip's War, rather than bringing the demise of the white man in New England, signaled instead the beginning of the end for the Indian tribes.

CONCLUSION

ALMOST one hundred years ago the eminent New England historian John Gorham Palfrey prefaced his chapters on King Philip's War with a brief evaluation of Indian-white relations up to that event. Much that Palfrey wrote is open to criticism: his undisguised contempt for Indian intelligence and character, his unmistakable Protestant bias, his unabashed filiopiety. But at least the clergyman-historian was unencumbered by the myriad myths that have grown up since his time to cloud our understanding of the Puritans and their treatment of the New England Indians. Not all historians since the mid-nineteenth century have fallen prey to these myths — Herbert L. Osgood and Charles M. Andrews were too well grounded in primary sources to succumb at all — but the majority of writers have tended to ascribe the "typical" frontier pattern to one area of the country where it does not apply, or to ascribe to the New England Puritans certain attitudes and characteristics that they simply did not possess.

The sources of the misconceptions are difficult to trace. The writings of Helen Hunt Jackson, the frontier thesis of Frederick Jackson Turner, and only recently the sharp reaction in America against racial intolerance probably have all had a share in creating a number of assumptions that may be valid for other places and other times but have little application to the New England frontier before King Philip's War. Similarly, it is through innumerable writers that we have inherited those notions about "Puritanism" which Samuel Eliot Morison, Perry Miller, Edmund Morgan and others have labored so hard to dispel. Still myths die hard, and once established, the patterns and prejudices quickly descend from historian to popularizer and from popularizer to the general public. In any event, the traditional approaches to the story of the Puritan and the American Indian have been characterized more by hindsight than by insight.

The root of the misunderstanding—for historians and laymen alike—may lie in a faulty interpretation of cultural interaction in seventeenth-century New England. What occurred in the Puritan colonies was less a clash of cultural opposites than the inexorable expansion of one system at the expense—and sometimes at the invitation—of the other. The Puritans were politically united (on most issues), militarily strong, culturally aggressive, and rapidly increasing in number. The Indians—in a relative, not an absolute, sense—were politically fragmented, militarily weak, culturally tolerant (except occasionally to adopted captives), and rapidly decreasing in number. It was probably inevitable, therefore, that Puritan settlements would expand into Indian territory and that Puritan institutions would increasingly dominate New England. In no American mainland colony did the natives succeed in thwarting, for any appreciable time, the relentless pressure of European encroachment, and in almost every colony the colonists were encouraged by some of the Indians to settle, expand, and rule. The important question is therefore not whether the Puritans should have settled in New England or expanded their initial footholds—domination by the Puritans or some other European group would have come eventually—but how humanely and justly they introduced their brand of western civilization into the neolithic world of the American Indian.

Even without a disparity of cultures, Puritan and Indian
might have found ground for animosity in concepts of racial purity or racial superiority, had either held such notions. Some historians have wrenched Puritan rhetoric out
of its context and given it a racist meaning that was never
there. Other historians have waxed loquacious over the Indians' "pride of race" — a conception unknown to the natives of seventeenth century New England. And implicit in
the historian's argument that the natives defeated themselves in the long run by their inability to join together
against the white man is a belief that they *should* have acted
together as a race. To argue in this fashion is to be far more
race-minded than Puritans or Indians ever were. They, unlike many of their descendants, saw that considerations of
justice, religion, humanity, political policy, economic well-
being, or even the lure of technological progress, were more
valid reasons for determining actions and allegiances than
the chance assignment to a particular ethnic category.

The whole matter of Indian participation in the wars of
seventeenth century New England is a case in point. From
Massasoit's revelation of Corbitant's scheme against the
Pilgrims in 1621, to the reports of Ninigret's conspiracies in
the forties and fifties, to the dramatic disclosures made on
the eve of King Philip's War, it was the red man who
warned his white neighbor of impending attack. When war
did come, the Indians played a still more conspicuous role as
allies to the settlers. The reader will recall the contributions
made by the native confederates of the Puritans to the outcome of the Pequot conflict and King Philip's War. After
Mason's opening victory against the Pequots at Mystic —
where he was aided by Mohegans, Narragansetts, and Eastern Niantics — the surviving enemies had been prey to almost every tribe in New England; and in the struggle with

Philip, the colonial ranks were swelled by native cohorts. In both wars the assistance of friendly Indians as scouts and guides, while less dramatic, was perhaps equally important to the cause of the settlers: witness for example the contribution of Wequash in leading Mason's army undetected to Mystic Fort. Finally, it should not be forgotten that the three men who posed the greatest challenge to Puritan security in the seventeenth century were slain by fellow Indians: Sassacus by the Mohawks, Miantonomo by Uncas, and Philip by one of his former subjects.

In peacetime as in war, many of the natives of New England identified their interests and loyalties with those of the colonists. Ever since Squanto attached himself to the Pilgrim Fathers, a significant number of Indians chose to cast their lot, in part at least, with the white man's society. The manner and degree varied. Large numbers of natives came no closer than to mesh their economic habits with the more prosperous economy of the Puritans, or to make use of some of the tools, trinkets, or garments of the English. Others looked to the colonies for military protection or for arbitration in native disputes. The praying Indians went still further toward assimilation in the Puritan culture and accepted its deepest religious convictions. Finally, a few natives tried to merge their lives completely with colonial society by joining its communities and adopting all its customs and values.

In choosing to live partly or wholly in the white man's way, the American Indian was being neither weak nor disloyal to his own heritage. There is no reason to expect the member of a primitive society to forego the alluring offerings of a wealthier and more cosmopolitan civilization. To be on the side of westernization is not necessarily to be right; to resist it, on the other hand, is not necessarily noble. While there is a fascination in studying primitive cultures, there is no reason to expect the participants in those cultures to remain stagnant in the face of better alternatives. No society of any appreciable magnitude has ever chosen to reject "westernization," nor has western civilization itself remained static. Adaptation, amalgamation, and integration have been the hallmarks of human change, not only in the material realm but in human rights and social justice. There is no reason why the Indians of New England should not have shared in this almost universal trend if they so chose. There is some evidence that a far greater number of them would have thrown off the shackles of the Stone Age if their sachems had not been so reluctant to jeopardize their own power and wealth.

The tragedy is that in the long run the red man of New England succeeded neither in amalgamation nor in resistance. Rather, by 1750 the Indian had almost disappeared from the New England scene. There is therefore a temptation to suspect that Puritan policy subtly aimed at exterminating or utterly subduing the native. But here again, the myth is easier to repeat than to support. The fact that one ethnic group deteriorated while another flourished in a given area is not proof of a causal relationship. The rise of the white man and the subsequent decline of the red man are unquestionably interrelated, but only in rather subtle and unconscious ways. Perhaps the best way of understanding the interplay of forces is to restate some of the things that the New Englander did *not* do to the native.

(1) The Puritan did not push the New England Indian off his land. The myth of the early colonist as a land-grabber is one of the most persistent, for on the surface it has an immediate aura of validity. The red man once owned all the land, now he owns little or none: hence, the Puritan

must have tricked, cajoled, or forced the Indian out of his birthright.

But does this *prima facie* evidence accord with the ascertainable facts? The Indian did not hold that the entire continent belonged to him; it was rather the white man who introduced the idea that it was a red man's continent that purchase alone could transform into the domain of the white. The Indian only knew that he had enough land for himself and his tribe; the remainder was as truly *vacuum domicilium* to him as it was to the Puritan. The native therefore did not object to the occupation of proximate territory by European settlers, so long as the immigrants came as friends rather than foes. Hence the Wampanoags did not contest Pilgrim settlement at Plymouth and the Massachusetts did not object to the establishment of English towns around Boston Harbor. If the white man should desire indisputable possession of territory over which some tribe had an ancient claim, the sachems were ever ready to relinquish their title for a payment — a payment that sometimes appeared modest in European eyes, but that usually accorded with the values of Algonquian society. Deeds were carefully drawn, signed only after translation by a competent interpreter (as often as not an Indian), and filed with responsible colonial officials.*

(2) The Puritan did *not* deplete the food sources of the natives. The supply of meat unquestionably diminished as an increasing English population raised the demand while it reduced the forest areas. But it had not been on game that the Indian subsisted, but upon vegetable and grain crops, only supplemented by seafood and meat. There is simply no

---

* For a documented discussion of land tenure concepts and acquisition, see pages 109-115.

evidence, and even less logic, to support a charge that the seventeenth century Puritan colonists deprived the red man of a food supply, on which, in fact, the Indian had not been dependent in the first place.*

(3) The Puritan did *not* upset the Indian's economic pattern by underpaying him for goods and services. The Indian parted with two major trade commodities: fur and land. Fur, an item he had never considered of great marketable value, suddenly came into demand with the arrival of the settlers, thus bringing a new source of wealth to the Indian. His new prosperity, in turn, permitted him to obtain items —both native and imported — which he desired.

The sale of land, of course, imposed no hardship on a people who subsisted primarily on agricultural crops. The area actually devoted to gardens was an infinitesimal fraction of the New England soil. Most of the rest — excepting village sites, favorite fishing and trapping areas, and the like — was surplus land to the Indians. In 1620 there were more than four square miles of land for every Indian man, woman, and child in New England. It is not surprising, therefore, that the natives were glad to sell some of it to the newcomers. Moreover, the deeds of sale clearly indicate that the native usually retained the right to hunt and fish; sometimes he even retained the right to cultivate crops, though this occurred less frequently because the Indian rarely parted with cultivated land. Finally, the Puritan colonies followed the English custom of allowing the public to hunt and fish on unfenced land.†

And what was the Indian receiving in exchange for his land and his furs? A familiar theme in American historical literature has the white trader enticing the Indian out of his

* See pages 30-32.
† See pages 108-109.

magnificent forest heritage with a glitter of glass beads and a splash of pretty colored cloth — or far worse, a whiff of strong waters. Trinkets, of course, were often exchanged, and to the real satisfaction of their new native possessors; very real also was the liquor trade. But the inventories of New England merchants and traders reveal a steady flow of solid goods into the Indian economy — of new tools and materials far superior to anything the Algonquian had known, and wampum that served as currency for whites as well as Indians. (The increase in the value of wampum stands, in itself, as an example of the invigorating effect upon the native economy of English settlement.)* That the white man, particularly in the twentieth century, should think hoes, hatchets, and cloth less valuable than land does not alter the fact that the seventeenth century Indian believed he was getting a bargain. And it could easily be argued that the red man's sense of values in cherishing functional tools and textiles was more commendable than the white man's craving for beaver skins that served no better purpose than to adorn the top of his head. In any event, the fact of frequent and voluntary sale is conclusive evidence that neither side thought it was being cheated. It is a peculiar theory of economic morality that judges the equity of a barter by the value of the commodities three centuries later.

(4) The Puritan did *not* kill off the Indians in a series of protracted military actions. True, the Pequot tribe sustained heavy losses in 1637; the Wampanoags, Narragansetts, Nipmucs, and Pocumtucks suffered similarly in 1676. Yet the total casualties of the two "Indian wars" account for at most fifteen or twenty per cent of the decline in native population. And, as has been noted above, so many of the na-

---

* See pages 220-224.

tives fought on the English side in both wars that neither
struggle can be described accurately as Puritan wars against
the Indians. What casualties the Puritan inflicted on some of
the Indians of New England, he inflicted with the aid and
encouragement of an equal number of others. Statistical accuracy is impossible in such a matter, but it is not unlikely
that Puritan militia killed fewer natives in the years 1620-
1676 than did their red allies. It is also important to remember that intertribal rivalries played a major role in bringing
on the wars. John Oldham was killed by Narragansett subjects, probably for trading with the Pequots; Cutshamekin
of the Massachusetts tribe may have fired the first fatal shot
of the Pequot War; while the River tribes, Narragansetts,
and Mohegans all were eager for revenge on Sassacus's
tribe. King Philip's War was less related to intertribal rivalry, but it is perhaps significant that it was sparked by the
assassination of one Indian by several others, presumably
under Philip's direction.* [27]

(5) The Puritan did *not* drive the Indian to despair
through repeated injustices and cruelties. Certainly, colonial laws were framed by Puritans on Puritan premises, and
of course were in large part determined by intelligent self-
interest. Examples include colonial and intercolonial regulations against war; prohibition of the sale of firearms, other
weapons, and liquor to Indians; and temporary wartime restrictions on the travel of unaccompanied natives into areas
settled by colonists. But such rules were intended for the
safety of all, and they seem to have had the general endorsement of native leaders. The prohibition against war, for example, was favored by all except those who, at any given
moment, desired to wage war.

---

* See Chapter V *passim*, and pages 313-314.

Most New England Indians, however, were rarely affected by the Puritan legal machinery unless they voluntarily submitted to it. When whole tribes, through their sachems, agreed by written treaty to obey the government and laws of a particular colony, or when an individual native signified his desire to join white society, they became citizens of the colony in almost the same sense that white settlers were citizens. They obeyed the law or paid the prescribed penalty. The subject Indian was treated differently, to be sure, in that he was occasionally the object of such special legislation as exemption from military service or the restrictions imposed on the praying Indians during Philip's War. Under certain circumstances, then, he was the victim of discrimination. But for the seventeenth century, these were unusually mild proscriptions on a people that was not only an ethnic minority but a religious and political minority as well. And in each instance of discriminatory legislation, the motive was security, not social or religious bias.

Many tribes had little contact with colonial laws, encountering only those passed by the Confederation of New England or by the individual colonies for insuring the public peace. Occasionally an individual native from an autonomous tribe would become involved as plaintiff, defendant, or witness in litigation resulting from assault, trespass, or some other crime. To the extent that he rarely saw Indians on the jury, he was deprived of equal treatment before the law. But problems of language and learning made the native an unlikely jury prospect, although three of the Puritan colonies did at times seat Indian jurors in cases in which both principals were Indians.

When the Indian came to the Puritans' courts for civil or criminal cases, he could expect just treatment. It would be a mistake to gauge the fairness of the Puritan legal system on the basis of whether it distributed favorable verdicts in equal numbers to red men and white. A host of variants might create an understandable numerical imbalance. Indians, for example, owned far less personal property than English settlers, and it is not surprising that when an Indian and an Englishman were pitted against each other in cases of theft, the Indian was usually the defendant and more often than not was found guilty. On the other hand, since the natives owned far fewer cattle and swine than the whites, it was usually the native who was plaintiff and won the verdict in charges concerning the destruction of property by livestock. Case by case, the New England court records reveal no apparent discrimination against the Indian. A white plaintiff was not assured of a favorable decision, nor an Indian plaintiff of an adverse one.

Certainly in respect to punishments the Indian was not treated more harshly than the colonist. Murder of a white by an Indian merited the death penalty, and so did the reverse. For other crimes the Indian was punished in the customary ways: stocks, whipping, fines, imprisonment; and there is no evidence that such penalties were inflicted with greater harshness or magnitude on the Indian than on his white neighbor. That Indian prisoners of war were sometimes enslaved is by modern standards the blackest of marks against Puritan society, and it is slight mitigation that this was a common custom in the seventeenth century — among red men and whites alike. It is equally distressing that Puritan courts occasionally sold captives and debtors to the West Indies. Still, it is of some significance, though small consolation, that this was usually a military safeguard rather than a judicial sentence, and that the few who were sold out of the colonies during peacetime were victims of the Puritan search for a punishment comparable to banishment that could be applied to a chronic transgressor. It is significant too that war captives and prisoners sold for default of debts who were kept as slaves within New England were treated as indentured servants, and most of them probably did not serve more than a few years.*

(6) Finally, the Puritan was *not* indifferent to the natives' physical and spiritual well-being. Attempts to ameliorate hardships among the Indians appear to have been sincere and commendable. Edward Winslow's medical ministrations in the 1620's and the Massachusetts settlers' aid in the early 1630's are cases in point.

Equally sincere, but far less commendable to the modern observer, were Puritan missionary efforts.† John Eliot and his cohorts aimed unabashedly at the complete destruction of Indian culture, and they enjoyed some success in the praying towns and with a few scattered individuals. Whether such actions are praiseworthy or deplorable depends on subjective judgments: concerning the utility of literacy and classical learning, the validity of English social norms (monogamy, for example), the importance of certain signs of conformity (clothing, for example), and the efficacy of reformed Protestantism. In any event, the Puritans' efforts to "civilize" and Christianize were genuine attempts to share what *they* considered God's true faith and right ways, and the missionaries relied overwhelmingly on persuasion rather than coercion.

*   *   *

THAT the New England frontier exhibited a pattern of interracial relations far different from the one so frequent on later frontiers is a tribute to both the individual Puritan and

---

* See Chapter VII.
† See Chapters IX-XI *passim.*

to the character of his society. The explanation for the contrast undoubtedly lies largely in the nature of Puritanism itself. The immigrants to New England between 1620 and 1675 brought with them a theology and a polity that stressed social responsibility and high moral standards, and if some did not live up to those expectations, the bulk of the settlers did. Thus New England society was highly self-disciplined from the start. The Puritans who came to America had a clear idea of their mission, and they did not intend to let it be diverted from within or without. They knew what kind of rules they wanted to impose on themselves and needed no directives from London to insure an orderly community.

The character of New England society profited also from certain convictions that were especially, though not exclusively, Puritan. Foremost, perhaps, was the prevailing belief that the Indians were children of Old Zion who had strayed — theologically as well as geographically — and were therefore to be treated as potential converts rather than as implacable foes. Important, too, was the absence of a conscious racial distinction: the Indian, in Puritan eyes, was not the product of a different race but of a different culture. Finally, the English heritage of the settlers made more likely a government of laws rather than of men, especially in the hands of a highly educated and disciplined society. Thus Puritanism, bolstered by English traditions and beliefs, gave a unique cast to the New England frontier.

In many ways Puritanism manifested in New England both its vigor and its restraint. The settlers' economic system expanded rapidly but seldom to the point of exploiting its baser opportunities by defrauding the Indian or by interfering with his liberties; commercial restrictions were placed on the white man alone. The legal system of the New England colonies also expanded, but here again, usually within careful limits of procedure and impartiality. And the propagation of the Gospel was carried out under similar controls. The Puritan missionaries approached their task with energy, but they did not let their enthusiasm degenerate into forced conversions or persecution of heathens.

As Puritan society expanded, its controls kept pace, checking any boisterous frontiersmen, curbing the inclinations of the occasional vicious settler, thwarting the designs of the inevitable avaricious trader. When the first decades had passed and the English colonies were clearly dominant in their region, there was no decline in the supervision of land transactions, liquor and arms sale, or in the impartiality of justice. At times there were mistakes — as under Endicott in 1636; at times there were evasions — as the illicit sales of firearms and liquor show; but during most of the period before Philip's War, the Puritan colonies expanded peacefully and moderately, with both native and New Englander enjoying the security of a well-regulated frontier.

But the very self-discipline of Puritanism, as well as the superior technology of European society, made it inevitable that the English community would soon displace the Indian tribes as the predominant force in the area. Discipline kept the colonies tightly knit and cooperative. Indian society, by contrast, had no unity in politics, in purpose, or even, perhaps, in language. As time passed, then, the Puritan world grew stronger and more pervasive, the Indian society grew weaker and less influential — especially on its own members. Helping this process to take place and helping to make it redound to the credit of the Puritans is the fact that

the self-restraint of the New England colonies witnessed remarkably few lapses, and those lapses usually met censure
from the Puritans themselves.

*   *   *

IT was not through threat of starvation, or demon rum, or
the greed and malice of white settlers that so many of the
Indians were eliminated from New England, but through
three agencies: disease, war, and migration. Most important, probably, was disease, for from the first coming of the
white man the Indian was exposed to a number of new sick-
nesses to which he was highly susceptible. Even before the
Pilgrims arrived, disease had swept away one-third or more
of the native population. Subsequent epidemics reduced it
still further. The new maladies struck down friend and foe
alike; if anything they showed a perverse preference for the
native who had taken up the white man's ways. For example, Squanto died less than two years after adhering to the
Plymouth settlers, Indian students in English schools rarely
lasted much longer, and the praying Indians suffered heavily
too. On the other hand, those Indians who were partially or
wholly segregated from the white man did not incur as high
mortality rates as did those who mingled more directly with
colonial society. It is ironic that the Puritans of New England, innocent of so many of the charges against them,
should unwittingly cause the devastation of their Indian
neighbors through communicable disease.

Of war, enough has already been said to make it clear
that armed conflicts resulted in heavy casualties but were
certainly not solely responsible for the sharp decline in Indian population. Nor were they ever simple clashes of
white man against red. On the other hand, since warfare
ordinarily takes the lives of young men, and since inter-

tribal warfare continued to add its toll to the list of victims, the final effect of seventeenth century conflict was a serious check on the native population. These wars, of course, continued into the eighteenth century, and helped to maintain the steady decline of native population after 1675.

Finally, many Indians from fear of diseases, from wartime necessity, or from a desire to escape the challenge of the new era, moved west and north to areas still untouched by the European. But others remained behind to meet the spreading influence of the more advanced society. Much like the white frontiersmen of the eighteenth and nineteenth centuries, the New England Indian responded in a variety of ways to "civilization's" intrusion into his area. Some, especially the tribal leaders who had enjoyed great power under the old regime, resisted the new ways. Others eagerly took them up, while still others remained where they were born and quietly ignored all innovation.

* * *

FROM the perspective of the 1960's, it is easy to detect sins of omission in the Puritan's conduct of Indian affairs, and there is much we can point to that he did with less tact and judgment than a later generation could desire. But at the same time, it is hard to chastise the Puritans for failing to do better a job that their contemporaries did not perform as well. The record of the New England colonies, when tested comparatively rather than absolutely, becomes another credit on their list of achievements in the New World. The suspicion and hostility of the pre-Pilgrim period was changed during the early decades of Puritan settlement into an atmosphere of amity and cooperation, and that atmosphere remained prevalent until 1675. There were exceptions, of course. It would have been too much to expect any two large groups of seventeenth century mortals to live in such proximity without occasional friction. The Indian tribes had not been able to live together peaceably before the European came, the European nations could not live together peaceably on either side of the Atlantic, and even within the Puritan colonies there was something less than complete tranquillity. This made it unlikely that natives and New Englanders, separated by vast differences in political, economic, religious, and social patterns, could share the same corner of the continent without occasional clashes of interests and arms. But what is most significant is that when troubled times came, the division of forces was not along purely ethnic lines. Red man and white had enough in common to pick their quarrels over issues rather than over skin color. This, in itself, is a sign that the New England Puritans had treated the Indians not as a race apart, but as fellow sinners in God's great universe. It also makes more poignant the ultimate failure of the Puritans' mission to the wilderness.

Appendices

Treaty of Peace and Alliance Between Chief Massasoit of the Wampanoags and Governor Carver of Plymouth, 22 March 1621 [*Heath*, Mourt's Relation, 56-57].

1. That neither he nor any of his should injure or do hurt to any of our people.

2. And if any of his did hurt to any of ours, he should send the offender, that we might punish him.

3. That if any of our tools were taken away when our people were at work, he should cause them to be restored, and if ours did any harm to any of his, we would do the like to them.

4. If any did unjustly war against him, we would aid him; if any did war against us, he should aid us.

5. He should send to his neighbor confederates, to certify them of this, that they might not wrong us; but might be likewise comprised in the conditions of peace.

6. That when their men came to us, they should leave their bows and arrows behind them, as we should do our pieces when we came to them.

Lastly, that doing thus, King James would esteem of him as his friend and ally.

Treaty of Hartford, 21 September 1638
[R.I. Hist. Soc. Coll., *III. 177-178*].

ARTICLES BETWEEN THE INGLISH IN CONNECTICUT AND THE INDIAN SACHEMS

A Covenant and Agreement between the English Inhabiting the Jurisdiction of the River of Connecticut of the one part, and Miantinomy the chief Sachem of the Narragansetts in the behalf of himself and the other Sachems there; and Poquim or Uncas the chief Sachim of the Indians called the Mohegans in the behalf of himself and the Sachims under him, as Followeth, at Hartford the 21st of September, 1638.

Imp'r. There is a peace and a Familiarity made between the sd Miantinome and Narragansett Indians and the sd Poquim and Mohegan Indians, and all former Injuryes and wrongs offered each to other Remitted and Burryed and never to be renued any more from henceforth.

2. It is agreed if there fall out Injuryes and wrongs for fuetur to be done or committed Each to other or their men, they shall not presently Revenge it But they are to appeal to the English and they are to decide the same, and the determination of the English to stand And they are each to do as is by the English sett down and if the one or the other shall Refuse to do, it shall be lawfull for the English to Compel him and to side and take part if they see cause, against the obstinate or Refusing party.

3. It is agreed and a conclusion of peace and friendship made between the sd Miantinome and sd Narragansetts and the sd Poquim and the sd Mohegans as long as they carry themselves orderly and give no just cause of offence and that they nor either of them do shelter any that may be Enemyes to the English that shall or formerly have had hand in murdering or killing any English man or woman or consented thereunto, They or either of them shall as soon as they can either bring the chief

Sachem of our late enemies the Peaquots that had the chief
hand in killing the English, to the sd English, or take of their
heads, As also for those murderers that are now agreed upon
amongst us that are living they shall as soon as they can possibly
take off their heads, if they may be in their custody or Else
whensoever they or any of them shall come Amongst them or
to their wigwams or any where if they can by any means come
by them.

4. And whereas there be or is reported for to be by the sd
Narragansetts and Mohegans 200 Peaquots living that are men
besides squawes and paposes. The English do give unto Miantinome and the Narragansetts to make up the number of Eighty
with the Eleven they have already, and to Poquime his number,
and that after they the Peaquots shall be divided as abovesd,
shall no more be called Peaquots but Narragansetts and Mohegans and as their men and either of them are to pay for every
Sanop one fathom of wampome peage and for every youth
half so much — and for every Sanop papoose one hand to be
paid at Killing time of Corn at Connecticut yearly and shall not
suffer them for to live in the country that was formerly theirs
but is now the Englishes by conquest neither shall the Narra-
gansets nor Mohegans possess any part of the Peaquot country
without leave from the English And it is always expected that
the English Captives are forthwith to be delivered to the English, such as belong to the Connecticut to the Sachems there,
And such as belong to the Massachusetts; the sd agreements are
to be kept invoylably by the parties abovesd and if any make
breach of them the other two may joyn and make warr upon
such as shall break the same, unless satisfaction be made being
Reasonably Required.

The Mark of MIANTINOMMY,
The Marks of POQUIAM alias UNKAS.
      JOHN HAINES,
      ROG'R LUDLOW,
      EDW'RD HOPKINS.

APPENDIX III

Submission of the Massachusetts sub-tribes to the
Massachusetts Bay Colony, 8 March 1644 [Mass.
Col. Rec., *II, 55*].

Wee have and by these presents do voluntarily, and without
any constraint or perswasion, but of our owne free motion,
put ourselves, our subjects, lands, and estates under the government and jurisdiction of the Massachusets, to bee governed
and protected by them, according to their just lawes and orders,
so farr as wee shalbee made capable of understanding them;
and wee do promise for ourselves, and all our subjects, and all
our posterity, to bee true and faithfull to the said government,
and ayding to the maintenance thereof, to our best ability, and
from time to time to give speedy notice of any conspiracy,
attempt, or evill intension of any which wee shall know or
heareof against the same; and wee do promise to bee willing
from time to time to bee instructed in the knowledge and worship of God. In witnes whereof wee have hereunto put our
hands the 8th of the first month, anno 1643-1644

> CUTSHAMACHE,
> NASHOWANON,
> WOSSAMEGON,
> MASKANOMETT,
> SQUA SACHIM.

The section pertaining to Indians in the second code of laws of Massachusetts Bay Colony, 1648 [Farrand, Laws and Liberties of Massachusetts, 28-29].

Indians.

It is ordered by Authorities of this Court; that no person whatsoever shall henceforth buy land of any Indian, without licence first had & obtained of the General Court: and if any shall offend heerin, such land so bought shall be forfeited to the Countrie.

Nor shall any man within this Jurisdiction directly or indirectly amend, repair, or cause to be ammended or repaired any gun, small or great, belonging to any Indian, nor shall indeavour the same. Nor shall sell or give to any Indian, directly or indirectly anysuch gun, or any gun-powder, shot or lead, or shot-mould, or any militarie weapons or armour: upon payn of ten pounds fine, at the least for everie such offence: and that the court of Assistants shall have power to increase the Fine; or to impose corporall punishment (where a Fine cannot be had) at their discretion.

It is also ordered by the Authoritie aforesaid that everie town shall have power to restrein all Indians from profaning the Lords day.

2. *Whereas it appeareth to this Court that notwithstanding the former laws, made against selling of guns, powder and Amunition to the Indians, they are yet supplyed by indirect means, it is therefore ordered by this Court and Authoritie thereof;*

That if any person after publication heerof, shall sell, give or barter any gun or guns, powder, bullets, shot or lead to any Indian whatsoever, or unto any person inhabiting out of this Jurisdiction without licence of this Court, or the court of As-

sistants, or some two Magistrates, he shall forfeit for everie gun
so sold, given or bartered ten pounds: and for everie pound
of powder five pounds: and for everie pound of bullets, shot
or lead fourty shillings: and so proportionably for any greater
or lesser quantitie.

3. It is ordered by this Court and Authoritie therof, that
in all places, the English and such others as co-inhabit within
our Jurisdiction shall keep their cattle from destroying the
Indians corn, in any ground where they have right to plant;
and if anyof their corn be destroyed for want of fencing, or
hearding; the town shall make satisfaction, and shall have
power among themselves to lay the charge where the occasion
of the damage did arise. Provided that the Indians shall make
proof that the cattle of such a town, farm, or person did the
damage. And for encouragement of the Indians toward the
fencing in of their corn fields, such towns, farms or persons,
whose cattle may annoy them that way, shall direct, assist and
help them in felling of trees, ryving, and sharpening of rayls,
& holing of posts: allowing one Englishman to three or more
Indians. And shall also draw the fencing into place for them,
and allow one man a day or two toward the setting up the same,
and either lend or sell them tools to finish it. Provided that such
Indians, to whom the Countrie, or any town hath given, or
shall give ground to plant upon, or that shall purchase ground
of the English shall fence such their corn fields or ground at
their own charge as the English doe or should doe; and if any
Indians refuse to fence their corn ground (being tendred help
as aforesaid) in the presence and hearing of any Magistrate or
selected Townsmen being met together they shall keep off all
cattle or lose one half of their damages.

And it is also ordered that if any harm be done at any time
by the Indians unto the English in their cattle; the Governour
or Deputie Governour with two of the Assistants or any three
Magistrates or any County Court may order satisfaction according to law and justice.

4. *Considering that one end in planting these parts was to propagate the true Religion unto the Indians: and that divers of them are become subjects to the English and have ingaged themselves to be willing and ready to understand the law of God, it is therfore ordered and decreed,*

That such necessary and wholsom Laws, which are in force, and may be made from time to time, to reduce them to civilitie of life shall be once in the year (if the times be safe) made known to them, by such fit persons as the General Court shall nominate, having the help of some able Interpreter with them.

Considering also that interpretation of tongues is appointed of God for propagating the Truth: and may therfore have a blessed successe in the hearts of others in due season, it is therfore farther ordered and decreed,

That two Ministers shall be chosen by the Elders of the Churches everie year at the Court of Election, and so be sent with the consent of their Churches (with whomsoever will freely offer themselves to accompany them in that service) to make known the heavenly counsell of God among the Indians in most familiar manner, by the help of some able Interpreter; as may be most available to bring them unto the knowledge of the truth, and their conversation to the Rules of Jesus Christ. And for that end that somthing be allowed them by the General Court, to give away freely unto those Indians whom they shall perceive most willing & ready to be instructed by them.

And it is farther ordered and decreed by this Court that no Indian shall at any time *powaw*, or performe outward worship to their false gods: or to the devil in any part of our Jurisdiction; whether they be such as shall dwell heer, or shall come hither: and if any transgresse this Law, the *Powawer* shall pay five pounds; the Procurer five pounds; and every other countenancing by his presence or otherwise being of age of discretion twenty shillings.

Rules for the Praying Indians at Concord, Massachusetts, January 1647 [Mass. Hist. Soc. Coll., *3 ser. IV, 39-40*].

Conclusions and Orders made and agreed upon by divers Sachims and other principall men amongst the Indians at Concord, *in the end of the eleventh moneth, An. 1646.*

1. That everyone that shall abuse themselves with wine or strong liquors, shall pay for every time so abusing themselves, 20 s.
2. That there shall be no more *Pawwowing* amongst the *Indians.* And if any shall hereafter *Pawwow*, both he that shall *Powwow*, & he that shall procure him to *Powwow*, shall pay 20 s apeece.
3. They doe desire that they may be stirred up to seek after God.
4. They desire they may understand the wiles of Satan, and grow out of love with his suggestions, and temptations.
5. That they may fall upon some better course to improve their time, then formerly.
6. That they may be brought to the sight of the sinne of lying, and whosoever shall be found faulty herein shall pay for the first offence 5 s. the second 10 s. the third 20 s.
7. Whosoever shall steale any thing from another, shall restore fourfold.
8. They desire that no *Indian* hereafter shall have any more but one wife.
9. They desire to prevent falling out of *Indians* one with another, and that they may live quietly one by another.
10. That they may labour after humility, and not be proud.
11. That when *Indians* doe wrong one to another, they may be lyable to censure by *fine* or the like, as the *English* are.

12. That they pay their debts to the *English*.
13. That they doe observe the Lords-Day, and whosoever shall prophane it shall pay 20 s.
14. That there shall not be allowance to *pick lice*, as formerly, and eate them, and whosoever shall offend in this case shall pay for every louse a penny.
15. They weill weare their *haire* comely, as the *English* do, and whosoever shall offend herein shall pay 5 s.
16. They intend to reforme themselves, in their former greasing themselves, under the Penalty of 5 s. for every default.
17. They doe all resolve to set up prayer in their *wigwams*, and to seek to God both before and after meats.
18. If any commit the sinne of fornication, being single persons, the man shall pay 20 s and the woman 10 s.
19. If any man lie with a beast he shall die.
20. Whosoever shall play at their former games shall pay 10 s.
21. Whosoever shall commit adultery shall be put to death.
22. Wilfull murder shall be punished with death.
23. They shall not disguise themselves in their mournings, as formerly, nor shall they keep a great noyse by howling.
24. The old Ceremony of the Maide walking alone and living apart so many dayes 20 s.
25. No *Indian* shall take an English mans *Canooe* without leave under the penaltie of 5 s.
26. No *Indian* shall come into any *English* mans house except he first knock: and this they expect from the *English*.
27. Whosoever beats his wife shall pay 20 s.
28. If any *Indian* shall fall out with, and beats another *Indian*, he shall pay 20 s.
29. They desire they may bee a towne, and either to dwell on this side the *Beare Swamp*, or at the east side of Mr. *Flints Pond*.

APPENDIX VI

Example of an unrestricted deed of land; no rights are retained by the Indians [Original in John Carter Brown Library, Providence; reprinted in R.I. Col. Rec., I, 130-131].

Deed from Miantonomi to Randall Holden, John Greene and others of Shawomet, now known as Warwick, January, 12, 1642.

Know all men: that I, Myantonomy, Cheefe Sachem of the Nanheygansett, have sould unto the persons heare named, one parsell of lands with all the right and privileges thereoff whatsoever, lyinge uppon the west syde of that part of the sea called Sowhomes Bay, from Copassanatuxett, over against a little Iland in the sayd Bay, being the North bounds, and the outmost point of that neck of land called Shawhomett; beinge the South bounds ffrom the sea shoare of each boundary uppon a straight lyne westward twentie miles. I say I have truly sould this parsell of lande above sayde, the proportion whereof is according to the mapp under written or drawne, being the forme of it unto Randall Houlden, John Greene, John Wickes, ffrancis Weston, Samuell Gorton, Richard Waterman, John Warner, Richard Carder, Sampson Shotten, Robert Potter, William Wuddall, ffor one hundreth and fortie foure ffathom of wampumpeage. I say I have sould it, and possession of it given unto the men above sayed, with the ffree and joynt consent of the present inhabitants, being natives, as it appeares by their hands hereunto annexed.

Dated the twelfth day of January, 1642. Beinge enacted uppon the above sayed parsell of land in the presence off

PUMHOMM   [his mark, a pipe]
JANO   [his mark, a bird]
JOHN GREENE, Jun'r

MYANTONOMY,
Sachem of Shawhomett,
[his mark, a vertical bow and arrow]
TOTANOMANS,
his marke, [a musket].

APPENDIX VII

*Example of a restricted deed of land; certain rights
are retained by the Indians* [Ply. Col. Rec., *II,
130-131*].

An agreement made the 17th of May, 1648, betweene Paupmunnuck, with the consent of his brother, and all the rest of his associats on the one part, and Captaine Myles Standish in the behalfe of the inhabitants of Barnestable on the other part, as followeth, viz: —

That the said Paupmunnucke hath, with the free and full consent of his said brother and associats, freely, fully, and absolutely bargained and sould unto the said Captaine Myles Standish in the behalfe and for the use of the inhabytants of Barnstable aforesaid, all his and thayer right, title, and intereste in all his and thayer lands lying and beeing within the precincts of Barnstable afforesaid, faring upon the sea, commonly called the South Sea, buting home to Janno his land eastward, and a little beyond a brooke, called the First Hearing Brooke, weastward, and to Nepoyetums and Seqqunneks lands northward, exsepting thirty acars which hee the said Paupmunnuck hath retained to the proper use and behoofe of himselfe, his brother, and associates, for and in consideration of 2 brasse kittells and one bushell of Indian corn, to bee dewly and trewly payed unto him, the said Paupmunnuck by the said inhabytants of Barnstable, between the date heerof and November next inseuing; allso, one halfe part of so mutch fence as will fence in the thirty acars of land afforesaid for the said Paupmunnuck.

to bee dewly and trewly made by the laste of Aprill next in-
sewing the date heerof; allso, the said Paupmunnck and his
associates shall have free leave and liberty to hunt in the said
lands, provided thay give notice to the said inhabitants before
thay sett any trappes, as allso fully and diligenttly to see all
thair trappes evry day, that soe in case any are taken or in-
trapped therin, thaye shall speedyli lett them out, and acquaint
the said inhabytants forthwith therof; as allso to acquainte
them if thay shall perceive any cattell to have broken out of
thayer trapps before thay come unto them.

In wittnes of all and singuler the preemises heerof, thay have
heerunto sett thayer hands the day and yeare above written.

All which conditions, in case thay doe not dilligently observe,
thay shall pay whatsoever damage comes to any mans cattell
through thayer default heerin.

Notes

I: ANTECEDENTS

1. James Rosier, "A True Relation of the Voyage of Captaine George Waymouth," in Henry S. Burrage, ed., *Early English and French Voyages* (New York, 1906), 391; Ferdinando Gorges, "Brief Narration . . . ," in *Maine Hist. Soc. Coll.*, 1 ser. II (1847), 17 (2nd pagination); Henry S. Burrage, *The Beginnings of Colonial Maine, 1602-1628* (Portland, 1914), 48-53.
2. Carolyn Thomas Foreman, *Indians Abroad, 1493-1938* (Norman, Oklahoma, 1943), 15. The first American Indians to see England had been brought over by Cabot in 1497.
3. Gorges, "Brief Narration," 17 (2nd pagination).
4. Prior to 1588, Englishmen frequently fished off Newfoundland, since that territory was believed to be within Portugal's domain; when they ventured farther south they usually did not let it be known, for the southern part of the continent was claimed by Spain — with whom England had a treaty of amity. The defeat of the Armada in 1588 permitted England to explore the Spanish claim without fear of major reprisal, although Spain still occasionally attempted to enforce her prerogative by seizing vessels and incarcerating trespassers. Samuel Purchas, *Hakluytus Posthumus, or Purchas His Pilgrims* (20 vols., Glasgow, 1905-1907), XIX, 284-297; Henry O. Thayer, *The Sagadahoc Colony* (Portland, 1892), 164-166; William I. Roberts, "The Fur Trade of New England in the Seventeenth Century" (unpublished Ph.D. dissertation, University of Pennsylvania, 1958), 2-3.
5. For treatments of the various developments that led to English colonization, see especially Charles H. Levermore, ed., *Forerunners and Competitors of the Pilgrims and Puritans* (2 vols., Brooklyn, 1912), I, ch. 1; Louis B. Wright, *Religion and Empire: The Alliance Between Piety and Commerce in English Expansion, 1558-1625* (Chapel Hill, N.C., 1943), *passim;* Wallace Notestein, *The English People on the Eve of Colonization, 1603-1630* (New York, 1954), ch. 21.

6. John Brereton, "A Briefe and True Relation," in H. S. Burrage, *Early English and French Voyages*, 329-340; "Documents Relating to Captain Bartholomew Gosnold's Voyage to America, A.D. 1602," in *Mass. Hist. Soc. Coll.*, 3 ser. VIII (1843), 75-79; H. S. Burrage, *Beginnings of Colonial Maine*, 19.

7. "Documents Relating to Gosnold's Voyage," 80-81.

8. Bartholomew Gosnold to his father (7 Sept. 1607) in *ibid.*, 70-72; *ibid.*, 98; Brereton, "A Briefe and True Relation," 327-328.

9. Purchas, *Purchas His Pilgrims*, *passim*; John Smith, *True Travels* (2 vols., Richmond, 1819), I, 108; H. S. Burrage, *Beginnings of Colonial Maine*, 23; Wright, *Religion and Empire*, chs. 2, 5; A. L. Rowse, *Elizabethans and America* (New York, 1959), 59-60.

10. Martin Pring, "A Voyage Set out from the Citie of Bristoll," in H. S. Burrage, *Early English and French Voyages*, 347-351.

11. Charles M. Andrews, *The Colonial Period of American History* (4 vols., New Haven, 1934-1938), I, 79.

12. Alexander Brown, ed., *Genesis of the United States* (2 vols., Boston, 1890), I, 26. Rosier's account, "A True Relation of the Voyage of Captaine George Waymouth, 1605 . . . ," is in H. S. Burrage, *Early English and French Voyages*, 353-394, and in *Mass. Hist. Soc. Coll.*, 3 ser. VIII, 125-158.

13. Rosier, "True Relation," 377-378, 388, 391. Champlain, who visited the area soon after Waymouth departed, was told by the natives that some fishermen recently had killed five Indians. Presumably Champlain's informants referred to the five men taken to England by Waymouth. [Samuel de Champlain], *Voyages of Samuel de Champlain, 1604-1618*, edited by W. L. Grant (New York, 1907), 77.

14. Gorges, "Brief Narration," 17 (2nd pagination).

15. Pedro de Zuñiga to King of Spain (6 March 1606) in Brown, *Genesis of the United States*, I, 46.

16. Rosier, "True Relation," 391-392; James P. Baxter, ed., *Sir Ferdinando Gorges and His Province of Maine* (3 vols. [*Publications of the Prince Society*, XVIII-XX], Boston, 1890), II, 80.

17. Ferdinando Gorges, "A Brief Relation of the Discovery and Plantation of New England," in *Mass. Hist. Soc. Coll.*, 2 ser. IX (1823), 3; Gorges, "Brief Narration," 18-19 (2nd pagination); Purchas, *Purchas His Pilgrims*, XIX, 284; Thayer, *Sagadahoc Colony*, 164-166; Andrews, *Colonial Period*, I, 80. At least one of the Indians was eventually retrieved (Gorges, "Brief Narration," 26 [2nd pagination]).

18. Gorges, "Brief Relation," 3; Gorges, "Brief Narration," 19 (2nd pagination); William Strachey, *Historie of Travell into Virginia Britania*, edited by Louis B. Wright and Virginia Freund (London, 1953), 164.

19. Gorges, "Brief Narration," 21 (2nd pagination); Brown, *Genesis of the United States*, II, 969.

20. Strachey, *Historie of Travell into Virginia Britania*, 165; "A Relation of a Voyage to Sagadahoc," in H. S. Burrage, *Early English and French Voyages*, 408; Andrews, *Colonial Period*, I, 91.

21. Strachey, *Historie of Travell into Virginia Britania*, 172; Gorges, "Brief Narration," 21-22 (2nd pagination); Charles E. Banks, "New Documents Relating to the Popham Expedition, 1607," in *Proceedings of the American Antiquarian Society*, new ser. XXXIX (1929), 313; Gorges to Earl of Salisbury (7 Feb. 1607) in Baxter, *Gorges and Maine*, III, 161.

22. Strachey, *Historie of Travell into Virginia Britania*, 170-173; Popham to James I (13 Dec. 1607) in Thayer, *Sagadahoc Colony*, 118.

23. Gorges to Earl of Salisbury (2 Dec. 1607) in Baxter, *Gorges and Maine*, III, 158-159; Banks, "New Documents," 312; Gorges, "Brief Relation," 4; Strachey, *Historie of Travell into Virginia Britania*, 173.

24. Biard to the Reverend Father Provincial at Paris (31 Jan. 1612) in Reuben Gold Thwaites, ed., *Jesuit Relations and Allied Documents* (73 vols., New York, 1959), II, 45, 47; Gorges to Earl of Salisbury (3 Dec. 1607) in Baxter, *Gorges and Maine*, III, 158; Thayer, *Sagadahoc Colony*, 120. See also *The Popham Colony: A Discussion of Its Historical Claims* (Boston, 1866), *passim*.

25. William W. Hening, ed., *The Statutes at Large: Being the Laws of Virginia . . .* (13 vols., Richmond, 1819-1823), I, 74.

26. Gorges, "Brief Relation," 4-5; Gorges, "Brief Narration," 23, 35 (2nd pagination); John Smith, *Works*, edited by Edward Arber (Birmingham, England, 1884), 597; Andrews, *Colonial Period*, I, 148-149.

27. Smith, *Works*, 219, 696-698, 701; Gorges, "Brief Narration," 25-28 (2nd pagination); Gorges, "Brief Relation," 5-7.

28. Smith, *Works*, 699; Gorges, "Brief Relation," 6. According to Gorges, as soon as it was "understood that they were *Americans*, and found to be unapt for their use, [the Spanish] would not meddle with them."

29. Gorges, "Brief Relation," 6; Thomas Dermer to [?] (30 June 1620) in William Bradford, *History of Plymouth Plantation*, edited by Worthington C. Ford (2 vols., Boston, 1912), I, 207-208; *A Journal of the Pilgrims at Plymouth [Mourt's Relation]*, edited by Dwight B. Heath (New York, 1963), 52, 70; Champlin Burrage, ed., *John Pory's Lost Description of Plymouth Colony . . .* (Boston and New York, 1918), 43.

30. Smith, *Works*, 697-698, 731-732; John Smith, "New England Trials," in *Chronicles of the Pilgrim Fathers* ([Everyman's Library] London and New York, n.d.), 245; Gorges, "Brief Relation," 7; R. V. Coleman, *The First Frontier* (New York, 1948), 121; Bradford Smith, *Captain John Smith* (Philadelphia, 1953), chs. 9, 13. Cf. Samuel G. Drake, *The Aboriginal Races of North America [Book of the Indians]* (15th ed., Philadelphia, 1859), 83.

31. See, for example, [Edward Johnson], *Johnson's Wonder-Working Providence*, edited by J. Franklin Jameson (New York, 1910), 23-26; Bradford, *History of Plymouth Plantation*, I, 52-68, 121-124; "Arguments for the Plantation of New England" in Allyn B. Forbes, ed., *Winthrop Papers* (5 vols., Boston, 1929-1947), II, 106-149. See also

John Gorham Palfrey, *History of New England* (5 vols., Boston, 1865-1890), I, chs. 3, 4, and 7; Perry Miller, *Errand into the Wilderness* (Cambridge, Mass., 1956), ch. 1; and James Truslow Adams, *The Founding of New England* (Boston, 1921), ch. 4.

32. Edward Winslow, "Winslow's Brief Narration," in *Chronicles of the Pilgrim Fathers* (Everyman's Library), 360; [Robert Cushman], "Cushman's Discourse," in Alexander Young, ed., *Chronicles of the Pilgrim Fathers* (Boston, 1844), 256-261.

33. For a contrary view of the Puritans' attitude toward the Indians, see Roy Harvey Pearce, *The Savages of America: A Study of the Indian and the Idea of Civilization* (Baltimore, 1953), 19-25.

34. [Roger Williams], *The Complete Writings of Roger Williams* (7 vols., New York, 1963), I, 84; Henry Whitfield, ed., "The Light appearing more and more towards the perfect Day . . . ," in *Mass. Hist. Soc. Coll.*, 3 ser. IV (1834), 119, 127-128; Edward Winslow, "The Glorious Progress of the Gospel, amongst the Indians in New England," in *ibid.*, 72-74, 93-95; and Drake, *Aboriginal Races*, 22-26.

35. Cotton Mather, *Magnalia Christi Americana* (2 vols., Hartford, 1820), I, 503, 506.

36. See, for example, Williams, *Complete Writings*, I, 140.

37. See, for example, Johnson, *Wonder-Working Providence*, 40-42; [John White], *The Planters Plea, or the Grounds of Plantations Examined . . .* (London, 1630 [Facsism. Rockport, Massachusetts, 1930]), 25. Thomas Morton agreed that the plague was intended to clear the way for the Gospel (Thomas Morton, *The New English Canaan*, edited by Charles Francis Adams, Jr. [Boston, 1883], 120-134).

38. Gorges, "Brief Narration," 24 (2nd pagination). One Frenchman died of the plague, according to John Smith, "New England's Trials," 251.

39. The best discussion of the plague is in Bradford, *History of Plymouth Plantation*, I, 221n. See also Charles Francis Adams, Jr., *Three Episodes in Massachusetts History* (2 vols., Boston, 1896), I, 104; Oliver Wendell Holmes, "The Medical Profession in Massachusetts," in Massachusetts Historical Society, *Early History of Massachusetts* (Boston, 1869), 260-261; John Duffy, *Epidemics in Colonial America* (Baton Rouge, Louisiana, 1953), 43, 141; Robert Austin Warner, "The Southern New England Indians to 1725: A Study in Culture Contact" (unpublished Ph.D. dissertation, Yale University, 1935), 284-285.

40. Thomas Dermer to Samuel Purchas (ca. fall 1619) in *Purchas His Pilgrims*, XIX, 129-130; T. Morton, *New English Canaan*, 132-133. Estimates of the casualties vary widely, with a mortality of one-third representing the most conservative judgment. Robert Cushman doubted that one in 20 had survived (Young, *Chronicles of the Pilgrim Fathers*, 258), while John White believed that in many areas 99 of 100 had died (*Planter's Plea*, 25). Writing at the end of the century, Cotton Mather used Cushman's figure (*Magnalia Christi Americana*, I, 49). See also Smith, *Works*, 933; John Josselyn, "An Account of Two Voyages to New-England," in *Mass. Hist. Soc.*

Coll., 3 ser. III (1833), 293-294; Emmanuel Altham to Sir Edward Altham (Sept. 1623) in Sydney V. James, Jr., ed., *Three Visitors to Early Plymouth* (Plimouth Plantation, Mass., 1963), 29; Phinehas Pratt, "A Declaration of the Affairs of the English People that First Inhabited New England," in *Mass. Hist. Soc. Coll.*, 4 ser. IV (1858), 479.

41. Daniel Gookin, "Historical Collections of the Indians in New England," in *Mass. Hist. Soc. Coll.*, 1 ser. I (1792), 148; Bradford, *History of Plymouth Plantation*, I, 242; Johnson, *Wonder-Working Providence*, 40-42; John Winthrop, "Diverse Objects," in *Winthrop Papers*, II, 141; and Ferdinando Gorges, "Description of New England," in Baxter, *Gorges and Maine*, II, 77.

42. Bradford, *History of Plymouth Plantation*, I, 202.

43. *Ibid.*, 202-206; *Mourt's Relation*, 55; John Josselyn, "Chronological Observations of America, From the Year of the World to the Year of Christ, 1673," in *Mass. Hist. Soc. Coll.*, 3 ser. III (1833), 374; T. Morton, *New English Canaan*, 244; Gorges, "Brief Narration," 17 (2nd pagination); Gorges, "Brief Relation," 7-9; C. Burrage, *John Pory's Lost Description of Plymouth*, 43; Thomas Dermer to Samuel Purchas (ca. fall 1619) in *Purchas His Pilgrims*, XIX, 129-130; J. N. Kinnicut, "The Plymouth Settlement and Tisquantum," in *Proceedings of the Mass. Hist. Soc.*, XLVIII (1914-1915), 103-118; Samuel Eliot Morison, "Squanto," in *Dictionary of American Biography*; H. S. Burrage, *Early English and French Voyages*, 394; Baxter, *Gorges and Maine*, I, 104. Cf. Drake, *Aboriginal Races*, 69-71.

44. Gorges, "Brief Narration," 25 (2nd pagination); Foreman, *Indians Abroad*, 15-28.

45. Act II, sc. 2.

46. Great Britain, Public Record Office, *Calendar of State Papers, Colonial Series, America and the West Indies*, I (London, 1860), 18; Foreman, *Indians Abroad*, ch. II. Some Englishmen seem to have never viewed the Indian as anything but a curio. As late as 1632 a London correspondent of John Winthrop, Jr., asked him "to send over some of your Indian Creatures alive when you may best, as one brought over a Squirrel . . . and one a Rattlesnake Skin with the rattle." Henry Jacie to John Winthrop, Jr. (9 Jan. 1632) in *Winthrop Papers*, III, 58.

47. There is no way of knowing how familiar the early Puritans were with the available literature on the American Indian. It can be presumed, however, that most of the leaders would have read some or all of the travel accounts published by Hakluyt, Purchas, Smith, and others (e.g., see Emmanuel Altham to Sir Edward Altham [Sept. 1623] in James, *Three Visitors to Early Plymouth*, 33). They may also have availed themselves of the works of Las Casas and other non-English observers. On such matters, however, Puritan writings are annoyingly silent.

II: THE INDIANS OF NEW ENGLAND

1. Paul Le Jeune, "Brief Relation of the Journey to New France," in Reuben Gold Thwaites, ed., *The Jesuit Relations and Allied Documents* (73 vols., New York, 1959), VI, 27. See also Regina Flannery, *An Analysis of Coastal Algonquian Culture* (Catholic University of America Anthropological Series, no. 7, 1939).

2. James Mooney, "The Aboriginal Population of America North of Mexico," in *Smithsonian Miscellaneous Collections*, LXXX, no. 7 (1928), 2.

3. *Ibid.*, 4-22. I have computed the Indian population density on the assumption that there were 18,000 natives — a generous figure — in New England in 1620. There were then probably 850,000 in the entire area of the future United States, or about .28 per square mile, including the virtually uninhabited mountain and desert areas.

4. David I. Bushnell, Jr., "Tribal Migrations East of the Mississippi," in *Smithsonian Miscellaneous Collections*, LXXXIX, no. 12 (1934), 2-9, and maps 1-4.

5. See, for example, [Roger Williams], *The Complete Writings of Roger Williams* (7 vols., New York, 1963), I, 84; [William Wood], *Wood's New-England's Prospect* (Boston, 1865), 104.

6. John Eliot to Richard Baxter (20 June 1669) in F. J. Powicke, ed., "Some Unpublished Correspondence of the Rev. Richard Baxter and the Rev. John Eliot, 'the Apostle to the American Indians,' 1656-1682," in *Bulletin of the John Rylands Library*, XV (1931), 453-454; Edward Winslow, "Good Newes from New England," in Edward Arber, ed., *The Story of the Pilgrim Fathers* (London, 1897), 591; Williams, *Complete Writings*, I, 80; Thomas Shepard, "The Clear Sun-shine of the Gospel Breaking Forth upon the Indians in New-England," in *Mass. Hist. Soc. Coll.*, 3 ser. IV (1834), 43; Daniel Gookin, "Historical Collections of the Indians in New England," in *ibid.*, 1 ser. I (1792), 149; Wood, *New-England's Prospect*, 102-103; Albert Gallatin, "A Synopsis of the Indian Tribes of North America," in *Transactions and Collections of the American Antiquarian Society [Archaeologia Americana]*, II (1836), 33-36; Frank G. Speck, "Native Tribes and Dialects of Connecticut: A Mohegan-Pequot Diary," in *Bureau of American Ethnology*, 43rd Annual Report (1924-1925), 212; Froelich G. Rainey, "A Compilation of Historical Data Contributing to the Ethnography of Connecticut and Southern New England Indians," in *Bulletin of the Archeological Society of Connecticut*, reprint no. 3 (March 1956, originally published April 1936), 6.

7. For example, Francis Higginson, *New-Englands Plantation* (Salem, 1908), 105; John Winthrop, "Reasons to be Considered, and Objections with Answers," in Allyn B. Forbes, ed., *Winthrop Papers* (5 vols., Boston, 1929-1947), II, 141.

8. Williams, *Complete Writings*, I, 134-135; Wood, *New-England's Prospect*, 101.

9. Williams, *Complete Writings*, I, 134-135, 175-176, 197-199; Wood, *New-England's Prospect*, 27-40, 101; Thomas Morton, *The New English Canaan*, edited by Charles Francis Adams, Jr. (Boston, 1883), 160-161, 192-193, 221-227; John Josselyn, "An Account of Two Voyages to New-England," in *Mass. Hist. Soc. Coll.*, 3 ser. III (1833), 296, 302-307; Emmanuel Altham to Sir Edward Altham (Sept. 1623) in Sydney, V. James, Jr., ed., *Three Visitors to Early Plymouth* (Plimouth Plantation, Mass., 1963), 25, 28.

10. Williams, *Complete Writings*, I, 183-184; Wood, *New-England's Prospect*, 13; Gookin, "Historical Collections," 149; Rainey, "Ethnography of Connecticut," 10-15.

11. M. K. Bennet, "The Food Economy of the New England Indians, 1605-1675," in *The Journal of Political Economy*, LXIII (1955), 369-395.

12. Williams, *Complete Writings*, I, 222-223; Gookin, "Historical Collections," 154; William H. Whitmore, ed., *John Dunton's Letters from New England* (Boston, 1867), 218-220; Josselyn, "Account of Two Voyages," 308-309.

13. Some authorities indicate a distinction between Sachem and Sagamore, but the evidence to the contrary is overwhelming. See, for example, Edward Winslow, "The Glorious Progress of the Gospel, amongst the Indians in New England," in *Mass. Hist. Soc. Coll.*, 3 ser. IV (1834), 78, 82; Wood, *New-England's Prospect*, 113 (not paginated); Higginson, *New-Englands Plantation*, 105; T. Morton, *New English Canaan*, 205; David Pulsifer, ed., *Acts of the Commissioners of the United Colonies* (2 vols., *Records of the Colony of New Plymouth*, IX-X [Boston, 1859]), I, 28, 30, 32 and *passim*. Cf. Thomas Lechford, "Plain Dealing: or, Newes from New-England," in *Mass. Hist. Soc. Coll.*, 3 ser. III (1833), 103; "Dudley's Letter to the Countess of Lincoln," in Alexander Young, ed., *Chronicles of the First Planters of the Colony of Massachusetts Bay . . .* (Boston, 1846), 305; and John Smith, *Works*, edited by Edward Arber (Birmingham, England, 1884), 939.

14. Whitmore, *John Dunton's Letters*, 219; Wood, *New-England's Prospect*, 89-90; Rainey, "Ethnography of Connecticut," 33-34.

15. Winslow, "Good Newes from New England," 586-587; Williams, *Complete Writings*, I, 224; Wood, *New-England's Prospect*, 90; Shepard, "Clear Sun-shine of the Gospel," 38; T. Morton, *New English Canaan*, 205; Frank G. Speck, *Territorial Subdivisions and Boundaries of the Wampanoag, Massachusetts, and Nauset Indians* (Museum of the American Indian, Heye Foundation, *Indian Notes and Monographs*, no. 44 [New York, 1928]), 30-31.

16. Whitmore, *John Dunton's Letters*, 220; Winslow, "Good News from New England," 587-588; Williams, *Complete Writings*, I, 226, 253;

Gookin, "Historical Collections," 154; Wood, *New-England's Pros-pect*, 89-90; Speck, *Territorial Subdivisions*, 16-18.

17. Williams, *Complete Writings*, I, 180; Speck, *Territorial Subdivisions*, 16-18; Henry Whitfield, "The Light appearing more and more to-wards the perfect Day . . . ," in *Mass. Hist. Soc. Coll.*, 3 ser. IV (1834), 139.

18. Wood, *New-England's Prospect*, 92-94; Williams, *Complete Writings*, I, 211-212, 272; Gookin, "Historical Collections," 154; Lechford, "Plain Dealing," 104; T. Morton, *New English Canaan*, 150-152; Shepard, "Clear Sun-shine of the Gospel," 38; Winslow, "Glorious Progress of the Gospel," 77; Whitfield, "The Light Appearing," 113-116; [John Wilson?], "The Day-Breaking, if not the Sun-Rising of the Gospell . . . ," in *Mass. Hist. Soc. Coll.*, 3 ser. IV (1834), 19-20; Francis Parkman, *The Jesuits in North America in the Seven-teenth Century* (New Library Edition, Boston, 1905), 29-30. For sim-ilar practices among the Mohawks, see "Narrative of a Journey into the Mohawk and Oneida Country, 1634-1635," in J. Franklin Jame-son, ed., *Narratives of New Netherland, 1609-1664* (New York, 1909), 152-153.

19. Gookin, "Historical Collections," 154; Wilson, "The Day-Breaking," 19-20; Thomas Mayhew to Henry Whitfield (16 Oct. 1651) in Whit-field, "Strength out of Weaknesse; or a Glorious Manifestation of the Further Progresse of the Gospel among the Indians in New-Eng-land," in *Mass. Hist. Soc. Coll.*, 3 ser. IV (1834), 185-187; Frederick Webb Hodge, ed., *Handbook of American Indians North of Mexico* (2 vols., Washington, 1907), II, 303; Rainey, "Ethnography of Con-necticut," 41.

20. Roger Williams to John Winthrop (28 Feb. 1638) in *Winthrop Pa-pers*, IV, 17. Williams, *Complete Writings*, I, 109-110, 151, 164, 171, 188, 191, 208-210; Gookin, "Historical Collections," 154; Wood, *New-England's Prospect*, 92; Lechford, "Plain Dealing," 105; Whitfield, "The Light Appearing," 111; Higginson, *New-Englands Plantation*, 36; [William Morrell], "Morrell's Poem on New England," in *Mass. Hist. Soc. Coll.*, 1 ser. I (1792), 138; John Eliot and Thomas May-hew, Jr., "Tears of Repentance: Or, a Further Narrative of the Prog-ress of the Gospel amongst the Indians in New-England," in *ibid.*, 3 ser. IV (1834), 202.

21. Williams, *Complete Writings*, 95, 108, 154; Wood, *New-England's Prospect*, 105; John Eliot to Edward Winslow (12 Nov. 1648) in Winslow, "Glorious Progess of the Gospel," 82.

22. See, for example, Ferdinando Gorges, "Brief Narration," in *Maine Hist. Soc. Coll.*, 1 ser. II (1847), 24, 28 (2nd pagination).

23. Wood, *New-England's Prospect*, 66, 95, 101; Increase Mather, *A Relation of the Troubles which have hapned in New-England By reason of the Indians there*, edited by Samuel G. Drake under the title, *Early History of New England* (Boston, 1864), 182*n*; Rainey, "Ethnography of Connecticut," 25-27.

24. Wood, *New-England's Prospect*, 94-95; Philip Vincent, "A True Relation of the Late Battel Fought in New England between the English and the Pequet Salvages," in *Mass. Hist. Soc. Coll.*, 3 ser. VI (1837), 38-39; Josselyn, "Account of Two Voyages," 309-310.

25. Williams, *Complete Writings*, I, 264.

26. Wood, *New-England's Prospect*, 95; John Underhill, "News from America," in *Mass. Hist. Soc. Coll.*, 3 ser. VI (1837), 26; John Mason, "A Brief History of the Pequot War," in *ibid.*, 2 ser. VIII (1826), 142.

27. T. Morton, *New English Canaan*, 153-157; George T. Hunt, *The Wars of the Iroquois: A Study in Intertribal Trade Relations* (Madison, 1960), 19.

28. Josselyn, "Account of Two Voyages," 309-310; Rainey, "Ethnography of Connecticut," 28-29. Torture of captives was common among tribes in eastern North America. See Nathaniel Knowles, "The Torture of Captives by the Indians of Eastern North America," in *Proceedings of the American Philosophical Association*, LXXXII (1940), 151-225.

29. Williams, *Complete Writings*, I, 138, 140, 264; Wood, *New-England's Prospect*, 95. Cf. Marc Lescarbot, *The History of New France*, edited by W. L. Grant (3 vols., Toronto, 1907-1914), II, 124, III, 263-272.

30. Wood, *New-England's Prospect*, 70; Josselyn, "Account of Two Voyages," 294; "Documents Relating to Captain Bartholomew Gosnold's Voyage to America, A.D. 1602," in *Mass. Hist. Soc. Coll.*, 3 ser. VIII (1843), 71; [Samuel de Champlain], *Voyages of Samuel de Champlain, 1604-1618*, edited by W. L. Grant (New York, 1907), 61, 73.

31. Williams, *Complete Writings*, I, 140; T. Morton, *New English Canaan*, 147; Lechford, "Plain Dealing," 103; Morrell, "New England," 135; Wood, *New-England's Prospect*, 71.

32. Wood, *New-England's Prospect*, 86. Present day descendants of the New England Indians are probably darker than their ancestors because of the extensive miscegenation with Negroes that has taken place since the seventeenth century.

33. *Ibid.*, 74, 104; Williams, *Complete Writings*, I, 244, 266, 274-275; Lechford, "Plain Dealing," 103; T. Morton, *New English Canaan*, 170; Gookin, "Historical Collections," 153.

34. Wood, *New-England's Prospect*, 77-79, 82-83; Williams, *Complete Writings*, I, 91, 96, 98, 160; T. Morton, *New English Canaan*, 137; Gookin, "Historical Collections," 153; Morrell, "New England," 132. Cf. Nicholas Perrot, "Memoir on the Manners, Customs, and Religion of the Savages of North America," in Emma Helen Blair, trans. and ed., *The Indian Tribes of the Upper Mississippi Valley and Region of the Great Lakes*, I (Cleveland, 1911), 132-135.

35. [John Winthrop], *Winthrop's Journal*, edited by James K. Hosmer (2 vols., New York, 1908), I, 63, 142, II, 33; Wood, *New-England's Prospect*, 78-82; Williams, *Complete Writings*, I, 156-157, 161.

36. Williams, *Complete Writings*, VII, 35; E[dward] W[inslow] to [George Morton?] (11 Dec. 1621) in *A Journal of the Pilgrims at Plymouth* [*Mourt's Relation*], edited by Dwight B. Heath (New York, 1963), 82; T. Morton, *New English Canaan*, 161.

37. Josselyn, "Account of Two Voyages," 295; Williams, *Complete Writings*, I, 162, 225; Gookin, "Historical Collections," 149-150; Morrell, "New England," 131. See also Champlain, *Voyages*, 73. Roger Williams's opinion of the natives seems to have fluctuated drastically. For his less favorable views see, for example, his letters to John Winthrop in *Winthrop Papers*, III, 444-445, 451, IV, 26, 39; and to other members of the Winthrop family in *ibid.*, V, 251, 289, 326-327.

38. Lechford, "Plain Dealing," 103; Morrell, "New England," 131; Wood, *New-England's Prospect*, 88, 105; Gookin, "Historical Collections," 141, 178; Shepard, "Clear Sun-shine of the Gospel," 59. Cf. Lescarbot, *History of New France*, III, 195, 217.

39. Williams, *Complete Writings*, I, 225; T. Morton, *New English Canaan*, 174; Josselyn, "Account of Two Voyages," 304; Gookin, "Historical Collections," 151; Daniel Gookin, "An Historical Account of the Doings and Sufferings of the Christian Indians in New England, in the Years 1675, 1676, 1677," in *Transactions and Collections of the American Antiquarian Society* [*Archaeologia Americana*], II (1836), 515.

40. Wood, *New-England's Prospect*, 105-106; Williams, *Complete Writings*, I, 120-127, 134-135; Gookin, "Historical Collections," 149-150, 191; Higginson, *New-Englands Plantation*, 35; T. Morton, *New English Canaan*, 134-135; Josselyn, "Account of Two Voyages," 295-296; Champlain, *Voyages*, 96; Rainey, "Ethnography of Connecticut," 19-20; Charles C. Willoughy, *Antiquities of the New England Indians* (Cambridge, Massachusetts, 1935), 289-292. Excellent models of Algonquian buildings can be seen at the Peabody Museum of Harvard University.

41. Williams, *Complete Writings*, I, 120-125; T. Morton, *New English Canaan*, 135; Gookin, "Historical Collections," 150; Champlain, *Voyages*, 96; Wood, *New-England's Prospect*, 106; *Mourt's Relation*, 66-67; Rainey, "Ethnography of Connecticut," 20-21.

42. T. Morton, *New English Canaan*, 141-142; Winslow, "Good Newes from New England," 590-591; Williams, *Complete Writings*, I, 203-205; Wood, *New-England's Prospect*, 72-73; Josselyn, "Account of Two Voyages," 297-298; Emmanuel Altham to Sir Edward Altham (Sept. 1623) in James, *Three Visitors to Early Plymouth*, 30; [Edward Johnson], *Johnson's Wonder-Working Providence*, edited by J. Franklin Jameson (New York, 1910), 262; Rainey, "Ethnography of Connecticut," 15-17.

43. Wood, *New-England's Prospect*, 71-73; Gookin, "Historical Collections," 153; Shepard, "Clear Sun-shine of the Gospel," 40.

44. Martin Pring, "A Voyage Set out from the Citie of Bristoll," in

Henry S. Burrage, ed., *Early English and French Voyages* (New York, 1906), 347; "Documents Relating to Gosnold's Voyage," 74-75; Wood, *New-England's Prospect*, 74.

45. Wood, *New-England's Prospect*, 105-109; Lechford, "Plain Dealing," 103; Josselyn, "Account of Two Voyages," 303-304; Williams, *Complete Writings*, I, 183; Morrell, "New England," 136.

46. Gookin, "Historical Collections," 151-152; T. Morton, *New English Canaan*, 159; Williams, *Complete Writings*, I, 191-192; Wood, *New-England's Prospect*, 101; Champlain, *Voyages*, 66.

47. Williams, *Complete Writings*, I, 194.

48. *Ibid.*, 188, 197-199; Wood, *New-England's Prospect*, 98-100.

49. Williams, *Complete Writings*, I, 158, 254-258; Wood, *New-England's Prospect*, 74, 95-98; Josselyn, "Account of Two Voyages," 57; Gookin, "Historical Collections," 153.

50. Wood, *New-England's Prospect*, 63.

51. Although this classification of tribes is not based on any single primary or secondary source, it conforms in general to that in John R. Swanton, *The Indian Tribes of North America* (Smithsonian Institution, Bureau of American Ethnology, Bulletin no. 145 [Washington, 1952]), 13-22.

52. *Ibid.*, 13-15; James P. Baxter, "The Abnakis and their Ethnic Relations," in *Collections and Proceedings of the Maine Hist. Soc.*, 2 ser. III (1892), 21-40; Hodge, *Handbook of American Indians*, I, 2-6.

53. Mooney, "Aboriginal Population," 4; Swanton, *Indian Tribes of North America*, 13-15; Wood, *New-England's Prospect*, 67-68. Cf. Wendell S. Hadlock, "War Among the Northeast Woodland Indians," in *American Anthropologist*, new ser. XLIX (1947), 204-221.

54. Frank G. Speck, "The Eastern Algonkian Wabanaki Confederacy," in *American Anthropologist*, new ser. XVII (1915), 289-305.

55. Gookin, "Historical Collections," 149; Mooney, "Aboriginal Population," 4; Swanton, *Indian Tribes of North America*, 17-18; Hodge, *Handbook of American Indians*, II, 225-226.

56. Gookin, "Historical Collections," 148; Mooney, "Aboriginal Population," 4; Speck, *Territorial Subdivisions*, 94-105; Hodge, *Handbook of American Indians*, I, 816-817; Swanton, *Indian Tribes of North America*, 19-20. I have deviated from Hodge's spelling of the tribal name in order to make it coincide with the commonly accepted form.

57. Gookin, "Historical Collections," 148; Samuel G. Drake, *The Aboriginal Races of North America* [*Book of the Indians*] (15th edition, Philadelphia, 1859), 81-85; Hodge, *Handbook of American Indians*, II, 903-904; Speck, *Territorial Subdivisions*, 51-88, 114-115; Swanton, *Indian Tribes of North America*, 24-26.

58. Gookin, "Historical Collections," 147-148; Drake, *Aboriginal Races*, 117-118; Hodge, *Handbook of American Indians*, II, 28-30; Swanton, *Indian Tribes of North America*, 27-29.

59. Wood, *New-England's Prospect*, 69-70; Gookin, "Historical Collec-

tions," 147; John W. DeForest, *History of the Indians of Connecticut* (Hartford, 1852), 59-62; Swanton, *Indian Tribes of North America*, 31-33.

60. Williams, *Complete Writings*, I, 82*n*, 263.

61. The group that seceded from the Pequots in 1636 may have been a band of the tribe which had retained the Mohegan name. See the Dutch map of 1616 reprinted in John Romeyn Brodhead, *Documents Relative to the Colonial History of New York*, edited by E. B. O'Callaghan (15 vols., Albany, 1853-1857), I, 12-13.

62. Hodge, *Handbook of American Indians*, II, 74-75; Swanton, *Indian Tribes of North America*, 22-23; Roger Williams to Massachusetts General Court (7 May 1668) in Williams, *Complete Writings*, VI, 326.

63. Sylvester Judd, *History of Hadley* (new edition, Springfield, 1905), 114-115; Hodge, *Handbook of American Indians*, II, 270; Swanton, *Indian Tribes of North America*, 23-24.

64. Rainey, "Ethnography of Connecticut," 4, 7-8; Swanton, *Indian Tribes of North America*, 33, 44-48.

65. Hodge, *Handbook of American Indians*, II, 40-41; Swanton, *Indian Tribes of North America*, 21-22.

66. E. M. Ruttenber, *History of the Indian Tribes of Hudson's River* (Albany, 1872), 41-44; Hodge, *Handbook of American Indians*, I, 786-789, II, 913.

67. Swanton, *Indian Tribes of North America*, 42-43.

68. Wood, *New-England's Prospect*, 64-66; Williams, *Complete Writings*, I, 102*n*, 105, 138; Williams to John Winthrop (24 Oct. 1636) in *Winthrop Papers*, III, 318; same to same (3 July 1637) in *ibid.*, 438; Gookin, "Historical Collections," 161-163; Thwaites, *Jesuit Relations*, XXXVI, 103-105; Johannes Megapolensis, "A Short Account of the Mohawk Indians . . . ," in Jameson, *Narratives of New Netherland*, 174-175. According to Reverend Megapolensis, "the common people eat the arms, buttocks and trunk, but the chiefs eat the head and heart."

69. William Bradford, *History of Plymouth Plantation*, edited by Worthington C. Ford (2 vols., Boston, 1912), I, 206-208; *Mourt's Relation*, 52, 70.

70. I. Mather, *Relation of the Troubles*, 59.

71. Phinehas Pratt, "A Declaration of the Affairs of the English People that First Inhabited New England," in *Mass. Hist. Soc. Coll.*, 4 ser. IV (1858), 479; T. Morton, *New English Canaan*, 130-132; Bradford, *History of Plymouth Plantation*, I, 210-211; Drake, *Aboriginal Races*, 80-81, 84-85. See also Great Britain, Public Record Office, *Calendar of State Papers, Colonial Series, America and the West Indies*, I (London, 1860), 111.

72. Wood, *New-England's Prospect*, 82.

73. Williams, *Complete Writings*, I, 83, 207-208; Morrell, "New England," 138.

74. Williams, *Complete Writings*, I, 147.
75. *Ibid.*, 81-83.

III: PILGRIM PRECEDENTS, 1620-1630

1. William Bradford, *History of Plymouth Plantation*, edited by Worthington C. Ford (2 vols., Boston, 1912), I, 57.
2. *Ibid.*, 207-210; *A Journal of the Pilgrims at Plymouth* [*Mourt's Relation*], edited by Dwight B. Heath (New York, 1963), 52; Phinehas Pratt, "A Declaration of the Affairs of the English People that First Inhabited New England," in *Mass. Hist. Soc. Coll.*, 4 ser. IV (1858), 479; Ferdinando Gorges, "Brief Narration," in *Maine Hist. Soc. Coll.*, 1 ser. II (1872), 30-31 (2nd pagination); Emmanuel Altham to Sir Edward Altham (Sept. 1623) in Sydney V. James, Jr., ed., *Three Visitors to Early Plymouth* (Plimoth Plantation, Mass., 1963), 27; Increase Mather, *A Relation of the Troubles which have hapned in New England By reason of the Indians there*, edited by Samuel G. Drake under the title *Early History of New England* (Boston, 1864), 59-62.
3. *Mourt's Relation*, 18-21; Bradford, *History of Plymouth Plantation*, I, 162-164.
4. *Mourt's Relation*, 21-24, 26; Bradford, *History of Plymouth Plantation*, I, 164-167.
5. *Mourt's Relation*, 21-34.
6. *Ibid.*, 34-37; Bradford, *History of Plymouth Plantation*, I, 167-173.
7. *Mourt's Relation*, 38-41; Bradford, *History of Plymouth Plantation*, I, 173-177.
8. [Robert Cushman], "Cushman's Discourse," in Alexander Young, ed., *Chronicles of the Pilgrim Fathers* (Boston, 1844), 258; Thomas Prince, *Chronological History of New England* (5 vols. in 1, Edinburgh, 1887), III, 38-39; *Mourt's Relation*, 42-50; Bradford, *History of Plymouth Plantation*, I, 192-196.
9. *Mourt's Relation*, 42-48.
10. *Ibid.*, 49-50; Emmanuel Altham to Sir Edward Altham (Sept. 1623) in James, *Three Visitors to Early Plymouth*, 24.
11. *Mourt's Relation*, 50-53; Bradford, *History of Plymouth Plantation*, I, 198-199.
12. *Mourt's Relation*, 53-54.
13. *Ibid.*, 55.
14. *Ibid.*, 55-59.
15. The full text of the treaty is given in *Mourt's Relation*, 56-57, reprinted on page 339 above as Appendix I. Slightly different versions can be found in Bradford, *History of Plymouth Plantation*, I, 201-202, and in Nathaniel Morton, *New-Englands Memoriall* (Boston, 1903), 24.
16. *Mourt's Relation*, 57-58. For another contemporary description of

Chief Massasoit see Emmanuel Altham to Sir Edward Altham (Sept. 1623) in James, *Three Visitors to Early Plymouth*, 30.

17. *Mourt's Relation*, 58. The character of the Wampanoag-Narragansett enmity at this time is not clear. Presumably it was part of the ancient rivalry between neighboring independent tribes. However, many years later Roger Williams reported that Massasoit had been subject to the Narragansetts for some time prior to 1621 and on the arrival of the Pilgrims tried to use the new English colony as an unwitting ally in a bid for autonomy. See [Roger Williams], *The Complete Writings of Roger Williams* (7 vols., New York, 1963), VI, 316.

18. *Mourt's Relation*, 60-62; Bradford, *History of Plymouth Plantation*, I, 219.

19. *Mourt's Relation*, 62-67.

20. *Ibid.*, 65-66.

21. *Ibid.*, 69-71; Bradford, *History of Plymouth Plantation*, I, 222-225.

22. *Mourt's Relation*, 71-73; Bradford, *History of Plymouth Plantation*, I, 225. Samoset disappeared from history almost as mysteriously as he entered it. No mention is made of him in the Pilgrim chronicles after the spring of 1621. On his subsequent career, see *ibid.*, 199n.

23. *Mourt's Relation*, 73-74; Bradford, *History of Plymouth Plantation*, I, 225-226.

24. *Mourt's Relation*, 74-76.

25. Bradford, *History of Plymouth Plantation*, I, 226-227; Prince, *Chronological History of New England*, III, 47-48. For the text of the submission see N. Morton, *New-Englands Memoriall*, 29. See also Samuel G. Drake, *The Aboriginal Races of North America* [*Book of the Indians*] (15th edition, Philadelphia, 1859), 94.

26. Edward Winslow, "Good Newes from New England," in Edward Arber, ed., *The Story of the Pilgrim Fathers . . .* (London, 1897), 527-528; Bradford, *History of Plymouth Plantation*, I, 252-254; I. Mather, *Relation of the Troubles*, 72-73.

27. E[dward] W[inslow] to [George Morton?] (11 Dec. 1621) in *Mourt's Relation*, 82-83.

28. *Ibid.*, 83; Emmanuel Altham to Sir Edward Altham (Sept. 1623) in James, *Three Visitors to Early Plymouth*, 30; Champlin Burrage, ed., *John Pory's Lost Description of Plymouth Colony . . .* (Boston, 1918), 42-43; I. Mather, *Relation of the Troubles*, 107-109; [Isaac de Rasieres], "Letter of Isaac de Rasieres to Samuel Bloomaert, 1628 (?)," in J. Franklin Jameson, ed., *Narratives of New Netherland, 1609-1664* (New York, 1909), 113.

29. *Mourt's Relation*, 77-80; Bradford, *History of Plymouth Plantation*, I, 228-229.

30. Winslow, "Good Newes from New England," 517-520; Bradford, *History of Plymouth Plantation*, I, 240-241. Cf. C. Burrage, *John Pory's Lost Description of Plymouth*, 44.

31. Winslow, "Good Newes from New England," 523-527; Bradford, *History of Plymouth Plantation*, I, 252-254.

32. Winslow, "Good Newes from New England," 525-526.
33. *Ibid.*, 527; Bradford, *History of Plymouth Plantation*, I, 255. See also C. Burrage, *John Pory's Lost Description of Plymouth*, 43-44.
34. Winslow, "Good Newes from New England," 532-533; I. Mather, *Relation of the Troubles*, 82-84.
35. The corn-buying expeditions are narrated in detail in Winslow, "Good Newes from New England," 533-541, and in Bradford, *History of Plymouth Plantation*, I, 276-284.
36. Winslow, "Good Newes from New England," 559-560; Bradford, *History of Plymouth Plantation*, I, 284-287.
37. Winslow, "Good Newes from New England," 547-550.
38. *Ibid.*, 550-552, 555.
39. *Ibid.*, 555-556; Bradford, *History of Plymouth Plantation*, I, 292-293; Emmanuel Altham to Sir Edward Altham (Sept. 1623) in James, *Three Visitors to Early Plymouth*, 30-31.
40. Winslow, "Good Newes from New England," 559-564; Bradford, *History of Plymouth Plantation*, I, 288-291; Pratt, "Declaration," 482; Thomas Morton, *The New English Canaan*, edited by Charles Francis Adams, Jr. (Boston, 1883), 96, 251n. See also Adams's *Three Episodes in Massachusetts History* (2 vols., Boston, 1896), 79-82.
41. Pratt, "Declaration," 474-487; Winslow, "Good Newes from New England," 530, 561-562, 572-573; Bradford, *History of Plymouth Plantation*, I, 276, 293-294; Great Britain, Public Record Office, *Calendar of State Papers, Colonial Series, America and the West Indies*, I (London, 1860), 31.
42. Winslow, "Good Newes from New England," 567-574; Emmanuel Altham to Sir Edward Altham (Sept. 1623) in James, *Three Visitors to Early Plymouth*, 31-32; I. Mather, *Relation of the Troubles*, 91-93. Cf. T. Morton, *New English Canaan*, 252-255.
43. Winslow, "Good Newes from New England," 572-575.
44. C. F. Adams, *Three Episodes*, I, 196; Bradford to Gorges (15 June 1627) in "Governor Bradford's Letter Book," *Mass. Hist. Soc. Coll.*, 1 ser. III (1794), 57. Cf. Christopher Levett, "A Voyage to New England," in *Maine Hist. Soc. Coll.*, 1 ser. II (1847), 96-97.
45. William Bradford to Sir Ferdinando Gorges (9 June 1626) in "Governor Bradford's Letter Book," 64; Bradford, *History of Plymouth Plantation*, II, 44-45.
46. Bradford to Gorges (9 June 1628) in "Governor Bradford's Letter Book," 64.
47. See, for example, Samuel G. Drake, *The History and Antiquities of Boston . . .* (2 vols., Boston, 1856), I, 48-49; James Truslow Adams, *The Founding of New England* (Boston, 1921), 109-113; Charles M. Andrews, *The Colonial Period of American History* (4 vols., New Haven, 1934-1938), I, 332-334, 362-363; and George F. Willison, *Saints and Strangers* (New York, 1945), 274-284 and *passim*.
48. Bradford, *History of Plymouth Plantation*, II, 48.
49. C. F. Adams, *Three Episodes*, I, 200.

50. Bradford to the Council for New England (9 June 1628) in "Governor Bradford's Letter Book," 62; Bradford to Sir Ferdinando Gorges (9 June 1628) in *ibid.*, 63; Bradford, *History of Plymouth Plantation*, II, 46-58. Cf. T. Morton, *New English Canaan*, 276-287.

IV: THE EXPANSION OF NEW ENGLAND, 1630-1636

1. [Edward Johnson], *Johnson's Wonder-Working Providence* (New York, 1910), 48; Frederick Webb Hodge, ed., *Handbook of American Indians North of Mexico* (2 vols., Washington, 1907), I, 816.
2. Johnson, *Wonder-Working Providence*, 78-79.
3. Matthew Craddock to Endicott (16 Feb. 1629) in Nathaniel B. Shurtleff, ed., *Records of the Governor and Company of The Massachusetts Bay in New England* (5 vols., Boston, 1853-1854), I, 384-385. Hereafter cited as *Mass. Col. Rec.*
4. Massachusetts Bay Company to Endicott (17 April 1629) in *ibid.*, 386-394.
5. *Ibid.*, 396; Francis Higginson, *New-Englands Plantation* (Salem, 1908), 107.
6. "The Early Records of Charlestown," in Alexander Young, ed., *Chronicles of the First Planters of the Colony of Massachusetts Bay from 1623 to 1636* (Boston, 1846), 377; Increase Mather, *A Relation of the Troubles which have hapned in New-England, By reason of the Indians there*, edited by Samuel G. Drake under the title *Early History of New England* (Boston, 1864), 105; Thomas Prince, *Chronological History of New England* (5 vols. in 1, Edinburgh, 1887), IV, 67-68.
7. Higginson, *New-Englands Plantation*, 107-108.
8. Thomas Wiggin to John Cocke (ca. Nov. 1632) in *Mass. Hist. Soc. Coll.*, 3 ser. VIII (1843), 322; John Winthrop to Sir Nathaniel Riche (22 May 1634) in Allyn B. Forbes, ed., *Winthrop Papers* (5 vols., Boston, 1929-1947), III, 166; Evarts B. Greene and Virginia D. Harrington, *American Population Before the Federal Census of 1790* (New York, 1932), 8-13.
9. Joseph B. Felt, "Statistics of Population in Massachusetts," in *American Statistical Association Collections*, I (1897), 143.
10. John Josselyn, "Chronological Observations of America, From the year of the World to the year of Christ, 1673," in *Mass. Hist. Soc. Coll.*, 3 ser. III (1833), 381. Josselyn's figure seems high in the light of other contemporary estimates. See Greene and Harrington, *American Population*, 8-13.
11. [John Winthrop], *Winthrop's Journal*, edited by James K. Hosmer (2 vols., New York, 1908), I, 50; William Hubbard, *A General History of New England*, in *Mass. Hist. Soc. Coll.*, 2 ser. V-VI (1815), 130, 145-146; Higginson, *New-Englands Plantation*, 105. See also Thomas Wiggin to Secretary Coke (19 Nov. 1632) in Great Britain,

Public Record Office, *Calendar of State Papers, Colonial Series, America and the West Indies,* I (London, 1860), 156.

12. John Eliot to Sir Simonds D'Ewes (18 Sept. 1633) in Franklin M. Wright, "A College First Proposed . . . ," in *Harvard Library Bulletin,* VIII (1954), 272; [William Wood], *Wood's New-England's Prospect* (Boston, 1865), 64; and Higginson, *New-Englands Plantation,* 106.

13. For example, see Winthrop, *Journal,* I, 56, 62, 65.

14. Joseph Dudley to Countess of Lincoln (12 March 1631) in Young, *Chronicles of the First Planters,* 322-323; [Roger Clap], "Captain Roger Clap's Memoirs," in *ibid.,* 352-353.

15. Winthrop, *Journal,* I, 66-67; Hubbard, *General History,* 145.

16. Dudley to Countess of Lincoln (12 March 1631) in Young, *Chronicles of the First Planters,* 321-322; *Mass. Col. Rec.,* I, 75; I. Mather, *Relation of the Troubles,* 106.

17. *Mass. Col. Rec.,* I, 84, 91, 92, 100, 102, 121; Winthrop, *Journal,* I, 67, 68.

18. *Mass. Col. Rec.,* I, 87-89, 121; Winthrop, *Journal,* I, 64; Edward Howes to John Winthrop, Jr. (26 March 1632) in *Winthrop Papers,* III, 74.

19. *Mass. Col. Rec.,* I, 76, 118, 127.

20. *Ibid.,* 99; Winthrop, *Journal,* I, 90; Hubbard, *General History,* 145.

21. Winthrop, *Journal,* I, 60; Joseph Dudley to Countess of Lincoln (12 March 1631), in Young, *Chronicles of the First Planters,* 339-340; *Mass. Col. Rec.,* I, 85.

22. For example, see *Mass. Col. Rec.,* I, 87.

23. *Ibid.,* 90, 96; Winthrop, *Journal,* I, 90.

24. *Mass. Col. Rec.,* I, 125, 137, 138, 146-147.

25. I. Mather, *Relation of the Troubles,* 110-111; Johnson, *Wonder-Working Providence,* 79; Winthrop, *Journal,* I, 111, 114-115, 118; John Winter to Robert Trelawney (10 Aug. 1634) in James P. Baxter, ed., *The Trelawney Papers* (*Documentary History of the State of Maine,* III [1884]), 47.

26. Johnson, *Wonder-Working Providence,* 79-80; Winthrop, *Journal,* I, 111, 114-115; William Bradford, *History of Plymouth Plantation,* edited by Worthington C. Ford (2 vols., Boston, 1912), II, 193-195.

27. Winthrop, *Journal,* I, 118; Bradford, *History of Plymouth Plantation,* II, 194-195; "Early Records of Charlestown," 386.

28. John Winthrop to John Endicott (3 Jan. 1634) in *Winthrop Papers,* III, 149; "Early Records of Charlestown," 387. See also I. Mather, *Relation of the Troubles,* 110-111; Johnson, *Wonder-Working Providence,* 79; Winthrop to Sir Nathaniel Rich (22 May 1634) in *Winthrop Papers,* III, 167; Winthrop to Sir Simonds D'Ewes (21 July 1634) in *ibid.,* 171-172.

29. Edward Winslow, "Good Newes from New England," in Edward Arber, ed., *The Story of the Pilgrim Fathers* (London, 1897), 587. [Roger Williams], *The Complete Writings of Roger Williams* (7

vols., New York, 1963), I, 180; Frank G. Speck, "The Family Hunting Band as the Basis of Algonkian Social Organization," in *American Anthropologist*, new ser., XVII (1915), 289-305; Frank G. Speck and Loren C. Eisely, "Significance of Hunting Territory Systems of the Algonkian in Social Theory," in *ibid.*, XLI (1939), 277; John M. Cooper, "Is the Algonquian Family Hunting Ground System Pre-Columbian?" in *ibid.*, 66-90; A. L. Kroeber, "Nature of the Land-Holding Group," in *Ethnohistory*, II (1955), 303; Anthony F. C. Wallace, "Political Organization and Land Tenure Among the Northeastern Indians, 1600-1830," in *Southwestern Journal of Anthropology*, XIII (1957), 311*n*.

30. For an account of the confusion that sometimes resulted from disputed Indian titles, see Douglas E. Leach, *Flintlock and Tomahawk: New England in King Philip's War* (New York, 1958), 15-16.

31. Frank G. Speck, *Territorial Subdivisions and Boundaries of the Wampanoag, Massachusett, and Nauset Indians* (Museum of the American Indian, Heye Foundation, *Indian Notes and Monographs*, no. 44 [New York, 1928]), 30-32. See also the sources listed in note 29 above.

32. Nathaniel B. Shurtleff and David Pulsifer, eds., *Records of the Colony of New Plymouth* (12 vols., Boston, 1855-1861), XI, 41, 183, 185; *Mass. Col. Rec.*, I, 112; John R. Bartlett, ed., *Records of the Colony of Rhode Island and Providence Plantations in New England* (10 vols., Providence, 1856-1865), I, 236, 403-404; J. Hammond Trumbull, ed., *Public Records of the Colony of Connecticut* (15 vols., Hartford, 1850-1890), I, 402; Charles J. Hoadley, ed., *Records of the Colony or Jurisdiction of New Haven . . .* (Hartford, 1858), 27, 200. Hereafter cited as *Ply. Col. Rec.*, *R.I. Col. Rec.*, *Conn. Col. Rec.*, and *New Haven Col. Rec.*, I.

33. See, for example, Harry A. Wright, ed., *Indian Deeds of Hampden County* (Springfield, Mass., 1905), *passim; Suffolk Deeds* (14 vols., Boston, 1880-1906), *passim; Mass. Col. Rec.*, II, 159-160; Massachusetts Archives (Massachusetts State Library), XXX, 1, 4, 15, 33; Massachusetts Historical Society, Miscellaneous Bound MSS, I, 40, 50, 75; Massachusetts Historical Society, Miscellaneous Photostats, Boxes, I-VIII, X-XV, *passim;* Massachusetts Historical Society, Miscellaneous Unbound MSS, Box I, *passim;* Connecticut Archives (Connecticut State Library), Indians (1 ser.), I, 27, 28, 30; Connecticut Archives, Towns and Lands, I (part I), 67c; *Ply. Col. Rec.*, II, 130-131; *R.I. Col. Rec.*, I, 450*n;* Rhode Island Historical Society, RIHS MSS, Eddy Papers, Shepley Papers, Peck Papers, and Miscellaneous MSS, all *passim.*

34. See, for example, *Ply. Col. Rec.*, V, 37-38; Josiah Winslow to Commissioners of the United Colonies (1 May 1676) in William Hubbard, *A Narrative of the Troubles with the Indians in New-England, From the first Planting thereof to the present Time*, edited by Samuel G.

Drake under the title, *The History of the Indian Wars in New England* . . . (2 vols., Roxbury, Mass., 1865), I, 56-57.

35. *Winthrop Papers*, V, 4-5.

36. *Conn. Col. Rec.*, I, 186; David Pulsifer, ed., *Acts of the Commissioners of the United Colonies of New England* (2 vols. [*Ply. Col. Rec.*, IX-X], Boston, 1859), II, 144; Roger Williams to John Winthrop (10 July 1637) in Williams, *Complete Writings*, VI, 43-44; Wallace, "Political Organizations and Land Tenure among the Northeastern Indians," 311-312.

37. Puritan courts were alert to protect Indian land titles. See, for example, Pulsifer, *Acts of the Commissioners*, I, 73, 103-104; *Ply. Col. Rec.*, III, 101; *Conn. Col. Rec.*, I, 309-310; *Mass. Col. Rec.*, IV (2), 529.

38. Pulsifer, *Acts of the Commissioners*, I, 175; Winthrop, *Journal*, II, 331.

39. Pulsifer, *Acts of the Commissioners*, I, 112, II, 13; *New Haven Col. Rec.*, I, 518.

40. For example, John Cotton, *God's Promise to His Plantations* (*Old South Leaflets*, III, no. 53 [Boston, n.d.]), 6; *A Journal of the Pilgrims at Plymouth* [*Mourt's Relation*], edited by Dwight B. Heath (New York, 1963), 91-92. It is important to note that the Puritans applied this regulation to their own landholdings as well as to the Indians' (*Mass. Col. Rec.*, I, 114; "Essay on the Ordering of Towns," in *Winthrop Papers*, III, 182). And on at least one occasion it was used as a rationalization for dispossessing the Dutch. See David Pietersz de Vries, "Korte Historiael Ende Journaels Aenteyckeninge," in J. Franklin Jameson, ed., *Narratives of New Netherland, 1609-1664* New York, 1909), 203.

41. John Winthrop, "Reasons to be Considered, and Objections with Answers," in *Winthrop Papers*, II, 141; *Mass. Col. Rec.*, IV (1), 102. See also Winthrop, *Journal*, I, 294, 306; Winthrop to John Endicott (3 Jan. 1634) in *Winthrop Papers*, III, 146-149; Winthrop to [John Wheelwright?] (ca. March 1639) in *ibid.*, IV, 101-102; John Cotton, *The Bloudy Tenent Washed, And Made White in the Bloud of the Lambe* (London, 1647), 27 (2nd pagination); Pulsifer, *Acts of the Commissioners*, II, 13.

42. Williams, *Complete Writings*, I, 180; *Mass. Col. Rec.*, IV (2), 213.

43. For an example of the distortions that can result from dabbling in Puritan rhetoric, see Roy Harvey Pearce, *The Savages of America: A Study of the Indian and the Idea of Civilization* (Baltimore, 1953), 19-35.

44. James P. Baxter, ed., *Sir Ferdinando Gorges and His Province of Maine* (3 vols. [*Publications of the Prince Society*, XVIII-XX], Boston, 1890), III, 310; Amandus Johnson, *The Swedish Settlements on the Delaware* (2 vols., New York, 1911), I, 573.

45. For a somewhat different interpretation of the Puritan viewpoint, see Chester E. Eisinger, "The Puritans' Justification for Taking the Land," in *Essex Institute Hist. Coll.* LXXXIV (1948), 131-143. It will be

interesting to see what sort of justification is devised if American spacemen discover a sparse population of neolithic *Homo sapiens* on some strategic planet. The seemingly egocentric and imperialistic rationalizations of our ancestors may yet enjoy a revival.

46. Thomas Morton, *The New English Canaan*, edited by Charles Francis Adams, Jr. (Boston, 1883), 133.

47. For example, Winthrop, *Journal*, I, 294, 306; Deposition of John Wheelwright (15 April 1666) in Pequot Library Collection, Yale University Library.

48. J. S. Clark, "Did the Pilgrims Wrong the Indians?" in *The Congregational Quarterly*, I (1859), 129-135; David Bushnell, "The Treatment of the Indians in Plymouth Colony," in *New England Quarterly*, XXVI (1953), 193-218. Cf. John Easton, "A Relacion of the Indyan Warre," in Charles H. Lincoln, ed., *Narratives of the Indian Wars* (New York, 1913), 11.

49. See Massachusetts Historical Society, Miscellaneous Unbound MSS, Box I, for a deed by Philip dated 28 Sept. 1672; and Boston Atheneum, MSS (Miscellaneous) L1, I (1652-1799), no. 16 for one dated 1 Nov. 1672.

50. Josiah Winslow to Commissioners of the United Colonies (1 May 1676) in Hubbard, *Narrative of the Troubles*, I, 56-57.

51. Massachusetts Bay Company to John Endicott (17 April 1631) in *Mass. Col. Rec.*, I, 394.

52. Joseph Dudley to Countess of Lincoln (12 March 1631) in Young, *Chronicles of the First Planters*, 372-374; Johnson, *Wonder-Working Providence*, 111-112; *Mass. Col. Rec.*, I, 112, 114, 117, 151-152.

53. John W. DeForest, *History of the Indians of Connecticut* (Hartford, 1852), 59-62.

54. Bradford, *History of Plymouth Plantation*, II, 164-171.

55. *Ibid.*, 166-167, 216-224; Winthrop, *Journal*, I, 61, 108, 132-134, 163; Charles M. Andrews, *The Colonial Period of American History* (4 vols., New Haven, 1934-1938), II, 67-91. According to Winthrop (*Journal*, I, 61) one of the Indians who came to Boston from Connecticut to solicit settlers was Jack Straw, "who had lived in England and had served Sir Walter Raleigh."

56. Lion Gardiner, *A History of the Pequot War* (Cincinnati, 1860), 8-9.

57. Williams to John Mason (22 June 1670) in Williams, *Complete Writings*, VI, 335; Howard M. Chapin, *Documentary History of Rhode Island* (2 vols., Providence, 1916-1919), I, 14-15, 18-19, 103; *R.I. Col. Rec.*, I, 18.

58. Perry Miller, "Roger Williams: An Essay in Interpretation," in Williams, *Complete Works*, VII, 21-25.

59. James Ernst, *Roger Williams: New England Firebrand* (New York, 1932), 80; Samuel Hugh Brockunier, *The Irrepressible Democrat: Roger Williams* (New York, 1940), 49-50; Perry Miller, *Roger Williams: His Contribution to the American Tradition* (New York,

1962), 51-52. See also William Christie MacLeod, *The American In-dian Frontier* (New York, 1928), 199-201.
60. Winthrop, *Journal*, I, 116-117, 142; Williams, *Complete Writings*, I, 324-325; Ola E. Winslow, *Master Roger Williams: A Biography* (New York, 1957), 107-112.
61. John Winthrop to John Endicott (3 Jan. 1634) in *Winthrop Papers*, III, 149; Williams, *Complete Writings*, I, 180, IV, 461-462.
62. Williams, *Complete Writings*, I, 180, IV, 461; Cotton, *The Bloudy Tenent Washed*, 27 (2nd pagination).

V: THE PEQUOT WAR, 1637

1. See, for example, Timothy Dwight, *Greenfield Hill: A Poem in Seven Parts* (New York, 1794), Bk. IV; Samuel G. Drake, *The Aboriginal Races of North America* [*Book of the Indians*] (15th ed., Philadel-phia, 1859), 170-171.
2. For an explanation of Melville's knowledge of the war and his reasons for selecting the name of the tribe see *Moby Dick*, edited by Luther S. Mansfield and Howard P. Vincent (New York, 1952), 68, 631-633.
3. William Bradford, *History of Plymouth Plantation*, edited by Worth-ington C. Ford (2 vols., Boston, 1912), II, 232-234; William Hubbard, *A Narrative of the Troubles with the Indians in New England, From the first Planting thereof to the Present Time*, edited by Samuel G. Drake under the title *The History of the Indian Wars in New Eng-land* . . . (2 vols., Roxbury, 1865), II, 7.
4. [John Winthrop], *Winthrop's Journal*, edited by James K. Hosmer (2 vols., New York, 1908), I, 108; Bradford, *History of Plymouth Plantation*, II, 190-192; [Roger Clap], "Captain Roger Clap's Mem-oirs," in Alexander Young, ed., *Chronicles of the First Planters of the Colony of Massachusetts Bay, from 1623 to 1636* (Boston, 1846), 363; Nathaniel B. Shurtleff, ed., *Records of the Governor and Com-pany of the Massachusetts Bay in New England* (5 vols., Boston, 1853-1854), I, 108. Hereafter cited as *Mass. Col. Rec.*
5. Bradford, *History of Plymouth Plantation*, II, 191-192; Winthrop, *Journal*, I, 118; Clap, "Memoirs," 363.
6. Some of the Puritans were undoubtedly angered by reports that the Indians had roasted Stone alive. Clap, "Memoirs," 363.
7. John Winthrop to John Winthrop, Jr. (12 Dec. 1634) in Allyn B. Forbes, ed., *Winthrop Papers* (5 vols., Boston, 1929-1947), III, 177; Bradford, *History of Plymouth Plantation*, II, 232-234; Winthrop, *Journal*, I, 138-140.
8. Winthrop, *Journal*, I, 138; John Winthrop to William Bradford (ca. March 1635) and same to same (12 March 1635) in Bradford, *History of Plymouth Plantation*, II, 233-234; Increase Mather, *A Relation of the Troubles, which have hapned in New-England By reason of the*

Indians there, edited by Samuel G. Drake under the title *Early History of New England* (Boston, 1864), 179. See also the sources cited in the previous note.

9. Jonathan Brewster to John Winthrop, Jr. (18 June 1636) in *Winthrop Papers*, III, 270-272; John Winthrop to Sir Simonds D'Ewes (24 June 1636) in *ibid.*, 276; Henry Vane to John Winthrop, Jr. (1 July 1636) in *ibid.*, 282-283; Colony of Massachusetts Bay to John Winthrop, Jr. (4 July 1636) in *ibid.*, 284-285; I. Mather, *Relation of the Troubles*, 159-160.

10. Winthrop, *Journal*, I, 183-184; Thomas Cobbet, "A Narrative of New England's Deliverances," in *New England Historical and Genealogical Register*, VII (1853), 211-212.

11. Winthrop, *Journal*, I, 184-185; Bradford, *History of Plymouth Plantation*, II, 234-235; Hubbard, *Narrative of the Troubles*, II, 11.

12. [Edward Johnson], *Johnson's Wonder-Working Providence*, edited by J. Franklin Jameson (New York, 1910), 162-163; Winthrop, *Journal*, I, 186.

13. Winthrop, *Journal*, I, 186-187.

14. *Ibid.*, 187-188; John Underhill, "News from America," in *Mass. Hist. Soc. Coll.*, 3 ser. VI (1837), 7. Underhill, who left the only eyewitness account of the expedition, reported that fourteen Indians were killed and forty wounded on Block Island. Winthrop (*Journal*, I, 188) related that the Narragansetts believed only one Block Islander had died. Cf. I. Mather, *Relation of the Troubles*, 161.

15. Lion Gardiner, *A History of the Pequot War* (Cincinnati, 1860), 12. Gardiner was never convinced that the Narragansetts were not the real villains of Oldham's murder, and he could therefore see little justification in a campaign against the Pequots (*ibid.*, 23-24).

16. Underhill, "News from America," 7.

17. *Ibid.*, 7-10; Winthrop, *Journal*, I, 188-189.

18. Winthrop (*Journal*, I, 189) indicates that there were no English casualties, but Underhill ("News from America," 11) tells of one wounded in the leg, while *Mass. Col. Rec.*, I, 183, shows a grant of £5 to a man "in regard of the losse of his eye in the voyage to Block Iland."

19. Gardiner, *A History of the Pequot War*, 13. Winthrop also mentions Cutshamekin's role, but only as incidental to the clash with the Pequots (*Journal*, I, 189-190). Underhill ("News from America," 11) reported "certain numbers of theirs slain and many wounded." See also Hubbard, *Narrative of the Troubles*, II, 14-15, and John Mason, "A Brief History of the Pequot War," in *Mass. Hist. Soc. Coll.*, 2 ser. VIII (1826), 131, who assert that only one Pequot was killed but make no mention of Cutshamekin.

20. Lion Gardiner to John Winthrop, Jr. (6 Nov. 1636) in *Winthrop Papers*, III, 319-321; Winthrop, *Journal*, I, 191; Gardiner, *A History of the Pequot War*, 13-15.

21. Lion Gardiner to John Winthrop, Jr. (23 March 1637) in *Winthrop Papers*, III, 381-382; Gardiner, *A History of the Pequot War*, 15-18; Winthrop, *Journal*, I, 208; Mason, "Brief History," 131. Mason says he brought twenty men, but his estimates are consistently high, and subsequent events make Gardiner's figure seem more plausible.

22. Mason, "Brief History," 123; Bradford, *History of Plymouth Plantation*, II, 247; Hubbard, *Narrative of the Troubles*, II, 16; Winthrop, *Journal*, I, 190.

23. Roger Williams to General Court of Massachusetts (Oct. 1651) in [Roger Williams], *The Complete Writings of Roger Williams* (7 vols., New York, 1963), VI, 231-232; Williams to John Mason (22 June 1670) in *ibid.*, 338.

24. Winthrop, *Journal*, I, 192-194, 212. Roger Williams later claimed that the Narragansetts also were responsible for convincing the Mohegans to support the English cause. Williams to Massachusetts General Court (5 Oct. 1654) in Williams, *Complete Writings*, VI, 274.

25. Winthrop, *Journal*, I, 194; Underhill, "News from America," 15; [John Hull], *The Diaries of John Hull, Mintmaster and Treasurer of the Colony of Massachusetts Bay* (*Transactions and Collections of the American Antiquarian Society*, III [1850]), 171.

26. Lion Gardiner to John Winthrop, Jr. (23 March 1637) in *Winthrop Papers*, III, 382; Edward Winslow to John Winthrop (17 April 1637) in *ibid.*, 391-392.

27. Underhill, "News from America," 12; Winthrop (*Journal*, I, 212) reported that the loan of the Massachusetts troops to Saybrook was partly to thwart Dutch designs on the fort.

28. Underhill, "News from America," 12; Mason, "Brief History," 131-132; Johnson, *Wonder-Working Providence*, 149; Winthrop, *Journal*, I, 213; Hubbard, *Narrative of the Troubles*, II, 12. The captives were redeemed a month later by some Dutch traders. I. Mather, *Relation of the Troubles*, 177.

29. *Mass. Col. Rec.*, I, 192; J. Hammond Trumbull, ed., *Public Records of the Colony of Connecticut* (15 vols., Hartford, 1850-1890), I, 9. Hereafter cited as *Conn. Col. Rec.*

30. Winthrop, *Journal*, II, 115-116; Gardiner, *History of the Pequot War*, 23-24; Johnson, *Wonder-Working Providence*, 164n.

31. Williams to John Winthrop (*ca.* Sept. 1636) in *Winthrop Papers*, III, 298. The text of the letter strongly suggests that it is misdated in the published collection. It was probably written in early August. See also Hull, *Diaries*, 171-172.

32. See, for example, Great Britain, Public Record Office, *Calendar of State Papers, Colonial Series, America and the West Indies*, I (London, 1860), 239.

33. Thomas Hooker to John Winthrop (Spring 1637) in *Winthrop Papers*, III, 407.

34. *Conn. Col. Rec.*, I, 3-4; *Mass. Col. Rec.*, I, 186-188, 192; Nathaniel B.

Shurtleff and David Pulsifer, eds., *Records of the Colony of New Plymouth* (12 vols., Boston, 1855-1861), I, 38. Hereafter cited as *Ply. Col. Rec.*

35. Thomas Hooker to John Winthrop (Spring 1637) in *Winthrop Papers*, III, 408; *Conn. Col. Rec.*, I, 7-10; Mason, "Brief History," 122, 151-152.

36. *Mass. Col. Rec.*, I, 192; Winthrop, *Journal*, I, 194.

37. Bradford, *History of Plymouth Plantation*, II, 242-248; Winthrop, *Journal*, I, 213-214; *Ply. Col. Rec.*, I, 60; Hubbard, *Narrative of the Troubles*, II, 18. No Plymouth troops participated in the war at any stage.

38. Hubbard, *Narrative of the Troubles*, II, 18.

39. Mason, "Brief History," 133. The colonists' confidence in Uncas had probably been shaken by a report that he had sheltered Pequot women and children at the time of the Endicott expedition. Roger Williams to John Winthrop (9 Sept. 1637) in *Winthrop Papers*, III, 496.

40. I. Mather, *Relation of the Troubles*, 167; Mason, "Brief History," 133; Underhill, "News from America," 16; Gardiner, *History of the Pequot War*, 21; Philip Vincent, "A True Relation of the Late Battel Fought in New England, between the English and the Pequet Salvages," in *Mass. Hist. Soc. Coll.*, 3 ser. VI (1837), 36; Roger Ludlow to William Pynchon (17 [May] 1637) in "Pincheon Papers," in *Mass. Hist. Soc. Coll.*, 2 ser. VIII (1826), 235-237.

41. Underhill, "News from America," 16-17.

42. *Ibid.*, 17-18; Gardiner, *History of the Pequot War*, 19; Mason, "Brief History," 133; Winthrop, *Journal*, I, 219; Johnson, *Wonder-Working Providence*, 149. On the Pequots' sources of guns see Lion Gardiner to John Winthrop, Jr. (7 Nov. 1636) in *Winthrop Papers*, III, 321; and I. Mather, *Relation of the Troubles*, 182.

43. Mason, "Brief History," 134.

44. *Ibid.*, 134-135.

45. *Ibid.*, 135-136; I. Mather, *Relation of the Troubles*, 169-171. Mason's strategy bears a striking resemblance to a plan previously devised by Miantonomo and transmitted to Governor Winthrop by Roger Williams less than two weeks before Mason arrived at Narragansett. See Williams to Winthrop (15 May 1637) in *Winthrop Papers*, III, 413-414. Apparently Mason thought his army was large enough to destroy the Pequots, for he declined to wait for a force of forty Massachusetts soldiers under Captain Patrick, then at New Providence. Hubbard, *Narrative of the Troubles*, II, 22-23.

46. Mason, "Brief History," 138-141.

47. *Ibid.*; Underhill, "News from America," 23-24, 38-39. Williams reported to John Winthrop (*ca.* 2 June 1637) in *Winthrop Papers*, III, 427, that "the Quinnihticut English had yellow but not enough."

48. Mason, "Brief History," 141; Underhill, "News from America," 25, 38; Winthrop, *Journal*, I, 220; [Thomas Shepard], "Thomas Shepard's

Memoir of his own Life," in Young, *Chronicles of the First Planters*, 550. Cf. I. Mather, *Relation of the Troubles*, 171. On the fate of the captives, see Thomas Hutchinson, *The History of the Colony and Province of Massachusetts Bay*, edited by L. S. Mayo (3 vols., Cambridge, 1936), I, 70.

49. Mason, "Brief History," 140-141; Underhill, "News from America," 25.

50. Mason, "Brief History," 142-144; Winthrop, *Journal*, I, 222. I. Mather, *Relation of the Troubles*, 169, reported that the Pequots may have lost as many men trying to block Mason's retreat as they had lost at Mystic fort.

51. Mason, "Brief History," 145; Williams to Winthrop (*ca.* 2 June 1637) in *Winthrop Papers*, III, 427.

52. Hubbard, *Narrative of the Troubles*, II, 30; Winthrop, *Journal*, I, 225. According to Hubbard, John Gallop dumped thirty Pequot warriors into the harbor to drown (*Narrative of the Troubles*, II, 30). This is not corroborated by any other source.

53. Gardiner, *History of the Pequot War*, 22.

54. Mason, "Brief History," 145; Roger Williams to John Winthrop (*ca.* 30 June 1637) in *Winthrop Papers*, III, 436-437; Israel Stoughton to the Governor and Council of Massachusetts (14 Aug. 1637) in *ibid.*, 482; Edward Winslow to John Winthrop (5 June 1637) in *ibid.*, 428.

55. Richard Davenport to Hugh Peter (*ca.* 17 July 1637) in *Winthrop Papers*, III, 452; Winthrop, *Journal*, I, 226; I. Mather, *Relation of the Troubles*, 173; Drake, *Aboriginal Races*, 150-151.

56. Richard Davenport to Hugh Peter (*ca.* 17 July 1637) in *Winthrop Papers*, III, 453-454; John Winthrop to William Bradford (28 July 1637) in *ibid.*, 456-457; Winthrop, *Journal*, I, 227; Mason, "Brief History," 148; Hubbard, *Narrative of the Troubles*, II, 36. It is Hubbard who relates the brutal slaughter in the swamp, based on reports from "some that are yet living and worthy of Credit." Cf. I. Mather, *Relation of the Troubles*, 175-176.

57. William Hilton to John Winthrop (14 July 1637) in *Winthrop Papers*, III, 449; John Winthrop to William Bradford (28 July 1637) in *ibid.*, 457; Mason, "Brief History," 148; Winthrop, *Journal*, I, 230.

58. Winthrop, *Journal*, I, 229; [William Wood], *Wood's New-England's Prospect* (Boston, 1865), 64. Bradford, *History of Plymouth Plantation*, II, 258, reported a rumor that the Narragansetts had bribed the Mohawks to slay Sassacus.

59. Mason, "Brief History," 148.

60. For the text of the treaty see Appendix II, where it is reprinted from Elisha R. Potter, Jr., *The Early History of Narragansett* (R.I., Hist. Soc. Coll., III [1835]), 177-178. For details of the negotiations see Roger Williams to John Winthrop (*ca.* 10-21 Sept. 1638) in *Winthrop Papers*, IV, 58-60.

61. Mason, "Brief History," 148. Satisfaction for the loss of the mare was

not achieved until the 1660's, and then only after interminable negotiations and threats of coercion.

62. Connecticut's assumption of the role of spokesman for all the English
colonies soon aroused the ire of Massachusetts Bay and contributed
to the growing friction between the two colonies. See Winthrop,
Journal, I, 289.

63. A few Pequots may have wandered south to Pennsylvania and Virginia. See *ibid.*, II, 56-57, and William C. MacLeod, *The American
Indian Frontier* (New York, 1928), 216.

64. Mason, "Brief History," 148-151. For earlier Puritan grievances against
the Narragansetts see Israel Stoughton to John Winthrop (*ca.* 6 July
1637) in *Winthrop Papers*, III, 441-444.

65. *Conn. Col. Rec.*, I, 12-14.

66. *Ibid.*, 10; Winthrop, *Journal*, I, 238.

67. *Conn. Col. Rec.*, I, 70-71, 313.

68. Evarts B. Greene and Virginia D. Harrington, *American Population
Before the Federal Census of 1790* (New York, 1932), 47.

VI: PURITAN POLICY: CONFEDERATION AND
THE INDIANS, 1638-1675

1. [John Winthrop], *Winthrop's Journal*, edited by James K. Hosmer
(2 vols., New York, 1908), I, 271.

2. *Ibid.*, 6, 64; William Bradford, *History of Plymouth Plantation*, edited
by Worthington C. Ford (2 vols., Boston, 1912), II, 353; Bradford to
John Winthrop (29 June 1640) in Allyn B. Forbes, ed., *Winthrop
Papers* (5 vols., Boston, 1929-1947), IV, 258-259.

3. Winthrop, *Journal*, II, 7, 14-15.

4. See Evarts B. Greene and Virginia D. Harrington, *American Population Before the Federal Census of 1790* (New York, 1932), 13. I
estimate the Indian population of New England to have been not
more than 10,000 in 1635.

5. For example, Winthrop, *Journal*, II, 7, 74.

6. Miantonomo had ceded Block Island to Massachusetts in November
1637, and the natives were required to make tribute payments for
several years. The Bay Colony also received occasional gifts of
wampum or furs from other tribes. See *ibid.*, I, 238, 266, 269, 299, 305;
Nathaniel B. Shurtleff, ed., *Records of the Governor and Company
of the Massachusetts Bay in New England* (5 vols., Boston, 1853-
1854), I, 323. Hereafter cited as *Mass. Col. Rec.*

7. Winthrop, *Journal*, II, 74; J. Hammond Trumbull, ed., *Public Records
of the Colony of Connecticut* (15 vols., Hartford, 1850-1890), I, 73
(hereafter cited as *Conn. Col. Rec.*); "Relation of the Indian Plot," in
Mass. Hist. Soc. Coll., 3 ser. III, 161-164; John Haynes to John
Winthrop (1 Dec. 1643) in *Winthrop Papers*, IV, 418; John Mason
to John Winthrop (1 Dec. 1643) in *ibid.*, 419.

8. Winthrop, *Journal*, II, 74-76.
9. *Ibid.*, 79.
10. For a thorough treatment of the creation of the Confederation see Harry M. Ward, *The United Colonies of New England, 1643-1690* (New York, 1961), ch. II.
11. That the Indians might take advantage of the turmoil in the mother country to launch a concerted attack was well demonstrated by the Virginia massacre of 1644, in which three hundred colonists were slaughtered. See Winthrop, *Journal*, II, 167-168.
12. David Pulsifer, ed., *Acts of the Commissioners of the United Colonies* (2 vols. [*Records of the Colony of New Plymouth*, IX-X], Boston, 1859), I, 6.
13. For example, Samuel G. Drake concluded that "in the biography of Uncas, there is as much, perhaps, to censure regarding the acts of the English, as in any other article of Indian history." *The Aboriginal Races of North America* [*Book of the Indians*] (15th ed., Philadelphia, 1859), 144, 163. Cf. John Gorham Palfrey, *History of New England* (5 vols., 1865-1890), II, 128*n*.
14. Evidence of the Puritans' realistic estimation of Uncas can be seen in John Haynes to John Winthrop, Jr. (*ca.* 20 Sept. 1648) in *Winthrop Papers*, V, 256, and in Thomas James to John Winthrop, Jr. (4 Apr. 1654) in "Trumbull Papers," in *Mass. Hist. Soc. Coll.*, 5 ser. IX (1885), 6-7.
15. Pulsifer, *Acts of the Commissioners*, I, 10-11; [Edward Johnson], *Johnson's Wonder-Working Providence*, edited by J. Franklin Jameson (New York, 1910), 220-221; Increase Mather, *A Relation of the Troubles which have hapned in New-England By reason of the Indians there*, edited by Samuel G. Drake under the title *Early History of New England* (Boston, 1864), 188-189.
16. Pulsifer, *Acts of the Commissioners*, I, 10-11.
17. *Ibid.*; I. Mather, *Relation of the Troubles*, 189.
18. Pulsifer, *Acts of the Commissioners*, I, 11; I. Mather, *Relation of the Troubles*, 190.
19. Johnson, *Wonder-Working Providence*, 220-222; Winthrop, *Journal*, II, 134.
20. Winthrop, *Journal*, II, 134-135; I. Mather, *Relation of the Troubles*, 190.
21. Pulsifer, *Acts of the Commissioners*, I, 10-11.
22. *Ibid.*, 11-12; Winthrop, *Journal*, II, 135; William L. Stone, *Uncas and Miantonomo* (New York, 1842), 107-112.
23. Uncas was not permitted to take his prisoner until the Connecticut Commissioners had safely returned from Boston. Winthrop, *Journal*, II, 135-136.
24. See Drake, *Aboriginal Races*, 129-130, for a full discussion of the reliability of the legend. It has been perpetuated by Benjamin Trumbull, *History of Connecticut* (2 vols., New Haven, 1818), I, 135; and John Fiske, *Beginnings of New England* (Boston, 1898), 171.

25. Johnson, *Wonder-Working Providence*, 222; Pulsifer, *Acts of the Commissioners*, I, 14-15.

26. Pulsifer, *Acts of the Commissioners*, I, 14-15, 51-52; Winthrop, *Journal*, II, 135; I. Mather, *Relation of the Troubles*, 190.

27. Winthrop, *Journal*, II, 143; Pulsifer, *Acts of the Commissioners*, II, 415; John Haynes to John Winthrop (17 Jan. 1644) in *Winthrop Papers*, IV, 507.

28. Pulsifer, *Acts of the Commissioners*, II, 415-416; Great Britain, Public Record Office, *Calendar of State Papers, Colonial Series, America and the West Indies*, I (London, 1860), 326. For a highly unorthodox view of colonial authority see William Pynchon to Thomas Dudley (5 July 1648) in Henry Morris, *Early History of Springfield, 1636-1675* (Springfield, Mass., 1876), 68.

29. Pulsifer, *Acts of the Commissioners*, I, 17-18, 28-29, 33; Winthrop, *Journal*, II, 204.

30. Pulsifer, *Acts of the Commissioners*, I, 32-40; I. Mather, *Relation of the Troubles*, 196; Edward Winslow to John Winthrop (28 March 1645) in *Winthrop Papers*, V, 17-18; Thomas Peters to John Winthrop (*ca.* May 1645) in *ibid.*, 19.

31. Pulsifer, *Acts of the Commissioners*, I, 44.

32. *Ibid.*, 46-48.

33. *Ibid.*, 32, 42-47, 49.

34. *Ibid.*, 86; I. Mather, *Relation of the Troubles*, 208.

35. Pulsifer, *Acts of the Commissioners*, I, 74-75; I. Mather, *Relation of the Troubles*, 197-198.

36. *Ibid.*, 199-200; Winthrop, *Journal*, II, 349; Pulsifer, *Acts of the Commissioners*, I, 75-76.

37. In 1648 the Mohawks were believed to have 400 guns. Pulsifer, *Acts of the Commissioners*, I, 116.

38. *Ibid.*; I. Mather, *Relation of the Troubles*, 210.

39. Pulsifer, *Acts of the Commissioners*, I, 144, 145, 169; John Mason to the Commissioners (June 1649) in *ibid.*, II, 416. Particularly galling to the colonists was Ninigret's boast, made in 1645 to Thomas Stanton, that "no Englishman should step out of his doore to pisse, but he should be killed." That this rankled the Puritans is attested by the frequency with which it is repeated in their chronicles. See *ibid.*, 54, 87-88; Bradford, *History of Plymouth Plantation*, II, 379-380; I. Mather, *Relation of the Troubles*, 208. According to the records of the Commissioners, Ninigret did not deny making the statement but claimed that he had been provoked into anger by the colonial messengers.

40. Pulsifer, *Acts of the Commissioners*, I, 168-169.

41. I. Mather, *Relation of the Troubles*, 218; Alan W. Trelease, *Indian Affairs in Colonial New York: The Seventeenth Century* (New York, 1960), 96-102; Pulsifer, *Acts of the Commissioners*, II, 10-11. The colonists even feared that the Dutch were supplying arms to

Uncas (John Endicott to Peter Stuyvesant [28 March 1653] in *ibid.*, 426).

42. Pulsifer, *Acts of the Commissioners*, II, 13, 23-24, 57, 94-95; I. Mather, *Relation of the Troubles*, 217-219.

43. Pulsifer, *Acts of the Commissioners*, II, 25-27, 35-73 passim.

44. *Ibid.*, 74, 98, 101.

45. *Ibid.*, 114, 125, 430; Roger Williams to General Court of Massachusetts Bay (5 Oct. 1654) in John R. Bartlett, ed., *Records of the Colony of Rhode Island and Providence Plantations in New England* (10 vols., Providence, 1856-1865), I, 296-297.

46. Pulsifer, *Acts of the Commissioners*, II, 131-132.

47. *Ibid.*, 147-148. Although Willard apparently fulfilled his instructions, he was severely reprimanded for not dealing more strictly with Ninigret. The Commissioners feared they would have to send repeated expeditions so long as the Niantics were allowed to violate their covenants with so little penalty. See *ibid.*, 148-149; I. Mather, *Relation of the Troubles*, 222.

48. Drake, *Aboriginal Races*, 136-144; Pulsifer, *Acts of the Commissioners*, II, 150-151.

49. Ward, *United Colonies of New England*, 195-196.

50. *Conn. Col. Rec.*, I, 292; Pulsifer, *Acts of the Commissioners*, I, 97-98; II, 134, 142-143, 168. So far did the Commissioners go toward resurrecting the tribe that provisions were made for rearming it in the event it was invaded by hostile tribes. *Ibid.*, II, 193.

51. *Ibid.*, 168.

52. *Ibid.*, 199, 226, 284, 329; *Conn. Col. Rec.*, II, 548-550.

53. Pulsifer, *Acts of the Commissioners*, II, 283, 304-305, 321, 326-327, 332, 450.

54. A particularly serious clash took place between some of the New England tribes and Mohawks in the 1660's, in which the former sustained very heavy losses. This war began in 1664 and was not concluded until Dutch and English officials arranged a settlement in 1671. See Daniel Gookin, "Historical Collections of the Indians in New England," in *Mass. Hist. Soc. Coll.*, 1 ser. I (1792), 164-167; John Eliot, *A Brief Narrative of the Progress of the Gospel Among the Indians of New England, 1670* (Boston, 1868), 30; Massachusetts Historical Society, Winthrop Papers MSS, I, 19; II, 155; VIII, 2.

55. For example, Pulsifer, *Acts of the Commissioners*, II, 129-130; I. Mather, *Relation of the Troubles*, 223-224.

56. John Pynchon to John Winthrop, Jr. (16 Feb. 1658) in Massachusetts Historical Society, Winthrop Papers MSS, VII, 135; John Eliot to John Endicott (28 March 1661) in Charles Deane, "Report on the Belknap Donation," in *Publications of the Mas. Hist. Soc.*, III (1855-1858), 312-313; Pulsifer, *Acts of the Commissioners*, I, 101; II, 191, 196, 200, 222-248, 268, 429-430; Drake, *Aboriginal Races*, 162-165; *Conn. Col. Rec.*, I, 301-302.

57. Pulsifer, *Acts of the Commissioners*, I, 21; II, 196.
58. *Ibid.*, 225-226, 285, 297.
59. *Ibid.*, 284-285.
60. See, for example, *ibid.*, I, 74, 98, 100, 102; II, 159, 200; I. Mather, *Relation of the Troubles*, 194, 217. Roger Williams to John Winthrop, Jr. (10 Oct. 1648) in *Winthrop Papers*, V, 267-268; same to same (13 June 1675) in Roger Williams, *The Complete Writings of Roger Williams* (7 vols., New York, 1963), VI, 363-364; Thomas James to John Winthrop, Jr. (4 Apr. 1654) in "Trumbull Papers," 6-7; Winthrop, *Journal*, II, 131; Massachusetts Archives, XXX, 85a, 86; Connecticut Archives, Indians (1st ser.), I, 8.
61. I. Mather, *Relation of the Troubles*, 207n; Pulsifer, *Acts of the Commissioners*, I, 89.
62. Winthrop, *Journal*, II, 76.
63. Pulsifer, *Acts of the Commissioners*, II, 58, 114; I. Mather, *Relation of the Troubles*, 223-224.
64. For example, Pulsifer, *Acts of the Commissioners*, I, 17, 167; II, 375.
65. *Ibid.*, I, 102; II, 376.
66. For example, *ibid.*, I, 39.

VII: PURITAN POLICY
LAWS AND LITIGATION, 1620-1675

1. Figures for the English population are discussed in Evarts B. Greene and Virginia D. Harrington, *American Population Before the Federal Census of 1790* (New York, 1932), 9; and Stella H. Sutherland, *Population Distribution in Colonial America* (New York, 1936), 32. Cf. Richard Le Baron Bowen, *Early Rehoboth* (3 vols., Rehoboth, Mass., 1945), I, 20-24. My estimate of Indian numbers is based on indications of native population contained in various seventeenth century works, such as Daniel Gookin, "Historical Collections of the Indians in New England," in *Mass. Hist. Soc. Coll.*, 1 ser. I (1792), 195 and *passim*, as well as the later estimates in James Mooney, "The Aboriginal Population of America North of Mexico," in *Smithsonian Miscellaneous Collections*, LXXX, no. 7 (Washington, 1928), 3, and John R. Swanton, *The Indian Tribes of North America* (Washington, 1952), 13-32. Cf. Joseph B. Felt, "Statistics of Population in Massachusetts," in *American Statistical Association Collections*, I (1845), 182-190.
2. There are no legislative records for Plymouth Colony prior to 1633. See, however, Nathaniel B. Shurtleff and David Pulsifer, eds., *Records of the Colony of New Plymouth in New England* (12 vols., Boston, 1855-1861), XI, 41, hereafter cited as *Ply. Col. Rec.*; and [Isaac de Rasieres], "Letter of Isaac de Rasieres to Samuel Bloomaert, 1628 (?)," in J. Franklin Jameson, ed., *Narratives of New Netherland, 1609-1664* (New York, 1909), 112-113.
3. [John Winthrop], *Winthrop's Journal*, edited by James K. Hosmer

(2 vols., New York, 1908), II, 156, 159, 160, 169, 223; David Pulsifer, *Acts of the Commissioners of the United Colonies of New England* (2 vols., [*Ply. Col. Rec.*, IX-X], Boston, 1859), II, 142. Although Connecticut had title to the Pequot lands, the Commissioners acted as administrative agents until the 1660's.

4. Nathaniel B. Shurtleff, ed., *Records of the Governor and Company of the Massachusetts Bay in New England* (5 vols., Boston, 1853-1854), II, 176, hereafter cited as *Mass. Col. Rec.*; William H. Whitmore, ed., *The Colonial Laws of Massachusetts* [1641-1672] (Boston, 1889), 162-163; and by the same editor, *The Colonial Laws of Massachusetts* [1672-1686] (Boston, 1887), 77, hereafter cited as Whitmore, *Colonial Laws of Mass.*, I and II.

5. *Mass. Col. Rec.*, II, 84, 178, 188; Gookin, "Historical Collections," 177-180; Whitmore, *Colonial Laws of Mass.*, I, 162-163; II, 77.

6. *Ply Col. Rec.*, IV, 80.

7. For example, see *Ply. Col. Rec.*, III, 133-134; J. Hammond Trumbull, ed., *Public Records of the Colony of Connecticut* (15 vols., Hartford, 1850-1890), I, 294; Charles J. Hoadley, ed., *Records of the Colony and Plantation of New Haven, from 1638 to 1649* (Hartford, 1857), 134. Hereafter cited as *Conn. Col. Rec.* and *New Haven Col. Rec.*, I.

8. *Conn. Col. Rec.*, I, 14; Whitmore, *Colonial Laws of Mass.*, II, 74, 76-77. Cf. Charles Thornton Libby, ed., *Province and Court Records of Maine* (4 vols., Portland, 1928-1958), I, 3, in which the Councilors of the Province of New Somersetshire in 1636 "ordered that every planter or Inhabitant shall doe his best indevor to apprehend, execut or kill any Indian that hath binne known to murder any Engish, kill their Cattell or any waie spoyle their goods or doe them violence and will not mack satisfaction." It is important to note, however, that Maine was at that time the semi-feudal domain of Sir Ferdinando Gorges and was in no sense part of the Puritan enterprise.

9. There were, of course, occasional individual assaults against Indians, but Englishmen who perpetrated such illegal actions were condemned by the Puritan authorities and punished if caught. See, for example, Winthrop, *Journal*, I, 98; *Ply. Col. Rec.*, III, 74.

10. John R. Bartlett, ed., *Records of the Colony of Rhode Island and Providence Plantations in New England* (10 vols., Providence, 1856-1865), II, 509 (hereafter cited as *R.I. Col. Rec.*); *Records of the Court of Assistants of the Colony of the Massachusetts Bay, 1630-1692* (3 vols., Boston, 1901-1908), I, 22; *Ply. Col. Rec.*, V, 167-168.

11. *R.I. Col. Rec.*, II, 509; *Ply. Col. Rec.*, XI, 236.

12. *R.I. Col. Rec.*, II, 362; *Ply. Col. Rec.*, II, 118; III, 180, 192; IV, 8; V, 110.

13. Samuel Eliot Morison, ed., *Records of the Suffolk County Court, 1671-1680* (2 vols. [*Publications of the Colonial Society of Massachusetts, Collections*, XXIX-XXX], Boston, 1933), I, 485. See also John Easton, "A Relacion of the Indyan Warre," in Charles H. Lincoln, ed., *Narratives of the Indian Wars* (New York, 1913), 11.

14. All of the extant records of Puritan courts, both inferior and superior, are replete with actions in which the court's decision favored the Indian litigant. For example, see Joseph H. Smith, ed., *Colonial Justice in Western Massachusetts, 1639-1702: The Pynchon Court Record* (Cambridge, Mass., 1961), 217, 233, 243, 268; Morison, *Suffolk Court Rec.*, I, 183, 485; George F. Dow, ed., *Records and Files of the Quarterly Courts of Essex County, Massachusetts* (8 vols., Salem, 1911), III, 366, 400; *Rec. Mass. Court of Assistants*, I, 53; *Mass. Col. Rec.*, I, 92, 100, 172; *Ply. Col. Rec.*, I, 99, 103; II, 20, 89; III, 74, 90-91, 101, 106, 119-120; VII, 171.

15. Winthrop, *Journal*, II, 156, 160, 169, 223.

16. *Mass. Col. Rec.*, III, 365-366; IV (1), 210.

17. *Conn. Col. Rec.*, I, 19, 350, 529.

18. *Ibid.*, I, 79, 80; *Mass. Col. Rec.*, II, 16; *R.I. Col. Rec.*, I, 155; *New Haven Col. Rec.*, II, 593; *Ply. Col. Rec.*, XI, 32, 229.

19. For example, *Ply. Col. Rec.*, IV, 11, 17; *Mass. Col. Rec.*, I, 312; III, 308; *Conn. Col. Rec.*, I, 49, 182, 224; Dow, *Essex Court Rec.*, I, 233.

20. *R.I. Col. Rec.*, I, 186, 221-222.

21. Actions against colonists for the sale of forbidden articles are abundant in every court record. A glance at the entries under "Crimes" in the indexes of the published records will reveal the high frequency of this type of litigation. On the Connecticut forced labor law see *Conn. Col. Rec.*, II, 257, 576.

22. For example, *Ply. Col. Rec.*, III, 21, 89, 132, 192; Whitmore, *Colonial Laws of Mass.*, II, 76-77; Max Farrand, intro., *The Laws and Liberties of Massachusetts* (reprinted from the copy of the 1648 edition in the Henry E. Huntington Library [Cambridge, Mass., 1929]), 28-29. For an extract from the 1648 laws see Appendix III.

23. *R.I. Col. Rec.*, I, 484; *Conn. Col. Rec.*, I, 299, 316.

24. *New Haven Col. Rec.*, I, 3; *R.I. Col. Rec.*, I, 80; *Conn. Col. Rec.*, I, 46.

25. For example, Smith, *Pynchon Court Rec.*, 223-224, 274; Morison, *Suffolk Court Rec.*, I, 255, 485; Dow, *Essex Court Rec.*, V, 139; *Ply. Col. Rec.*, III, 90-91, 179, 209; V, 27, 69, 100-101, 151-152.

26. *Ply. Col. Rec.*, V, 151-152; *R.I. Col. Rec.*, I, 412-413.

27. See note 17 in Chapter IV; also *Ply. Col. Rec.*, II, 89; Dow, *Essex Court Rec.*, II, 335.

28. Morison, *Suffolk Court Rec.*, I, 404; *Ply. Col. Rec.*, II, 60; IV, 17, 57, 82-83, 190-191; V, 22; *Conn. Col. Rec.*, I, 226; Samuel Eliot Morison, *Builders of the Bay Colony* (Boston, 1930), 298.

29. *Mass. Col. Rec.*, I, 143; IV (2), 512-513; *R.I. Col. Rec.*, II, 172.

30. Smith, *Pynchon Court Rec.*, 223; *Ply. Col. Rec.*, II, 99, 103; III, 74; IV, 177-178; V, 31, 152; Dow, *Essex Court Rec.*, III, 400.

31. *New Haven Col. Rec.*, II, 208; *Ply. Col. Rec.*, III, 138; IV, 51, 136-137, 179; Smith, *Pynchon Court Rec.*, 246; Morison, *Suffolk Court Rec.*, I, 147-148, 404; Dow, *Essex Court Rec.*, IV, 230-232; V, 400.

32. William Bradford, *History of Plymouth Plantation*, edited by Worth-

ington C. Ford (2 vols., Boston, 1912), II, 263-268; *Ply. Col. Rec.*, I, 96-97; Winthrop, *Journal*, I, 273-274; [Roger Williams], *The Complete Writings of Roger Williams* (7 vols., New York, 1963), I, 209; Roger Williams to John Winthrop (*ca.* 1 Aug. 1638) in Allyn B. Forbes, ed., *Winthrop Papers* (5 vols., Boston, 1929-1947), IV, 48-50; same to same (14 Aug. 1638) in *ibid.*, 52-53; same to same (*ca.* 10-21 Sept. 1638) in *ibid.*, 60.

33. For example, see *New Haven Col. Rec.*, I, 22-24, 135, 146; II, 458-463; Dow, *Essex Court Rec.*, IV, 174; *Rec. Mass. Court of Assistants*, I, 52-54; Winthrop, *Journal*, II, 193.

34. *Conn. Col. Rec.*, I, 225, 294; *Mass. Col. Rec.*, IV (2), 414; Winthrop, *Journal*, I, 69, 82, 119; [William Wood], *Wood's New-England's Prospect* (Boston, 1865), 68.

35. John Mason, "A Brief History of the Pequot War," in *Mass. Hist. Soc. Coll.*, 2 ser. VIII (1826), 132; Winthrop, *Journal*, I, 265.

36. *Conn. Col. Rec.*, I, 19.

37. *Ibid.*, 19-20; Winthrop, *Journal*, I, 265-266: Sherman W. Adams and Henry R. Stiles, *The History of Ancient Wethersfield, Connecticut* (2 vols., New York, 1904), I, 68-70; II, 882-884.

38. *Conn. Col. Rec.*, I, 19-20.

39. For example, *Ply. Col. Rec.*, III, 180; V, 31, 107, 163; Morison, *Suffolk Court Rec.*, I, 183-184; Dow, *Essex Court Rec.*, I, 337; Winthrop, *Journal*, I, 67; Roger Williams to John Winthrop (*ca.* 26 Oct. 1637) in *Winthrop Papers*, III, 500-501.

40. *Ply. Col. Rec.*, I, 132; John Josselyn, "An Account of Two Voyages to New-England," in *Mass. Hist. Soc. Coll.*, 3 ser. III (1833), 294.

41. *New Haven Col. Rec.*, II, 543; *R.I. Col. Rec.*, II, 427; *Rec. Mass. Court of Assistants*, III, 210; Dow, *Essex Court Rec.*, 230-232.

42. Morison, *Suffolk Court Rec.*, I, 485; Dow, *Essex Court Rec.*, II, 58; *Mass. Col. Rec.*, IV (2), 407; *Rec. Mass. Court of Assistants*, I, 21-22; III, 216-217.

43. For a compilation of "warning out notices" issued during the colonial period by one Puritan community, see Bowen, *Early Rehoboth*, II, 133-166. Cf. Josiah Henry Benton, *Warning Out in New England* (Boston, 1911), *passim*.

44. Most of the colonists appear to have condoned the sale of war captives, although at least two leading spokesmen objected. See Roger Williams to John Winthrop (31 July 1637) in *Winthrop Papers*, III, 459; John Eliot to Governor and Council of War of Massachusetts (13 Aug. 1675) in Pulsifer, *Acts of the Commissioners*, II, 451-453.

45. *R.I. Col. Rec.*, I, 412-413; *Ply. Col. Rec.*, V, 151-152; Morison, *Suffolk Court Rec.*, I, 548.

46. *Ply. Col. Rec.*, XI, 237; Whitmore, *Colonial Laws of Mass.*, I, 52-53, 125; II, 10, 26; Almon Wheeler Lauber, *Indian Slavery in the Colonial Times within the Present Limits of the United States* (New York, 1913), 295.

47. Winthrop, *Journal*, I, 225-226; Mason, "Brief History," 148; Williams

to John Winthrop (*ca.* 21 June 1637), in *Winthrop Papers*, III, 434.
Williams, however, requested a captive for himself (Williams to John
Winthrop [31 July 1637] in *ibid.*, 459).

48. See *Roxbury Records* (*Sixth Report of the* [*Boston*] *Record Commissioners* [2nd ed., Boston, 1884]), 173. The nature of slavery —
both Negro and Indian — is difficult to determine for the period
before 1700. See Bernard C. Steiner, *History of Slavery in Connecticut* (*Johns Hopkins University Studies in Historical and Political
Science*, 11 ser. IX-X [Baltimore, 1893]), 9-11; and Lorenzo Johnston
Greene, *The Negro in Colonial New England, 1620-1776* (New
York, 1942), 17-20, 167-168.

49. *Mass. Col. Rec.*, III, 281.

50. The minutes of the General Court of Massachusetts for March 4,
1635, state that "the matter of marriage betweixte Englishe and Indeans is referd to after consideration" (*Mass. Col. Rec.*, I, 140). But
there is no evidence that it was taken up again by Massachusetts or
by any other New England Colony.

51. *Conn. Col. Rec.*, I, 78, II, 401; *Ply. Col. Rec.*, V, 163; Roger Williams
to John Winthrop (*ca.* 26 Oct. 1637) in *Winthrop Papers*, III, 500-
501; same to same (*ca.* 10 Jan. 1638) in *ibid.*, IV, 7; William Cod-
dington to John Winthrop (22 May 1640) in *ibid.*, 247.

VIII: COMMERCIAL RELATIONS, 1620-1675

1. William I. Roberts, "The Fur Trade of New England in the Seventeenth Century" (unpublished Ph.D. dissertation, University of Pennsylvania, 1958), 1-15.

2. [Roger Williams], *The Complete Writings of Roger Williams* (7
vols., New York, 1963), I, 239; George T. Hunt, *The Wars of the
Iroquois: A Study in Intertribal Trade Relations* (Madison, Wiscon-
sin, 1960), 17-18.

3. Roberts, "Fur Trade of New England," 25-32; Francis X. Moloney,
The Fur Trade in New England, 1620-1676 (Cambridge, Mass., 1931),
20-26.

4. William Bradford, *History of Plymouth Plantation*, edited by Worth-
ington C. Ford (2 vols, Boston, 1912), II, 41-43; [Isaac de Rasieres],
"Letter of Isaac de Rasieres to Samuel Bloomaert, 1628 (?)" in J.
Franklin Jameson, ed., *Narratives of New Netherland, 1609-1664*
(New York, 1909), 109-110.

5. Bradford, *History of Plymouth Plantation*, II, 40-41; Moloney, *Fur
Trade*, 26-27; Ruth A. McIntyre, *Debts Hopeful and Desperate: Financing the Plymouth Colony* (Plimouth Plantation, Mass., 1963),
49-52.

6. Moloney, *Fur Trade*, 28, 41; Bradford, *History of Plymouth Plantation*, II, 229.

7. John Winthrop to Nathaniel Rich (22 May 1634) in Allyn B. Forbes,
ed., *Winthrop Papers* (5 vols., Boston, 1929-1947), III, 167.

8. Bradford, *History of Plymouth Plantation*, II, 172-173.
9. [Edward Johnson], *Johnson's Wonder-Working Providence*, edited by J. Franklin Jameson (New York, 1910), 40, 64.
10. Roberts, "Fur Trade," 80-89; Moloney, *Fur Trade*, 50; Richard S. Dunn, *Puritans and Yankees: The Winthrop Dynasty of New England, 1630-1717* (Princeton, 1962), 83; Arthur H. Buffington, "New England and the Western Fur Trade, 1629-1675," in *Publications of the Colonial Society of Massachusetts, Transactions*, XVIII (1915-1916), 161-162.
11. Moloney, *Fur Trade*, 67-78; Bernard Bailyn, *The New England Merchants in the Seventeenth Century* (Cambridge, Mass., 1955), 26-28.
12. Moloney, *Fur Trade*, 50-61; Sylvester Judd, "The Fur Trade on Connecticut River in the Seventeenth Century," in *New England Historical and Genealogical Register*, XI (1857), 217-219; Samuel Eliot Morison, "William Pynchon, The Founder of Springfield," in *Proceedings of the Mass. Hist. Soc.*, LXIV (1930-1932), 67-107.
13. Moloney, *Fur Trade*, 46-49; Thomas Stanton to John Winthrop, Jr. (15 May 1649) in *Winthrop Papers*, V, 344.
14. Charles J. Hoadley, ed., *Records of the Colony and Plantation of New Haven from 1638 to 1649* (Hartford, 1857), 43. Hereafter cited as *New Haven Col. Rec.*, I.
15. Bailyn, *New England Merchants*, 57-58; John Gorham Palfrey, *History of New England* (5 vols., Boston, 1865-1890), II, 232; Isabel M. Calder, *The New Haven Colony* (New Haven, 1934), 77-78; Amandus Johnson, *The Swedish Settlements on the Delaware, 1638-1664* (2 vols., New York, 1911), I, 208-215; Charles M. Andrews, *The Colonial Period of American History* (4 vols., New Haven, 1934-1938), II, 167-172. On the quantity of beaver in the New Haven area cf. Samuel Maverick, "A Briefe Discription of New England and the Severall Townes Therein," in *New England Historical and Genealogical Register*, XXXIX (1885), 48.
16. Bailyn, *New England Merchants*, 58-60; Samuel Hugh Brockunier, *The Irrepressible Democrat: Roger Williams* (New York, 1940), 108-109, 184-186.
17. Judd, "Fur Trade," 219; Thomas Morton, *The New English Canaan*, edited by Charles Francis Adams, Jr. (Boston, 1883), 205-210.
18. Daniel Gookin, "Historical Collections of the Indians of New England" in *Mass. Hist. Soc. Coll.*, 1 ser. I (1792), 151-152; Williams, *Complete Writings*, I, 240; John Winthrop, Jr. to John Winthrop (28 March 1631) in *Winthrop Papers*, III, 21; same to same (30 April 1631) in *ibid.*, 32; Francis Kirby to John Winthrop, Jr. (26 Feb. 1634) in *ibid.*, 150; Company of Husbandmen to members in New England (8 March 1632) in *ibid.*, III, 69; Agreement of John Webb with John Winthrop, Jr. (21 Dec. 1648) in *ibid.*, V, 293; Receipt of Robert Bartlett (28 Feb. 1649) in *ibid.*, 313; Nathaniel Bouton, ed., *Provincial Papers: Documents and Records Relating to the Province New-Hampshire*, I (Concord, 1867), 76; James P. Baxter, ed., *The*

Trelawney Papers (*Documentary History of the State of Maine*, III [Portland, 1884]), 37.

19. William B. Weeden, *Indian Money as a Factor in New England Civilization* (*Johns Hopkins University Studies in Historical and Political Science*, 2 ser. VIII-IX [Baltimore, 1884]), 15.

20. John Eliot to Richard Baxter (20 June 1669), in F. J. Powicke, ed., "Some Unpublished Correspondence of the Rev. Richard Baxter and the Rev. John Eliot, 'the Apostle to the American Indians,' 1656-1682," in *Bulletin of the John Rylands Library*, XV, (1931), 454-455.

21. Weeden, *Indian Money*, 9-18; Williams, *Complete Writings*, I, 233-241; Gookin, "Historical Collections," 152; T. Morton, *New English Canaan*, 157-158; Frederick Webb Hodge, ed., *Handbook of American Indians North of Mexico* (2 vols., Washington, 1907), II, 904-909.

22. Williams, *Complete Writings*, I, 233, 240; T. Morton, *New English Canaan*, 157-158; Gookin, "Historical Collections," 152. For an illustrated description of the various types of wampum see Charles C. Willoughby, *Antiquities of the New England Indians* (Cambridge, 1935), 266-275.

23. Nathaniel B. Shurtleff, ed., *Records of the Governor and Company of the Massachusetts Bay in New England* (5 vols., Boston, 1853-1854), I, 208, 302, 329; II, 279; IV (1), 36; J. Hammond Trumbull, ed., *Public Records of the Colony of Connecticut* (15 vols., Hartford, 1850-1890), I, 61; II, 25; *New Haven Col. Rec.*, I, 175-176, 183, 211, 436; Nathaniel B. Shurtleff and David Pulsifer, eds., *Records of the Colony of New Plymouth* (12 vols., Boston, 1855-1861), XI, 57, 128; John R. Bartlett, *Records of the Colony of Rhode Island and Providence Plantations in New England* (10 vols., Providence, 1856-1865), I, 217, 400, 474. Hereafter cited as *Mass. Col. Rec.*, *Conn. Col. Rec.*, *Ply. Col. Rev.*, and *R.I. Col. Rec.*

24. David Pulsifer, ed., *Acts of the Commissioners of the United Colonies* (2 vols. [*Ply. Col. Rec.*, IX-X], Boston, 1857), I, 136-137; Williams, *Complete Writings*, I, 240-241; Joseph B. Felt, *An Historical Account of Massachusetts Currency* (Boston, 1839), 2-54 *passim*, 249; Weeden, *Indian Money*, 28-29; *Conn. Col. Rec.*, I, 179, 546; *Mass. Col. Rec.*, II, 261; *R.I. Col. Rec.*, I, 155-217; *New Haven Col. Rec.*, I, 217; William Pynchon to Stephen Day (8 Oct. 1644) in *Winthrop Papers*, IV, 495; Benjamin Negus to John Winthrop, Jr. (12 April 1649) in *ibid.*, V, 331.

25. William B. Weeden, *Economic and Social History of New England* (2 vols., Boston, 1890), I, 40-44; Williams, *Complete Writings*, I, 235.

26. Weeden, *Economic and Social History*, I, 42-44; [Sarah K. Knight], *The Journal of Madame Knight* (Boston, 1920), 40-41; *Conn. Col. Rec.*, I, 497; *New Haven Col. Rec.*, II, 346-347. See also Frank G. Speck, "The Functions of Wampum Among the Eastern Algonquian," in *American Anthropological Association, Memoirs*, VI (1919), 56-66.

27. Williams, *Complete Writings*, I, 242-243.
28. *Mass. Col. Rec.*, IV (1), 291.
29. *Mass. Col. Rec.*, I, 55, 96, 179; II, 60, 225; IV (1), 354; IV (2), 398-399, 548; *Conn. Col. Rec.*, I, 20, 79; II, 119; *New Haven Col. Rec.*, I, 43; *R.I. Col. Rec.*, I, 62, 90, 123, 230; *Boston Town Records, 1634-1660, and the Book of Possessions* (*Second Report of the Records Commissioners* [Boston, 1881]), part 1, 65; Judd, "Fur Trade," 217.
30. [John Winthrop], *Winthrop's Journal*, edited by James K. Hosmer (2 vols., New York, 1908), II, 326; Moloney, *Fur Trade*, 102.
31. Clarence S. Brigham, ed., *British Royal Proclamations Relating to America, 1603-1783* (*Transactions and Collections of the American Antiquarian Society*, XII [Cambridge, 1911]), 33-34, 66-68.
32. [William Bradford], "Bradford's Verse History of New England," in *Mass. Hist. Soc. Coll.*, 1 ser. III (1794), 82-83.
33. Williams, *Complete Writings*, I, 175, 261; [Thomas Lechford], *Note-Book Kept by Thomas Lechford . . .* (*Transactions and Collections of the American Antiquarian Society*, VII [1885]), 104; John Josselyn, "An Account of Two Voyages to New-England," in *Mass. Hist. Soc. Coll.*, 3 ser. III (1833), 309; *Mass. Col. Rec.*, I, 195; II, 16; IV (1), 21; *Ply. Col. Rec.*, II, 8; III, 4, 102; *Conn. Col. Rec.*, I, 1, 79, 80, 197-198; II, 119, 271; *R.I. Col. Rec.*, I, 155, 210, 320, 332; *New Haven Col. Rec.*, I, 60; Hunt, *Wars of the Iroquois*, 165-175.
34. Ronald O. MacFarlane, "Indian Relations in New England, 1620-1760: A Study of a Regulated Frontier" (unpublished Ph.D. dissertation, Harvard University, 1933), ch. IX.
35. *Mass. Col. Rec.*, IV (2), 364-366; *Conn. Col. Rec.*, II, 119; *Ply. Col. Rec.*, V, 11-12; XI, 184-185; Moloney, *Fur Trade*, 103. During King Philip's War, Plymouth made selling guns to the Indians a capital crime (*Ply. Col. Rec.*, V, 173).
36. Gookin, "Historical Collections," 151; *R.I. Col. Rec.*, I, 219, 279, 308, 338, 413; II, 486-487, 500-502; *Ply. Col. Rec.*, III, 60-61, 75; IV, 32; *New Haven Col. Rec.*, II, 195, 219, 299; *Mass. Col. Rec.*, I, 106, 197, 316, 323; II, 85, 258; III, 369, 425-426; IV (1), 117, 201, 289; IV (2), 297, 564; *Conn. Col. Rec.*, I, 254-255, 263, 338, 354; II, 257.
37. *Ply. Col. Rec.*, IV, 93; X, 158; *Mass. Col. Rec.*, IV (1) 255-256, 277; *Conn. Col. Rec.*, I, 284; II, 238; *New Haven Col. Rec.*, II, 217.
38. *New Haven Col. Rec.*, I, 3; *Conn. Col. Rec.*, I, 95, 530-531; *R.I. Col. Rec.*, I, 153; *Ply. Col. Rec.*, IX, 149.
39. Williams, *Complete Writings*, I, 246-247; *Conn. Col. Rec.*, I, 95; II, 252.
40. Buffington, "Fur Trade," 162-173; Moloney, *Fur Trade*, 114-116; Hunt, *Wars of the Iroquois*, 36; Judd, "Fur Trade," 218-219.
41. Winthrop, *Journal*, II, 328; Williams to John Winthrop, Jr. (12 July 1654) in Williams, *Complete Writings*, VI, 261.
42. Bailyn, *New England Merchants*, 46, 54-55; Moloney, *Fur Trade*, 76, 83-91.

43. Gookin, "Historical Collections," 151-152; [William Wood], *Wood's New-England's Prospect* (Boston, 1865), 87; Bradford, *History of Plymouth Plantation*, I, 283.

IX: EARLY MISSIONARY ACTIVITY, 1620-1650

1. Samuel Eliot Morison, *Builders of the Bay Colony* (Boston, 1930), 289; William Bradford, *History of Plymouth Plantation*, edited by Worthington C. Ford (2 vols., Boston, 1912), I, 52-55; Francis Higginson, *New-Englands Plantation* (Salem, 1908), 59; John Winthrop, "General Conclusions and Particular Considerations," in Allyn B. Forbes, ed., *Winthrop Papers* (5 vols., Boston, 1929-1947), II, 126; Great Britain, Public Record Office, *Calendar of State Papers, Colonial Series, America and the West Indies*, I (London, 1860), 111.

2. Nathaniel B. Shurtleff, ed., *Records of the Governor and Company of the Massachusetts Bay in New England* (5 vols., Boston, 1853-1854), I, 17, 352 (hereafter cited as *Mass. Col. Rec.*); Samuel Symonds to John Winthrop (6 Jan. 1647) in *Winthrop Papers*, V, 126.

3. See, for example, the contemporary criticisms cited in Justin Winsor, ed., *The Memorial History of Boston* (4 vols., Boston, 1880-1881), I, 244, 258, and William Kellaway, *The New England Company, 1649-1776* (New York, 1962), 4. Also Richard Baxter to John Eliot (20 Jan. 1657) in F. J. Powicke, ed., "Some Unpublished Correspondence of the Rev. Richard Baxter and the Rev. John Eliot, 'the Apostle to the American Indians,' 1656-1682," in *Bulletin of the John Rylands Library*, XV (1931), 156; Eliot to Baxter (7 Oct. 1657) in *ibid.*, 157-158.

4. Hopkins to Winthrop (25 Feb. 1633) in *Winthrop Papers*, III, 106; Thomas Shepard, "The Clear Sun-shine of the Gospel Breaking Forth upon the Indians in New-England," in *Mass. Hist. Soc. Coll.*, 3 ser. IV (1834), 66-67; Kellaway, *New England Company*, 6-7.

5. *Ibid.*, 5-6.

6. [Roger Williams], *The Complete Writings of Roger Williams* (7 vols., New York, 1963), I, 220-221; VII, 31-41.

7. Bradford, *History of Plymouth Plantation*, I, 367-369; Winsor, *Memorial History of Boston*, I, 258; Morison, *Builders of the Bay Colony*, 289-290.

8. Bradford, *History of Plymouth Plantation*, I, 283; *New England's First Fruits: with Divers other Special Matters Concerning That Country* (Sabin's Reprints, Quarto Series, no. VII [New York, 1865]), 4-5; George F. Willison, *Saints and Strangers* (New York, 1945), 314.

9. *New England's First Fruits*, 5-11; Edward Howes to John Winthrop, Jr. (26 March 1632) in *Winthrop Papers*, III, 174; [Edward Johnson], *Johnson's Wonder-Working Providence*, edited by J. Franklin Jameson (New York, 1910), 79-80; Morison, *Builders of the Bay Colony*,

290; John Gorham Palfrey, *History of New England* (5 vols., Boston, 1865-1890), II, 187-188.

10. [John Winthrop], *Winthrop's Journal*, edited by James K. Hosmer (2 vols., New York, 1908), II, 69; Williams, *Complete Writings*, I, 26-27; *New England's First Fruits*, 11-14.

11. Edward Winslow, "The Glorious Progress of the Gospel, amongst the Indians in New England," in *Mass. Hist. Soc. Coll.*, 3 ser. IV (1834), 75.

12. Franklin B. Hough, ed., *Papers Relating to the Island of Nantucket . . . Martha's Vineyard and other Island adjacent . . .* (Albany, 1856), 1-4; Daniel Gookin, "Historical Collections of the Indians in New England," in *Mass. Hist. Soc. Coll.*, 1 ser. I (1792), 201-202; Palfrey, *History of New England*, II, 196, 339.

13. Henry Whitfield, ed., The Light appearing more and more towards the perfect Day . . . ," in *Mass. Hist. Soc. Coll.*, 3 ser. IV (1834), 100-147.

14. *Ibid.*, 109-115; Winslow, "Glorious Progress of the Gospel," 77-78.

15. Winthrop, *Journal*, II, 156; *Mass. Col. Rec.*, II, 84, 134, 178-179.

16. Cotton Mather, *Magnalia Christi Americana* (2 vols., Hartford, 1820), I, 479-481; Morison, *Builders of the Bay Colony*, 291; George P. Winship, intro. and ed., *The New England Company of 1649 and John Eliot* (Boston, 1920), vii-viii; Convers Francis, *Life of John Eliot, The Apostle to the Indians* (New York, 1856), 3-9.

17. Winthrop, *Journal*, I, 94-95; Francis S. Drake, *The Town of Roxbury* (*Records Relating to the Early History of Boston*, XXXIV [Boston, 1905]), 10-11; Morison, *Builders of the Bay Colony*, 292-294. For examples of contemporary estimates of Eliot see William H. Whitmore, ed., *John Dunton's Letters from New England* (Boston, 1867), 192-193; [Jasper Danckaerts], *The Journal of Jasper Danckaerts*, edited by Bartlett B. James and J. Franklin Jameson (New York, 1913), 263-271.

18. John Eliot, "The Indian Grammar Begun," in *Mass. Hist. Soc. Coll.*, 2 ser. IX (1823), 312; Winslow, "Glorious Progress of the Gospel," 90; William W. Tooker, *John Eliot's First Indian Teacher and Interpreter . . .* (New York, 1896), 14-17; *New England's First Fruits*, 10-11.

19. Shepard, "Clear Sun-shine of the Gospel," 64; Francis, *Life of John Eliot*, 40-45.

20. [John Wilson?], "The Day-Breaking, if not the Sun-Rising of the Gospell with the Indians in New-England," in *Mass. Hist. Soc. Coll.*, 3 ser. IV (1834), 1-24; Gookin, "Historical Collections," 168-169.

21. Wilson, "Day-Breaking, if not the Sun-Rising," 3-4.

22. *Ibid.*, 4-8.

23. *Ibid.*, 8-14.

24. *Ibid.*, 17-23; Gookin, "Historical Collections," 169; F. Drake, *Town of Roxbury*, 180.

25. Shepard, "Clear Sun-shine of the Gospel," 37-41; see also Appendix V.

26. Shepard, "Clear Sun-shine of the Gospel," 45-46; Winthrop, *Journal*, II, 324.
27. Shepard, "Clear Sun-shine of the Gospel," 47-48, 62-63; Winslow, "Glorious Progress of the Gospel," 82-83.
28. Whitfield, "The Light appearing," 133-134.
29. Shepard, "Clear Sun-shine of the Gospel," 59.
30. Winthrop, *Journal*, II, 31; Raymond P. Stearns, *The Strenuous Puritan: Hugh Peter, 1598-1660* (Urbana, Illinois, 1954), ch. VII; same author, "The Weld-Peter Mission to England," in *Publications of the Colonial Society of Massachusetts, Transactions*, XXXII (1933-1937), 188-246; Kellaway, *New England Company*, 9-11.
31. *New England's First Fruits*; see note 8 above. On its authorship see Stearns, "The Weld-Peter Mission," 218-220.
32. Thomas Welde, "Innocency Cleared," in *New-England Historical and Geneological Register*, XXXVI (1882), 68; Kellaway, *New England Company*, 9-10.
33. Both pamphlets have been reprinted in *Mass. Hist. Soc. Coll.*, 3 ser. IV (1834); see notes 4 and 20 above.
34. Gookin, "Historical Collections," 212; Kellaway, *New England Company*, 10-13.
35. Leo F. Stock, ed., *Proceedings and Debates of the British Parliaments Respecting North America*, I (Washington, 1924), 203-210.
36. "Glorious Progress of the Gospel"; see note 11 above.
37. Ebenezer Hazard, *Historical Collections* (2 vols., Philadelphia, 1792), I, 635; Kellaway, *New England Company*, 12-16.
38. Winslow, "Glorious Progress of the Gospel," 75.
39. John Eliot to William Steele (8 Dec. 1652) in Columbia University Library, Miscellaneous MSS pertaining to John Eliot from the Library of Congress (microfilm); Shepard, "Clear Sun-shine of the Gospel," 42-43; Palfrey, *History of New England*, II, 340.
40. Shepard, "Clear Sun-shine of the Gospel," 50; Whitfield, "The Light appearing," 113-116, 147.
41. Winslow, "Glorious Progress of the Gospel," 83, 88; Shepard, "Clear Sun-shine of the Gospel," 38, 51, 62; Wilson, "The Day-Breaking, if not the Sun-Rising," 15-16, 19; Whitfield, "The Light appearing," 113. Waban was not actually a sachem, but was apparently an influential figure in his village. Eliot to William Steele (8 Dec. 1652) in Columbia University Library, Miscellaneous MSS . . . (microfilm).
42. Winslow, "Glorious Progress of the Gospel," 81, 88.

X: MISSIONARY EFFORTS: YEARS OF GROWTH, 1650-1665

1. Thomas Shepard, "The Clear Sun-shine of the Gospel, Breaking Forth upon the Indians in New-England," in *Mass. Hist. Soc. Coll.*, 3 ser. IV (1834), 50; Edward Winslow, "The Glorious Progress of the Gospel, amongst the Indians in New England," in *ibid.*, 87-88.

2. John Eliot and Thomas Mayhew, Jr., "Tears of Repentance: Or, A Further Narrative of the Progress of the Gospel amongst the Indians in New-England," in *Mass. Hist. Soc. Coll.*, 3 ser. IV (1834), 223; John Eliot, "A Late and Further Manifestation of the Progress of the Gospel amongst the Indians in New-England," in *ibid.*, 269-270.

3. Shepard, "Clear Sun-shine of the Gospel," 48-49, 59; Nathaniel B. Shurtleff, ed., *Records of the Governor and Company of the Massachusetts Bay in New England* (5 vols., Boston, 1853-1854), II, 188, 189 (hereafter cited as *Mass. Col. Rec.*); Francis S. Drake, *The Town of Roxbury* (*Records Relating to the Early History of Boston*, XXXIV [Boston, 1905]), 181.

4. Winslow, "Glorious Progress of the Gospel," 87; Shepard, "Clear Sunshine of the Gospel," 62.

5. Winslow, "Glorious Progress of the Gospel," 81, 86; Henry Whitfield, ed., "The Light appearing more and more towards the perfect Day. Or, A farther Discovery of the present state of the Indians in New-England, Concerning the Progresse of the Gospel amongst them," in *Mass. Hist. Soc. Coll.*, 3 ser. IV (1834), 134; Justin Winsor, ed., *The Memorial History of Boston* (4 vols., Boston, 1880-1881), I, 262-265.

6. *Mass. Col. Rec.*, II, 166, 189; [John Wilson?], "The Day-Breaking, if not the Sun-Rising of the Gospell with the Indians in New-England," in *Mass. Hist. Soc. Coll.*, 3 ser. IV (1834), 8; Samuel Eliot Morison, *Builders of the Bay Colony* (Boston, 1930), 295-296; John Gorham Palfrey, *History of New England* (5 vols., Boston, 1865-1890), II, 193-194.

7. Whitfield, "The Light appearing," 138-141.

8. *Ibid.*, 137-138; Eliot, "A Late and Further Manifestation," 270; Palfrey, *History of New England*, II, 336-337.

9. Henry Whitfield, "Strength out of Weaknesse; or a Glorious Manifestation of the Further Progresse of the Gospel among the Indians in New-England," in *Mass. Hist. Soc. Coll.*, 3 ser. IV (1834), 167; Daniel Gookin, "Historical Collections of the Indians in New-England," in *ibid.*, 1 ser. I (1792), 180; Eliot and Mayhew, "Tears of Repentance," 227; William Biglow, *History of the Town of Natick, Mass.* (Boston, 1830), 21-23.

10. Whitfield, "Strength out of Weaknesse," 177-178, 190-191; Gookin, "Historical Collections," 181.

11. Whitfield, "The Light appearing," 127; John Eliot to Jonathan Hanmer (19 July 1652) in Wilberforce Eames, ed., *John Eliot and the Indians, 1652-1657, Being Letters Addressed to Rev. Jonathan Hanmer of Barnstaple, England* (New York, 1915), 7.

12. Whitfield, "Strength out of Weaknesse," 171; Eliot, "A Late and Further Manifestation," 271.

13. Exodus 18:17-18.

14. Whitfield, "Strength out of Weaknesse," 171-174.

15. Eliot and Mayhew, "Tears of Repentance," 228-240.

16. *Ibid.*, 244-245. John Eliot to William Steele (8 Dec. 1652) in Columbia University Library, Miscellaneous MSS pertaining to John Eliot from the Library of Congress (microfilm).

17. Eliot, "A Late and Further Manifestation," 271.

18. "Tears of Repentance"; see note 2 above.

19. Eliot, "A Late and Further Manifestation," 271.

20. *Ibid.*, 272-275; Winsor, *Memorial History of Boston*, I, 268. A famous story, probably apocryphal, relates that one Indian judge's formula for handling drunkards was to "tie um all up, and whip um plaintiff, whip um fendant and whip um witness." Biglow, *History of Natick*, 85.

21. Eliot, "A Late and Further Manifestation," 272-276; Eliot to Jonathan Hanmer (28 Aug. 1654) in Eames, *John Eliot and the Indians*, 22.

22. Eliot, "A Late and Further Manifestation," 270-271; Gookin, "Historical Collections," 166; Eliot to Major Atherton (4 June 1657) in *Mass. Hist. Soc. Coll.*, 1 ser. II (1793), 9; Eliot to William Steele (8 Dec. 1652) in Columbia University Library, Miscellaneous MSS . . . (microfilm).

23. Ebenezer Hazard, *Historical Collections* (2 vols., Philadelphia, 1792), I, 635; Gookin, "Historical Collections," 212-213; George P. Winship, intro. and ed., *The New England Company of 1649 and John Eliot* (Boston, 1920), xiv-xix, xxxiii-xxxvii; William Kellaway, *The New England Company, 1649-1776* (New York, 1962), 21-40.

24. David Pulsifer, ed., *Acts of the Commissioners of the United Colonies of New England* (2 vols., [*Records of the Colony of New Plymouth*, IX-X], Boston, 1859), I, 162-163, 192-199; Kellaway, *New England Company*, 67-72.

25. *Mass. Col. Rec.*, IV (1), 234; Pulsifer, *Acts of the Commissioners*, II, 118-123, 135-139; Winship, *New England Company and Eliot*, xxxvii, lv-lvii; Kellaway, *New England Company*, 66-73.

26. John Eliot to Edward Winslow (10 Oct. 1654) in Columbia University Library, Miscellaneous MSS . . . (microfilm); Eliot's Account of Expenditures, 1649-1652, in *ibid.*; F. J. Powicke, "Some Unpublished Correspondence of the Rev. Richard Baxter and the Rev. John Eliot, 'the Apostle to the Indians,' 1652-1682," in *Bulletin of the John Rylands Library*, XV (1931), 138-176, 442-466 *passim;* [John Eliot], "Letters from Rev. John Eliot of Roxbury, to Hon. Robert Boyle," in *Mass. Hist. Soc. Coll.*, 1 ser. III (1794), 177-188 *passim;* Winship, *New England Company and Eliot*, xxii-xxvii; Morison, *Builders of the Bay Colony*, 308-311; Kellaway, *New England Company*, 93-94.

27. Whitfield, "Strength out of Weaknesse," 195; Eliot and Mayhew, "Tears of Repentance," 222; Palfrey, *History of New-England*, II, 334-335; Winship, *New England Company and Eliot*, xxii-xxvii, liii; Kellaway, *New England Company*, 22-26, 30-36, 62-64; cf. Raymond P. Stearns, *The Strenuous Puritan: Hugh Peter, 1598-1660* (Urbana, Illinois, 1954), 173-183; same author, "The Weld-Peter Mission to

England," in *Publications of the Colonial Society of Massachusetts, Transactions*, XXXII (1933-1937), 236-246.

28. Winship, *New England Company and Eliot*, xxiv, lxix; Whitfield, "The Light appearing," 128, 144.
29. [Richard Baxter], *Reliquiae Baxterianae* . . . (London, 1696), 290; Morison, *Builders of the Bay Colony*, 310-311; Kellaway, *New England Company*, 41-47.
30. Great Britain, Public Record Office, *Calendar of State Papers, Colonial Series, America and the West Indies*, V (London, 1880), 11; Kellaway, *New England Company*, 46.
31. *Ibid.*, 47-49; *Dictionary of National Biography*, VI, 118-123.
32. Winship, *New England Company and Eliot*, lviii-lix; Kellaway, *New England Company*, 73-80.
33. Wilson, "The Day-Breaking, if not the Sun-Rising," 11; Pulsifer, *Acts of the Commissioners*, II, 105; Morison, *Builders of the Bay Colony*, 312; Winship, *New England Company and Eliot*, 34.
34. Whitfield, "Strength out of Weaknesse," 169, 178; Kellaway, *New England Company*, 122.
35. Pulsifer, *Acts of the Commissioners*, II, 120; Edward Reynolds, ed., *A Further Accompt of the Progresse of the Gospel amongst the Indians in New England, and of the Means used Effectually to Advance the Same*, reprinted in Sabin's Reprints, Quarto Series, no. VI, under the title *A Further Manifestation of the Progress of the Gospel among the Indians in New England* (New York, 1865), 1.
36. Abraham Pierson, "Some Helps for the Indians: A Catechism," in *Conn. Hist. Soc. Coll.* III (1895), 12.
37. Kellaway, *New England Company*, 127.
38. Whitfield, "Strength out of Weaknesse," 167-168; Reynolds, *A Further Accompt*, 3, 21; Winship, *New England Company and Eliot*, xlvii-xlviii; Morison, *Builders of the Bay Colony*, 312-313.
39. Reynolds, *A Further Accompt*, 3; Winship, *New England Company and Eliot*, 71, 74; Morison, *Builders of the Bay Colony*, 313-314.
40. Gookin, "Historical Collections," 174; Winsor, *Memorial History of Boston*, I, 470-473; Winship, *New England Company and Eliot*, 111; same author, *The First American Bible* (Boston, 1929), 15-20; Morison, *Builders of the Bay Colony*, 313-314.
41. James C. Pilling, *Bibliography of the Algonquian Languages* (Washington, 1891), 127-184; Pulsifer, *Acts of the Commissioners*, II, 119; Winsor, *Memorial History of Boston*, I, 271, 473-478. A copy of the Lord's Prayer in Algonquian is in Massachusetts Historical Society, Miscellaneous Bound MSS, II (1663-1674).
42. Winsor, *Memorial History of Boston*, I, 470-479.

XI: MISSIONARY EFFORTS: YEARS OF HARVEST,
1665-1675

1. David Pulsifer, ed., *Acts of the Commissioners of the United Colonies* (2 vols. [*Records of the Colony of New Plymouth*, IX-X], Boston, 1859), II, 285.
2. *Harvard College Records* (*Publications of the Colonial Society of Massachusetts, Collections*, XV-XVI [1925]), I, 40, 181; Samuel Eliot Morison, *Harvard College in the Seventeenth Century* (2 vols., Cambridge, 1936), I, 6, 340.
3. Pulsifer, *Acts of the Commissioners*, II, 128-129, 228, 252, 288-289; Morison, *Harvard in the Seventeenth Century*, I, 357-358.
4. William Kellaway, *The New England Company, 1649-1776* (New York, 1961), 101.
5. *Harvard College Records*, I, lxxxii-lxxxv, lxxxvii; Pulsifer, *Acts of the Commissioners*, II, 105, 107, 128-129; Daniel Gookin, "Historical Collections of the Indians in New England," in *Mass. Hist. Soc. Coll.*, 1 ser. I (1792), 176. For a full discussion of the Indian College building and a conjectural drawing of it (reprinted above, p. 283), see Morison, *Harvard in the Seventeenth Century*, I, 342-344.
6. Gookin, "Historical Collections," 217; John Josselyn, "Two Voyages to New-England," in *Mass. Hist. Soc. Coll.*, 3 ser. III (1833), 310-311.
7. Gookin, "Historical Collections," 173; Morison, *Harvard in the Seventeenth Century*, I, 352-357.
8. [Nathaniel Saltonstall], "The Present State of New England," in Charles H. Lincoln, ed., *Narratives of the Indian Wars* (New York, 1913), 24, 31; Increase Mather, *A Relation of the Troubles which have hapned in New-England By reason of the Indians there*, edited by Samuel G. Drake under the title *Early History of New England* (Boston, 1864), 234-235; Morison, *Harvard in the Seventeenth Century*, I, 352-353.
9. *Harvard College Records*, I, 85; Commissioners of the United Colonies to Robert Boyle (13 Sept. 1665) in John W. Ford, ed., *Some Correspondence Between the Governors and Treasurers of the New England Company . . . and the Commissioners of the United Colonies . . .* (London, 1896), 13-14; Gookin, "Historical Collections," 173; John L. Sibley, *Biographical Sketches of Graduates of Harvard University*, II (Cambridge, Mass., 1881), 201-203.
10. *Harvard College Records*, I, 352.
11. [John Winthrop], *Winthrop's Journal*, edited by James K. Hosmer (2 vols., New York, 1908), II, 224.
12. Commissioners of the United Colonies to Robert Boyle (7 Sept. 1659) in Pulsifer, *Acts of the Commissioners*, II, 217; same to same (10 Sept. 1662) in *ibid.*, 275; same to same (13 Sept. 1655), in Ford, *Some Correspondence*, 14; Gookin, "Historical Collections," 172-173, 217; Justin Winsor, ed., *The Memorial History of Boston* (4 vols., Boston, 1880-

1881), I, 497; Samuel Eliot Morison, *The Founding of Harvard College* (Cambridge, Mass., 1935), 313-314. For President Chauncey's testimony on the Indian scholars see the certificate appended to John Eliot, *A further Account of the progress of the Gospel Amongst the Indians In New England* . . . (London, 1660).

13. Nathaniel B. Shurtleff, ed., *Records of the Governor and Company of the Massachusetts Bay in New England* (5 vols., Boston, 1853-1854), IV (2), 199. Hereafter cited as *Mass. Col. Rec.*

14. Henry Whitfield, ed., "The Light appearing more and more towards the perfect Day. Or, A Farther Discovery of the present state of the Indians in New-England, Concerning the Progresse of the Gospel amongst them," in *Mass. Hist. Soc. Coll.*, 3 ser. IV (1834), 121-122, 144; John Eliot, *A Brief Narrative of the Progress of the Gospel among the Indians of New England, 1670* (Boston, 1868), 23.

15. Henry Whitfield, "Strength out of Weaknesse; or a Glorious Manifestation of the Further Progresse of the Gospel among the Indians in New-England," in *Mass. Hist. Soc. Coll.*, 3 ser. IV (1834), 168-169; John Eliot and Jonathan Mayhew, Jr., "Tears of Repentance: Or, A Further Narrative of the Progress of the Gospel amongst the Indians in New-England," in *ibid.*, 208.

16. Pulsifer, *Acts of the Commissioners*, II, 277-279. For other annual accounts see, for example, *ibid.*, 205-206, 218-220, 244-246, 261-263.

17. Gookin, "Historical Collections," 143, 220-222.

18. John Josselyn, "Chronological Observations of America, From the year of the World to the year of Christ, 1673," in *Mass Hist. Soc. Coll.*, 3 ser. III (1833), 385; Whitfield, "Strength out of Weaknesse," 162; Gookin, "Historical Collections," 172.

19. For a convenient list of all who served as Commissioners, with brief biographical accounts of each, see Harry M. Ward, *The United Colonies of New England, 1643-1690* (New York, 1961), 400-411.

20. Eliot, *Brief Narrative*, 24-25; Gookin, "Historical Collections," 180-184.

21. Eliot, *Brief Narrative*, 25-32; Gookin, "Historical Collections," 166, 184-189. See also [John Eliot], "An Account of Indian Churches in New England . . . ," in *Mass. Hist. Soc. Coll.*, 1 ser. X (1809), 124-129; and Samuel G. Drake, *The Aboriginal Races of North America* [*Book of the Indians*] (15th ed., Philadelphia, 1859), 178-179.

22. Eliot, *Brief Narrative*, 27-28; Gookin, "Historical Collections," 185-186; Daniel Gookin, "An Historical Account of the Doings and Sufferings of the Christian Indians in New England, in the Years 1675, 1676, 1677," in *Transactions and Collections of the American Antiquarian Society* [*Archaeologia Americana*], II (1836), 429-534 *passim.*

23. Gookin, "Historical Collections," 186-188; Eliot, *Brief Narrative*, 29-30; Drake, *Aboriginal Races*, 109-110.

24. Eliot, *Brief Narrative*, 28-29; Gookin, "Historical Collections," 184, 188.

25. Whitfield, "The Light appearing," 130; Whitfield, "Strength out of

Weaknesse," 170-171; Eliot, *Brief Narrative*, 31-32; Eliot, "An Account of Indian Churches," 128; Cf. Gookin, "Historical Collections," 188-189.

26. Gookin, "Historical Collections," 189-194.

27. *Ibid.*, 194-195.

28. *Mass. Col. Rec.*, IV (1), 334, IV (2), 34; Gookin, "Historical Collections," 177-178, 192; Eliot, "An Account of Indian Churches," 128-129; Kellaway, *New England Company*, 105-106.

29. Gookin, "Historical Collections," 177-178; William H. Whitmore, ed., *The Colonial Laws of Massachusetts* [*1672-1686*] (Boston, 1887), 77.

30. Franklin B. Hough, ed., *Papers Relating to the Island of Nantucket . . . Martha's Vineyard and other Islands adjacent . . .* (Albany, 1856), ix-xv.

31. Whitfield, "Strength out of Weaknesse," 188; Eliot and Mayhew, "Tears of Repentance," 202-203.

32. Edward Reynolds, ed., *A Further Accompt of the Progresse of the Gospel amongst the Indians in New England, and of the Means used Effectually to Advance the Same*, in Sabin's Reprints, Quarto Series, no. VI, under the title *A Further Manifestation of the Progress of the Gospel among the Indians in New England* (New York, 1865), 7; Eliot, *Brief Narrative*, 20-22; Gookin, "Historical Collections," 202-204, 217; Thomas Mayhew, Sr. to John Winthrop, Jr. (*ca.* 1658) in "Winthrop Papers," in *Mass. Hist. Soc. Coll.*, 4 ser. VII (1865), 34; same to same (29 Aug. 1659) in *ibid.*, 36-37.

33. Gookin, "Historical Collections," 204-207.

34. Eliot, *Brief Narrative*, 20; Eliot, "An Account of Indian Churches," 126-127.

35. Thomas Mayhew to Daniel Gookin (1 Sept. 1674) in Gookin, "Historical Collections," 204-207; Eliot, "An Account of Indian Churches," 126-127.

36. Cotton Mather, *Magnalia Christi Americana* (2 vols., Hartford, 1820), I, 514; Gookin, "Historical Collections," 200; William Hubbard, *A Narrative of the Troubles with the Indians in New England, From the First Planting thereof to the Present Time*, edited by Samuel G. Drake under the title *The History of the Indian Wars in New England . . .* (2 vols., Roxbury, Mass., 1865), I, 46-47.

37. Edward Winslow, "The Glorious Progress of the Gospel, amongst the Indians in New England," in *Mass. Hist. Soc. Coll.*, 3 ser. IV (1834), 81; Whitfield, "Strength out of Weaknesse," 162, 180-181, 184, 194; Eliot, *Brief Narrative*, 19-20.

38. Eliot, *Brief Narrative*, 19-20; David Bushnell, "The Treatment of the Indians in Plymouth Colony," in *New England Quarterly*, XXVI (1953), 207-208; Kellaway, *New England Company*, 105.

39. Richard Bourne to Daniel Gookin (1 Sept. 1674) in Gookin, "Historical Collections," 196-199; Gideon Hawley, "Biographical and Topographical Anecdotes respecting Sandwich and Marshpee . . . ," in *Mass. Hist. Soc. Coll.*, 1 ser. III (1794), 188-191.

40. *Ibid.*, 198-199; John Cotton, Jr., to Gookin in *ibid.*, 199-200.
41. Bushnell, "Treatment of the Indians in Plymouth Colony," 208.
42. J. Hammond Trumbull, ed., *Public Records of the Colony of Connecticut* (15 vols., Hartford, 1850-1890), I, 531; II, 8. Hereafter cited as *Conn. Col. Rec.*
43. Rev. James Fitch to Daniel Gookin (20 Nov. 1674) in Gookin, "Historical Collections," 208-209. Cf. John Eliot to Commissioners of the United Colonies (4 Sept. 1671) in [John Eliot], "Letters of John Eliot the Apostle," in *Publications of the Massachusetts Historical Society*, XVII (1879-1880), 248.
44. Gookin, "Historical Collections," 207; Pulsifer, *Acts of the Commissioners*, II, 134, 167, 262; Kellaway, *New England Company*, 103.
45. Gookin, "Historical Collections," 210; Whitfield, "Strength out of Weaknesse," 170; Thomas Shepard, "The Clear Sun-shine of the Gospel Breaking Forth upon the Indians in New-England," in *Mass. Hist. Soc. Coll.*, 3 ser. IV (1834), 61.
46. John Eliot to Edward Winslow (21 Oct. 1650) in Whitfield, "The Light appearing," 135-137.
47. [Roger Williams], *The Complete Writings of Roger Williams* (7 vols., New York, 1963), I, 214-222.
48. George P. Winship, intro. and ed., *The New England Company of 1649 and John Eliot* (Boston, 1920), 32.
49. For example, see Gookin, "Historical Collections," 185, 186; John Eliot to Thomas Shepard (24 Sept. 1649) in Shepard, "Clear Sun-shine of the Gospel," 59; Daniel Gookin to Commissioners of the United Colonies (27 Aug. 1664) in *Conn. Col. Rec.*, III, 481-482.
50. Gookin, "Historical Collections," 188.
51. For complete lists of missionaries and commissioners see Frederick L. Weis, "The New England Company of 1649 and Its Missionary Enterprises," in *Publications of the Colonial Society of Massachusetts, Transactions*, XXXVIII (1947-1951), 198-200, 207-213.
52. Kellaway, *New England Company*, 207-208.

XII: EPILOGUE AND CONCLUSION

1. Daniel Gookin, "An Historical Account of the Doings and Sufferings of the Christian Indians in New England, in the Years 1675, 1676, 1677," in *Transactions and Collections of the American Antiquarian Society [Archaeologia Americana]*, II (1836), 438.
2. Nathaniel B. Shurtleff and David Pulsifer, eds., *Records of the Colony of New Plymouth* (12 vols., Boston, 1855-1861), XI, 237. Hereafter cited as *Ply. Col. Rec.* The embargo had been removed twice before, in 1665 and 1669 (*ibid.*, 215, 225).
3. Douglas E. Leach, *Flintlock and Tomahawk: New England in King Philip's War* (New York, 1958).
4. For example, see James Truslow Adams, *The Founding of New Eng-*

land (Boston, 1921), 338-343; George F. Willison, *Saints and Strangers* (New York, 1945), 390-394; Ruth Murray Underhill, *Red Man's America* (Chicago, 1953), 74-78; Roy Harvey Pearce, *The Savages of America: A Study of the Indian and the Idea of Civilization* (Baltimore, 1953), 19-22; Richard S. Dunn, *Puritans and Yankees: The Winthrop Dynasty of New England, 1630-1717* (Princeton, 1962), 206. Recent popularized accounts are even more flagrant in their distortions; for example, George Howe, *Mount Hope: A New England Chronicle* (New York, 1959), 28-33, and Alvin M. Josephy, *The Patriot Chiefs: A Chronicle of Indian Leadership* (New York, 1961), 35-40.

5. Leach also suggests that the Indian was chafing under the Puritans' version of justice and was gradually accumulating grievances that could only be settled by war. For evidence against the Puritans from an old enemy, see Samuel Gorton to John Winthrop, Jr. (11 Sept. 1675) in "Winthrop Papers," *Mass. Hist. Soc. Coll.,* 4 ser. VII (1865), 630-631.

6. Roger Williams to John Winthrop, Jr. (28 May 1664) in [Roger Williams], *The Complete Writings of Roger Williams* (7 vols., New York, 1963), VI, 319. For a review of the machinations of the Atherton Company see Douglas E. Leach, "The Causes and Effects of King Philip's War" (unpublished Ph.D. dissertation, Harvard University, 1952), 113-120, and Dunn, *Puritans and Yankees, passim.* Most of the pertinent sources are in "Trumbull Papers," *Mass. Hist. Soc. Coll.,* 5 ser. IX (1885) *passim;* John R. Bartlett, ed., *Records of the Colony of Rhode Island and Providence Plantations* (10 vols., Providence, 1856-1865), I, 462-473; J. Hammond Trumbull, ed., *Public Records of the Colony of Connecticut* (15 vols., Hartford, 1850-1890), II, 541-545; and Elisha R. Potter, Jr., *The Early History of Narragansett* (*R.I. Hist. Soc. Coll.,* III [1835]), *passim.*

7. Deeds can be found in Boston Athenaeum Miscellaneous MSS, L1, I (1652-1799), no. 16, and Massachusetts Historical Society, Miscellaneous Unbound MSS, Box I. The most judicious brief treatment of the causes of King Philip's War can be found in David Bushnell, "The Treatment of the Indians in Plymouth Colony," in *New England Quarterly,* XXVI (1953), 208-215.

8. Leach, *Flintlock and Tomahawk,* ch. VII.

9. Ninigret sent the head of a Wampanoag to Fitz-John Winthrop as a sign of Niantic loyalty. Winthrop to [?] (28 July 1675) in "Winthrop Papers," *Mass. Hist. Soc. Coll.,* 6 ser. III (1889), 447.

10. Gookin, "Doings and Sufferings of the Christian Indians," 436.

11. *Ibid.*

12. *Ibid.,* 442-445.

13. *Ibid.,* 449-450; Nathaniel B. Shurtleff, *Records of the Governor and Company of the Massachusetts Bay in New England* (5 vols., Boston, 1853-1854), V, 46-47; hereafter cited as *Mass. Col. Rec.*

14. Gookin, "Doings and Sufferings of the Christian Indians," 451-452.

15. *Ibid.*, 455-461; *Records of the Court of Assistants of the Colony of Massachusetts Bay, 1630-1692* (3 vols., Boston, 1901-1908), I, 52-55; [Nathaniel Saltonstall], "The Present State of New England," in Charles H. Lincoln, ed., *Narratives of the Indian Wars* (New York, 1913), 40-41.

16. *Mass. Col. Rec.*, V, 57, 64; Gookin, "Doings and Sufferings of the Christian Indians," 462-463, 472-474, 485-486, 491-492, 497; John Eliot to Robert Boyle (17 Oct. 1675) in [John Eliot], "Letters of John Eliot the Apostle," in *Proceedings of the Mass. Hist. Soc.*, XVII (1879-1880), 251-252.

17. Gookin, "Doings and Sufferings of the Christian Indians," 443-444, 460-466, 491.

18. *Ibid.*, 451, 475. So vigorously did some Bostonians vent their wrath on the protectors of the Christian Indians that in April 1676 Eliot and Gookin were "accidentally" run down by a boat in Boston Harbor. *Roxbury Records (Sixth Report of the [Boston] Record Commissioners*, 2nd ed. [Boston, 1884]), 193; Samuel Eliot Morison, ed., *Records of the Suffolk County Court, 1671-1680* (2 vols. [*Publications of the Colonial Society of Massachusetts, Collections*, XXIX-XXX], Boston, 1933), II, 695-697.

19. *Rec. Mass. Court of Assistants*, I, 71-73; Gookin, "Doings and Sufferings of the Christian Indians," 513-514.

20. For example, see Gookin, "Doings and Sufferings of the Christian Indians," 491-492, 519; and John Eliot to Robert Boyle (23 Oct. 1677) in [John Eliot], "Letters from Rev. John Eliot of Roxbury, to Hon. Robert Boyle," in *Mass. Hist. Soc. Coll.*, 1 ser. III (1794), 179.

21. Gookin, "Doings and Sufferings of the Christian Indians," 486, 491, 507-508, 516; [Mary Rowlandson], "Narrative of the Captivity of Mrs. Mary Rowlandson," in Lincoln, *Narratives of the Indian Wars*, 151.

22. Leach, *Flintlock and Tomahawk*, ch. XII. Most seventeenth century sources credit an Indian with killing Philip. However, cf. Richard Hutchinson, "The Warr in New England Visibly Ended," in Lincoln, *Narratives of the Indian Wars*, 105.

23. Leach, *Flintlock and Tomahawk*, ch. XIII. On the number of Indian casualties see [Nathaniel Saltonstall], "A New and Further Narrative of the State of New England," in Lincoln, *Narratives of the Indian Wars*, 97.

24. *Roxbury Records*, 195-196.

25. William Biglow, *History of the Town of Natick . . .* (Boston, 1830), 28, 33, 45.

26. Frederick Webb Hodge, ed., *Handbook of the American Indians North of Mexico* (2 vols., Washington, 1907), II, 637-638; William Kellaway, *The New England Company, 1649-1776* (New York, 1962), 269-276.

27. For an example of how some historians have grossly distorted the evidence on the causes and nature of the wars of 1637 and 1675, see

Peter Oliver, *The Puritan Commonwealth* (Boston, 1856), 100-153. The extent to which such a misreading of the evidence can be carried may be found in George McAleer, *An Hour with the Puritans and Pilgrims* (Worcester, Mass., 1908), 30-35, 43-44.

Bibliography

A NOTE ON SOURCES

TO THE everlasting gratitude of students of American colonial history, New Englanders have long been in the habit of publishing almost every scrap of primary material that pertains to their early history. The Winthrop family papers, the Massachusetts and Connecticut archives, and a few smaller collections are the only manuscript sources of major significance for a study of the Puritans' relations with the Indians from 1620 to 1675 which remain in manuscript — and even these have been published in part. Accordingly, although MANUSCRIPT SOURCES are listed first in the following bibliography, the most valuable materials for this study are those listed under the headings of PUBLIC RECORDS and SEVENTEENTH CENTURY SOURCES.

In addition to the usual bibliographical aids, a few special guides have proved useful, in particular Frederick J. Dockstadter, *The American Indian in Graduate Studies: A Bibliography of Theses and Dissertations* (Contributions from the Museum of the American Indian, Heye Foundation, XV [New York, 1957]); William Fenton, L. H. Butterfield, and Wilcomb E. Washburn, *American Indian and White Relations to 1830: Needs and Opportunties for Study* (Chapel Hill, 1957); and George Peter Murdock, *Ethnographic Bibliography of North America* (3rd ed., New Haven, 1960).

MANUSCRIPT SOURCES

Boston Athenaeum
  Miscellaneous MSS, I

Boston Public Library
  Cotton and Prince Papers
  Cotton Papers, Part VII

Columbia University Library
  Miscellaneous MSS Pertaining to John Eliot, from the Library of
    Congress (Microfilm)

Connecticut Historical Society
  Indian Deeds
  Edwin Stearns MSS
  Annie E. Trumbull Papers

Connecticut State Library
  Connecticut Archives
      Indians (first series), I
      Indians (second series), I-II
      Ecclesiastical Affairs, I, IX
      Crimes and Misdemeanors (first series)
      Miscellaneous (first series)
      Private Controversies, V
      Towns and Lands (first series), I
  Connecticut Colonial County Court and Probate Records, I-III
  New Haven County Court Records, I
  New London County Court Records, I-III
  R. C. Winthrop Collection

John Carter Brown Library
  Deed to Warwick, Rhode Island

Massachusetts Historical Society
  Davis Papers, I
  William C. Endicott Letters, Box I
  Miscellaneous Bound MSS, I-II
  Miscellaneous Photostats, Boxes I-VIII, X-XV
  Miscellaneous Unbound MSS, Box I
  Otis Papers, Box I
  Saltonstall Papers, I
  Trumbull Papers
  Winslow Papers, I
  Winthrop Papers

Massachusetts State Library
  Massachusetts Archives

Rhode Island Historical Society
    Deed of Nunaquoquit Neck
    Miscellaneous MSS
    Peck MSS
    Private Papers of Samuel Eddy
    Shepley MSS
    RIHS MSS

Rhode Island State Library
    Rhode Island Archives

Yale University Library
    Pequot Library Collection

PUBLIC RECORDS

Bartlett, John R., ed. *Records of the Colony of Rhode Island and Providence Plantations in New England.* 10 vols. Providence, 1856-1865.

Boston Records, 1634-1660, and the Book of Possessions. (*Second Report of the [Boston] Record Commissioners.*) 2nd ed. Boston, 1881.

Bouton, Nathaniel, ed. *Provincial Papers: Documents and Records Relating to the Province of New-Hampshire.* Vol. I. Concord, 1867.

Brigham, Clarence S., ed. *British Royal Proclamations Relating to America, 1603-1783.* (*Transactions and Collections of the American Antiquarian Society,* XII.) Cambridge, Mass., 1911.

——, ed. *The Early Records of Portsmouth [Rhode Island].* Providence, 1901.

Burt, Henry M., ed. *The First Century of Springfield: The Official Records from 1636 to 1736.* 2 vols. Springfield, Mass., 1898.

Dexter, Franklin Bowditch, ed. *New Haven Town Records.* 2 vols. (*Ancient Town Records,* I-II.) New Haven, 1917-1919.

Dorchester, Town Records. (*Fourth Report of the [Boston] Records Commissioners.*) Boston, 1880.

Dow, George F., ed. *Records and Files of the Quarterly Courts of Essex County, Massachusetts.* 8 vols. Salem, 1911-1921.

Early Records of the Town of Providence, The. Vol. I. Providence, 1892.

Early Records of the Town of Warwick [Rhode Island], The. Edited by [Howard M. Chapin]. Providence, 1926.

Farrand, Max, intro. *The Laws and Liberties of Massachusetts.* (Reprinted from the copy of the 1648 edition in the Henry E. Huntington Library.) Cambridge, Mass., 1929.

Great Britain, Public Record Office. *Acts of the Privy Council of England, Colonial Series.* Edited by W. L. Grant and James Munro. Vol. I (1613-1680). Hereford, England, 1908.

——. *Calendar of State Papers, Colonial Series, America and the West Indies.* Edited by W. Noel Sainsbury. Vols. I, V, VII, IX (1574-1676). London, 1860-1889.

Hening, William Waller, ed. *The Statutes at Large: Being the Laws of Virginia from the First Session of the Legislature in the Year 1619.* 13 vols. Richmond, Va., 1819-1823.

Hoadly, Charles J., ed. *Records of the Colony and Plantation of New Haven, from 1638-1649.* Hartford, Conn., 1857.

———, ed. *Records of the Colony or Jurisdiction of New Haven, from May, 1653, to the Union.* Hartford, Conn., 1858.

Libby, Charles Thornton, ed. *Province and Court Records of Maine.* 4 vols. Portland, 1928-1958.

Morison, Samuel Eliot, ed. *Records of the Suffolk County Court, 1671-1680.* 2 vols. (*Publications of the Colonial Society of Massachusetts, Collections,* XXIX-XXX.) Boston, 1933.

Nourse, Henry S., ed. *The Early Records of Lancaster, Massachusetts, 1643-1725.* Lancaster, Mass., 1884.

Pulsifer, David, ed. *Acts of the Commissioners of the United Colonies.* 2 vols. (*Records of the Colony of New Plymouth,* IX-X.) Boston, 1859.

Records of the Court of Assistants of the Colony of the Massachusetts Bay, 1630-1692. 3 vols. Boston, 1901-1908.

Records of the Court of Trials of the Town of Warwick, R.I., 1659-1674. Providence, 1922.

Records of the Town of Plymouth. Vol. I. Plymouth, 1889.

Roxbury Records. (*Sixth Report of the [Boston] Record Commissioners.*) 2nd ed. Boston, 1884.

Shurtleff, Nathaniel E., ed. *Records of the Governor and Company of the Massachusetts Bay in New England.* 5 vols. Boston, 1853-1854.

———, and Pulsifer, David, eds. *Records of the Colony of New Plymouth.* 12 vols. Boston, 1855-1861.

Smith, Joseph H., ed. *Colonial Justice in Western Massachusetts, 1639-1702: The Pynchon Court Record.* Cambridge, Mass., 1961.

Stock, Leo F., ed. *Proceedings and Debates of the British Parliaments Respecting North America.* Vol. I. Washington, 1924.

Suffolk Deeds. 14 vols. Boston, 1880-1906.

"Town Records of Salem, 1634-1659," in *Essex Institute Historical Collections,* 2 ser. I (1869), part 1.

Trumbull, J. Hammond, ed. *Public Records of the Colony of Connecticut.* 15 vols. Hartford, Conn., 1850-1890.

Whitmore, William H., ed. *The Colonial Laws of Massachusetts [1672-1686].* Boston, 1887.

———, ed. *The Colonial Laws of Massachusetts [1641-1672].* Boston, 1889.

Wright, Harry A., ed. *Indian Deeds of Hampden County [Massachusetts].* Springfield, Mass., 1905.

SEVENTEENTH CENTURY SOURCES

Arber, Edward. *The Story of the Pilgrim Fathers, 1606-1623 A.D. as told by Themselves, their Friends, and their Enemies.* London, 1897.

Banks, Charles E. "New Documents Relating to the Popham Expedition,

1607," in *Proceedings of the American Antiquarian Society*, new series, XXXIX (1930), 307-334.

Baxter, James P., ed. *Sir Ferdinando Gorges and his Province of Maine.* (*Publications of the Prince Society*, XVIII-XX.) Boston, 1890.

———, ed. *The Trelawney Papers.* (*Documentary History of the State of Maine*, III.) Portland, 1884.

[Baxter, Richard]. *Reliquiae Baxterianae: or Mr. Richard Baxter's Narrative of the Most Memorable Passages of His Life and Times.* Edited by Mathew Sylvester. London, 1696.

[Boyle, Robert]. *The Works of the Honourable Robert Boyle.* 5 vols. London, 1744.

[Bradford, William]. "Bradford's Verse History of New England," in *Massachusetts Historical Society Collections*, 1 ser. III (1794), 77-84.

[———]. "Governour Bradford's Letter Book," in *Massachusetts Historical Society Collections*, 1 ser. III (1794), 27-76.

———. *History of Plymouth Plantation.* Edited by Worthington C. Ford. 2 vols. Boston, 1912.

Brereton, John. "Briefe and True Relation of the Discoverie of the North Part of Virginia," in Henry S. Burrage, ed. *Early English and French Voyages.* (*Original Narratives of Early American History.*) New York, 1906. Pp. 325-340.

Brodhead, John Romeyn. *Documents Relative to the Colonial History of the State of New York.* Edited by E. B. O'Callagahan. 15 vols. Albany, 1853-1887.

Brown, Alexander, ed. *Genesis of the United States.* 2 vols. Boston, 1890.

Burrage, Champlin, ed. *John Pory's Lost Description of Plymouth Colony in the Earliest Days of the Pilgrim Fathers.* Boston and New York, 1918.

Burrage, Henry S., ed. *Early English and French Voyages.* (*Original Narratives of Early American History.*) New York, 1906.

[Champlain, Samuel de]. *Voyages of Samuel de Champlain, 1604-1618.* Edited by W. L. Grant. (*Original Narratives of Early American History.*) New York, 1907.

Chapin, Howard M. *Documentary History of Rhode Island.* 2 vols. Providence, 1916.

Church, Thomas. *The History of Philip's War, Commonly Called the Great Indian War, of 1675 and 1676.* Edited by Samuel G. Drake. 2nd ed. Exeter, N.H., 1829.

[Clap, Roger]. "Captain Roger Clap's Memoirs," in Alexander Young, ed. *Chronicles of the First Planters of the Colony of Massachusetts Bay, from 1623 to 1636.* Boston, 1846. Pp. 343-368.

Cobbet, Thomas. "A Narrative of New England's Deliverances," in *New-England Historical and Genealogical Register*, VIII (1853), 209-219.

Cotton, John. *The Bloudy Tenent, Washed, and Made White in the Bloud of the Lambe.* London, 1647.

———. *Gods Promise to His Plantations.* (Old South Leaflets, III, no. 53.) Boston, n.d.

[Cotton, Josiah]. "A Supplement to New England's Memorial, by Another Hand," in *Chronicles of the Pilgrim Fathers* (Everyman's Library). London and New York, n.d. Pp. 225-228.

[Cushman, Robert]. "Cushman's Discourse," in Alexander Young, ed.
*Chronicles of the Pilgrim Fathers of the Colony of New Plymouth,
from 1602-1625.* 2nd ed. Boston, 1844. Pp. 253-268. Also in *Chronicles
of the Pilgrim Fathers* (Everyman's Library). London and New
York, n.d.

[Danckaerts, Jasper]. *The Journal of Jasper Danckaerts.* Edited by Bartlett B. James and J. Franklin Jameson. (*Original Narratives of Early
American History.*) New York, 1913.

"Documents of the Society for Promoting and Propagating the Gospel in
New England," in *New-England Historical and Genealogical Register,* XXXVI (1882), 371-376.

"Documents Relating to Captain Bartholomew Gosnold's Voyage to
America, A.D. 1602," in *Massachusetts Historical Society Collections,*
3 ser. VIII (1843), 69-123.

Drake, Samuel G. *Old Indian Chronicle . . . and Chronicles of the Indians.* Boston, 1836.

[Dudley, Joseph]. "Dudley's Letter to the Countess of Lincoln," in Alexander Young, ed. *Chronicles of the First Planters of the Colony of
Massachusetts Bay, from 1623 to 1636.* Boston, 1846. Pp. 301-311.

Eames, Wilberforce, ed. *John Eliot and the Indians, 1652-1657, Being
Letters Addressed to Rev. Jonathan Hanmer of Barnstaple, England.*
New York, 1915.

"Early Records of Charleston," in Alexander Young, ed., *Chronicles of
the First Planters of the Colony of Massachusetts Bay, from 1623 to
1636.* Boston, 1846. Pp. 369-387.

Easton, John. "A Relacion of the Indyan Warre," in Charles H. Lincoln,
ed. *Narratives of the Indian Wars.* (*Original Narratives of Early
American History.*) New York, 1913. Pp. 1-17.

[Eliot, John]. "An Account of Indian Churches in New England in a
Letter written A.D. 1673 By Rev. John Eliot of Roxbury," in *Massachusetts Historical Society Collections,* 1 ser. X (1809), 124-129.

——. *A Brief Narrative of the Progress of the Gospel among the Indians of New England, 1670.* Boston, 1868.

——. *A further Account of the progress of the Gospel Amongst the
Indians in New England: Being a Relation of the Confessions made
by several Indians. . . .* London, 1660.

——. "The Indian Grammar Begun," in *Massachusetts Historical Society Collections,* 2 ser. IX (1823), 243-312.

[——]. "John Eliot's Description of New England in 1650" in *Proceedings of the Massachusetts Historical Society,* 2 ser. II (1885-1886),
44-50.

——. "A Late and Further Manifestation of the Progress of the Gospel
amongst the Indians in New-England," in *Massachusetts Historical
Society Collections,* 3 ser. IV (1834), 261-288.

[———]. "Letters from Rev. John Eliot of Roxbury to Hon. Robert Boyle," in *Massachusetts Historical Society Collections*, I ser. III (1794), 177-188.

[———]. "Letters of John Eliot the Apostle," in *Proceedings of the Massachusetts Historical Society*, XVII (1879-1880), 245-253.

[———]. "Letters of the Rev. John Eliot, the Apostle to the Indians," in *New England Historical and Genealogical Register*, XXXVI (1882), 291-299.

[———]. Letter to Humphrey Atherton (4 June 1657), in *Massachusetts Historical Society Collections*, I ser. II (1793), 9.

———, and Mayhew, Thomas, Jr. "Tears of Repentance: Or, A Further Narrative of the Progress of the Gospel amongst the Indians in New-England." *Massachusetts Historical Society Collections*, 3 ser. IV (1834), 197-260.

Forbes, Allyn B., ed. *Winthrop Papers*. 5 vols. Boston, 1929-1947. For other published papers of the Winthrop family see "Winthrop Papers" below.

Ford, John W., ed. *Some Correspondence Between the Governors and Treasurers of the New England Company in London and the Commissioners of the United Colonies in America, the Missionaries of the Company and Others between the Years 1657 and 1712*. London, 1896.

Gardiner, Lion. *A History of the Pequot War*. Cincinnati, 1860.

Gookin, Daniel. "An Historical Account of the Doings and Sufferings of the Christian Indians in New England, in the Years of 1675, 1676, 1677," in *Transactions and Collections of the American Antiquarian Society [Archaeologia Americana]*, II (1836), 429-534.

———. "Historical Collections of the Indians in New England," in *Massachusetts Historical Society Collections*, I ser. I (1792), 141-226.

[Gorges, Ferdinando]. "A Brief Relation of the Discovery and Plantation of New England," in *Massachusetts Historical Society Collections*, 2 ser. IX (1823), 1-25.

———. "Brief Narration of the Original Undertakings of the Advancement of Plantations into the Parts of America . . . ," in *Maine Historical Society Collections*, I ser. II (1847), 1-65 (2nd pagination).

Harvard College Records. 2 vols. (*Publications of the Colonial Society of Massachusetts, Collections*, XV-XVI.) Boston, 1925.

Hazard, Ebenezer. *Historical Collections*. 2 vols. Philadelphia, 1792.

Higginson, Francis. *New-Englands Plantation*. Salem, 1908.

Hough, Franklin B. *Papers Relating to the Island of Nantucket, with Documents relating to the Original Settlement of that Island, Martha's Vineyard and other Islands adjacent, known as Dukes County, While under the Colony of New York*. Albany, 1865.

Hubbard, William. *A General History of New England*. (*Massachusetts Historical Society Collections*, 2 ser. V-VI.) Boston, 1815.

———. *A Narrative of the Troubles with the Indians in New-England, From the first Planting thereof to the present Time*. Edited by Sam-

uel G. Drake under the title *The History of the Indian Wars in
New England from the First Settlement to the Termination of the
War with King Philip, in 1677.* 2 vols. Roxbury, Mass., 1865.

[Hull, John]. *The Diaries of John Hull, Mintmaster and Treasurer of
the Colony of Massachusetts Bay.* (*Transactions and Collections of
the American Antiquarian Society,* III.) Cambridge, Mass., 1850.

Hutchinson, Richard. "The Warr in New England Visibly Ended," in
Charles H. Lincoln, ed. *Narratives of the Indian Wars.* (*Original
Narratives of Early American History.*) New York, 1913. Pp. 101-
106.

Hutchinson, Thomas, ed. *The Hutchinson Papers.* (*Publications of the
Prince Society,* II-III.) Albany, 1865.

"Instructions from the Church at Natick to William and Anthony," in
Massachusetts Historical Society Collections, 1 ser. VI (1799), 201-
205.

James, Sydney V., Jr., ed. *Three Visitors to Early Plymouth: Letters
About the Pilgrim Settlement in New England During Its First Seven
Years by John Pory, Emmanuel Altham, and Isaak de Rasieres.* Plim-
outh Plantation, Mass., 1963.

[Johnson, Edward]. *Johnson's Wonder-Working Providence.* Edited by
J. Franklin Jameson. (*Original Narratives of Early American History.*) New York, 1910.

Josselyn, John. "An Account of Two Voyages to New-England," in
Massachusetts Historical Society Collections, 3 ser. III (1833), 211-
354.

———. "Chronological Observations of America, From the year of the
World to the year of Christ, 1673," in *Massachusetts Historical Society Collections,* 3 ser. III (1833), 355-396.

———. "New Englands Rarities Discovered," in *Transactions and Collections of the American Antiquarian Society* [*Archaeologia Americana*], IV (1860), 130-238.

A Journal of the Pilgrims at Plymouth [*Mourt's Relation*]. Edited by
Dwight B. Heath. New York, 1963.

[de Laet, John]. "From the 'New World,' by John de Laet, 1625, 1630,
1633, 1640," in J. Franklin Jameson, ed. *Narratives of New Netherland, 1609-1664.* (*Original Narratives of Early American History.*)
New York, 1909.

[Lechford, Thomas]. *Note-Book Kept by Thomas Lechford, Esq., Lawyer, in Boston, Massachusetts Bay, from June 27, 1638, to July 29,
1641.* (*Transactions and Collections of the American Antiquarian
Society,* VII.) Cambridge, Mass., 1885.

———. "Plain Dealing: or, Newes from New-England," in *Massachusetts
Historical Society Collections,* 3 ser. III (1833), 55-128.

Lescarbot, Marc. *The History of New France.* 3 vols. Edited by W. L.
Grant. (*Publications of the Champlain Society,* I, VII, XI.) Toronto,
1907-1914.

Levermore, Charles Herbert, ed. *Forerunners and Competitors of the Pilgrims and Puritans.* 2 vols. Brooklyn, 1912.

Levett, Christopher. "A Voyage to New England," in *Maine Historical Society Collections,* 1 ser. II (1847), 73-109.

Mason, John. "A Brief History of the Pequot War," in *Massachusetts Historical Society Collections,* 2 ser. VIII (1826), 120-153.

Mather, Cotton. *Magnalia Christi Americana: or, the Ecclesiastical History of New-England from its First Planting in the Year 1620, unto the Year of our Lord, 1698.* 2 vols. Hartford, Conn., 1820.

Mather, Increase. *A Brief History of the War with the Indians in New England.* Edited by Samuel G. Drake under the title *The History of King Philip's War.* Albany, 1862.

———. *A Relation of the Troubles which have hapned in New-England By reason of the Indians there. From the Year 1614 to the Year 1675.* Edited by Samuel G. Drake under the title *Early History of New England.* Boston, 1864.

Maverick, Samuel. "A Brief Description of New England and the Severall Townes Therein," in *New-England Historical and Genealogical Register,* XXXIX (1885), 33-48.

Megapolensis, Johannes, Jr. "A Short Account of the Mohawk Indians . . . ," in J. Franklin Jameson, ed. *Narratives of New Netherland, 1609-1664.* (*Original Narratives of Early American History.*) New York, 1909. Pp. 163-180.

[Michaelus, Jonas]. "Letter of Reverend Jonas Michaelus, 1628," in J. Franklin Jameson, ed. *Narratives of New Netherland, 1609-1664.* (*Original Narratives of Early American History.*) New York, 1909. Pp. 117-134.

[Morrell, William]. "Morrell's Poem on New England," in *Massachusetts Historical Society Collections,* 1 ser. I (1792), 125-139.

Morton, Nathanial. *New-Englands Memoriall.* Boston, 1803. Also in *Chronicles of the Pilgrim Fathers* (Everyman's Library). London and New York, n.d.

Morton, Thomas. *The New English Canaan.* Edited by Charles Francis Adams, Jr. (*Publications of the Prince Society,* XIV.) Boston, 1883.

"Narrative of a Journey into the Mohawk and Oneida Country, 1634-1635," in J. Franklin Jameson, ed. *Narratives of New Netherland, 1609-1664.* (*Original Narratives of Early American History.*) New York, 1909. Pp. 135-164.

New England's First Fruits: with Divers other Special Matters Concerning that Country. Sabin's Reprints, Quarto Series, no. VII. New York, 1865.

Of the Conversion of Five Thousand and Nine Hundred East Indians . . . with a Post-Script of the Gospels good Successe also amongst the West-Indians, in New England. London, 1650.

Perrot, Nicholas. "Memoir on the Manners, Customs, and Religion of the Savages of North America," in Emma Helen Blair, trans. and ed.

The Indian Tribes of the Upper Mississippi Valley and Region of the Great Lakes, I. Cleveland, 1911.

Pierson, Abraham. "Some Helps for the Indian: A Catechism," in *Connecticut Historical Society Collections*, III (1895), 1-67.

"Pincheon Papers," in *Massachusetts Historical Society Collections*, 2 ser. VIII (1826), 228-249.

Powicke, F. J., ed. "Some Unpublished Correspondence of the Rev. Richard Baxter and the Rev. John Eliot, 'the Apostle to the American Indians,' 1656-1682," in *Bulletin of the John Rylands Library*, XV (1931), 138-176, 442-466.

Pratt, Phinehas. "A Declaration of the Affairs of the English People that First Inhabited New England," in *Massachusetts Historical Society Collections*, 4 ser. IV (1858), 474-487.

[Prince, Thomas]. Letters to and from Thomas Prince, in *Massachusetts Historical Society Collections*, 1 ser. VI (1799), 196-201.

Pring, Martin. "A Voyage Set Out from the Citie of Bristoll," in Henry S. Burrage, ed. *Early English and French Voyages. (Original Narratives of Early American History.)* New York, 1906. Pp. 341-352.

Purchas, Samuel. *Hakluytus Posthumus, or Purchas His Pilgrimes.* 20 vols. Glasgow, 1907.

[Pynchon, William]. "Letters of William Pynchon," in *Proceedings of the Massachusetts Historical Society*, XLVIII (1914-1915), 35-36.

[de Rasieres, Isaac]. "Letter of Isaac de Rasieres to Samuel Bloomaert, 1628 (?)," in J. Franklin Jameson, ed. *Narratives of New Netherland, 1609-1664. (Original Narratives of Early American History.)* New York, 1909. Pp. 97-115.

"Records of the Council for New England," in *Proceedings of the American Antiquarian Society*, XLVII (1867), 51-131.

"A Relation of a Voyage to Sagadahoc," in Henry S. Burrage, ed. *Early English and French Voyages. (Original Narratives of Early American History.)* New York, 1906. Pp. 395-419.

"Relation of the Indian Plot," in *Massachusetts Historical Society Collections*, 3 ser. III (1833), 161-164.

Reynolds, Edward, ed. *A Further Accompt of the Progresse of the Gospel amongst the Indians in New England, and of the Means used Effectually to Advance the Same.* Reprinted by Joseph Sabin (Sabin's Reprints, Quarto Series, no. VI) under the title *A Further Manifestation of the Progress of the Gospel among the Indians in New England.* New York, 1865.

Rosier, James. "A True Relation of the Voyage of Captaine George Waymouth," in Henry S. Burrage, ed. *Early English and French Voyages. (Original Narratives of Early American History.)* New York, 1906. Pp. 353-394.

[Rowlandson, Mary]. "Narrative of the Captivity of Mrs. Mary Rowlandson," in Charles H. Lincoln, ed. *Narratives of the Indian Wars. (Original Narratives of Early American History.)* New York, 1913. Pp. 107-167.

[Saltonstall, Nathaniel]. "A Continuation of the State of New England," in Charles H. Lincoln, ed. *Narratives of the Indian Wars. (Original Narratives of Early American History.)* New York, 1913. Pp. 51-74.
———. "A New and Further Narrative of the State of New England," in Charles H. Lincoln, ed. *Narratives of the Indian Wars. (Original Narratives of Early American History.)* New York, 1913. Pp. 75-99.
———. "The Present State of New England," in Charles H. Lincoln, ed. *Narratives of the Indian Wars. (Original Narratives of Early American History.)* New York, 1913. Pp. 19-50.
Shepard, Thomas. "The Clear Sun-shine of the Gospel Breaking Forth upon the Indians in New-England," in *Massachusetts Historical Society Collections,* 3 ser. IV (1834), 25-68.
———. "Thomas Shepard's Memoir of Himself," in Alexander Young, ed. *Chronicles of the First Planters of the Colony of Massachusetts Bay, from 1623-1636.* Boston, 1846. Pp. 497-558.
Smith, John. "New England's Trials," in *Chronicles of the Pilgrim Fathers* (Everyman's Library). London and New York, n.d. Pp. 241-266.
———. *The True Travels and Observations of Captain John Smith.* 2 vols. Richmond, Va. 1819.
———. *Works.* Edited by Edward Arber. Birmingham, England, 1884.
Strachey, William. *The Historie of Travell into Virginia Britania.* Edited by Louis B. Wright and Virginia Freund. London, 1953.
Thorowgood, Thomas. *Jewes in America, or, Probabilities that the Americans are of that Race.* London, 1650.
———. *Jews in America, or Probabilities that those Indians are Judaical, made more probable by some Additionals to the former Conjectures.* London, 1660.
Thwaites, Reuben Gold, ed. *The Jesuit Relations and Allied Documents.* 73 vols. New York, 1959.
"Trumbull Papers," in *Massachusetts Historical Society Collections,* 5 ser. IX (1885).
Underhill, John. "News from America," in *Massachusetts Historical Society Collections,* 3 ser. VI (1837), 1-28.
Vincent, Philip. "A True Relation of the Late Battel Fought in New England, between the English and the Pequet Salvages," in *Massachusetts Historical Society Collections,* 3 ser. VI (1837), 27-43.
[de Vries, David]. "From the 'Korte Historiael Ende Journaels Aenteyckeninge,'" in J. Franklin Jameson, ed. *Narratives of New Netherland, 1609-1664. (Original Narratives of Early American History.)* New York, 1909. Pp. 181-234.
[von Wassenaer, Nicholas]. "From the 'Historisch Verhael,' by Nicholas van Wassenaer, 1624-1630," in J. Franklin Jameson, ed. *Narratives of New Netherland, 1609-1664. (Original Narratives of Early American History.)* New York, 1909. Pp. 61-96.
Welde, Thomas. "Innocency Cleared," in *New-England Historical and Genealogical Register,* XXXVI (1882), 62-70.

[————]. "The Society for the Propagation of the Gospel in New England and the Rev. Thomas Welde," in *New-England Historical and Genealogical Register*, XXXIX (1885), 179-183.

[White, John]. *The Planters Plea, or the Grounds of Plantations Examined, and usuall Objections Answered*. London, 1630. Reprinted in facsimile by the Sandy Bay Historical Society and Musuem, Rockport, Mass., 1930.

Whitfield, Henry. "Strength out of Weaknesse; or a Glorious Manifestation of the Further Progresse of the Gospel among the Indians in New-England," in *Massachusetts Historical Society Collections*, 3 ser. IV (1834), 149-196.

————, ed. "The Light appearing more and more towards the perfect Day. Or, A farther Discovery of the present state of the Indians in New-England, Concerning the Progresse of the Gospel amongst them," in *Massachusetts Historical Society Collections*, 3 ser. IV (1834), 100-148.

Whitmore, William H., ed. *John Dunton's Letters from New England*. (*Publications of the Prince Society*, IV.) Boston, 1867.

[Williams, Roger]. *The Complete Writings of Roger Williams*. 7 vols. New York, 1963.

[Wilson, John?]. "The Day-Breaking, if not the Sun-Rising of the Gospell with the Indians in New-England," in *Massachusetts Historical Society Collections*, 3 ser. IV (1834), 1-24.

Winship, George P., intro. and ed. *The New England Company of 1649 and John Eliot*. (*Publications of the Prince Society*, XXXVI.) Boston, 1920.

Winslow, Edward. "The Glorious Progress of the Gospel, amongst the Indians in New England," in *Massachusetts Historical Society Collections*, 3 ser. IV (1834), 69-99.

————. "Good Newes from New England," in Edward Arber, ed. *The Story of the Pilgrim Fathers*. London, 1897. Pp. 509-600.

[————]. "Winslow's Brief Narration (Appended to 'Hypocrisie Unmasked,' 1646)," in *Chronicles of the Pilgrim Fathers* (Everyman's Library). London and New York, n.d. Pp. 358-364.

[Winthrop, John]. *A Short Story of the Rise, Reign, and Ruin of the Antinomians, Familists, and Libertines That Infected the Churches of New-England*. London, 1692.

[————]. *Winthrop's Journal, "History of New England," 1630-1649*: Edited by James K. Hosmer. 2 vols. (*Original Narratives of Early American History*.) New York, 1908.

"Winthrop Papers," in *Massachusetts Historical Society Collections*, 4 ser. VI-VII (1861-1865); 5 ser. I (1871), VIII (1882); 6 ser. III (1889), V (1892). For other published papers of the Winthrop family see Forbes, Allyn B., above.

[Wood, William]. *Wood's New-England's Prospect*. (*Publications of the Prince Society*, I.) Boston, 1865.

Wright, Franklin M. "A College First Proposed, 1633: Unpublished Letters of Apostles Eliot and William Hammond to Sir Simonds D'Ewes," in *Harvard Library Bulletin,* VIII (1954), 255-282.

Young, Alexander, ed. *Chronicles of the First Planters of the Colony of Massachusetts Bay, from 1623 to 1636.* Boston, 1846.

——, ed. *Chronicles of the Pilgrim Fathers of the Colony of Plymouth, from 1602 to 1625.* 2nd ed. Boston, 1844.

POST-SEVENTEENTH CENTURY: BOOKS

Adams, Charles Francis, Jr. *Three Episodes in Massachusetts History.* 2 vols. Boston, 1896.

Adams, James T. *The Founding of New England.* Boston, 1921.

Adams, Sherman W., and Stiles, Henry R. *The History of Ancient Wethersfield, Connecticut.* 2 vols. New York, 1904.

Akagi, Roy Hidemichi. *The Town Proprietors of the New England Colonies.* Philadelphia, 1924.

Andrews, Charles M. *The Colonial Period of American History.* 4 vols. New Haven, 1934-1938.

——. *The River Towns of Connecticut.* (*Johns Hopkins University Studies in Historical and Political Science,* VII.) Baltimore, 1889.

Bailyn, Bernard. *The New England Merchants in the Seventeenth Century.* Cambridge, Mass., 1955.

Benton, Josiah Henry. *Warning Out in New England.* Boston, 1911.

Bicknell, Thomas W. *Sowams: with Ancient Records of Sowams and Parts Adjacent.* New Haven, 1908.

Biglow, William. *History of the Town of Natick, Mass. From the Days of the Apostolic Eliot, MDCL, to the Present Time, MDCCCXXX.* Boston, 1830.

Billington, Ray Allen. *Westward Expansion: A History of the American Frontier.* 2nd ed. New York, 1960.

Bolton, Charles K. *The Real Founders of New England.* Boston, 1929.

Bouton, Nathaniel. *The History of Concord [New Hampshire]* . . . *with a History of the Ancient Pennacooks.* Concord, N. H., 1856.

Bowen, Richard Lebaron. *Early Rehoboth,* 3 vols. Rehoboth, Mass., 1946.

Brockunier, Samuel Hugh. *The Irrepressible Democrat: Roger Williams.* New York, 1940.

Brodhead, John Romeyn. *History of the State of New York.* 2nd ed. 2 vols. New York, 1859.

Burrage, Henry S. *The Beginnings of Colonial Maine, 1602-1658.* Portland, 1914.

[Busk, Henry William]. *A Sketch of the Origin and Recent History of The New England Company.* London, 1884.

Byington, Ezra Hoyt. *The Puritan as a Colonist and a Reformer.* Boston, 1899.

Calder, Isabel M. *The New Haven Colony.* (*Yale Historical Publications,* Miscellany vol. XXVIII.) New Haven, Conn., 1934.

Caulkins, Frances Manwaring. *History of New London, Connecticut.* New London, 1852.

——. *History of Norwich, Connecticut, from its Settlement in 1660 to January 1845.* Norwich, 1845.

Caverly, Robert B. *History of the Indian Wars of New England, with Eliot the Apostle Fifty Years in the Midst of Them.* Boston, 1882.

Coleman, R. V. *The First Frontier.* New York, 1948.

DeForest, John W. *History of the Indians of Connecticut.* Hartford, 1852.

Drake, Francis S. *Dictionary of American Biography.* Boston, 1872.

——. *The Town of Roxbury.* (*Records Relating to the Early History of Boston,* XXXIV.) Boston, 1905.

Drake, Samuel G. *The Aboriginal Races of North America* [*Book of the Indians*]. 15th ed. Philadelphia, 1859.

——. *The History and Antiquities of Boston, the Capital of Massachusetts and Metropolis of New England, From its Settlement in 1630, to the Year 1770.* 2 vols. Boston, 1856.

Duffy, John. *Epidemics in Colonial America.* Baton Rouge, La., 1953.

Dunn, Richard S. *Puritans and Yankees: The Winthrop Dynasty of New England, 1630-1717.* Princeton, N. J., 1962.

Dwight, Timothy. *Greenfield Hill.* New York, 1794.

Eggleston, Thomas. *The Story of the Pequot War.* New York, 1905.

Ellis, George E. *The Red Man and the White Man in North America: from Its Discovery to the Present Time.* Boston, 1882.

Ernst, James. *Roger Williams: New England Firebrand.* New York, 1932.

Flannery, Regina. *An Analysis of Coastal Algonquian Culture.* (Catholic University of America Anthropological Series, no. 7.) Washington, 1939.

Felt, Joseph B. *An Historical Account of Massachusetts Currency.* Boston, 1839.

——. *History of Ipswich, Essex, and Hamilton.* Cambridge, Mass., 1834.

Fiske, John. *The Beginnings of New England.* Boston, 1898.

Foreman, Carolyn Thomas. *Indians Abroad, 1493-1938.* Norman, Okla., 1943.

Francis, Convers. *Life of John Eliot, the Apostle to the Indians.* (The Library of American Biography, V.) New York, 1856.

Fuller, Oliver Payson. *The History of Warwick, Rhode Island.* Providence, 1875.

Goodwin, John A. *The Pilgrim Republic.* Boston, 1888.

Gookin, Frederick William. *Daniel Gookin, 1612-1687.* Chicago, 1912.

Greene, Evarts B., and Harrington, Virginia D. *American Population Before the Federal Census of 1790.* New York, 1932.

Greene, Lorenzo Johnston. *The Negro in Colonial New England. 1620-1776.* New York, 1942.

Hagan, William T. *American Indians.* Chicago, 1960.

——. *The Indian in American History.* (American Historical Association, Service Center for Teachers of History, Publication no. 50.) New York, 1963.

Hodge, Frederick Webb, ed. *Handbook of American Indians North of Mexico.* (Smithsonian Institution, Bureau of American Ethnology, Bulletin no. 30.) 2 vols. Washington, 1907.

Howe, George. *Mount Hope: A New England Chronicle.* New York, 1959.

Hunt, George T. *The Wars of the Iroquois: A Study in Intertribal Trade Relations.* Madison, Wis., 1960.

Hutchinson, Thomas. *The History of the Colony and Province of Massachusetts Bay.* 3 vols. Edited by L. S. Mayo. Cambridge, Mass., 1936.

Johnson, Amandus. *The Swedish Settlements on the Delaware, 1638-1664.* 2 vols. New York, 1911.

Johnson, Frederick, ed. *Man in Northeastern North America.* (Papers of the Robert S. Peabody Foundation for Archeology, III.) Andover, Mass., 1946.

Josephy, Alvin M. *The Patriot Chiefs: A Chronicle of Indian Leadership.* New York, 1961.

Judd, Sylvester. *History of Hadley.* New ed. Springfield, Mass., 1905.

Kellaway, William. *The New England Company, 1649-1776.* New York, 1962.

[Knight, Sarah K.]. *The Journal of Madame Knight.* Boston, 1920.

Lauber, Almon Wheeler. *Indian Slavery in the Colonial Times within the Present Limits of the United States.* New York, 1913.

Leach, Douglas Edward. *Flintlock and Tomahawk: New England in King Philip's War.* New York, 1958.

Lombard, Percival Hall. *The Aptucxet Trading Post.* Bourne, Mass., 1934.

Massachusetts Historical Society, *Early History of Massachusetts.* Boston, 1869.

McAleer, George. *An Hour with the Puritans and Pilgrims.* Worcester, Mass., 1908.

McIntyre, Ruth A. *Debts Hopeful and Desperate: Financing the Plymouth Colony.* Plimouth Plantation, Mass., 1963.

McKenney, Thomas L., and Hall, James. *The Indian Tribes of North America.* 3 vols. Edinburgh, 1934.

MacLeod, William C. *The American Indian Frontier.* New York, 1928.

Mason, Louis B. *The Life and Times of Major John Mason of Connecticut: 1600-1672.* New York and London, 1935.

Mayo, Lawrence Shaw. *John Endicott: A Biography.* Cambridge, Mass., 1936.

Melville, Herman. *Moby Dick.* Edited by Luther S. Mansfield and Howard P. Vincent. New York, 1952.

Miller, Perry. *Errand into the Wilderness.* Cambridge, Mass., 1956.

———. *Roger Williams: His Contribution to the American Tradition.* New York, 1962.

Moloney, Francis X. *The Fur Trade in New England, 1620-1676.* (Harvard Undergraduate Essays.) Cambridge, Mass., 1931.

Morison, Samuel Eliot. *Builders of the Bay Colony.* Boston, 1930.

———. *The Founding of Harvard College.* Cambridge, Mass., 1935.

———. *Harvard College in the Seventeenth Century.* 2 vols. Cambridge, Mass., 1936.

Morris, Henry. *Early History of Springfield, 1636-1675.* Springfield, Mass., 1876.

Notestein, Wallace. *The English People on the Eve of Colonization, 1603-1630.* New York, 1954.

Oliver, Peter. *The Puritan Commonwealth.* Boston, 1856.

Osgood, Herbert L. *The American Colonies in the Seventeenth Century.* 3 vols. New York, 1930.

Palfrey, John Gorham. *History of New England.* 5 vols. Boston, 1865-1890.

Parkman, Francis. *The Jesuits in North America in the Seventeenth Century. (France and England in North America,* II.) Boston, 1905.

Pearce, Roy Harvey. *The Savages of America: A Study of the Indian and the Idea of Civilization.* Baltimore, 1953.

Pilling, James C. *Bibliography of the Algonquian Languages.* (Smithsonian Institution, Bureau of American Ethnology, Bulletin no. 13.) Washington, 1891.

The Popham Colony: A Discussion of Its Historical Claims. Boston, 1866.

Potter, Elisha R., Jr. *The Early History of Narragansett. (Rhode Island Historical Society Collections,* III.) Providence, 1835.

Prince, Thomas. *A Chronological History of New England.* 5 volumes in one. Edinburgh, 1887.

Rowse, A. L. *The Elizabethans and America.* New York, 1959.

Ruttenber, E. M. *History of the Indian Tribes of Hudson's River.* Albany, 1872.

Savage, James. *A Genealogical Dictionary of the First Settlers of New England* . . . 4 vols. Boston, 1860.

Sheldon, George. *A History of Deerfield, Massachusetts . . . with a special study of the Indian Wars of the Connecticut Valley.* 2 vols. Deerfield, Mass., 1895-1896.

Shelley, Henry C. *John Underhill: Captain of New England and New Netherland.* New York, 1932.

Sibley, John L. *Biographical Sketches of Graduates of Harvard University.* Vol. II. Cambridge, Mass., 1881.

Smith, Bradford. *Captain John Smith.* Philadelphia, 1953.

Speck, Frank G. *Territorial Subdivisions and Boundaries of the Wampanoag, Massachusetts, and Nauset Indians.* (Museum of the American Indian, Heye Foundation, *Indian Notes and Monographs,* no. 44.) New York, 1928.

Spiess, Mathias. *The Indians of Connecticut* (Tercentenary Commission of the State of Connecticut, Committee on Historical Publications, Pamphlet no. 19.) New Haven, 1933.

Starkey, Marion L. *Land Where Our Fathers Died: The Settling of the Eastern Shores, 1607-1735.* New York, 1962.

Stearns, Raymond P. *The Strenuous Puritan: Hugh Peter, 1598-1660.* Urbana, Ill., 1954.

Steiner, Bernard C. *History of Slavery in Connecticut.* (*Johns Hopkins University Studies in Historical and Political Science,* 11 ser. IX-X.) Baltimore, 1893.

Stone, William L. *Uncas and Miantonomo.* New York, 1842.

Sutherland, Stella H. *Population Distribution in Colonial America.* New York, 1936.

Swanton, John R. *The Indian Tribes of North America.* (Smithsonian Institution, Bureau of American Ethnology, Bulletin no. 145.) Washington, 1952.

Sylvester, Herbert M. *Indian Wars of New England.* 3 vols. Boston, 1910.

Thayer, Henry O. *The Sagadahoc Colony.* Portland, Maine, 1892.

Tooker, William W. *John Eliot's First Indian Teacher and Interpreter, Cockenoe-de-Long Island, and the Story of his Career from the Early Records.* New York, 1896.

Trelease, Allen W. *Indian Affairs in Colonial New York: The Seventeenth Century.* Ithaca, N. Y., 1960.

Trumbull, Benjamin. *A Compendium of the Indian Wars in New England.* Edited by Frederick B. Hartranft. Hartford, 1926.

———. *History of Connecticut.* 2 vols. New Haven, 1818.

Trumbull, J. Hammond. *Origin and Early Progress of Indian Missions in New England.* Worcester, Mass., 1874.

Underhill, Ruth Murray. *Red Man's America: A History of Indians in the United States.* Chicago, 1953.

Ward, Harry M. *The United Colonies of New England, 1643-1690.* New York, 1961.

Weeden, William B. *Economic and Social History of New England, 1620-1789.* 2 vols. Boston, 1890.

———. *Indian Money as a Factor in New England Civilization.* (*Johns Hopkins University Studies in Historical and Political Science,* 2 ser. VIII-IX.) Baltimore, 1884.

Weeks, Alvin G. *Massasoit of the Wampanoags.* Fall River, Mass., 1919.

Willard, Joseph. *Willard Memoir, or The Life and Times of Major Simon Willard.* Boston, 1858.

Willison, George F. *Saints and Strangers.* New York, 1945.

Willoughby, Charles C. *Antiquities of the New England Indians.* Cambridge, Mass., 1935.

Winship, George Parker. *The First American Bible.* Boston, 1929.

Winslow, Ola Elizabeth. *Master Roger Williams: A Biography.* New York, 1957.

Winsor, Justin, ed. *The Memorial History of Boston.* 4 vols. Boston, 1880-1881.

———, ed. *Narrative and Critical History of America.* 8 vols. Boston, 1889.

Wright, Louis B. *Religion and Empire: The Alliance between Piety and Commerce in English Expansion, 1558-1625*. Chapel Hill, N. C., 1943.

POST-SEVENTEENTH CENTURY: ARTICLES

Banks, Charles Edward. "Thomas Morton of Merrymount," in *Publications of the Massachusetts Historical Society*, LVIII (1924-1925), 147-193.

Baxter, James P. "The Abnakis and their Ethnic Relations," in *Collections and Proceedings of the Maine Historical Society*, 2 ser. III (1892), 13-40.

Bennett, M. K. "The Food Economy of the New England Indians, 1605-1675," in *The Journal of Political Economy*, LXIII (1955), 369-397.

Buffington, Arthur H. "New England and the Western Fur Trade, 1629-1675," in *Publications of the Colonial Society of Massachusetts, Transactions*, XVIII (1915-1916), 160-192.

Bushnell, David. "The Treatment of the Indians in Plymouth Colony," in *New England Quarterly*, XXVI (1953), 193-218.

Bushnell, David I., Jr. "Tribal Migrations East of the Mississippi," in *Smithsonian Miscellaneous Collections*, LXXXIX (1934), no. 12.

Clark, J. S. "Did the Pilgrims Wrong the Indians?" in *The Congregational Quarterly*, I (1859), 129-135.

Cooper, John M. "Is the Algonquian Family Hunting Ground System Pre-Columbian?" in *American Anthropologist*, new ser. XLI (1939), 66-90.

Deane, Charles. "Report on the Belknap Donation," in *Publications of the Massachusetts Historical Society*, III (1855-1858), 286-328.

Eisinger, Chester E. "The Puritans' Justification for Taking the Land," in *Essex Institute Historical Collections*, LXXXIV (1948), 131-143.

Ellis, George E. "Life of John Mason," in *The Library of American Biography*. Edited by Jared Sparks. 2 ser. III (1855), 207-428.

Eno, Joel N. "The Puritans and the Indian Lands," in *The Magazine of History*, IV (1906), 274-281.

Felt, Joseph B. "Statistics of Population in Massachusetts," in *American Statistical Association Collections*, I (1845), 121-216.

Gallatin, Albert. "A Synopsis of the Indian Tribes of North America," in *Transactions and Collections of the American Antiquarian Society* [*Archaeologia Americana*], II (1836), 1-422.

Gilmore, Melvin R. "Indian Tribal Boundary-Lines and Monuments," in Museum of the American Indian, Heye Foundation, *Indian Notes*, V (1928), 59-63.

———. "Some Indian Ideas of Property," in Museum of the American Indian, Heye Foundation, *Indian Notes*, V (1928), 137-144.

Green, Samuel A. "Early History of Printing in New England," in *Proceedings of the Massachusetts Historical Society*, 2 ser. XI (1876-1897), 240-253.

Hadlock, Wendell S. "War Among the Northeastern Woodland Indians," in *American Anthropologist*, new ser. XLIX (1947), 204-221.

Hallett, L. F. "The Colonial Invasion of Hereditary Lands," in *Bulletin of the Massachusetts Archaeological Society*, XX (1959), 34-37.

Hawley, Gideon. "Biographical and Topographical Anecdotes respecting Sandwich and Marshpee, Jan. 1794," in *Massachusetts Historical Society Collections*, 1 ser. III (1794), 188-191.

Judd, Sylvester. "The Fur Trade on Connecticut River in the Seventeenth Century," in *New-England Historical and Genealogical Register*, XI (1857), 217-219.

Kinnicut, L. N. "The Plymouth Settlement and Tisquantum," in *Proceedings of the Massachusetts Historical Society*, XLVIII (1914-1915), 103-118.

Knowles, Nathaniel. "The Torture of Captives by the Indians of Eastern North America," in *Proceedings of the American Philosophical Society*, LXXXII (1940), 151-225.

Kroeber, A. L. "Nature of the Land-Holding Group," in *Ethnohistory*, II (1955), 303-314.

MacFarlane, Ronald O. "The Massachusetts Bay Truck-Houses in Diplomacy with the Indians," in *New England Quarterly*, XI (1938), 48-65.

Mooney, James. "The Aboriginal Population of America North of Mexico," in *Smithsonian Miscellaneous Collections*, LXXX (1928), no. 7.

Morison, Samuel Eliot. "Squanto," in *Dictionary of American Biography*.

———. "William Pynchon, The Founder of Springfield," in *Proceedings of the Massachusetts Historical Society*, LXIV (1930-1932), 67-107.

Paige, Lucius R. "Communications Respecting Marmaduke Johnson," in *Proceedings of the Massachusetts Historical Society*, XX (1882-1883), 265-268.

Rainey, Froelich G. "A Compilation of Historical Data Contributing to the Ethnography of Connecticut and Southern New England Indians," in *Bulletin of the Archeological Society of Connecticut*, reprint no. 3 (1956 [originally published April 1936]), 3-49.

Russell, Howard S. "New England Indian Agriculture," in *Bulletin of the Massachusetts Archaeological Society*, XXII (1961), 58-61.

Speck, Frank G. "The Eastern Algonkian Wabanaki Confederacy," in *American Anthropologist*, new ser. XVII (1915), 492-508.

———. "The Family Hunting Band as the Basis of Algonkian Social Organization," in *American Anthropologist*, new ser. XVII (1915), 289-305.

———. "The Functions of Wampum among the Eastern Algonkian," in *American Anthropological Association, Memoirs*, VI (1919), 3-71.

———. "Native Tribes and Dialects of Connecticut: A Mohegan-Pequot Diary," in *Bureau of American Ethnology*, 43rd Annual Report (1924-1925), 199-287.

———, and Eisely, Loren C. "Significance of Hunting Territory Systems of the Algonkian in Social Theory," in *American Anthropologist*, new ser. XLI (1939), 269-280.

Spiess, Mathias. "Podunk Indian Sites," in *Bulletins of the Archeological Society of Connecticut*, reprint numbers 4, 5, 6 (1962 [originally published December 1936, April 1937, March 1938]), 9-11.

Stearns, Raymond Phineas. "The Weld-Peter Mission to England," in *Publications of the Colonial Society of Massachusetts, Transactions*, XXXII (1933-1937), 188-246.

Vaughan, Alden T. "Pequots and Puritans: The Causes of the War of 1637," in *William and Mary Quarterly*, 3 ser. XXI (1964), 256-269.

Wallace, Anthony F. C. "Political Organization and Land Tenure Among the Northeastern Indians, 1600-1830," in *Southwestern Journal of Anthropology*, XIII (1957), 301-321.

Washburn, Wilcomb E. "The Moral and Legal Justification for Dispossessing the Indians," in James Morton Smith, ed. *Seventeenth Century America*. Chapel Hill, N. C., 1959.

Weis, Frederick L. "The New England Company of 1649 and Its Missionary Enterprises," in *Publications of the Colonial Society of Massachusetts, Transactions*, XXXVIII (1947-1951), 134-218.

UNPUBLISHED THESES AND DISSERTATIONS

James, Francis Goodwin. "Puritan Missionary Endeavors in Early New England." M.A. thesis, Yale University, 1938.

Leach, Douglas Edward. "The Causes and Effects of King Philip's War." Ph.D. dissertation, Harvard University, 1952.

MacFarlane, Ronald O. "Indian Relations in New England, 1620-1760: A Study of a Regulated Frontier." Ph.D. dissertation, Harvard University, 1933.

Roberts, William I. "The Fur Trade of New England in the Seventeenth Century." Ph.D. dissertation, University of Pennsylvania, 1958.

Warner, Robert Austin. "The Southern New England Indians to 1725: A Study in Culture Contact." Ph.D. dissertation, Yale University, 1935.

Wasserman, Maurice Marc. "The American Indian As Seen by the Seventeenth Century Chroniclers." Ph.D. dissertation, University of Pennsylvania, 1954.

Index

CPSIA information can be obtained at www.ICGtesting.com
Printed in the USA
LVOW07s0741121114

413174LV00003B/166/P